A–Z of Grand Prix Cars

This book is dedicated to the memory of David and Brenda Hodges, by their children Richard, Jane and Judy.

A–Z of GRAND PRIX CARS

David Hodges

The Crowood Press

First published in 2001 by
The Crowood Press Ltd
Ramsbury, Marlborough
Wiltshire SN8 2HR

British Library Cataloguing-in-Publication Data
A catalogue record for this book is available from the British Library.

ISBN 1 86126 339 2

Publisher's Acknowledgement
The publishers would like to thank Graham Robson and Charles Herridge for their assistance in completing the *A–Z of Grand Prix Cars* following the death of David Hodges.

Typefaces used: Goudy (*text*), Cheltenham (*headings*).

Typeset and designed by D & N Publishing
Baydon, Marlborough, Wiltshire.

Printed and bound in Great Britain by Bookcraft, Midsomer Norton.

Contents

Introduction

At the close of the twentieth century, Grand Prix racing was approaching its hundredth birthday – yet no-one had ever produced a complete directory on the teams that had been involved. David Hodges, who had been close to the Formula 1 scene for many years, set out to produce a definitive record – a comprehensive A–Z of every marque involved – and had almost completed the massive task before his untimely death in 1999.

It was arranged that the task should be completed and every attempt was made to remain entirely consistent with what David had already written. It is believed that this book is a vital, and important, record, of the very best of motor racing.

Grand Prix racing began with the running of the French Grand Prix, on the Circuit de la Sarthe, near Le Mans, in June 1906, and has become one of the biggest sports in the world by the end of the twentieth century.

Before then, town-to-town racing, followed by the Gordon Bennett races, had already inspired designers to get the very best out of the technology currently available to them. This book lists every make of car, and much detail about all of them, that competed thereafter, in National and International Grands Prix from 1906 to 2000. This, therefore, includes cars that were built to whatever Grand Prix regulations applied in any particular year: Formula A, Formula 1 since 1947, and those Formula 2 cars which were run in the 1952 and 1953 Grand Prix championship events.

The accompanying list also includes the cars that ran in the very early Grand Prize races in the United States, the *Coupe de l'Auto* cars that ran in the 1912 French Grand Prix, cars built for Grand Prix and F1 events that did not actually start in Grands Prix (but whose existence and purpose was well known – such as Cosworth, DAMS, Trossi and Walker–Climax) – and a variety of post-1947 F1 cars that ran in

non-championship races, both in Europe and in South Africa.

It does not include several other classes of cars such as:

- The sports cars that ran in races called 'Grand Prix' – such as the German 'Grand Prix' races of 1926–1931, and the French 'Grand Prix' races of 1936, 1937 and 1949.
- Cars run in the German 'Grand Prix' when it was only an F2 race (except for 1952 and 1953 as stated above).
- Cars which ran in the F2 category within a Grand Prix where F2 was a separate classification.
- USAC cars from the brief period where, for FIA political reasons, the Indianapolis 500 race was made a 'Grand Prix World Championship' event.

Content

Unless it is understood how the regulations have changed from time to time, it would be impossible to see how and why a 1914 Mercedes could possibly relate to a Lotus-Climax of the 1960s, or to a latter-day Ferrari, or McLaren.

Accordingly, the various regulations that have applied over the years have been summarized in Appendix I. In the early days these seemed to change on an annual basis; in the late 1920s something approaching *formule libre* seemed to apply, and it was only in the last years of the last century that anything approaching stability was achieved. Invariably what each Formula was all about has had to be paraphrased: in the 1980s and 1990s, in particular, a lawyer's mind, and cunning, was needed to read through the many rules that applied, and to get the best out of them!

The principal section is a marque-by-marque A–Z listing. Within each marque

entry the various types of car are described in chronological order; as the years passed, it gradually became easier to delineate the various models by their project codes, or those by which they were advertised.

Within the space available, these entries normally recall the mechanical make-up, the designer, the racing career of a type, and the most notable drivers associated with them. In some cases, of marginal makes, one humble paragraph is enough to tell the story, but in the case of famous constructors like Ferrari, a separate book would almost have been in order.

Lastly, and for the sake of completeness, tables of World Championship winning drivers and marques have been included as appendices, although because these were only initiated in the 1950s, only half the story has been told.

At a glance, this book might seem to concentrate more on modern F1 cars than on the titanic machinery of the past, but this is an illusion. The reason, easy to check, but surprising, was that many more different cars have taken part in F1 racing since 1947 than ever attempted to win Grands Prix before 1939.

It is worth recalling that in the early days the French GP was, literally, *the* Grand Prix of that year, and that even in 1927 there were only five events, two of which were held in Italy. When the first 3-litre Championship ran in 1966 there were only nine World Championship rounds, though by 1976 (the year of the titanic Lauda–Hunt, Ferrari–McLaren battle), the full sixteen-race calendar had already been established. At one point in the 1990s, over forty cars wanted to start every race, which explains references to 'Pre-qualifying' and to 'The Wide-Awake Club', which served to reduce the numbers.

Well over 200 marques in less than 100 years! If Grand Prix racing still exists in twenty or even fifty years' time, how many new names will have appeared by then?

◆ A ◆

Abbott-Detroit

A pair of near-stock touring cars was entered in the 1911 Grand Prize at Savannah, to face professional teams running Grand Prix Fiats, Benz and Mercedes. The Abbott-Detroits were running at the end, but were flagged off, too far back to be classified (they would have been the second and third American cars to finish).

Acme

During its short life (1903–10) this Pennsylvania company made some impact on racing in the early (and sometimes wild) 24-hour races on dirt tracks and in stock chassis road races. Optimistically, it also entered a production-based straight six in the 1908 Grand Prize of the AC of America (usually known as the Savannah Grand Prize). This event was modelled on the Grand Prix and attracted leading European teams, so like the other local entries the Acme was outclassed. Driver Len Zengle was in last place when he retired on the seventh of sixteen laps.

AFM

Alex von Falkenhausen built the first AFM single-seater in 1949, following BMW lines – he had been a BMW development engineer – and in the following year several were run in German national races. When German entrants were admitted to International events again from 1950, AFMs appeared more widely in Formula 2 races, with no more than flashes of success. Something more was obviously needed if AFM was to be competitive in the championship Grands Prix run for F2 cars in 1952–53.

Before he closed the AFM business, von Falkenhausen worked towards this, fitting one car with a 1,993cc twin-cam V8, designed by Richard Küchen on the basis of an Abarth project. When it was behaving, this unit produced some 150bhp, which made the light AFM a useful contender in hill climbs. It did not have the stamina or reliability needed for longer races, and it failed to finish a Grand Prix in 1952 (in common with straight-six AFMs hopefully entered by other German teams). Stuck replaced the V8 with a six-cylinder Bristol (née BMW) engine for 1953; he qualified respectably for the German GP, but completed only one lap, then for AFM's last Grand Prix, at Monza, the car was embarrassingly slow and Stuck finished fourteenth.

AGS

Automobiles Gonfaronnaise Sportives' progression from national category constructor in 1970 to Formula 1 constructor in 1986 was conventional, but seldom successful, and it was quite in character that this little Grand Prix venture should fade away before the end of the 1991 season.

Henri Julien's first AGS cars were for *Formule France*, a Formula 3 car followed in 1972, then the first of five Formula 2 types (which were to win just three European F2 Championship races between them, including the last ever). An F3000 car led to the JH21C F1 one-off which made an inauspicious debut late in 1986.

A championship point scored in 1987 seemed encouraging, but there was to be only one more for AGS, in 1989. That year Cyril de Rouvre took control, with Julien retaining an association as a 'consultant'. Hugues de Chaunac became responsible for technical matters, and designer Christian Vanderpleyn gave way to Michel Costa (Claude Galopin took over from him for a short spell, but Costa, Vanderpleyn and Tolentino were to be credited with the last AGS cars). The team's base was in Provence, away from the racing mainstream.

In company terms, AGS failed in 1991. Italians Gabriele Rafanelli and Patrizio Cantu took over, but their recovery plans foundered as the team's dismal record of failing to qualify cars to start in Grands Prix races continued. Realistically, the little team's entries for the last two races of 1991 were withdrawn, and that spelled the end.

AFM V8 of 1950, Hans Stuck driving.

AGS JH23 of 1989, Gabriele Tarquini driving.

JH21C AGS entered the demanding world of Formula 1 at the 13th race of 1986, at Monza with the unlovely JH21C. Vanderpleyn made expedient use of Renault components, primarily a remodelled monocoque, suspension and gearbox. For power, AGS turned to the Motore Moderni V6. Ivan Capelli started the JH21C in the Italian and Portuguese GPs, each time retiring early.

JH22 This followed the 1986 car fairly closely, and was no more handsome. The major change was in the use of normally aspirated Cosworth DFZ engines. Pascal Fabre qualified to start eleven times in fourteen attempts; Roberto Moreno took his place for the last two races of 1987, and in Australia he finished sixth, to score AGS's first championship point.

One of the two cars built was later used as a test vehicle for the abortive Negre MGN01 W12 engine.

JH23 The 1988 AGS looked a better car, and first indications were that it was, especially in aspects such as handling. But the team's meagre resources meant that it was unable to build on initial promise. The chassis was new, and Vanderpleyn clothed it in slender and aerodynamically efficient bodywork; there was double wishbone pushrod suspension, DFZ engines were again used, and there were no Renault elements in the transmission. Philippe Streiff qualified to

start in every Grand Prix, although he was to finish only four times (for a best placing of ninth, in the Portuguese GP).

Personnel changes did nothing to improve the team's fortunes early in 1989, nor did Streiff's serious test accident. The JH24 was delayed, and two JH23s were uprated for Gabriele Tarquini. He qualified a JH23B for the opening races, and scored a point in the Mexican GP, but from the British GP onwards he failed to get an AGS (JH23B or JH24) to a grid. Joachim Winkelhock was entered for the first seven races, but never progressed beyond the pre-qualifying phase.

JH24 The 1989 AGS, designed by Clause Galopin, came in mid-season. Some components were carried over, and DFZ engines were still used, while there was a new and stiffer monocoque. Tarquini was joined by Yannick Dalmas for the last races, but neither driver managed to qualify a JH24.

The cars came out for the first two meetings of 1990, with the front suspension intended for the JH25. Dalmas did qualify to start in the Brazilian GP, only to retire when the front suspension failed.

JH25 Michel Costa was entrusted with this DFR-powered car, notably the sleekest AGS. The first appearance, at Imola, was a non-event; in the next thirteen race meetings, Tarquini got to grids four times, and finished one race (thirteenth

in Hungary), while Dalmas also qualified four times (best placing ninth in Spain). The team had to run JH25s with little revision in 1991. Tarquini managed eighth place in the opening race, then he qualified for just two more races. Johansson, Barbazza and Grouillard tried to qualify AGS JH25s for grids, but none succeeded.

JH26 Some work was done on this successor to the JH25, but it was abandoned early in 1991.

JH27 The first DFR-powered JH27 was just completed for its debut at Monza, but far from race-ready. A pair appeared for the next two races, when Barbazza and Grouillard failed to qualify by discouraging margins. A late September morning at Barcelona saw the last appearances of AGS F1 cars.

Aiden-Cooper

This one-off appeared in 1962 as an enterprising adaptation of the Cooper T59 F Junior car, by Hugh Aiden-Jones, a mechanic with the Anglo-American Racing Team. A Coventry Climax FPF engine was used, driving through a Cooper five-speed gearbox, but the major innovation was in the use of twin radiators in side pods flanking the engine, while the nose was elegantly pointed. However, before the end of the season the front radiator was reinstated.

The car was entered in eight non-championship races, to be driven by Ian Burgess. He qualified each time, usually well down grids, and his best results came in the Naples and Danish GPs, when he took fifth place in each event.

Alco

The American Locomotive Co built imposing and expensive road cars from a 1905 base of a Berliet licence, with its '60hp' straight six coming in 1908. The company test driver, Harry Grant, was convinced that the engine and its chassis had racing potential, but had to quit Alco to build an Alco racer. Its success meant that he rejoined the company as a works racing driver, and he repaid the compliment by winning America's premier road race, the Vanderbilt Cup, in 1909 and 1910. The car was a conventional chain-drive machine, and there have been suggestions that far from being the specified

9.5litre unit, its engine capacity handsomely exceeded the Vanderbilt 9.8litre limit!

Grant started this 'big black Alco' in the 1910 Grand Prize at Savannah, but failed to finish. However, his success in other races persuaded Alco to add two shaft-drive cars to its team in 1911. One of these featured in the fifth Grand Prize, one B. Taylor placing it third at Santa Monica in 1914. That was an independent entry, for Alco had unexpectedly abandoned car manufacture in 1913. One aged Alco Six started in the 1915 Grand Prize race at San Francisco, but was never prominent – this was a period when European Grand Prix cars with more advanced specifications ruled in US racing.

Alcyon

The ACF chose to publish a single result list for its 1912 Grand Prix and the concurrent *Coupe de l'Auto*, hence an Alcyon is credited with tenth place in a Grand Prix. The marque had entered second-level racing for several years, and its 1912 Coupe car was rated a leading competitor. It was a conventional 3litre machine hardly handsome with a solidly bluff nose. The trio entered in the 1912 GP/Coupe race performed well on the first day of the two-day event, but two then retired, leaving Arthur Duray to finish tenth – 4.5 hours behind the overall winner!

Alda

Fernand Charron was a leading driver in the period of heroic city-to-city races; he retired from racing in 1901, to concentrate on the CGV company he had set up with Girardot and Voigt (CGV has a niche place in motor sports history as it built a racing straight eight in 1903). By 1907 the cars were badged Charron, and this marque survived until 1930. But in 1912 Charron had launched Alda, and his new company entered racing in the following year, with a trio of 3litre cars in the *Coupe de l'Auto* (one placed sixth).

That led to a three-car Grand Prix team in 1914. The Alda was neat, with an ohc 4.4litre four-cylinder engine, but it did not stand out in a glittering field. The team's lead driver was Szisz, winner of the first Grand Prix in 1906, whose Alda carried the race number 1. He was fifteenth at the end of the first lap and dropped steadily down the order, to last on lap 11, and then at just over half-distance he retired. The other Aldas had already gone, from lowly positions.

Alfa Aitken

This British one-off started life as the Alfa Romeo Bimotore, and it was rebuilt as a conventional front-engined single-seater for Peter Aitken at the end of the 1930s. In 1947 Tony Rolt had a 3.4litre engine installed, and he ran it as a Formula 1 car until 1949. Generally it was not a success, save in the 1948 Zandvoort GP when Rolt was second in a heat and the final.

The Alfa Aitken was sold to a New Zealand entrant, and eventually returned to Britain, where it was rebuilt as a running Bimotore for the Donington Collection.

Alfa Romeo

See pp.10–15.

Alfa Special

One of the better 'specials' built in South Africa, primarily for a local Formula 1 series (that stipulated four-cylinder engines). It was also seen in full Grand Prix company. The Alfa Special had a space frame and, like some other local cars, used a modified Alfa Romeo Giulietta engine. Performances were more than respectable in some races contested by major European F1 teams, notably the 1962–63 Rand GPs. However, when it came to the South African GP at the end of 1963, the Alfa Special was some seven seconds off the pole pace set by Clark and did not feature in the race before it was retired with transmission failure. It was six seconds away from pole time in 1965, when De Klerk placed it tenth in his country's Grand Prix.

Alphi

A tiny Paris company, Alphi entered a car for the 1930 *formule libre* French Grand Prix, which was to have a grid made up of seventeen Bugattis and an odd assortment of other cars. The Alphi was basically the company's sports car, with a Cozette-supercharged CIME 1.5litre straight six. It was not ready for the race, but it was completed and survived as a museum exhibit.

Alpine

Two Alpine Formula 1 cars were built, a decade apart, and neither was raced. Jean Redele, who had formed Alpine in 1951 and remained in control as it effectively became Renault's racing arm in the 1960s, apparently did not authorize the 1968 F1 car to proceed beyond the project stage. But it did, and was tested by Mauro Bianchi at Zandvoort, in secret but seemingly with discouraging results. It was largely conventional, save in the suspension where a curious upper wishbones arrangement was intended to keep wheels absolutely upright at all times. A Gordini-prepared V8 drove through a Hewland gearbox. After tests it was set aside.

continued on p.15

Alpine A500, with turbo Renault V6. Built in 1976 but never raced.

Alfa Romeo had a long and honourable Grand Prix history, which almost started in 1914 while the company was still A.L.F.A. and ended in 1985, as Ferrari became Fiat's only Formula 1 racing arm. Between these low points, Alfa Romeo teams were dominantly successful at times in the 1920s, 1930s and 1950s, with cars that were 'classics' by any yardstick.

Industrialist Nicola Romeo acquired a majority shareholding in A.L.F.A. in 1915, and the company became Alfa Romeo in 1918. Test driver Ugo Sivocci soon introduced Enzo Ferrari to Romeo, and he was to be closely involved with Alfa Romeo racing activities for almost two decades – through most of the 1930s, the 'official' cars were run by Scuderia Ferrari. Alfa Romeo had a majority shareholding in that team then. Great designers associated with the marque's racing cars were Vittorio Jano and Gioacchino Colombo; unhappily some of the others, from first to last, were not of the same calibre. There were outstanding conventional cars – P2, Tipo B, 158/159 – and some adventurous types, such as the Bimotore (which were the first racing cars built by Ferrari) and the mid-engined Tipo 512.

The 158/159 set the standard as Grand Prix racing resumed after the Second World War, and in the first World Championship seasons. That supremacy could not last, and Ferrari eventually toppled

the proud Alfas. Some Alfa engines were used in Formula 1 cars built in South Africa in the 1960s, then the company returned to the front rank as it supplied engines to the Brabham team. Its own cars followed from 1979, but the approach seemed more in tune with an earlier era than the technological forcing house of Formula 1 as the 1980s opened. Racing responsibility was in the hands of Autodelta, and its struggles mirrored the parent company's difficulties, which were eventually to be resolved after a Fiat takeover. Even if the future of its racing participation was not already uncertain, that spelled the end of the Grand Prix effort – Alfa Romeos were to be very successful in touring car racing in the 1990s, but although F1 engines were supplied to minor constructors such as Minardi and Osella until 1988, Alfa Romeo's glorious racing years were by then long in the past.

1914 GP Car Even the Alfa Romeo archives refer to this 4.5litre car as 'the 1914 GP car', although it was not completed in time to race in that year; after the First World War it was run in events such as the Targa Florio. Designed by Giuseppe Merosi, it appeared dated even in 1914, although the engine specification seemed promising, for the 4,490cc four-cylinder unit had twin overhead camshafts and two valves per cylinder. But its output of 88bhp was not competitive in 1914 GP terms.

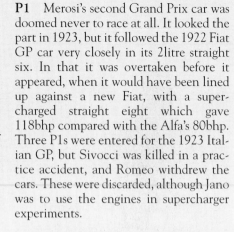

P1 Merosi's second Grand Prix car was doomed never to race at all. It looked the part in 1923, but it followed the 1922 Fiat GP car very closely in its 2litre straight six. In that it was overtaken before it appeared, when it would have been lined up against a new Fiat, with a supercharged straight eight which gave 118bhp compared with the Alfa's 80bhp. Three P1s were entered for the 1923 Italian GP, but Sivocci was killed in a practice accident, and Romeo withdrew the cars. These were discarded, although Jano was to use the engines in supercharger experiments.

P2 Ferrari was the go-between as Vittorio Jano was persuaded to turn his back on Fiat and join Alfa Romeo in 1923. He was to become chief designer three years later. Meanwhile his first Alfa design was the P2, which followed Fiat lines mechanically and had visual resemblances to the P1. The supercharged 1987cc straight eight of the P2 gave some 135bhp when it was first raced, and 155bhp in 1925. Chassis and semi-elliptic spring suspension were conventional, and had to be revised for the more powerful engines used when these three cars were raced in the late 1920s.

Antonio Ascari gave the P2 a debut race win, at Cremona, and then a full team was run in the 1924 French GP, which Campari won, before there was an Alfa 1-2-3 in the Italian GP. In 1925 riding mechanics were no longer called for, so Ascari's victory in the Belgian GP was the first in a single-handed drive (Campari was second, and Alfa domination was so complete that the cars were cleaned during the race!). Ascari's fatal accident in the French GP meant withdrawal from the race. An Italian GP victory meant that a laurel wreath was added to the Alfa Romeo badge.

In 1926 the P2s were run in *formule libre* races, then in the free formula Grands Prix in 1928–30 (the last year they were run by Scuderia Ferrari). Engines were enlarged to 2,006cc, to give some 175bhp. These cars were hardly a match for later Bugattis and Maseratis, but there were highlights (notably when Varzi ended Bugatti's run of Targa Florio victories), and Nuvolari raced P2s in their last season.

Tipo A Jano's approach to the next pure racing Alfa was economical, which was

Alfa Romeo P1 of 1923, Ugo Sivocci driving.

(Above) Alfa Romeo P2, as raced in the late 1920s, Antonio Ascari driving.

(Right) Alfa Romeo Monza, Monaco GP 1933.

appropriate for 1931. This Tipo A had two straight-six engines mounted side-by-side, with a combined capacity of 3,504cc and an output of 230bhp, to give a 240kmph/150mph top speed. There were parallel transmission systems, with one gear lever for two gearboxes. Luigi Arcangeli's fatal crash at Monza meant that the team withdrew its first entry for the Tipo A; later these cars were successful in major Italian races and hill climbs, but generally the Monza was preferred.

Monza Effectively, this was a short-chassis version of the 8C 2300 sports car, with 2.3litre engine developed to give 165bhp (later 178bhp), and normally run with the 'mechanic space' partly faired. Campari and Nuvolari shared one to win the ten-hour Italian GP in 1931, and there were top-three placings in other GPs.

Independent entrants raced Monzas after 1931, and Scuderia Ferrari had to use them through the first half of 1933 as Alfa Romeo withheld the Tipo B. Engines were bored out to 2.55litres (180bhp). There were encouraging results (2-3-4-5-6 for assorted Alfas in the French GP, for example) but by the late summer Alfa Romeo had sensibly released the Tipo B to Ferrari.

Tipo B ('P3') The 'two-seat body' was laid to rest in the 1932 Grand Prix regulations, and the first monoposto GP car was Vittorio Jano's outstanding Tipo B, which became known as P3 as it reflected enthusiasts' assessments that here was a true successor to the P2. The engine was a 2,654cc supercharged version of the straight eight, made up of two blocks of four cylinders with a one-piece cylinder head. The transmission was inspired by the Tipo A; the differential was immediately behind the gearbox, and two angled propeller shafts took the power to twin bevel final drives (thus the differential was sprung weight, and the rear axle was light). There was nothing novel in the suspension or the narrow channel-section chassis, while the body was slim and elegant.

Nuvolari won the 1932 Italian and French GPs, and three Italian regional races; Carraciola won the German GP and the Monza GP in a Tipo B. Then Alfa Romeo withdrew the cars, releasing them to Ferrari in the summer of 1933, when Fagioli and Chiron each used them to win three races.

For the 750kg (1,650lb) formula, the width at the cockpit had to be increased while the engines were bored out to 2,905cc (power was raised from 215bhp to 255bhp – not enough to compete with the new German cars). The Alfa Romeos won the first full confrontation, in the French GP, and also won at Monaco and in a string of secondary races.

For 1935 a Dubonnet independent front suspension was used, with revised rear suspension, and so were 3.2litre engines. The last great race for the Tipo B came as Nuvolari drove one to a sensational victory in the German GP. There were secondary successes as the Tipo B faded from the GP scene, although there were appearances in sport car guise and one was raced in the Indianapolis 500 in 1939, 1940 and as the Don Lee Spl in 1946–47.

Incidentally, the Tipo B provided the basis for the Bimotore, designed by Luigi Bazzi and built by Ferrari in 1935. A lengthened Tipo B chassis carried a straight eight ahead of the cockpit and another behind it. Chiron and Nuvolari drove to creditable places in *formule libre* races, and the Italian set class records in a 6.4litre Bimotore.

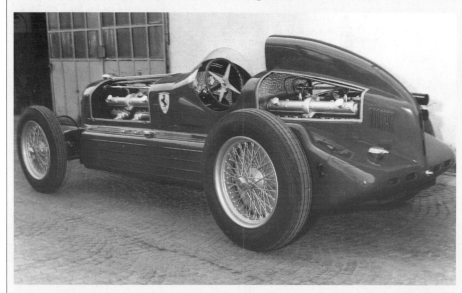

Alfa Romeo Bimotore of 1935, with two engines and 6.3litres.

8C 35 This was an interim car, pending completion of a 12-cylinder engine. It had the straight eight, with bore increased to give a 3.8litre capacity. The suspension was independent all round, with a swing axle at the rear. The cars were fast on occasion in 1935, but fragile.

12C 36 Outwardly this was similar to the 8C 35, for save in details such as exhausts it used the same body, on the same running gear. The 4.1litre 60-degree V12 gave 370bhp, some 40bhp more than the 3.8litre straight eight, but as much as 150bhp less than the Auto Union's monstrous 6litre engine.

Nevertheless, in the hands of Nuvolari the 12C 36 did beat the German cars in 1936, in the Penya Rhin, Hungarian and Milan Grands Prix. He also won the Vanderbilt Cup in one. In 1937 he won the secondary Circuit of Milan race, but generally these cars were outclassed.

Alfa Romeo Tipo 12C, Nuvolari driving in the 1937 German GP.

12C 37 Introduced in mid-1937, this car 'looked right', but was not right. It had a 4,495cc 430bhp version of the V12, and it had handling shortcomings. Jano was held responsible, and left Alfa Romeo.

308 In 1938 Scuderia Ferrari broke its ties with Alfa, while Alfa Corse soon despaired, and did not contest all Grands Prix. Three cars were available to the team, all with similar tubular chassis and suspension, independent all round with swing axles and integral gearboxes at the rear. The 308 had the long-used straight eight in 2,991cc form, developing 295bhp – not enough to challenge the German teams. A 308 accident led Nuvolari to turn away from Alfa Romeo. 308s won odd secondary races in 1938–39, and after the Second World War. They were used by independents as well as Alfa Corse.

312 This used a 3litre version of the V12, giving some 320bhp. Giuseppe Farina twice finished second behind Mercedes in 312s in 1938, but this was not a significant car.

316 The V16 alternative was seldom seen, although Farina did drive one to second place in the 1938 Italian GP. Its 2,958cc engine had twin crankshafts, and the claimed output was 440bhp.

162 This car was to be a fresh-start Alfa Romeo, designed by Wilfredo Ricart (his arrival at Alfa was a prime reason for Ferrari's departure). It had low and purposeful lines, and a 135-degree, two-stage supercharged, dohc V16, for which 490bhp was claimed. The intention was to have it raceworthy for 1940.

512 Another unraced car, inspired by Auto Union designs, which even at rest in the Alfa Romeo museum looks as if it should have had potential. Under Ricart's direction, Colombo designed a car with a 1,490cc supercharged flat 12 behind the cockpit. A central fuel tank led to an upright driving position. It was

(Above) Alfa Romeo Tipo 512, mid-engined, completed in 1941 but never raced.

completed sluggishly, and not tested until 1943.

158/159 The dominant car of the first World Championship seasons – even in 1949, when it was not raced, its presence in the background worried other teams – this design was initiated by Ferrari for *vetturetta* racing, the 'second division' of the period. It was designed by Colombo along straightforward lines, with an oval-tube chassis and independent chassis following other 1938 racing Alfas. The power unit was a dohc supercharged straight eight, in effect half of the V16, which gave 195bhp when it was first raced. These 158s, then known as Alfettas, were raced ten times in 1938–40, when they won six times.

The cars were hidden away in 1943, then brought out to race again in 1946. The two first run retired, but then the GP des Nations at Geneva saw the first of a

Alfa Romeo Tipo 158, Varzi driving in the Swiss GP of 1947.

long sequence of victories (Farina headed a 1-2-3 in that race). By that time two-stage supercharging had been adopted, and power was up to 254bhp; a year later the quoted figure was 310bhp.

In 1947 the team contested four races, Varzi (twice), Wimille and Trossi driving the winning 158s. In 1948 Wimille won three races, Trossi one, and there were no defeats. For several reasons (cost and the R&D commitment to bread-and-butter models among them) Alfa withdrew from racing in 1949. In the first World Championship season, 1950, the team won all of the eleven races it entered – Farina won six, and the first drivers' title, while Fangio won five.

To meet the Ferrari challenge in 1951, there were new cars – 159s, some with de Dion rear ends – and the engine was taken to and beyond its limits with raised supercharger pressures (the superchargers in turn had to be driven, and that sapped outright power). Up to 400bhp was the realistic maximum, although as much as 425bhp was produced by the ultimate 159M. In the French GP, Fangio and Fagioli shared a 159 to secure the 27th consecutive victory for the 158/159. Then came defeat, by Ferrari, in the British GP. But Fangio secured the championship with a last-gasp win, in the Spanish GP.

160 Late in 1952 a hack 159 (one of the de Dion cars) was tested at Monza with a cockpit behind the rear axle. The experiment was hardly conclusive, but the idea was carried forward by Giuseppe Busso to the planning stage for a car for the 2.5litre Formula. This 160 would have been an extraordinary machine. It was to be a four-wheel drive car with a flat 12 engine (the only major component built, although apparently it was not even bench-tested), a backbone chassis comprising a large-diameter tube with the transmission running inside it, and the engine used as a stressed member. The supposed advantages of sitting the driver at the rear, outside the wheelbase, were unproven. At least it would have removed the weakness of a large hole for the driver in the middle of the car – later a drawback in first-generation space frame cars – and the intrepid pilot would have had an unrivalled view of impending accidents.

177 Some South African constructors used Alfa Romeo engines in the 1960s, and the company made a modest return as the 1970s opened, supplying sports-car based V8s to McLaren and March, then developing a flat twelve F1 engine from a unit that had sports-car origins. This was used by Brabham in 1976–78, and it was followed by a V12 for 1979. That year Brabham turned away from the Alfa units (actually designed and produced by Carlo Chiti's Autodelta concern).

There seemed an inevitability as Autodelta, and hence Alfa Romeo, edged back towards full F1 participation. This came gradually, and although the Tipo 177 ran its first tests in 1978 it did not race until late Spring 1979. It appeared substantial rather than elegant, and used the 2,995cc 115-12 V12; the claimed output was 520bhp. The 177 was raced three times, Bruno Giacomelli retiring it twice and finishing seventeenth in the French GP.

179 Autodelta felt its way into Formula 1 with the one-off 177, and in Autumn 1979 its 179 appeared, and for the last races of the season there was a two-car team. The 179 had the Type 1260 V12, rated at 525bhp. The car was revised for 1980, and through the year became increasingly competitive, especially in Giacomelli's hands. Patrick Depailler was killed in a test accident at Hockenheim. Giacomelli was joined by Andretti for 1981, but just as Autodelta seemed to come to terms with 'sliding skirts' it was wrong-footed by a ban on these devices and the hydropneumatic suspension lowering system. At least its WC points score reached ten.

Alfa Romeo 179 of 1979–80, with V12 engine. Brambilla driving in the US GP of 1979.

Alfa Romeo 183T of 1983, Andrea de Cesaris driving.

The 179D which came in mid-1981 was no more successful. A late 179F had a carbon-fire monocoque, and in 1982 a 179 was tested with a turbocharged 1.5litre V8. Meanwhile, in 1981 Gerard Ducarouge had joined, and influenced design work.

182/182T Although the 182 looked as bulky as the 179, it had a lighter British-built carbon-fibre monocoque. The first cars were powered by a 530bhp version of the V12. These sometimes showed promise, but as frequently cars were damaged by the accident-prone Andrea de Cesaris (at least he led the Long Beach race from pole before crashing). In 1982 de Cesaris and Giacomelli mustered seven points.

The 182T appeared late that year, although it was not raced. The 890 90-degree turbocharged V8 was rated at 600bhp. Its narrower monocoque had been seen on a V12-powered car, but the 182T still looked hefty.

183T This was a 'flat-bottom' derivative of the 182T; its 1983 season was promising – de Cesaris was second in the German and South African GPs, and with Baldi scored eighteen points for Alfa Romeo. The team had actually become Euroracing Alfa Romeo, although Autodelta continued to build the cars. Ducarouge left under a cloud, and Luigi Marmiroli took his place. In 1984, incidentally, Paolo Pavanello of Euroracing was to ease out Chiti.

184T Marmiroli designed this slimmer car, with up-to-the-minute suspension and the turbo engine rated at 670bhp. But fortunes slipped, with Patrese's third place in the 1984 Italian GP the highlight (Patrese and Cheever scored eleven points that year – Alfa's last in championship racing). The 184Ts had to be used again in 1985, as the 185T derivative was a failure.

185T John Gentry undertook this reworking of the 184T, principal changes being in the suspension. However, he left before development work started, and by mid-season Euroracing had abandoned the car.

That season was the last for the Alfa Romeo cars in Grand Prix racing and, sadly, through the 1980s achievements had not remotely lived up to the marque's illustrious past.

continued from p.9

The second car was the forerunner of the Renault turbocharged F1 cars of the late 1970s, and its *Laboratoire* name gives a clue to the intensity of the preparations for that programme. This A500 was designed by André de Cortanze, using A442 sports-racing car suspension and a 1.5litre turbo V6 developed by Castaing and Dudot, with Alpine's first monocoque. It was tested at French circuits and at Jarama in 1976. A range of body variations was tried, such as a bulky full-width nose and conventional front wing arrangement and air intakes atop the engine cover or alongside it. This test vehicle served its purpose in Renault's F1 programme, and oddly was the last Alpine to be laid down before the company was wholly absorbed by Renault.

Alta

Geoffrey Taylor's tiny company built sports cars in the 1930s, and its first single-seater *voiturette* late in that decade, when a 3litre Grand Prix car was also planned. One of the 1.5litre cars started in the 1938 Donington Grand Prix, distinguishing itself only by dropping its engine oil at the hairpin, to the embarrassment of some of the drivers of German GP cars.

Immediately after the end of the Second World War Taylor started work on a 1.5litre supercharged GP car. This took shape slowly, and the first car did not appear at a race meeting until 1948 (in the Isle of Man). Two more followed, at yearly intervals. The tubular chassis was conventional, but the double wishbone independent suspension was complemented by rubber block springing, which was to prove inconsistent. The engine was a 1,485cc

(78 × 78mm) four-cylinder unit with single-stage supercharging; the third car had two-stage supercharging, and the engine was credited with 230bhp. An Alta four-speed gearbox was used.

George Abecassis gave the first car its race debut, and its first Grand Prix was that year's Swiss event. Modest success came in 1949, when the first car was seventh in the British GP and the second was seventh in Belgium. The owner of the

Alta of 1949, George Abecassis driving in the French GP.

Alta ahead of Talbot at the 1950 British GP, Geoffrey Crossley driving the Alta, Johnny Claes the Talbot.

third car, Joe Kelly, achieved a notable third placing in the 1952 Ulster Trophy; this car became the basis of Kelly's Irish Racing Automobile (IRA) F2 car in 1952.

Alta entered that 2litre category with another straightforward car, still using rubber springing. Its 1,970cc (83.5 × 90mm) engine was rated at 140bhp in 1951, and 150bhp in 1952, in the last two Alta cars. These were never really competitive (Peter Whitehead's seventh place in a heat of the 1951 Monza GP was the best International result). The engines were used in more successful Cooper and HWM chassis.

Late in 1952 Alta announced a 90-degree dohc fuel-injection 2,470cc (75 × 70mm) V8 for the 2.5litre formula that was to come in 1954. Its estimated output was 260bhp, and the intention was to offer it to other constructors, as well as to use it in an Alta chassis that was also stillborn. The only Alta 2.5litre GP units completed and raced were the four-cylinder engines supplied to Connaught.

Alvis

In the mid-1920s Alvis turned to front-wheel drive for its competition cars, and followed this pattern in a pair of Grand Prix cars in 1926. These were powered by a 1,497cc straight eight with horizontally opposed valves and a camshaft on each side of the engine and a Roots-type supercharger; it developed some 100bhp. The channel-section chassis was conventional, but as well as independent front suspension there were inboard front brakes. The entry for the first British Grand Prix was withdrawn, as the cars were not ready (they were run in another Brooklands race later in the year, without success).

The engine was revised for 1927, primarily with orthodox overhead camshafts. In this form it gave perhaps 125bhp. The single car entered for the British Grand Prix was withdrawn after practice … so the Alvis Grand Prix cars never did start in a Grand Prix.

Amon

By common consent, Chris Amon was unlucky never to win a World Championship race – he certainly deserved to, with Ferrari and Matra at least, among the eleven marques he drove for. He was no more fortunate in his 1974 venture as a

Alvis, with front-wheel drive, hitting a sand bank at Brooklands.

Amon AF101, Chris Amon driving.

constructor, although judgements in that sphere could be questioned.

With backing from John Dalton, Amon commissioned a design by Gordon Fowell. One AF101 was completed, from components made by John Thompson and assembled by Amon's little team. The car was complex, with a slim aluminium monocoque and torsion-bar suspension with inboard brakes all round (outboard at the front after the car's only race). DFV engines were used. The car appeared unusual, and although the aerodynamic work by Tom Boyce was reckoned to be sound, substantial changes were to be made to the nose.

In tests and race practice sessions there were component failures, and a crash when Larry Perkins was driving at the Nürburgring. The AF101 started in just one race, the 1974 Spanish GP, when Amon retired at quarter-distance with brakeshaft failure.

Andrea Moda

Few Grand Prix ventures have started so inauspiciously, or ended in such ignominy. Andrea Moda Formula (AMF) flickered on the Formula 1 fringe in 1992, born of shoe magnate Andrea Sassetti's ambitions and on the back of the hapless Coloni team, whose negligible assets Sassetti had acquired after the 1991 season. Resources were far from adequate, and the first setback came when the team's attempt to run Coloni C4Bs in the first race was rejected by FISA. An existing Nick Wirth design was adopted for the

Andrea Moda S921, and mechanics were working to complete two cars in the Mexico City paddock as the second Grand Prix meeting of the year got under way (the cars did not run in qualifying sessions).

The S921 was conventional, with double wishbone suspension all round, powered by the Judd GV V10 which drove through a transverse gearbox.

The first nominated drivers, Caffi and Bertaggia, quit the team in Mexico; Roberto Moreno qualified to start just once (from the back of the Monaco grid, and completed eleven racing laps), while he failed to pre-qualify to take part in timed practice six times, and failed to qualify for grids twice; Perry McCarthy was never given a reasonable chance by the team, and reached the qualification phase only once in the eight times he was entered.

Ironically, McCarthy qualified for timed practice at the Belgian GP meeting, when bailiffs arrived on the second day and removed Sassetti from the circuit. The next meeting, at Monza, saw FISA exclude Andrea Moda from the championship for bringing it into disrepute.

Apollon

This name was used by the Swiss Jolly Club for its 1977 Italian Grand Prix entry for Loris Kessel. It was in fact a Williams FW03 with some body revisions. Predictably the combination was off the pace at Monza, Kessel failing to qualify for the last row of the grid by more than six seconds.

Aquila Italiana

In the late Edwardian years, Aquila Italiana designer Giulio Cesare Cappa laid out some advanced engines for the company's touring cars. These were seen in competitions in 1913, and a year later in the first (and only) Aquila Italiana Grand Prix car. This was a good-looking machine, low-built in the then new fashion, with an sohc straight six. Only one of the projected trio was completed in time for the Grand Prix at Lyon; driven by Bartolomeo Costantini, it retired on the second lap with engine failure. Aquila Italiana car production ended in 1917. Cappa went on to design successful Fiat GP cars.

Arrol-Johnston

This Scottish company never built a Grand Prix car as such, but one of its three rather pedestrian cars run in the 1912 *Coupe de l'Auto* was classified ninth in the concurrent Grand Prix, albeit over four hours behind the winning Peugeot. The Arrol-Johnston was not far removed from the company's touring model, and was unusual by 1912 for its radiator-behind-engine layout. It was distinguished in the Dieppe race by Gordon tartan colours, which the French authorities prescribed as Scottish racing colours!

Arrows

See pp.19–23.

Arzani-Volpini

One of the Maserati-Milano F1 cars of 1950 was reworked by Edigio Arzani and Gianpaolo Volpini for amateur driver Mario Alborghetti to race in the next Formula 1, in 1955. The ladder chassis was retained, with double wishbone independent front suspension and a de Dion rear axle. The 1.5litre engine of the original car had, of course, been supercharged, and in the Arzani-Volpini a normally aspirated Maserati 'four' enlarged to 2,492cc was used. Attractive new bodywork, on Maserati 250F lines, gave the impression that this was an up-to-date GP car.

Its one race start was in the non-championship Pau GP, where the inexperienced Alborghetti was fatally injured in a crash. The car was rebuilt and entered for the 1955 Italian GP, but it failed to appear at Monza.

Andrea Moda of 1992, Roberto Moreno driving at Monaco.

Arrows survived through two decades of World Championship racing on a record of little achievement, sometimes deserving better, through changes of ownership and even a passing name change. Its origins were in management disagreements in the Shadow team late in 1977; Jackie Oliver and Alan Rees left to form another team, and were joined by designer Tony Southgate and draughtsman Dave Wass. Financial backing came from Italian Franco Ambrosio. The initial letters of their surnames were arranged to form the team's name, with an added 'R' to make a word. A base was set up at Milton Keynes.

There a Grand Prix car was designed and built within the 60 days available before the second championship race of 1978 – an important deadline, for an Arrow had to contest it in order that the team qualified for FOCA membership, and its tangible benefits. Inevitably, perhaps, the FA1 resembled the Shadow DN9, and the judgement in a London High Court case found that 40 per cent of the components had been copied, so the cars had to be destroyed. Anticipating this, Southgate had a replacement in hand, and the A1 was ready as the court case ended!

The Arrows story then followed fairly predictable lines, with some good cars and some mediocre ones, seldom with sponsorship that was any more than adequate. Dave Wass took over as designer from 1981–86, when Ross Brawn took his place until 1989. By that time only Oliver and Rees of the original management team remained, and the Japanese Footwork Group had acquired a major shareholding. Its principal, Watara Ohashi, was prepared to spend, to win the World Championship. As far as Arrows was concerned, there was a price: by 1991 the team was Footwork, and that lasted until the end of 1993.

Track fortunes hardly improved. 'Second-line' BMW turbo engines had not been competitive, nor were Cosworth customer units at the end of the 1980s. A Porsche V12 was hopeless, and with it in 1991 the team hit bottom, scoring no championship points for the only time in its history.

Oliver regained control in 1994, and two years later Tom Walkinshaw took a substantial holding, and control of the team. Alan Jenkins had been designing competent cars since Brawn left, but what Arrows still did not have in the 1990s was a competitive engine – Mugen, Ford, Hart, Yamaha and Arrows's own

Arrows A2 of 1979.

unit were used. A great moment came in 1997 when an Arrows, driven by Damon Hill, led a Grand Prix for the first time since the team's second race, in 1978.

At the end of the century, though, Arrows was still flattering, but not delivering. Finance always seemed to be a problem – there was little worthwhile sponsorship on the car in 1998 and 1999, and a promised massive input of funds from a shadowy Nigerian never materialized – but for 2000 the high-profile mobile phone company, Orange, came on board to brighten up the image *and* the company's prospects.

By 2000, and aided by a very effective new aerodynamic package, the car's potential was better than it had been for a decade. If only Arrows had a 'works' engine supply, and could hold on to their star engineers ...

FA1 This car looked promising, with a slim monocoque, double ground effects wing sections, and purposeful lines. There was rocker arm and wishbone suspension, with upper and lower links and radius rods at the rear. DFV engines and Hewland gearboxes were used.

Patrese led during Arrows's first race, in South Africa, before retiring, scored

the team's first point at Long Beach and was second in the Swedish GP before the cars had to be broken up.

A1 The second 1978 Arrows had some resemblance to the first, but the undercar airflow was improved, largely as the rear suspension elements were mounted inboard. Patrese was fourth in the Canadian GP in an A1, and the team ended its first season in ninth place in the Constructors' Championship, with eleven points. A1B was a revised version for 1979, primarily with modified suspension and aerodynamic detailing. The best race placing was Patrese's fifth in Belgium, while Mass scored a single point at Monaco.

A2 This singular car led to raised eyebrows in the Dijon paddock before its race debut, and its shortcomings were soon recognized (Mass was later to score two sixth placings with A2s, and that seemed remarkable). Arrows liked references to the bullet nose, although the appellation 'doodlebug' was more apt. Engine and gearbox were tilted up at the rear, to permit a full-width undercar aerofoil section, overall lines were rounded and seemed bulky (although that impression was misleading),

(Above) Arrows A3 of 1980, Rolf Stommelen driving.

(Below) Arrows A4 at the 1982 Austrian GP, Mauri Baldi driving.

front suspension members were faired. This wing car suffered from 'porpoising' – generous downforce was there, but it was not properly employed.

A3 Southgate and Wass got the aerodynamics right in this car for 1980, Wass then got the revisions right as the ban on ground effects came in 1981, but like other teams Arrows was then caught out by Brabham's suspension lowering device. That apart, the A3 had top rocker arm/lower wishbone suspension all round. There was the usual Cosworth/Hewland combination at the back.

In 1980 Patrese placed an A3 second at Long Beach, but then scored only one more point in the season, while Mass contributed four. In 1981 Patrese scored ten points early in the year; team mate Stohr's best finish was seventh, in Holland.

A4 Necessarily an economic design, this was a compact wing car for 1982. It had Arrows's first honeycomb monocoque. Surer and Baldi scored five points, Henton none in his three drives for the team.

A5 A one-off car that was raced only three times in 1982 (best finish was Surer's seventh in the USA). It was lighter than the A4 and had pullrod suspension. There

were resemblances to the Williams FW08. This car was converted to the 'flat bottom' A6 specification in 1983.

A6 Save that it was a 'flat bottom' car from the outset, the A6 was in a line of evolution, handicapped as Arrows resources would not run to carbon-fibre monocoques and the team still used DFVs. Marc Surer scored the team's only points (four) early in 1983, Serra twice came close to scoring, but generally these cars were mid-field runners.

Three of them were used in the first races of 1984, effectively standing in until the BMW-powered Arrows became raceworthy. Thierry Boutsen scored three points with an A6 – as many as he and Marc Surer were to collect with A7s later in the year.

A7 When Arrows obtained turbo engines in 1984 they were not top-spec works BMW units, and lack of freedom in positioning the ancillaries compromised the A7 design. That in any case had the built-in drawback of too much A6 technology – its use was enforced by lack of time – which was not really adequate for the greater power of the engines.

A8 The A8 was an up-to-the-minute turbo car, with a carbon-fibre monocoque, pushrod front suspension and pullrod rear suspension, and Arrows's own installations for the Mader-prepared BMW engines and ancillaries. In most respects this was the best Arrows since the first Southgate cars, Boutsen and Berger scoring fourteen points (giving Arrows eighth place in the Constructors' Championship) in 1985; Boutsen's second place at Imola was the best single performance.

The cars had to be used again in 1986, when they were no longer competitive and Christian Danner scored Arrows's only point.

A9 Wass's last Arrows design appeared bulky alongside the A8, and turned out to be a one-off that was raced only three times, in the second half of 1986.

A10 Arrows entered a new period in 1987, with adequate sponsorship from USF&G, while Ross Brawn joined from Lola to take on the design role. Megatron, a USF&G company, became responsible for the 'upright' BMW engines; these were renamed Megatron, but failed to match the Honda V6 turbos that became dominant that year. The car followed conventional lines, for example in its pushrod suspension. It was refined as the A10B for 1988, most notably as Mader developed the engine to meet the restricted boost/lower fuel allowance regulations (power was down to perhaps 650bhp compared with more than 800bhp in 1987, but reliability was improved).

Derek Warwick and Eddie Cheever were the team's drivers, harvesting eleven points in 1987, then twenty-three points in 1988 – Arrows's best ever scores, and good for equal fourth place in the Constructor's Championship.

A11 In this slim car, Arrows reverted to Cosworth V8 engines, this time the DFR (giving 600bhp at most in 1989). The car had a carbon fibre/honeycomb composite chassis, suspension on A10 lines, and a transverse six-speed gearbox. It looked good on the 1989 grids, and although it was hardly competitive the team did accumulate

thirteen points (Cheever scored six, and the best race placing, third in the US Grand Prix, while Warwick scored seven).

Entered by Footwork Arrows Racing, revised cars designated A11B were run in 1990. James Robinson simplified the fuel system around a central cell, introduced a new front suspension, and changed details. Cosworth DFRs were still used. The new driver pairing was Alboreto and Caffi, the latter scoring the team's only points, two at Monaco (Schneider also had two fruitless drives).

For the early 1991 races, chassis were modified (as A11Cs) to accommodate a Porsche V12, for which Footwork had high hopes.

Arrows A8, with BMW turbo power, in the 1985 Monaco GP.

Footwork became the entrant in 1991, but the Arrows's numerical designation sequence was continued.

FA12 This was Alan Jenkins's first design for Arrows and followed fashion in the front wing pylon-suspended under the nose. The name 'Porsche' appeared on the engine cover, and getting the German power unit for the first time cost Watara Ohashi a lot of dollars. But from the outset it was only too obvious that this overweight 80-degree V12 was unreliable and – on paper or in a car – none too powerful. In mid-season the cars had to be adapted to use Cosworth DFRs. That

called for a system of transfer gears, as the power take-off was in the middle of the V12; the 'temporary' use of the DFR lasted to the end of the season, when drivers (Alboreto, Caffi and Johansson) often struggled to qualify, and the team recorded a zero in championship points terms.

FA13 Jenkins's approach to the 1992 car was cautious, for the setbacks of 1991 meant that the team was among the pre-qualifying small fry. Save for the front wing, the car looked similar to the FA12, but there were substantial differences, to accommodate a Mugen (Honda) 72-degree V10 and a Footwork Xtrac six-speed transverse gearbox.

Albereto's six points pulled the team back to respectability, and Suzuki failed to qualify only twice (his best race finish was seventh).

Once again the chassis had to be uprated for the start of a new season, FA13Bs being run in two 1993 races. Modifications were actually minuscule. Warwick had rejoined, and finished both races (once classified although he had spun off).

FA14 The 1993 car was lighter, still with Mugen V10s, and from the early summer with an active suspension system 'bought-in' from McLaren. This was soon sorted out, and with it the cars were competitive.

But now there were unlucky incidents, so the year's points tally was four, scored by Warwick in two races (Suzuki managed only four finishes).

FA15 Footwork lingered as the entrant's name in 1994, but otherwise had no involvement, and Arrows had to live with modest sponsorship again. Moreover, there were no Mugen engines – another outcome of a Far Eastern economic downturn. Jenkins produced a neat design around the Cosworth HB V8. Hasty reactions to Senna's fatal accident brought precipitate changes in the F1 regulations, and those affecting aerodynamics caught out Arrows. Late in the summer, Christian Fittipaldi and Gianni Morbidelli did place fourth and fifth in the German GP, and between them scored nine points.

FA16 The 1995 car was laid out for the compact Hart 830 72-degree V8, and other major departures were in the rear suspension and longitudinal six-speed gearbox. Suspension variations were to be tried during the year. Finance was again a handicap, and the two drivers who brought money to the team were hardly top calibre. The presence of Inoue and Papis meant that Morbidelli was sometimes side-lined, but he scored the team's five points, four of them when he was third in the 1995 Australian GP.

FA17 This was laid down for the first season of the Tom Walkinshaw regime, 1996, when the team was moved to Leafield and there were many personnel changes, most notably Jenkins's departure. Frank Dernie took his place, to inherit another neat Hart-powered design. This had a six-speed longitudinal semi-automatic

Arrows (Footwork-Arrows) FA13, with Mugen-Honda power, 1992.

gearbox. Little development work was put into it in an essentially transitional year, when Jos Verstappen scored Arrows's only point.

A18 Dernie laid out this car, then he left as John Barnard was brought in as technical director. The car had a 'high-nose' silhouette, and less obviously had considerable stiffening from the cockpit back. Judd-developed Yamaha 72-degree V10s drove through the longitudinal six-speed semi-automatic 'box.

The first part of the 1997 season was beset by problems, then Damon Hill led the Hungarian GP convincingly before finishing second – rare achievements in Arrows's history! Hill scored only one

other point, and Pedro Diniz contributed two, giving Arrows nine points and eighth place in the Constructors' Championship.

A19 Although sleek, and beautifully detailed, as John Barnard's cars always tend to be, the A19 was late on the scene, virtually untested before the first race – and only scored three points throughout the 1998 season. Before the end of the year Barnard had moved on (this time to consult with Prost), and development stagnated.

Compared with the A18, the big change was to buy in power by the Hart V10, and to secure its future Tom Walkinshaw bought that company during the year and renamed the engine an 'Arrows',

Arrows FA16 of 1995, Hart V8-powered.

though that did not mean there was any more power. In theory this meant that there would be more reliability than with the troublesome Yamaha of yore – but it took months to achieve that end. The A19's other principal novelties were a gearbox with a carbon-fibre casing, and front suspension with horizontal torsion bars mounted within the chassis.

Damon Hill having moved on (to end his F1 career with Jordan), Mika Salo became the lead driver, which was encouraging, while rent-a-drive Pedro Diniz also proved to be surprisingly fleet. During 1998 too many engine problems spoiled the finishing record, and there were only three Championship points, so the team could only hope for better fortune in 1999.

A20 Because of their very restricted financial status, Arrows could afford to make only minimal changes for the 1999 season, so the 'new' A20 was little more than a lightly modified A19. For the same reason the Hart V10 engine, which was always designed and built by a plucky little concern, received little development, and even that dried up by mid-season, by which time Tom Walkinshaw had announced a change to Renault 'customer' power for 2000.

Financial input promised by Nigerian entrepreneur Malik Ado Ibrahim was a chimera that never materialized, so the miracle was that Arrows could continue to start every race of the 1999 season.

Team recruit Pedro de la Rosa amazed everyone by scoring one Championship point in the first race – Australia – but that was that, and it was never added to throughout the rest of the year. Toranosuke Takagi, supposedly rapid, was always a disappointment, and was not retained.

A21 Buoyed up by the announcement of good financial backing from Orange and the use of old but sturdy Supertec/Renault V10 engines, Arrows predicted great things for their new car for the 2000 season.

Arrows A18 of 1997, powered by Yamaha V10.

Designed by technical director Mike Coughlan, and aided by ex-Stewart aerodynamicist Eghbal Hamidy, it bore visual similarities to the 1999 Stewart SF-3 and was thought to be far superior in aerodynamic qualities to any previous Arrows. Supertec/Renault claimed to have upgraded the engine to 780bhp, while the entire design and aura of the latest machine was claimed to be a great step forward.

Points, at least, were scored, but the team was still wallowing in seventh place in the standings, and few could understand the move to updated Peugeot V12 engines that was proposed for 2001.

Arrows A20 of 1999, with Hart V10 engine.

Assegai

A South African one-off from the early 1960s, this space-frame car was built by Tony Kotze, and had notably slim lines. Like some of its contemporaries it was powered by a modified Alfa Romeo Giulietta engine, but unlike them it was entered in only one full Formula 1 race. Kotze failed in his attempt to qualify it for that 1962 Rand GP at Kyalami.

Aston-Butterworth

Bill Aston built a pair of F2 cars on Cooper lines in 1952, one for his own use and the second for Robin Montgomerie-Charrington. These had box-section chassis and transverse leaf spring independent suspension, and the low and compact power unit meant that Aston could give the cars very attractive body lines. When he failed to buy a German engine, Aston turned to Butterworth's AJB air-cooled flat four that rated no more than 140bhp. In the transmission a four-speed MG gearbox was used.

These cars were not at their best on fast circuits – in 1952 for example, Montgomerie-Charrington's best practice lap at Reims was 18sec off pole pace, while at Silverstone in the following year Aston was 24sec away from Moss's pole time. The best showing in a title race came in the 1952 European GP at Spa, when Montgomerie-Charrington ran as high as seventh before retiring.

Aston-Butterworth, driven by Robin Montgomerie-Charrington in 1952 with AJB flat-four engine.

Aston Martin

In racing, Aston Martin has almost invariably been associated with sports cars, and its two Grand Prix ventures enjoyed little success. The first, in 1922, involved cars that were not Grand Prix cars *per se*, while in the 1950s an entry into Formula 1 with cars based on sports-car design and practices soon seem ill-judged.

The lead-in to the 1950s programme came in the form of a 2.9litre single-seater based on the DB3S sports-racer that was raced in New Zealand in 1956.

Formula 1 cars based on the DBR sports cars followed, but as priority was given to the sports car programme, these did not race until the end of the decade – too late, since the era of the front-engined Grand Prix car had passed. Achievements declined from a promising start, with a few reasonable results coming in Tasman series races, when the cars were run with 3litre engines. In that form, they have been splendid attractions in more recent historic racing.

1922 Count Louis Zborowski financed the construction of two 1.5litre cars for a race in the Isle of Man, but as they were not ready for that, the pair became Grand Prix cars. In that guise they were handicapped from the outset, with 1,486cc engines when the 1922 Grand Prix capacity limit was 2litres. The dohc, 16-valve, four-cylinder engine was designed by Marcel Gremillon and credited with 55bhp. a channel-section chassis was carried on semi-elliptic springs (which also had to support some ballast, as the cars weighed in below the 750kg (1,654lb) minimum.

In the French GP at Strasbourg, Clive Gallop ran as high as sixth in one of the Astons before retiring at half distance (Zborowski had kept pace with him earlier, before retiring). Zborowski finished second in the 1.5litre GP de Penya Rhin at Barcelona. He drove the third car, built in 1923, to a similar result in that year's Barcelona race, and Gallop raced it at the Sitges track.

Aston Martin GP car of 1922, Clive Gallop driving.

Aston Martin DBR4/250 of 1959, Carroll Shelby driving at Silverstone.

The second car became the basis of the Halford Special (qv), while the first was road-equipped with a replacement engine.

DBR4/250 This car's long gestation period told heavily against it when it was eventually raced. It followed mid-1950s lines, and by the end of that decade the perception of a racing car had changed vastly. The chassis was a narrow version of the Aston sports car's, initially with torsion bar springing (coil springs were substituted at the front during development). This was the last Grand Prix car to be raced with a de Dion rear axle, although Ferrari toyed with this arrangement in the 1970s. The 2,492cc F1 version of the straight six gave 250bhp, hardly a competitive output in 1959. The car was substantially overweight and there were reliability problems.

The first outing promised much, when Roy Salvadori was second in the 1959 International Trophy at Silverstone. But in championship races, Salvadori and Carroll Shelby were never well placed on grids and the best race finishes were sixth, achieved by Salvadori in Britain and Portugal.

DBR5 This 1960 derivative of the DBR4 was smaller and substantially lighter (by some 135kg/298lb 'dry') than the four 1959 cars. Some of the weight saving was due to the adoption of a Maserati transaxle. The second of the pair built had independent rear suspension. New cylinder heads made for a loss of power, and fuel injection hardly compensated for this.

This time there was little promise in the first race, again at Silverstone, while poor practice showings meant that the first Grand Prix entry, in Holland, was withdrawn. The two cars did run in the British GP, when Trintignant finished eleventh and Salvadori retired. Aston Martin then turned away from Formula 1.

ATS (D)

Hans-Gunther Schmid entered Grand Prix racing to promote his ATS (Auto Technik Spezialzubehor) specialist wheels company, and soon gained a paddock reputation for idiosyncrasy and autocratic methods that undermined his team as well as his ambitions for it. Good drivers served ATS – Jarier, Lammers, Mass, Rosberg, Surer and Winkelhock, while Gerhard Berger started his F1 career with the team – and notable team managers who suffered short periods with ATS included Caldwell, Collins, Elford, Opert and Ramirez.

Schmid took a short route into World Championship racing when he acquired the cars and equipment of the defunct Penske team. An erstwhile PC4 appeared in ATS colours at Long Beach in April 1977, when Jean-Pierre Jarier perhaps gave a misleading impression of the new team's potential by finishing sixth in the US Grand Prix West. Then the March F1 team and its important FOCA membership was taken over in 1978, when seven drivers tried ATS team cars and failed to muster a point between them.

From 1979 ATS ran its own original cars, and too often floundered. It did get BMW turbo engines for 1983–84, and they were used in potentially good cars. But that potential was squandered. BMW's refusal to supply engines for 1985 was sufficient reason for Schmid to close down the operation. In eight seasons it had accumulated jut eight Constructors' Championship points.

ATS (Germany) HS-1 of 1978, Jochen Mass at the wheel.

ATS (Germany) D6 of 1983–84, with BMW turbo power. Manfred Winkelhock driving.

HS-1 The Penske PC4 was reworked by Robin Herd, and redesigned HS-1 for the 1978 season. However, this was basically an ageing design, and drivers good, bad and indifferent struggled to qualify an ATS for races. No points were scored (Mass came closest, finishing seventh in the Brazilian GP).

D1 This was a further uprating of the PC4/HS-1, by John Gentry and Gustav Brunner that appeared for the late-1978 races. It looked quite promising as Rosberg qualified for a mid-grid position at its first outing (at Watkins Glen), but the pairing faded to a last-row place for the next race.

D2–D4 The D2 was credited to Gentry, Brunner and Nigel Stroud, with aerodynamic work by Giacomo Caliri. It very closely resembled the Lotus 79 in its body lines, and in its suspension. Cosworth DFVs were still used, almost as a matter of course among lesser constructors at that time, with Hewland gearboxes. Handling let it down, badly. In mid-season they laid out a new monocoque and revised the suspension for a single car designated D3. In a wet race at Watkins Glen, Stuck drove it to finish fifth.

Two more D3s were built for 1980, and then remodelled as D4s by Brunner and Tim Wardrop to produce an ATS that was fractionally shorter and wider and for all the world looked like a Williams FW07. Four more were completed, and two of these were most widely used. Marc Surer finished five times in eleven starts, and his seventh place in Brazil was ATS's best in 1980.

D4s were run in the opening races of 1981, Jan Lammers qualifying twice in four attempts and finishing one race in eleventh place.

HGS1/D5 Hervé Guilpin designed the outwardly attractive HGS1, but this started life with an ineffectual hydro-pneumatic suspension system. Moreover, its debut at Imola coincided with manager Jo Ramirez quitting the team, and he was soon followed by Lammers. Slim Borgudd drove for the rest of the year, starting in seven races, and scoring a point in the British GP.

Two of the cars were modified by Don Halliday and run as D5s in 1982. Winkelhock was fifth in Brazil, Salazar fifth at Imola, to give ATS its highest points score (four) and eleventh place in the Constructors' Championship.

D6–D7 ATS had BMW turbo engines for 1983, and the Brünner-designed D6 was ready before the season opened. This car was genuinely new, with a carbon-fibre monocoque that also formed the cockpit upper bodywork and double-wishbone pullrod suspension.

Achievements did not reflect the qualities of this up-to-the-minute car – Winkelhock finished four times in fourteen starts, with a best final placing eighth in the Grand Prix of Europe. Slight modifications led to the D7 in 1984, when Winkelhock and Berger recorded five finishes, the best being Berger's sixth place at Monza (which did not even earn the team a point, as it ran a single car).

Herr Schmid closed down the operation, but was to return to Formula 1 in 1988 with the Rial team.

ATS (I)

Automobili Turismo e Sport seemed to have the right credentials for a specialist high-performance car constructor in the

ATS (Italy) car of 1963, with Phil Hill driving.

early 1960s – primarily sound financial backing and disaffected Ferrari executives to run the company. Its immediate programme when it was set up in 1961 included a Formula 1 car to challenge Ferrari, to be designed by erstwhile Ferrari chief engineer Carlo Chiti. He always worked quickly, perhaps in this case too quickly.

The first T100 was ready for tests late in 1962, when the space frame was found to lack rigidity (tubes had to be added around the engine bay before the car's first race, and these had to be cut before an engine could be lifted out!). The 1,494cc 90-degree V8 was rated at 190bhp. A Colotti six-speed gearbox was used. Outwardly, this was a dumpy car, and in its details suggested low-grade workmanship.

The race debut came at the 1963 Belgian GP, when the car was hopelessly off the pace. Phil Hill and Giancarlo Baghetti did their best at five Grand Prix meetings that year; component, engine or transmission failures usually led to transmission failures, but at least both cars were classified at Monza, eleventh, and fifteenth in the Italian GP.

A 1964 successor was laid down, but not built. The team, and soon ATS, were closed down. One T100 was developed in 1964 by Alf Francis, as the Derrington-Francis (qv).

Austin

Herbert Austin raced early in the century, driving a Wolseley in the 1902 Paris–Vienna race (retiring after the first section), and after forming the company bearing his name in 1906 he committed it to enter a team in the 1908 Grand Prix. Two cars of the Austin trio finished – the first British cars to be placed in a Grand Prix.

The '100hp' Austin was wholly conventional, with a chassis derived from a touring model and a T-head straight six following the company's largest production engine. This 9,655cc unit had an estimated output of 117bhp at 1,500rpm. Two of the four cars built had chain final drive, two had shaft drive – an approach prompted by the supposed fragility of live axles.

At Dieppe in July 1908 these Austins were not expected to match thoroughbred racing cars, and they were outclassed in the Grand Prix. Dario Resta crashed two in practice, and one good race car was made out of the two wrecks, and Resta placed it nineteenth. JTC Moore-Brabazon finished

Austin Grand Prix car of 1908, which raced only once.

eighteenth in a sister car, Wright retired the other after four laps with a seized engine.

The cars were then sold, and Moore-Brabazon's survives as an exhibit at the Heritage Motor Centre. Austin did not return to the Grand Prix, although the company was active in lesser racing for many years.

Austro-Daimler

Austro-Daimler never built a Grand Prix car, so its inclusion here is marginal. Entries from the erstwhile Central Powers were not accepted in some countries in the years following the First World War, but Italian organizers were happy to see German and Austrian cars in their races. So an Austro-Daimler entry was accepted for the second Italian GP in 1922 (the first to be run at Monza), to help swell the grid towards a double figure. A pair of Sascha Austro-Daimlers had run (without distinction) in the *Gran Premio de Vetturette* that was the main race when the circuit in the royal park was opened a week earlier, and the Grand Prix entry was presumably two Saschas with the larger engines sometimes fitted. They were withdrawn after Kuhn was killed in one, in a test accident on the then shallow Monza banking.

Auto Union

The Auto Union combine was set up in mid-1932 by Rasmussen's companies Audi, DKW and Horch, and another weak Saxony manufacturer, Wanderer, was soon brought in. The merger was complete by the spring of 1933, the year that Hitler's Third Reich came into existence. The marque names were retained for the group's road cars, while in the 1930s 'Auto Union' was reserved for the Grand Prix cars carrying the interlinked rings badge still used by Audi. The management realized that badly needed publicity could be gained through racing and, more to the point, Hitler was already aware that racing success could be used to demonstrate German superiority. So the State was to make RM600,000 available to this end.

It was assumed that this would go to Mercedes-Benz, but in the event it was to be shared between two constructors at opposite ends of Germany: an Auto Union team was to battle with Mercedes through most of the 1930s, and despite its more limited resources was to achieve great success (it has been reckoned that less than a quarter of the cost was covered by State aid, although that also brought political and business input).

In 1933 the Porsche Buro had completed preliminary design work on a Grand Prix

Austro-Daimler of early 1920s, Dr Porsche (behind 'No. 46') the designer.

car, and this was to be adopted by Auto Union after Ferdinand Porsche had joined chairman Klaus von Oertzen and racing driver Hans Stuck in a presentation to Hitler. Subject to a satisfactory prototype test, this gained half of the direct State funds on offer.

That first car, known for a while as the P-Wagen, was revolutionary, and Stuck more than proved its potential in that test at Avus early in 1934. That year he was to drive Auto Unions to win three Grands Prix, three of the major hill climbs that were then so important, and also set records. The following year was less rewarding, but Berndt Rosemeyer joined the team, and won his first Grand Prix. The C-types were then largely dominant in his hands in 1936–37, and he was European champion (effectively World Champion) in 1936. Then his life was squandered in a record attempt on an autobahn early in 1938.

The team began to recover as Nuvolari was recruited, and soon came to terms with the more sophisticated D-type 3litre cars designed by Dr Robert Eberan von Eberhorst. The Italian was to win Auto Union's last Grand Prix, at Belgrade, on

the day that Britain and France declared war on Germany in September 1939.

Incidentally, there is a neat little car with strong Auto Union family characteristics in the Donington Collection. This is not the 'E-type Auto Union' which was the subject of speculation when it arrived in Britain, incomplete. Its 2litre V12 dates from around 1950, and the assumption is that it was built by one-time Auto Union people at DAMW Eisenach (where EMW sports cars were once produced) with an eye to the 1948–53 Formula 2.

Another footnote is called for. Because the Zwickau factory fell in the Soviet zone of Germany in 1945, the Auto Unions that had been hidden in nearby mines became Russian booty. Some were used for 'research' and most were eventually scrapped, so that for many years the C-type cutaway showchassis in a Munich museum that was eventually to be restored to running condition seemed to be the only survivor. Rumours of others persisted, and more than a quarter of a century after they disappeared into Russia, the first re-emerged. That 1938–39 car was restored in England, and it was followed by

a D-type with a C-type engine, built for hill climbs, that had languished in Latvia and was painstakingly rebuilt in England for Audi. a D-type was also rebuilt, then Audi commissioned a C-type replica, which made its debut at Goodwood in 1998, and was to be followed by more British-built replicas.

P-Wagen A-, B- and C-types Dr Porsche's design team (primarily Josef Kalles, engine; Karl Rabe, suspension; Erwin Kommenda, body) laid out a radical car for racing under 750kg (1,654lb) Formula regulations. It had a chassis of two main longitudinal tubes linked by cross members, independent front suspension with torsion bars, and transverse leaf sprung swing axle independent rear suspension. The engine was behind the cockpit and ahead of the rear axle, with a rear-mounted five-speed gearbox and a 210litre fuel tank between driver and engine. Some of the bodywork was in fabric, to save weight.

The engine was a 4.4litre all-alloy V16, with a Roots-type supercharger; a single central camshaft operated all 32 valves (inlets directly, exhausts via pushrods). Its initial rating was a modest 295bhp at 4,500rpm, with generous torque.

Stuck led the first races that Auto Union contested, and won the German, Swiss and Czechoslovak GPs in 1934.

The cars were modified for 1935, with torsion bars in place of the leaf springs at the rear and all-alloy bodywork (a streamlined version with enclosed cockpit was built for high-speed tracks). At the beginning of the season, these B-types had 4.95litre, 375bhp, engines, and by the summer a 5.6litre version had appeared. Stuck was consistently fastest in hill climbs, but there was little circuit success until late in the summer, when Varzi won at Pescara, Stuck won at Monza and Rosemeyer won the Masaryk (Czech) Grand Prix.

The 1936 C-type had a 6litre engine developing some 520bhp at 5,000rpm (a 6.3litre version was used in spring record runs). Rosemeyer won five races that year, Varzi won at Tripoli, and Stuck broke records in C-types. Mercedes did not contest a full season, and Auto Union achieved notable 1-2-3 triumphs in the Coppa Acerbo and the Swiss GP. The cars were little changed for 1937, when Rosemeyer won

Auto-Union Type A P-Wagen of 1934, with mid-mounted V16 engine.

four races, including the last of the 750kg (1,654lb) formula, at Donington, while Hasse and Stuck had earlier placed 1-2 in the Belgian GP.

Fourteen of these 750kg (1,654lb) cars were built, and the race achievement record was good. However, there seems to have been virtually no technical spin-off to the production car companies.

D-type For the 3litre supercharged/ 4.5litre unsupercharged formula that came into force in 1938, von Eberhorst laid down a more efficient and controllable car. Porsche's front suspension was retained, but a de Dion arrangement was introduced at the rear. The engine, more truly mid-mounted, was a three-cam V12 with a central camshaft operating the inlet valves and a single camshaft for the exhaust valves of each bank. In its first single-stage supercharged form the V12 was rated at 420bhp, but soon 460bhp was quoted. The cockpit was set further back from the front wheels, and fuel was carried in pannier tanks.

Rosemeyer had won ten times in his thirty-three starts for the team, so his death was a great blow. Auto Union did not enter a Grand Prix until the summer of 1938, and late in the year Nuvolari won the Italian and Donington GPs in D-types. Stuck still reliably delivered good placings, and climbed hills very quickly.

In 1939 power was boosted to 485bhp with two-stage supercharging, and attractive definitive bodies appeared on the last of the eleven D-types built. The success rate improved, notably when H.P. Muller won the French Grand Prix and then Nuvolari won that last race for Auto Union.

Auto-Union Type D of 1939, with 3litre V12 engine, Hans Stuck driving in the French GP.

BAF

Many Formula 1 projects have never progressed beyond a planning stage, and the BAF possibility of 1975 stands out only because it would have been the first F1 car designed by Adrian Reynard. It was conceived by Mike Keegan, owner of British Air Ferries (BAF), and his ambition was that it would be driven by his son Rupert. Reynard designed a 'Cosworth kit car', paying particular attention to the aerodynamic aspects, but it was set aside before the designated constructor, Hawke, cut metal. Rupert's talents were not quite up to Formula 1 standards at that stage in his career. Reynard was to become a prolific designer, involved with other F1 projects, as well as the production of hundreds of Reynard racing cars.

Baird-Griffin

Bobby Baird was an amateur driver, who first indulged his passion for heavily modified cars or 'specials' before planning an F1 car with Denis Griffin in 1951. This took shape along contemporary Maserati lines, and incorporated many Maserati components. The engine was a 4CLT unit, substantially reworked by Griffin, driving through a rear-mounted four-speed gearbox. The chassis was on straightforward tubular lines, the independent front suspension used proprietary parts, and there was a de Dion rear end.

This car was normally used in minor Irish events, after a debut foray to Goodwood in 1952 showed it to be less than competitive. Baird abandoned his plan to follow it with an F2 car eligible for the Grands Prix in 1952–53, preferring to buy a Cooper and a Ferrari. However, he was fatally injured in a sports-car accident at Snetterton in 1953.

Ballot

Etablissements Ballot entered racing in 1919 on the back of experience as an engine manufacturer (Delage was a customer) and did not build its first road car until 1921. It took fourth place at Indianapolis in 1919 with a 4.9litre straight eight, and in 1920 Ballots were second, fifth and seventh in the 500. These were 3litre cars, and that capacity limit also applied to the two Grands Prix run in 1921, so Ballot had a ready-made entry.

The cars were designed by Ernest Henry, famous for his pre-war Peugeots, and with war-time experience of work on the Bugatti aero engines. The 1919 cars had to be designed and built in less than four months, and Henry naturally drew on experience. The Ballots had channel-section chassis members, with rigid front and rear axles on semi-elliptics, and Hispano Suiza-type mechanical brakes. The 1920–21 engine was a scaled-down version of the 4.9litre straight eight, with four valves per cylinder and gear-driven twin overhead camshafts. The use of light alloys, for pistons and crankcase, probably came from Henry's Bugatti experience. The lubrication system was considered the weak feature of the design. Output in 1921 was 107bhp at 3,800rpm; a four-speed gearbox proved to be the only advantage Ballot pilots had as they faced the Duesenberg drivers.

Ralph de Palma finished second in one of the three cars run in the 1921 French GP, while Wagner was seventh. Goux and Chassagne then took first and second places in the Italian GP with a pair of these 3litre cars.

Third place in the 1921 French race had fallen to Goux in a 2litre four-cylinder Ballot. This was the forerunner of the 2LS limited-production sports car. Three of these appeared with odd cylindrical bodies in Grand Prix car guise for the 1922 French race. The engines were slightly improved, to give 90bhp (88bhp in 1921). These were nominally independent entries, and none finished the race. Ballot turned away from racing.

Ballot 2litre model of 1921.

Ballot 2litre model of 1922.

BAR

No new team ever came to Grand Prix racing with such a high profile – or with so many people wishing to see it fall flat on its face. Founded in 1998 to satisfy the ambition of a multinational tobacco company (British American Tobacco), British American Racing Grand Prix was well-financed, expensively equipped – and totally unsuccessful. When BAR reached the end of its first year, 1999, with no Championship points, virtually no-one was sorry.

Put together around the undoubtedly great driving talent of 1997 Champion Jacques Villeneuve, the BAR team built itself glossy headquarters in Brackley, near Silverstone, took over the Tyrrell team (swiftly extinguishing the merits and goodwill of that well-liked organization), drew in the hitherto shining talents of Reynard to engineer the cars, and used tens of millions of BAT dollars to get the show on the road.

Craig Pollock initially headed the group, Rick Gorne (of Reynard) became commercial director, while perhaps more importantly there were Adrian Reynard (whose cars had not previously entered the GP world) and Malcolm Oastler to engineer the cars. They were joined by key technical personnel from other teams.

There was a great deal of arrogance at first – the team forecast victory in its first race, and clashed with F1 supremo Bernie Ecclestone over colour schemes even before that race came along. It did not help that Craig Pollock, at once a team principal, and also Villeneuve's manager, showed no sign of the humility expected of all new F1 team personalities.

Hampered by having to use less-than-competitive Supertec (Renault) 'customer' V10s, and with no sign of drawing on Tyrrell's experience, BAR had an awful first season, and not even a clever deal with Honda, whereby true 'works' engines were available for 2000, made much improvement in the second year.

BAR, who had expected great things which could be advertised, were completely non-plussed, while Reynard, so successful at all levels under F1, were humiliated. Much change, much eating of humble pie, and a much more realistic approach to the challenges of F1, would be needed before BAR could even challenge for podium positions, let alone for victories.

For 2000, with a change to the use of a Honda V10, they were at least credible, though not competitive. Points were scored, and the predominantly white cars sometimes fought with Jordan and Benetton for minor placings, but there was still a long way to go to turn this '1999 Dream Team' into a Grand Prix winner.

BAR 01   Before the definitive BAR F1 car could be designed, the team ran a heavily modified Tyrrell 026 to develop systems and installations, but this test car never carried a BAR design code, and was merely a useful 'mule'.

When BAR showed their cars early in 1999, they proposed to run the two in different (cigarette-inspired) colour schemes, but FOCA regulations (and Bernie Ecclestone) soon stamped on that one. Instead they ran throughout the season with a different scheme on each side of the car, which made otherwise conventional cars look all the more ridiculous.

Without the muscle to attract a 'works' engine deal, BAR was obliged to share Supertec/Renault V10s with Williams and Benetton, but were at no time as competitive. Not even Jacques Villeneuve, who rarely got involved (in public, that is) in team politics, could make the difference, for the cars were unreliable. Front suspension, by vertical torsion bars tucked away out of sight, and coil springs at the rear, was totally conventional by late-1990s F1 standards.

Although the team contested all sixteen races, Villeneuve did not even record a finish until the twelfth of those races, his best finish being eighth in Italy. Zonta, of whom much had been expected, at least finished seven times, but never higher than eighth either. Mika Salo stood in for him three times early in the season while he recovered from injury.

2000 could not be worse – could it?

BAR 02   Full of contrition over their 1999 performance, BAR was positively humble about the prospects for their BAR 02 model for 2000. The livery, in particular, was more logical, for only '555' appeared on the cars, which were mainly white.

They were wise, for although the new car was not as abysmally slow or unreliable as in 1999, it was still nowhere near fast enough to fight for victories.

Technical chief Malcolm Oastler agreed that BAR 02 was an evolutionary development of BAR 01, slightly shorter in the wheelbase, and with new torsion bar rear suspension. There were also two other important differences – that it was fitted with a modern-generation Honda engine, fundamentally different, theoretically lighter and more powerful than the similar engine being used by Jordan in 2000, and with a new longitudinally positioned six-speed gearbox (which had been designed in conjunction with Xtrac).

BAR 01 Renault V10 of 1999, with different livery on either side.

This was the year in which BAR found itself fighting for credibility with Benetton and Jordan for fourth place in the Constructors' table, and making a far better fist of it than in 1999.

Beatrice

This simple team name gave no clues to its complexity, beyond, of course, the sponsor. One-time McLaren principals Teddy Mayer and Tyler Alexander came back to Formula 1 with, and were supported by, US race car entrant Carl Haas, who was also the Lola concessionaire from North America, and by Beatrice Corporation Inc. Lola was involved, although the cars were to be designed by ex-Williams engineer Neil Oatley and John Baldwin and built by FORCE (Formula One Race Car Engineering) at its own base. There was little Lola input, although Eric Broadley was among personalities at the 1985 launch in London.

The cars were also to be known as Beatrice-Lola, Lola-Haas, or simply as Lola. They were first run with Hart engines, and by the time the Cosworth-designed 1.5litre Ford turbo was ready for them in spring 1986 there had been management and policy changes at Beatrice, which meant that its support dwindled. The team did complete the season, but after its cars had competed in nineteen Grands Prix it was closed down at the end of 1986.

THL1 This wholly conventional car made its race debut at the 1985 Italian GP, when Alan Jones qualified it for the last row of the grid and retired after six laps – obviously, development time was needed. THL1 had a double wishbone pushrod suspension all round, with a Hart 415T four-cylinder engine giving perhaps 750bhp driving through a FORCE/Hewland six-speed gearbox. It was run until spring 1986, with minor modifications. Alan Jones was joined in 1986 by Patrick Tambay; they started in eight races in THL1s, with only one finish (Tambay's eighth in the 1986 Spanish GP).

THL2 Oatley's design was modified in detail for the more compact Cosworth-originated Ford-badged turbocharged V6, for which 900bhp was claimed. It seemed to be run with an eye to reliability rather than to exploit maximum power, but the team's retirement rate was still high (sixteen times in twenty-five race starts). The best placing was Jones' fourth in Austria, and the team scored eight points, for eighth place in the Constructors' Championship.

Bellasi

Swiss entrant-driver Silvio Moser commissioned this one-off from Vittorio Bellasi to replace the Brabham BT24 with which he had scored three World Championship points in 1968–69, as it was ruled out by a change in regulations that banned space-frame cars. Bellasi – a minor constructor – used components such as the suspension from Moser's Brabham, as well as its Cosworth DFV engine and Hewland gearbox. He produced a bulky monocoque car, with artisan rather than inspired qualities.

When it first appeared, for the 1970 Dutch GP, Moser failed to qualify for the grid. Three more attempts that year earned one start, in Austria, where Moser retired while running last. He brought the Bellasi out once in 1971, qualifying at Monza but retiring early in the Italian Grand Prix.

Benetton

See pp.34–37.

Bentley

Amazingly, a four-seater Bentley road car took part in one Grand Prix – the 246-mile French GP of September 1930. Even more amazingly, in the capable hands of Sir

Henry ('Tim') Birkin, it finished second to a Bugatti Type 35C!

To quote Laurence Pomeroy, from many decades ago:

> In periods of technical weakness it becomes possible for the series type high-performance car to compete with, and on occasions beat, the pure racing design.

By 1930 Grand Prix racing was in a state of chaos, not to say anarchy, so when the regulations for the French GP, at Pau, were published, Sir Henry saw that *formule libre* rules would apply, and promptly entered one of the supercharged 'blower' Bentleys which had recently begun racing in sports car events.

Except that this 'blower' Bentley had its wings and headlamps removed, and as much other equipment as possible was discarded, it was precisely the same as one of cars which Birkin had been racing in non-Grand Prix events during the season. With a vast, 118in wheelbase, and a start-line weight of no less than 4,650lb/2,114kg, it had a 240bhp 4.5litre four-cylinder single-overhead-cam-shaft engine, where the massive Roots-type supercharger poked out through the bottom of the lofty front-mounted radiator.

The rest of the car was pure 'vintage Bentley', with a four-speed gearbox separated from the engine, with the gear-change lever to the right of the driver's

legs, with 15.75in brake drums and a big, four-seater body.

Quite unsuitable for Grand Prix racing, one might have thought, but on a moderately fast circuit (this was not the 'town centre' Pau lap, incidentally, but a fast triangular 9.8-miler on the outskirts of town) it might stretch its legs and occasionally reach its top speed of 130mph (209kph).

Amazingly, it came within 206sec (in nearly three hours) of actually winning the French GP, where it finished a startling second behind Philippe ('Fifi') Etancelin's Bugatti Type 35C – 4.5litre being just overcome by a supercharged 2litre type.

Of the twenty-five starters in this race, fourteen were Type 35 Bugattis, though there were no Italian or Germany entries. Fifth after five laps, fourth after ten, and third on the fifteenth, Birkin finally took second place on lap 19, and held it to the close – one reason being that he enjoyed a non-stop run, needing neither fuel nor tyres at half-distance.

After nearly three hours, Etancelin's 'works' Bugatti Type 35C had averaged 90.37mph (145kph), with the Bentley averaging 88.50mph (142kph) – a quite sensational performance.

This, though, was a completely one-off occasion, for no Bentley ever again started an official Grand Prix.

Beatrice (Lola)-Ford THL2 of 1986, with turbo Cosworth V6 power, Patrick Tambay test-driving.

The Italian company entered Grand Prix racing as a sponsor with Tyrrell in 1983, switched to Alfa Romeo in 1984, then to Toleman. That team was struggling, and it was taken over by Benetton Formula Limited before the 1986 season. By the end of the decade it was a leading constructor, and it was never lower than fourth in the Constructors' Championship end-of-season tables from 1988 until 1997. And by that time, it was an Italian team.

There had been many other changes. Toleman manager Peter Collins initially remained in overall charge. Gordon Message was actual team manager, 'relieved' at times, by Joan Villadelpret in 1991 and from 1994. In 1989 Luciano Benetton invited Flavio Briatore to take over, apparently because of his success in setting up a chain of shops in the USA! For a while in the 1990s he worked in tandem with Tom Walkinshaw, who gave the team a new sense of purpose, and brought all its departments together at one base, Enstone. The Scot had gone by 1995, when Benetton won the Constructors' Championship and its lead driver Michael Schumacher was World Champion. Vastly experienced and professional motor sports manager Dave Richards joined in 1997, was put in control for 1998, but quit just before the end of that season. Meanwhile, Rory Byrne had continued in charge of design, answering to technical director John Barnard 1989–91, then to Ross Brawn.

Benetton attracted talented people, and perhaps it was more than coincidence that fortunes turned down in 1996 when Schumacher was enticed away to Ferrari. Brawn followed in 1997, when Pat Symonds took over as technical director; his design team was to be headed by Nick Wirth.

Benetton used engines from four manufacturers (five if the Mecachrome V10s labelled Playlife are separated from their Renault roots), and the cars have appeared in many bright colour schemes since the original 'United Colours of Benetton' display. For most of its history, its status had never been in dispute, although it was sometimes threatened.

B186 Work on the first Benetton started late in 1985, and early in the 1986 season the demands of development and completing the batch of cars were sometimes in conflict. The monocoque and some components were similar to those on the last Toleman, although nothing was carried over. Double wishbone suspension (pullrod at the front, pushrod at the rear) was used. A major change was in the use of BMW M12/13 turbo engines, more powerful than the Hart units in the last Tolemans, and that called for some strengthening in the development phase.

Both drivers scored in early races, but it was not until quite late in the season that the *équipe* 'came together', and in Mexico Berger scored the team's first Grand Prix victory. In its first season, Benetton was sixth in the Constructors' Championship.

B187 A switch to Cosworth-Ford V6 turbo engines meant that this car was also designed and built in a hurry, and its monocoque had to be strengthened. Pushrod suspension was used all round. In overall terms, Benetton performance improved, to fifth place in the Constructors' Championship with twenty-eight points (nine more than in 1986), but Boutsen's third in the Australian GP was its best single result.

B188 Normally aspirated Cosworth DFR engines were used in 1988, in a car that proved to be overweight and somewhat under-powered (that year the engine failed to deliver the 650bhp that was expected).

Nevertheless, in 1988 Boutsen finished third in six Grands Prix, Nannini third in two, and the team was third in the championship, with thirty-nine points.

Little changed, B188s were used in the first six races in 1989. Herbert scored in two races (five points) before he was replaced by Pirro, who scored just two points in the rest of the year. Meanwhile, Nannini scored eight points in B188s, before they were set aside.

The B188 was also used in 'active suspension' trials in 1988–89.

B189 There was a change to the light and compact Ford HB engine in this car, but there were teething problems to be solved before the B189 came into use (first at the French GP). Nannini scored well with it, racking up twenty-four points to add to those he scored with B188s; high points were his victory in Japan and second place in Australia.

Cars designated B189B, with some aerodynamic improvements, were used in the opening races in 1990, when Piquet twice scored points with them.

B190 A development of the B189, the 1990 Benetton was first raced in the San Marino GP (Nannini third, Piquet fifth). There was a new monocoque, the front suspension was new, and so were the aerodynamic appendages, while in 1990 the HB engine did produce 650bhp. Observers began to detect Barnard's influence, although he did not join Benetton until the design was virtually complete. Both drivers scored well, particularly as Piquet won the last two Grands Prix of 1990. That year Benetton accrued seventy-one points, for third place in the Constructors' Championship.

B190Bs were run in the opening races of 1991, Piquet finishing third and fifth.

B191 Once again a new Benetton was late, and development was in parallel with its first races – normally not a recipe for instant success, but Piquet did win the fifth race of the series, in Canada.

The B191 design was controlled by Barnard, who left in mid-season, just as

Benetton-BMW B186 of 1986, with Gerhard Berger driving.

Benetton-Ford B191 of 1991, with Nelson Piquet winning the Canadian GP.

TWR acquired an interest (some of Walkinshaw's men were to move in, including Ross Brawn, while Byrne returned after a brief absence).

There was another new monocoque, pushrod suspension all round (the 'active' system was not raced), an under-nose front aerofoil, and the Cosworth Ford HB rated 730bhp driving through Benetton's six-speed gearbox.

Piquet scored a third and some minor placings after his Canadian victory. Moreno scored eight points before he was dismissed to make way for Schumacher, plucked from Jordan by Walkinshaw despite legal haggles (the German scored four points in late season races). Benetton was fourth in the championship.

Schumacher scored with B191Bs, with uprated engines, in the first three races of 1992 (his 4-3-3 garnering eleven points, while Brundle retired each time).

B192 Under Brawn, Benetton stayed with (relative) simplicity in the 1992 car – for example with normal double wishbone pushrod suspension rather than an active system, and the normal six-speed gearbox rather than a semi-automatic 'box. Schumacher gave the new car a sensational baptism by finishing second in the Spanish GP; later he was second in Canada and Australia, and between these

races won his first Grand Prix, in Belgium. Brundle also scored a second place (at Monza) and was a respectable sixth in the drivers' table. Ninety-one points gave Benetton third place in the Constructors' Championship.

B193 On the technical side, Benetton made up ground on McLaren and Williams with its 1993 car, which had a 'B' designation from its first race, the European GP at Donington. In the first two races the team used B192s, substantially reworked and run as B193As. These had active suspension and semi-automatic transmission, revised systems and the works-status HB engines (initially shared with McLaren). Schumacher took third place in the Brazilian GP with a B193A.

The B193B had the technical features from these cars, and refined aerodynamics (its high nose meant that it stood out among front-running cars). There was no traction control.

Schumacher overshadowed team mate Patrese, for although they were respectively fourth and fifth on the drivers' championship table at the end of the year, thirty-two points separated them. Schumacher scored the only Benetton victory, in Portugal, and was second in five races. The team was again third in the other championship, with seventy-two points.

B194 This time a new Benetton was ready as the season opened. It was a simpler car, for some of the high-tech driver aids had been outlawed … but Benetton was reckoned to have used a form of traction control, after tests on the electronic 'black box' from a B194 run in the San Marino GP. The engine was the 75-degree V8 labelled Ford Zetec-R, which revved to 14,500rpm, then phenomenal for a V8. Benetton's six-speed gearbox was still used.

The brilliance of Schumacher was a great asset, two disqualifications notwithstanding. He won eight Grands Prix, was second twice, and clinched the title after a controversial collision with Hill in the last race. Verstappen garnered ten points, Lehto one, Herbert none as he joined for the last two races. Yet the constructors' title eluded the team, 103 points gaining it second place.

B195 Brawn and Byrne designed this car for the Renault RS7 67-degree V10, and this unfamiliar unit did cause some problems (for example with hydraulics) as well as give advantages – primarily, the team was on a par with its main rivals in power terms.

Defending his title, Schumacher won nine Grands Prix, to head the points table so clearly that he hardly needed the

Benetton-Ford B194 of 1994, J.J. Lehto test-driving.

scores from a second place and a third. Normally, the number two driver in a team running Schumacher would play a subdued role, but Johnny Herbert won two Grands Prix, and was fourth in the championship table. And Benetton convincingly beat Williams in the Constructors' Championship, with 137 points.

B196 The last Benetton design controlled by Brawn was developed from the B195, to meet new regulations framed to protect drivers. The engine was Renault's RS8, and in this car it drove through a seven-speed semi-automatic longitudinal gearbox. Reliability had been a strong asset in 1995, but the failure rate was higher in 1996. Beyond that, Schumacher left for Ferrari, Alesi and Berger joined from Ferrari. Alesi was second in four GPs, and with other placings scored forty-seven points for fourth place in the championship, while Berger was sixth with twenty-one points. The total put Benetton third on the constructors' table.

B197 Rory Byrne completed the B197 design before he responded to the call from Ferrari; technical director Pat Symonds took over. The car had no startling new features, although it was refined in areas such as the suspension, and it was intended to suit the team's 1997 drivers. Renault's RS9 engines were used, this time with six-speed gearboxes.

Technicalities were overshadowed by discord within the team, and at the end of

Benetton-Renault B195, Michael Schumacher driving – World Championship-winning combination.

the year Briatore left. Alesi scored thirty-six points, but his best placings were second (four times) while Berger did win the German GP and scored twenty-one points. While the Austrian was side-lined, Alexander Wurz stood in, and was third in the British GP. Yet again Benetton was third in the Constructors' Championship, but seemed to face a difficult period.

B198 Pat Symonds and chief designer Nick Wirth were primarily concerned with aerodynamic aspects on this car, for it had to run in the latest narrow-track/grooved-tyre period imposed by the new regulations. Their other concern, which could not be smoothed out by development, was a complete change of drivers, as Alesi and Berger had both moved out, to be replaced by youngsters Giancarlo Fisichella and Alexander Wurz.

Led until the end of the summer by Prodrive boss David Richards (who had joined late in 1997), the 1998 team lacked technical progress, if not direction. Even so, the new car had titanium and carbon fibre in the pushrod suspension, while the B197's torsion bars were discarded in favour of coil springs.

As before, the V10 engine was Renault's GC37-01, now a customer unit supplied by Mecachrome, and inexplicably known as a 'Playlife' by Benetton. It was no better than in 1997, and this showed.

As the months passed, Benetton lagged, this sometimes being due to the decision to run Bridgestone tyres (while most rivals stayed with Goodyear), and sometimes due to the young drivers' inexperience. Fifth in the Constructors' Championship, with thirty-three points, and no victories but two second places to Fisichella, was as much as could be expected.

B199 Looking back, one could almost foretell a poor 1999 season for Benetton and the B199, this obligingly being delivered. On the one hand, the much-respected David Richards had been replaced by a Benetton family member – Rocco Benetton, who knew little about F1 racing – and on the other, there were numerous high-tech gizmos at the start of the B199 programme which proved not to work.

Pat Symonds and Nick Wirth had slaved away at the B199, but it proved to be a real dog, little better when simplified than in early testing. The use of pushrod suspension all round (torsion bars at the front, coil springs at the rear) could not balance other failings.

As with Williams, Benetton was in any case inflicted by a down-for-competitive power 'Playlife' (Supertec – one-time Mecachrome) V10 engine, and a twin clutch scheme that was troublesome, but B199 was not only too heavy, but seemed to lack overall grip, and originally used a mechanical FTT (Front Torque Transfer) system between the front wheels – which seemed to be ineffective.

It was a pity, therefore, that Fisichella, in particular, could not show how fast he really was. Ninth in the Drivers' championship, he was only once on the podium, while Benetton dropped to sixth in the Constructors' series.

B199, for sure, would not provide a good base for the 2000 car – and did not.

B200 Benetton's strategy with B200 for the 2000 season was not only to simplify the overall design, but to get the new car out, and testing, a lot earlier than before. Launched in January, with a lot of time for testing, the latest car was placarded as simpler, lighter, and shorter than before. Significantly, there was no sign of the FTT or twin-clutch features which had both been dumped during 1999.

The B200 was 88lb/40kg lighter than the B199, and also had a revised aerodynamic package with a lower nose. Benetton also parroted Supertec's claims for more power from the ageing V10 engine.

The year 2000, though, was almost a repeat performance of 1999, in that the cars never looked like winning races, and were only occasionally to be seen in the top six: driver Wurz was a casualty, told well before the end of the season that he would not be re-hired. Throughout the season, the fight was with Jordan and BAR – for fourth place in the Constructors' table – which was a far cry from the heady mid-1990s when they won World Championships.

Being 'Best of the Renault-Supertec' runners was clearly not good enough for Renault, who took control of the team before the end of the year. For 2002, they announced Benetton's F1 name would disappear.

Benetton-Renault B198 of 1998.

Benz

Benz cars were used in the earliest races, but this pioneer company did not enter racing until 1907, when a team contested all the major European events except the (French) Grand Prix. However, there was a three-car entry for that team in 1908, when Benz was unlucky to lose its German rival Mercedes. The cars, and derivatives, were then successful in other events, notably in the USA. For 1923 Benz produced a most innovative Grand Prix car, with a rear-mounted engine and a finely streamlined body. German entrants were still not universally accepted, so this Benz ran in only one Grand Prix, at Monza in 1923, and little development work was carried through – more power was found in the engine, and sports-car equipment was added. By 1924 the economic situation was harsh, and there were signs that the company's future lay in strength through amalgamation; in 1926 it merged with Daimler to create the Mercedes-Benz marque.

1908 There were no novelties in the first Grand Prix Benz, which took shape along conservative lines under design director George Diehl; his lieutenants were Hans Nibel, who would become Mercedes Benz's technical director, and Belgian de Groulart, responsible for the engine. There was the usual pressed-steel chassis frame, with rigid axles and semi-elliptic springs, brakes to the rear wheels, typical open bodies differing from car to car but all with bolster tanks. The 12,076cc four-cylinder engine was rated at 120bhp (and was not the most powerful in the 1908 Grand Prix).

Benz's leading driver Victor Hémery ran with the leaders of the Grand Prix; he was actually leading during the first half, lost ground when his goggles were smashed,

(Above) Benz 1908 Grand Prix car. *(Below)* Benz Tropfenwagen, with mid-mounted engine of 1923.

then crawled to the finish with a burst rear tyre. Even so he was second, just ahead of team mate Hanriot, while Erle was seventh for Benz.

The engine was enlarged to 15litres, to give 158bhp (and the '150bhp Benz' label), and in this form Benz cars placed second and fourth in the US Grand Prize at Savannah in 1908, and Hémery was second again in 1910. These cars were successful in other events for several years. They were also the basis of the '200bhp Benz' record car and the Blitzen Benz; three of these cars were used in competition into the 1920s.

Tropfenwagen Benz made a tentative return to racing after the First World War with modified production cars, then built a sensational Grand Prix car that was tested in 1922 and raced in 1923. This was inspired by Edmund Rumpler's 'tear drop' saloon, and that Tropfenwagen nickname was applied to the racing car, more formally the RH.

This radical car had an extensively drilled lightweight chassis, with the engine behind the cockpit and some added bracing. At first there was all-round independent suspension, but a rigid front axle was substituted on the race cars, with a swing axle at the rear. Semi-elliptic springs were used front and rear. The body was finely streamlined, with the radiator projecting above it, aligned with the rear of the engine. That was a 1,997cc dohc straight six giving 80bhp at 4,500rpm – hardly a competitive output at a time when the supercharged car had arrived on the Grand Prix scene. It drove through a three-speed gearbox, behind the engine.

The Benz team contested only one Grand Prix, the European race at Monza in 1923. Supercharged Fiats dominated the event, but two of the Benz trio finished, fourth (Minoia) and fifth (Horner). After that the cars were run in local events in Germany, later as sports cars with wings and lights. Several of the principals associated with them were later involved with the Auto Union programme, while Hans Nibel and Max Wagner had prominent engineering roles with Mercedes-Benz.

Berta

In the mid-1970s Argentine constructor Oreste Berta laid down a Brabham-inspired single-seater to be powered by a V8 on DFV lines, initially with Formula 1 in mind. However, as the monocoque, body and other main components neared completion early in 1975 he sensibly set aside F1 ambitions, and looked towards Formula A (F5000) racing, then settled for local contests.

BKL

The Borgward-Kuhnke-Lotus appeared in 1963, when the two cars of Kurt Kuhnke's team failed to qualify for the first time. This should not have surprised Herr Kuhnke, for a Lotus 18 with a late-1950s Borgward Formula 2 engine was hardly a competitive proposition in the third season of the 1.5litre Formula 1. Two cars qualified for the non-championship Solitude GP in 1963–64, one at Karlskoga in 1963. Kuhnke entered one car for himself in the 1963 German GP, when he failed to qualify with a best practice lap in 11min 23.5sec – 1:21 slower than the back of the grid qualifier, and 3:37.7 off pole time!

Boro

The Ensign N175 (qv) was taken over and renamed by its Dutch sponsor H.B. Bewaking, after a disagreement late in 1976. It was entered as a Boro in six 1976 Grands Prix, run with inadequate resources, and driven by Larry Perkins. His best race placing was eighth in the Belgian GP. Brian Henton attempted two Grands Prix with it in 1977, to be excluded for a push start in Holland and failing to qualify in Italy.

Brabham

See pp.40–46.

Brasier

A year before the company entered Grand Prix racing, its founder Georges Richard left, so the confusion of names from earlier periods does not apply. In that year, 1905, Léon Théry won the last Gordon Bennett race for the company and for France, and Brasier seemed content to enter essentially similar cars for the first three Grands Prix.

So, its 1906 Grand Prix cars were conventional to a fault. Substantial chassis frames carried minimal bodywork, and ran on wooden-spoked artillery wheels, with brakes to the rear only. The engine was a four-cylinder unit (cylinders cast in pairs), with a capacity of 11,974cc, and chain final drive. The Brasiers were right on the 1,007kg (2,220lb) maximum weight limit. Their drivers and riding mechanics had no more protection than crews in the early city-to-city races. All three Brasiers were classified at the end of that two-day French race, Barillier fourth, Baras seventh and Pierry ninth, while Baras put in the fastest lap of the 103km (64 mile) circuit.

The 1907 cars had slightly smaller engines (11,874cc) and were fractionally shorter. The team again finished the Grand Prix intact, headed by Baras in third place, with Barillier seventh and Bablot twelfth.

continued on p.46

Brasier Grand Prix car of 1906.

BRABHAM

Jack Brabham and Ron Tauranac formed their company to build racing cars in 1961, as Motor Racing Developments (MRD), a name that was used by the last entrants of Brabham cars in 1992. In its first decades the team enjoyed glorious periods. Once Brabham's Cooper contract was ended he was free to use his own name, and from early 1962 Brabham Racing Developments built cars and the Brabham Racing Organization ran the works teams.

The first car was an MRD retrospectively numbered BT1, a Formula Junior one-off in 1961. The first Brabham, also for Formula Junior, was the BT2 and a Grand Prix car, BT3, came later in 1962. BT signified Brabham-Tauranac and was to prefix every Brabham type number through to the last car (incidentally, in the 1960s the cars were known as Repco-Brabhams).

Tauranac was a fine designer who exploited natural talents, and he seemed particularly skilled in space-frame cars – until his late Brabhams and the Ralts he built later showed that he was equally adept with other forms of construction.

The first hurdle for Brabham was passed when he scored championship points in his team's first season; the first of thirty-five Grand Prix victories for the marque came in 1964, when Dan Gurney drove a BT7 to win the French race, and then at Reims in 1966 Jack Brabham became the first driver to win a Grand Prix in a car bearing his name, and that year he also won the World Championship. His last Grand Prix victory in one of his own cars came in South Africa in 1970. He was to be knighted for his achievements.

Brabham retired at the end of the 1970 season and for a while Tauranac ran the team on a low-key basis, before selling out to B. (Bernie) C. Ecclestone at the end of 1971. The new owner played himself in fairly cautiously. Then, ever-perceptive, he entrusted Gordon Murray with the design role as Ralph Bellamy left after a brief tenure, and the team prospered again.

Murray's first two designs were particularly elegant, then Ecclestone's deal with Autodelta put him in the awkward position of having to design a car for the Alfa Romeo V12. The Brabham-Alfa partnership was not fruitful, although interesting at times, particularly with the 'fan-car' episode in 1978.

There was a return to elegance – and success – from 1980 with Cosworth and BMW engines. The last great season for Brabham cars came in 1983, when the marque's previous best score of four Grand Prix victories was equalled, although its one Constructors' Championship success was then in the distant past, in 1967. Its last victory came two years later, in France.

Ecclestone left, to concentrate his commercial acumen on the government of the sport. Brabham's new owner was apparently Swiss Joachim Luhti (the situation was clouded by legal squabbles) and he gained the breathing space of a year's sabbatical for the team, which was in decline.

An association with Yamaha seemed to promise a brighter future, but it just lasted through a difficult year, 1991. In the following year Motor Racing Developments Ltd was controlled by the Alolique Group, and was hopelessly under-funded. Reworked cars were altered for races, but were qualified only three times, twice by Damon Hill, who started his first Grands Prix with them. His eleventh place in the 1992 Hungarian GP was the last for a Brabham driver, and after 394 Grands Prix the marque simply faded away.

BT3 The first Formula 1 Brabham was neat and particularly workmanlike, a one-off designed early in 1962 and built in time to make its debut in the German GP in high summer. It had a space frame leading top wishbone/trailing lower wishbone front suspension and twin wishbones in the rear suspension, with outboard coil springs/dampers all round. Fuel was carried in tanks beside and behind the cockpit. A rear-mounted Coventry Climax V8 drove through a Colotti-Francis six-speed gearbox. Late in 1962, Brabham was fourth in the US Grand Prix – for the first time, a driver had scored points in his own car. It was modified for 1963, with a fuel-injection Coventry Climax V8 and a Hewland five-speed gearbox. It served for most of the year (Denny Hulme drove his first F1 races in it), then it was sold to Ian Raby, who ran it in a few F1 races with BRM V8. Together with the BT7s, it contributed to Brabham completing its first full season, 1963, in third place in the Constructors' Championship.

BT7 The BT7 was developed from the BT3, and was the car that really established Brabham as a leading Grand Prix contender. There was, of course, a space frame, the rear suspension layout was changed to upper wishbones and transverse links, the wheelbase was longer and the body a little more efficient in aerodynamic respects.

Coventry Climax FWMV 'flat crank' units giving 195bhp (an improvement of more than 10bhp) were used, with Hewland 'boxes. Just two cars were built, and that made the team's achievement record the more remarkable. Dan Gurney was fifth in the drivers' championship, with second places in the Dutch and South African GPs his best placings, while Brabham was seventh in the points standings.

The cars were slightly modified for 1964, when they were fast in qualifying but save for an International Trophy win for Brabham luck seemed against the team, until Gurney won the French GP at Rouen. He won again in Mexico. Although the team's points score was higher than in 1963, its championship position at the end of 1964 was one place lower, fourth. One of the cars was sold, the other occasionally being used by the works team in 1965.

BT11 Introduced as a customer version of the BT7, this car served independent entrants well, with BRM or Coventry Climax V8s, and the last two built were used by the Brabham team. Save for engine variations, the specification was similar to the BT7.

In 1964 Bob Anderson took third place in the Austrian GP with his Climax-engined car, and scored another point in Holland, while Jo Siffert in a Walker car was third in the USA and fourth in the German GP. He also won the non-championship race at Enna, and he repeated this victory a year later. Gurney placed one of the works pair second in the 1965 US and Mexican GPs, at the end of a generally disappointing season.

BT11s were adapted for the opening seasons of 3litre Grand Prix racing, when Anderson again scored points, with a 2.7litre Coventry Climax FPF in his car. Sadly, he was killed in a test accident at Silverstone in 1967 (John Taylor had a fatal accident in Bridges' BT11 at the Nürburgring in 1966).

BT19 This car turned out to be an historic one-off. Laid down for the Coventry Climax 1.5litre flat 16 in 1965, the chassis was put to one side as that engine was abandoned, then dusted down and modified for the Type 620 Repco V8, for the first season of the 3litre formula. And Jack Brabham drove it, to win the world championships.

Its space frame, strengthened in the cockpit area, and suspension followed normal Tauranac lines. In 2,994cc form, the engine produced almost 300bhp (wrongly thought by some pundits to be quite inadequate). It drove through Hewland HD, later DG, gearboxes. In 1966 he won the French GP with it, gaining the first championship race victory for a driver in a car bearing his name. He won the next three Grands Prix, scoring enough points to win the Drivers' Championship. Moreover, the marques title fell to Brabham.

The car was used in three 1967 GPs, when Brabham took second place with it in Holland, and it was also run by the works in non-title races.

BT20 This was a modestly improved version of the BT19 design, with minor changes including a longer wheelbase and wider track. Two were built and run in only eleven GPs by the works team. Hulme placed the first car third behind Brabham on that glorious day at Reims in 1966; the New Zealand driver won the 1967 Monaco GP in a BT20, giving the type its only championship race victory. The cars were sold, one to Guy Ligier, who scored a point with it in the 1967 German GP, the other to John Love. This one was sold on to Silvio Moser, who was fifth in the 1968 Dutch GP, then raced it with a DFV in 1969, when he was sixth in the US GP.

BT24 Deriving from the 1967 BT23A Tasman series car, this was another highly successful Brabham. It was built around an outstanding Tauranac space frame, was more compact than the BT20, and was powered by the Repco 740 V8. This gave no more than 300bhp while 400bhp was claimed for other 1967 engines, but it was reliable.

It was first raced in the Belgian GP in 1967, then Jack Brabham won two Grands Prix in BT24s and Hulme one. But Denny piled up fifty-one points, with three second places and three third places, whereas Jack scored only forty-eight in the Drivers' Championship.

The works team made little use of the three cars built after that season, and two were sold to independent entrants, Frank Williams and Silvio Moser.

BT26 The last Brabham car to have a tubular chassis, a hybrid affair with sheet stiffening, was handsome but let down by its engine. The Repco dohc unit, developed by John Judd and Norman Wilson, seemed to be an adequately powerful response to the DFV, but had several detail weaknesses. The reigning championship team scored points just twice in 1968. The car was revised to take the DFV engine in 1969, when a fourth was completed as a BT26A (Frank Williams had one). Jacky Ickx won the German and Canadian GPs for the team, while Courage was second in the USA in the Williams car. Their efforts gained second place for Brabham in the Constructors' Championship.

BT33 Ron Tauranac had to turn his back on space-frame F1 designs for 1970, as new regulations regarding fuel tanks meant monocoque chassis. He designed a simple sheet aluminium tub, with the main tanks in the flanks, and used the DFV as a stressed member. The front suspension had inboard coil spring/damper units. The body was smooth and neat, and the works car was run in odd turquoise colours (a second car with similar status in 1970 had white colours, for Stommelen's German backers). Jack Brabham won the first Grand Prix of the year, in South Africa, and that proved to be his last victory; mistakes cost him two more, and he retired at the end of the year. His team slipped to fourth in the championship.

Brabham-Repco BT26 of 1968, Jochen Rindt at the wheel.

Brabham-Ford BT26 of 1969, when big aerofoils were still legal.

41

The BT33s came out again in 1971, when little was achieved by works team or independent drivers (Brabham was ninth in the Constructors' Championship, with a mere five points), and with some updating one lingered on into 1972, and the Ecclestone era.

BT34 A distinctive one-off, the 'lobster claw' car for Graham Hill in 1971 had twin water radiators in nacelles ahead of the front wheels, with an adjustable aerofoil between them. Its flat sides were also unusual, as was the oil radiator protruding on the right flank, and the engine cover (not always used) with its twin shoulder air intakes. In his last F1 Brabham design, Tauranac used outboard suspension again. A DFV drove through a Hewland FG400 gearbox.

Hill drove it to his last F1 victory, in the 1971 Silverstone International Trophy,

and scored two championship points with it that year. It was slightly revised for 1972, when the colour scheme was largely white, and Carlos Reutemann drove it to win the non-championship Brazilian GP.

BT37 Ralph Bellamy's only F1 Brabham was an adaptation rather than a new design. Effectively, it was a lighter BT34 with a conventional nose radiator, and with modified rear suspension. The team

Brabham-Ford BT34 of 1971, Graham Hill driving.

Brabham-Ford BT44B of 1975, Carlos Reutemann driving.

was entering a new period in 1972, when it ran three types; its best placing with a BT37 was Reutemann's fourth in Canada. De Adamich matched that in the 1973 Belgian GP.

BT39 Tested in 1972 but never raced, this car used the monocoque and other components from the BT38 F2/F Atlantic customer car, with a Weslake Type 190 V12 engine. This harked back to the Gurney-Weslake F1 V12, and was developed with Ford encouragement, largely with sports car use in mind. Seemingly, it failed to develop the anticipated power.

BT42 The first of Gordon Murray's compact DFV-engined designs marked the opening of a new phase in Brabham history. It had an unusual pyramid cross section, and there should have been gains from a low frontal area and a clean airflow over the upper surfaces. The dual radiator was one detail recalling the immediate Brabham past, on the BT42 with a full-width nose. There was double wishbone front suspension, with upper and lower links at the rear.

Reutemann was third in BT42s in two 1973 Grands Prix and fourth in two, while Wilson Fittipaldi and de Adamich with a BT37 added points to give the marque fourth place in the Constructors' Championship. The cars came out again early in 1974, but were usually seen that year in independent hands. The only driver to score with one was John Watson, sixth at Monaco.

BT44 Murray refined his concept in the BT44, a slightly larger and prettier car. He introduced rising rate front suspension, with pullrods and partly inboard. Appearance did not mislead, for the aerodynamics were cleaner, from the nose to the high engine airbox.

The first victory for a Murray-designed F1 car fell to Reutemann in BT44/1 in South Africa, then the team encountered problems and he did not win again until late summer, in Austria, and then won the US GP. Rent-a-drive team mates contributed little, then Carlos Pace joined Brabham and showed his value with second place in the USA. Brabham was fifth in the championship. As BT44Bs in 1975 the cars had a stiffer monocoque, narrower front track and revised bodywork; still basically white, they had Martini's colourful stripes running fore and aft.

Pace won the Brazilian GP, and Reutemann the German GP in a somewhat erratic season (in part perhaps because the team's attention was turning to the BT45). BT44s were sold to John MacDonald's RAM team, which proved ineffectual and folded in mid-1976.

BT45 The alliance with Autodelta dated from 1974, and had commercial advantages for Brabham, not least in distinctly different engines, from the country of the team's main sponsor, and engines apparently supplied at no cost. But they were bulky boxer engines, thirsty, heavy and inconsistent (people accustomed to standardized DFVs were appalled to discover that parts were not always interchangeable between Alfa units). The paper output was 510bhp.

The BT45 had a wide monocoque, to match up with the flat-12 engine, which in turn was carried on pontoons extending back from the tub. There were revisions through the 1976 season, an early change seeing the deletion of the extraordinary high engine air intakes on the outer lines of the fuselage.

Pace's third place in the French GP was the best of a season that saw Brabham ninth in the championship, with nine points. Reutemann despaired, and moved to Ferrari before the end of the season. A lighter BT45B came for 1977, when Pace opened the season with second place in Argentina. His death in a flying accident was a blow. John Watson was second in France, Hans Stuck joined the team and was third in Germany and Austria. Brabham improved to fifth in the championship, with twenty-seven points.

Problems with a successor meant that the BT45 was uprated again for the first races in 1978, when Lauda was second in Argentina and third in Brazil, before the BT46 made its debut in South Africa.

BT46 In the BT46, Murray reverted to the 'pyramid' cross section, and that suited the engine shape, so that in spite of the Alfa unit's size the car's frontal area was not excessive. But the first BT46 captured attention for its heat exchanger radiators on the surfaces of the flanks. However, the airflow meant that this system for cooling water and oil did not work, and the BT46 had to be revised, with conventional nose radiators. Rising rate suspension was used, and there were integral jacks. The engines were optimistically rated at 520bhp.

Watson was third when the car was first raced in this form, in South Africa in 1978. But it was all too obvious that ground-effects cars were called for, and the heads of the boxer engine interfered with the airflow in a vital area. Murray's solution was the 'fan car', the BT46B.

In this highly controversial car, a large fan at the rear sucked air from the sealed

Brabham-Alfa Romeo BT46, with surface cooling. Shown in 1978, but never raced in this form.

(Above) Brabham-Alfa Romeo BT46B 'fan car', racing in Sweden 1978. It won, but was banned thereafter.

The 'cooling' fan of the Brabham BT46B actually helped provide downforce.

The BT48 proved to be a failure – at first, ground effects calculations seemed to be shown faulty – and it was to be an interim type as a DFV-powered car was soon under construction. There was a win in a non-championship race, but in the Grands Prix Lauda and Piquet accumulated just seven points in three scoring finishes with the cars, to give Brabham a humbling eighth place in the championship.

BT49 A crash programme saw this DFV-powered replacement for the hapless Alfa-engined cars built very quickly, and it was raced in the autumn events in 1979. A slightly lengthened version of the BT48 monocoque was used, with similar suspension. The V8 drove through a Brabham-Alfa six-speed gearbox, also carried over. The car was some 15kg (33lb) lighter – hardly enough to compensate for a paper loss of around 50bhp.

There were no race finishes in 1979, but Nelson Piquet won the fourth Grand Prix of 1980. There was an interlude while the compact Weismann gearbox was introduced, then Piquet won in Holland and Canada. He was second in the championship to Alan Jones, but scored all but one of the points that lifted Brabham to third in the Constructors' Championship (team mate Zunino contributed little, and Rebaque scored just one point).

engine bay through a horizontal radiator, thereby sucking the car down to the track. Two cars appeared for the Swedish GP, and Lauda won in one. Protests then saw to it that the cars were banned on the grounds that the fan was a moveable aerodynamic device (never mind that in advance Murray had convinced officials that the primary purpose of the fan was cooling).

The BT46C was brought in, at one meeting, and quickly discarded (it had the needle nose of the original BT46 and water radiators behind the front wheels). Through the rest of 1978, normal BT46s sometimes showed potential as 'the best of the rest' behind the Lotus 79, and Brabham was third in the championship.

BT47 A projected 'Phase 2' 'fan car' that was to have a more generous sealed under-car area. Work started, with the intention of racing the car late in 1978, but it was set aside after the BT46B was outlawed.

BT48 Autodelta produced a V12 very quickly, for a 1979 Brabham wing car. This 2,991cc twelve-cylinder unit incorporated parts from the flat 12, and it was used as a stressed member. A rating of 525bhp was quoted.

The monocoque was in aluminium, but with some carbon-fibre composite panels. The double wishbone suspension had inboard coil springs/dampers.

BT49C for 1981 was lighter, and had a hydro-pneumatic suspension system to circumvent a new ground clearance rule; this allowed a car to rise to the minimum heights as it slowed to stop, or was at rest, and predictably it led to wrangles! A change of tyres did not help, but with three Grand Prix victories and other good placings Piquet was World Champion, and with the eleven points scored by Rebaque, Brabham was runner-up in the makes championship.

The team was looking to a future with BMW engines, but ran BT49s in 'D' form early in 1982, and then in tandem with BT50s until the summer. The D was transmitted through Brabham gearboxes with Hewland internals. Additional fuel had to be carried. Outwardly, the higher body line behind the cockpit distinguished it from the BT49.

Early in 1982, the BMW-powered cars were disappointing, then Piquet unexpectedly won the Canadian GP. There were to be only three more scoring finishes for BT50s. But they still captured attention as the team introduced the fuel-stop ploy, which meant that cars could be run with lower fuel loads, on softer tyres.

BT51 A 'flat-bottom' ruling meant that this car was never raced – it was built

At the start of 1983, Piquet gave the BT52 a debut victory in the Brazilian GP, and later he was to win the Italian and European GPs, while Patrese won in South Africa. Their 72 points gave Brabham third place in the Constructors' Championship.

BT53 With larger side pods and aerodynamic changes, this appeared as a developed BT52, and that car was indeed the basis, and once again a 'B' designation was to come in mid-season. A ban on fuel stops meant that more fuel had to be carried. The engine gave as much as 850bhp, but unreliability became a sapping factor

Brabham-Ford BT49 of 1980, with Nelson Piquet driving.

lighter and lower, with a new monocoque. Carbon-fibre brakes were run, and so were 'water-cooled' brakes (a form of disposable ballast to circumvent weight regulations that set up more debate!). Protests against this ploy led to Piquet's win in Brazil being disallowed. Ricardo Patrese did win at Monaco, and after the Canadian GP the BT49 was retired.

BT50 Major components – suspension and monocoque, for example – were carried over to this car. It was powered by the BMW M12/13 turbocharged 1,499cc engine, which had been under development since 1980, sometimes painfully (reliability was to be elusive). It was to be raced before it was really ready, at BMW's insistence. The claimed output when a car was first run in public, at Silverstone in British GP tests, was 570bhp, and this

as a ground effects car with a small fuel capacity, intended to be used with fuel-stop strategies.

BT52 Another visually striking Brabham, with a rearward weight bias that was very obvious – there were no side pods, so from the rear of the cockpit forward it appeared very slender. The lower part of its monocoque was in sheet aluminium, the upper sections being moulded in carbon-fibre composites. A wide track and inboard coil springs/dampers emphasized its slim nose. Radiators flanked the engine bay, and a single-pylon rear wing complemented the delta-plan front aerofoil. Jacks were built in. The engine was in a steel frame, and gave some 640bhp in race trim, or up to 750bhp for qualifying. Modifications through the year justified a 'B' designation at its mid-point.

again, particularly with turbocharger failures.

There were two victories (Piquet winning the Canadian and USA(E) Grands Prix) but only twelve finishes in thirty-two starts, and the constructors' score was just over half the 1983 total (for fourth place).

BT54 Basically, the 1985 F1 Brabham followed the BT53, while the BMW engine was still rated at 850bhp in race trim but proved more reliable. However, there was a change to Pirelli tyres, and this was not an advance: Brabham shone only when track and weather conditions really suited the Italian rubber, and the French GP was the only race to fall to the team – Piquet's victory at Paul Ricard was to be the last for Brabham.

The team's score and championship position slipped, to twenty-six and fifth.

BT54s were used to gain back-to-back comparisons with the BT55 in 1986.

BT55 The distinctive 'low line' car's theoretical advantages, in aerodynamic respects and reduced frontal area, were not translated into track success. There was a carbon-fibre/Kevlar monocoque, and the tried suspension layout. The BMW engine was inclined at 72 degrees, and it did not function at all well in this 'lay-down' position. Beyond that, the seven-speed Weismann gearbox was not reliable.

Patrese scored the team's only points, two, with sixth places at Imola and Detroit. Brabham was ninth in the championship. Gordon Murray left.

BT56 Murray's associate of several years, David North, with Sergio Rinland and John Baldwin, were credited with this car. They were tied to the 'lay down' engine (Megatron had taken over the upright units), but the freakish lines of the BT55 gave way to good looks again.

In terms of results there was a modest recovery, Patrese and de Cesaris each scoring a third place, so that Brabham was one championship place better off, eighth with ten points.

BT58 In 1988 the Brabham team was granted a sabbatical while its affairs were sorted out. It was back in 1989 with a straightforward car designed by Rinland, using the Judd CV engine. The car lacked straight-line speed, but it proved competent, especially when Modena and Brundle finished 'in the points' at Monaco.

The BT58s were run again in the opening races of 1990, and Modena scored the team's only points of that year, two in the first Grand Prix.

BT59 This development of the BT58 by Rinland used much of that car's rear end, with extended bodywork and other detail differences, and it met new cockpit safety regulations. Judd EV engines were used, and a transverse gearbox came in mid-season, while lesser modifications were gradually introduced. These 1990 cars did not produce championship points.

One BT59 was sent to Japan, for Yamaha development work, and the BT59Y was used while the 1991 car was readied. BT59Y had the Yamaha OX99 V12. Neither driver scored with it, and the BT60Y appeared for the third Grand Prix.

BT60Y Rinland's Yamaha-powered car was smart, but the programme was under-resourced, and development time had to be devoted to rectification work. There was a composite monocoque, pushrod suspension all round, an underslung front aerofoil, and the V12 rated at 700bhp driving through a new transverse gearbox.

There was a point-scoring finish in Belgium by Blundell, and Brundle contributed two points with his Australian GP fifth place – Brabham's last scoring finish. It was ninth in the Constructors' Championship.

The cars had to be revamped for 1992, as BT60Bs with Judd GV V12 engines, for Yamaha chose to switch to Jordan. The lack of finance became desperate, and suppliers began to squeeze the team, so there was no meaningful development, rather a struggle to survive.

To that end, Giovanna Amati might have contributed a mite of publicity, but she failed to qualify to start a race. Eric van der Poele qualified once, failed to qualify nine times, and quit.

Damon Hill took the Italian lady's place, qualifying twice and finishing both races, sixteenth in Britain and eleventh in Hungary. That was the Brabham team's last Grand Prix, as its owners went into receivership.

continued from p.39

Engine capacity was reduced again in 1908 to 12,045cc (the formula imposed a 155mm stroke for four-cylinder engines). Otherwise, in specification and appearance, these last Brasiers showed every sign of design stagnation. That was reflected in performance: two cars failed to reach one-third distance, and Théry retired the last on the last lap. After that there were a few successes in minor events for the Brasiers.

BRM

See pp.47–51.

BRP

The British Racing Partnership was a leading independent team as the 1960s opened, formed in the late 1950s by Alfred Moss and Ken Gregory primarily to run cars for Stirling Moss, whose personal contracts meant that he could not drive for some main-line teams. It ran BRMs and Coopers in the closing 2.5litre formula years.

continued on p.51

BRP-BRM of 1964, Innes Ireland at the wheel.

British Racing Motors' fortunes fluctuated: it suffered a long period when the initials BRM became synonymous with failure, before change – not least in management – brought success, and then less fortunate developments led to a sad decline. BRM was formed in 1947 by Raymond Mays and Palin 'Peter' Berthon, who had made a success of ERA in the 1930s, and started to work towards a Grand Prix project during the Second World War. It was originally a research trust, to guide and co-ordinate as well as design a car.

This took shape slowly and when it did run, fears that it might be over-ambitious were borne out, yet Mays and Berthon persisted. BRM's seemingly never-ending string of failures became the butt of humour that was often sour, and alienated supporters (most notably Tony Vandervell, who did his own thing, and won Grands Prix before BRM). However, it made its contribution in drawing attention to motor racing in a country where the sport had been a minority interest.

Success eventually came, under another Grand Prix formula and after another series of setbacks. Into the 1.5litre years, the first half of the 1960s, prospects were much brighter. Sir Alfred Owen, an early backer who had actually bought BRM in 1952 but made the mistake of leaving Mays and Berthon in control, issued his famous 'win or close' ultimatum; there was a good car with a good engine, and in 1962 both championships fell to the team.

Then there was another false start, as the 3litre formula came into force. There were to be more victories, but inept management sapped the team in the 1970s.

Rubery Owen support was withdrawn in 1974, when Sir Alfred Owen died. Louis Stanley, who had effectively become manager by the sole qualification of marriage, proved quite ineffectual, and reduced the team to a hand-to-mouth existence as Stanley-BRM. The inevitable end came in 1977; others attempted to revive the marque in 1977, and more recently the initials have appeared on a sports car.

Type 15   The concept was wrong, but unfortunately the management stubbornly held to it, even after the formula to which the cars had been built was abandoned. Instead of straightforward simplicity, the first BRM was complex, and not just in its engine, where there was the justification of a target power output. The chassis echoed 1930s practices (but then

BRM V16 Type 15, as raced in 1951, with Reg Parnell at the wheel.

BRM V16 Type 15, further developed, with cooling slots and louvres. 1953 Albi race.

so did rivals' chassis), but the suspension incorporated oleo-pneumatic struts when coil springs/dampers would have served. There was a de Dion rear end. The infamous engine was a 1,488cc 135-degree V16 with centrifugal two-stage supercharging that, at least in its early years, had a very narrow power band. Various maximum power figures have been quoted, but by the time the Type 15 was raced 440bhp was the probable figure. The noise was, and is, extraordinary.

The cars ran in one Grand Prix, Parnell and Walker finishing fifth and seventh in the 1951 British race. Many other drivers, including the very best, drove them in secondary events, and few were flattering.

Although the 1.5litre/4.5litre Formula 1 virtually collapsed, two lightweight Mk II (P30) versions were built, and raced in *formule libre* events until 1955.

P25 This car for the 2.5litre formula also took shape slowly, and first appeared late in 1955. Outwardly it was a very neat little car. There was a multi-tube chassis, with some stressed panels, and Berthon stuck with oleo-pneumatic struts in the suspension (with double wishbones at the front and a de Dion rear axle). Another oddity was the single transmission disc brake at the rear. The engine was a 2,491cc over-square four-cylinder unit designed by Stuart Tresilian that initially gave almost 250bhp.

The cars failed in local events and their first Grand Prix outings. Expert consul-

tants were called in and, most importantly, Colin Chapman reworked the rear suspension, to incorporate coil springs/dampers. Later the chassis was to be revised, as a space frame.

A first victory eventually came, when Jean Behra won the non-title Caen GP in 1957. Then Harry Schell and Behra finished second and third in the 1958 Dutch GP.

The engine had to be revised for the obligatory AvGas fuel in 1958, output dropping from around 280bhp to 240bhp (some of the 'loss' due to changes that increased internal friction). At last a BRM won a championship Grand Prix, driven by Jo Bonnier in Holland. Altogether, the P25s earned thirty-seven championship points from starts in twenty-one Grands Prix. In 1960 the cars were cannibalized,

BRM 2.5litre P25 front-engined car, which raced from 1955 to 1959. This is the 1957 version.

parts being used in the rear-engined P48s – years later they were 're-converted' for historic racing!

P48 BRM responded surprisingly quickly to Cooper's lead in Grand Prix car layout, and late in 1959 the first P48 conversion of a P25 was running. The P25 front suspension and the front of the chassis was used, with the engine behind the driver and independent rear suspension. The single rear brake was retained. A Mk II with conventional outboard brakes, double wishbone and coil-spring rear suspension, and other refinements, was introduced in 1960. It had obvious potential, but luck seemed to run against it in races (just eight points were scored, by Bonnier and Hill).

P48/57 For the first season of 1.5litre Grand Prix, BRM had to use Coventry

BRM P48 mid-engined 2.5litre car, Graham Hill driving, British GP 1960.

Climax FPF engines in the Mk II cars. Despite the efforts of two talented drivers, Hill and Brooks, these were not competitive and BRM accumulated just seven championship points in 1961. The cars were sold to private owners, and two were to be fitted with BRM V8 engines.

P57   This was a slim and smooth car, save for the early aberration of separate exhausts pointing skywards. It was effective, too, with BRM's fuel-injected 1,482cc V8, designed by Berthon and developed by Aubrey Woods. It gave more than 180bhp at first, slightly more than the Coventry Climax V8 used by some rival constructors. The car had a space frame, with conventional suspension. BRM or Colotti gearboxes were used.

As the 1962 season opened, the team was successful in non-championship races. Then Graham Hill won the Dutch, German, Italian and South African GPs, and was champion driver while BRM won the constructors' title. Redemption in full!

The cars were used in 1963, with BRM six-speed gearboxes, in the early races and usually through the rest of the year. Notably, Hill and Ginther were first and second at Monaco. P57s were also sold to independent entrants.

P61   Following the appearance of the Lotus 25, Tony Rudd laid down this stressed-skin semi-monocoque car that was first taken to a GP meeting in Belgium (but not raced there). Usually, drivers preferred the older cars while handling problems, which stemmed from a tendency for the chassis to distort, were sorted out.

P261   This monocoque car was also known as the P61 MkII or P61/2 – whatever, it was handsome and purposeful in its dark colours, and the stressed-skin extensions to the central monocoque gave the level of stiffness required.

The first car was completed early in 1964, and the type served for three full seasons. The V8 delivered as much as 212bhp for the type's second season.

Hill and Ginther were first and second at Monaco again in 1964, when Hill also won the US GP again. He repeated these victories in 1965, when his team mate was Jackie Stewart, who scored his first GP victory at Monza. In those two seasons, Hill was second in the drivers'

BRM P57 1.5litre model, Graham Hill driving, Monaco 1962.

championship, BRM runner-up in the Constructors' Championship.

The engine was enlarged, as a '2litre' unit for Tasman racing, The 1,971cc version produced 270bhp, while the eventual 2,070cc version gave some 285bhp. P261s with enlarged engines were used in 1966, while BRM's first 3litre car was developed towards the race worthiness never fully achieved with it. Stewart drove one of these P261s to win at Monaco, bringing the type's GP victories score to six. Hill scored his seventeen points with them, Stewart his fourteen, and BRM slipped to fourth on the constructors' table. BRM ran these cars in the Tasman series again in 1967, then the team last used one in a Grand Prix in France, while independents ran them on into 1968.

P67   BRM was ahead of the pack with this four-wheel-drive one-off car, and one outcome was that it did not join the short-lived rush to build this type of car in the early 3litre years. It was designed by Mike Pilbeam, with a 1.5litre V8 reversed so that the clutch was just behind the cockpit. There was a centre differential on Ferguson lines and the drive was offset to the left. After tests, the P67 was entered for the 1964 British GP, but withdrawn after practice as Richard Attwood's times were not competitive. In 1967 it was sold for hill-climb use, and it was used successfully in this sport for the next two years.

P83   For the 3litre formula that came in 1966, BRM started to develop an over-complex engine, which Tony Rudd felt would be needed to deliver the power that pundits reckoned would be called for. In effect, this 2,988cc unit comprised two eight-cylinder horizontal engines, one above the other so that it was an H16. It was substantially overweight, even in its second 'lightweight' form; in its early form it seldom produced 400bhp, some 10 per cent below the target output, and it proved desperately unreliable.

The engine was a stressed member in the P83 chassis that was a monocoque following on from the successful 1.5litre cars. Because of the gross engine, the P83 was some 135kg (298lb) overweight, at best. First raced late in 1966, the car was occasionally quick, but in thirty-two starts it recorded only twelve finishes, the best performances being Stewart's second and Spence's fifth in the 1967 South African GP in 1968.

P126   Fortunately, BRM had a V12 in being in 1967. This was largely designed by Geoff Johnson, for Tasman and sports car use, but it was used in 2,998cc form in McLaren's M5A F1 car. The BRM to be powered by it was laid down for Tasman racing, and it was designed by Len Terry, whose company also built the chassis. There was a full monocoque, conventional suspension, and a Hewland gearbox. Initially, the 3litre V12 produced no

BRM P83 H16 3litre of 1966, Jackie Stewart at the wheel.

BRM P126, 3litre V12 of 1968. The driver is Pedro Rodriguez.

the Constructors' Championship, recorded in 1961, save for the zero Stanley-BRM years.

P139 This car was another failure at the end of the 1960s. It followed the P138 in some respects, with a monocoque designed by Alex Osborne. It was not race worthy early in the 1969 season, and was revised in mid-season. The only noteworthy placing was John Surtees's third in the USA at the end of the year. Meanwhile, personnel changes had become almost inevitable: Tony Rudd, a good servant of BRM, was dismissed, Tim Parnell became team manager and Tony Southgate became designer.

P153 Southgate's first BRM chassis was ready for the 1970 season, and it owed nothing to its hapless predecessors. It had a simple and light monocoque, and was distinguished by its broad flat nose and bulbous flanks housing bag tanks. The suspension was conventional, and brakes were outboard all round.

The V12 had been developed, by Aubrey Woods, to give up to 440bhp. Rodriguez drove a P153 to win the Belgian GP, averaging 149.94mph (241kmph) and BRM's seasonal points score of twenty-three was again respectable. The P153 was used in 1971, when a P153B (with P160 suspension) also appeared, despite the introduction of the P160.

P160 Evolution led to the P160, and in 1971 it was a very effective car; then it had to serve on, until four years later its competitive life was exhausted. It had lower lines than the P153, with a fine chisel nose, and the other outward change was in the colours, for BRM became the second team to whole-heartedly commit to sponsorship, shown in a restrained Yardley scheme.

In 1971 Siffert won the Austrian GP in a P160, Gethin the Italian GP – two very fast races. Beyond that, there were points-scoring finishes to give BRM second place in the Constructors' Championship, albeit its score (thirty-six) was less than half the total amassed by Tyrrell.

Sadly, Jo Siffert became the only driver to be killed racing a BRM, in a non-championship end-of-season race at Brands Hatch. Technical changes were few in 1972, and in any case were subordinate to muddled management moves. The P160B

more than 320bhp, and Cosworth DFV outputs were not matched until 1970; in revised forms, it was to serve BRM until the team collapsed. The P126 was a stand-in, while BRM built its own cars for the V12. Attwood placed one second at Monaco in 1968, and one of the cars was run by Parnell into 1969.

P133 Effectively, this was the BRM-built version of the P126, used in 1968–69. Pedro Rodriguez was second in the 1968 Belgian GP in a P133, and third in the Dutch and Canadian GPs.

P138 A lightweight development of the P133, with a revised monocoque and new suspension, a BRM gearbox, and in 1969 the 48-valve version of the V12 that produced some 400bhp but was not reliable. That year BRM scored only seven points, equalling its lowest-ever score in had the less attractive 'shovel' nose first seen in 1971, normally carried an engine air box, and wore Marlboro colours. A large team was run – Stanley's objective of five or six cars on a grid was not attained, but there were sometimes four scattered down grids before the sponsor restricted the team to three; fifty starts in championship races were recorded, to set against four scoring finishes – fourteen points for seventh place on the table. The bulk of those were gained as Jean-Pierre Beltoise won at Monaco, BRM's last Grand Prix victory, and a lucky one in that the Frenchman led from start to finish in pouring rain.

For 1973 the P160E had a deformable structure chassis, but there were no improvements in other areas, and generally the V12 was no longer competitive. A fourth in Canada (Beltoise) was the best result, and BRM's twelve points gave it equal fourteenth place with Ferrari. These cars were run again in 1974, alongside newer P201s.

P180 Southgate designed this car to have an excessive bias of weight to the rear – 30:70 – even locating the radiators alongside the gearbox, under the rear aerofoil. The monocoque followed low P160 lines. The experiment did not work. Handling was poor, the drivers generally preferred P160s. The two cars built were set aside, with just one race win (for Beltoise) in a non-championship race at Brands Hatch to their credit. But that was BRM's last victory of any sort.

P201 Mike Pilbeam's design was com-

BRM P160, 3litre V12 of 1972, driven by Jean-Pierre Beltoise.

pact, outwardly angular and hardly attractive. It relied on the aged V12, and it gained a reputation for good handling. Its debut race promised much, for Beltoise was second in the South African GP, driving the first of four cars to be completed. But after that, results fell away, and BRM's 1974 season produced ten points – the last scored by the marque.

The cars came out again in 1975, presented as Stanley-BRMs.

P207 Another Len Terry design, this

Stanley-BRM was outwardly smoother than the P201, but it also looked very bulky. As much as 480bhp was claimed for the V12, but the claim is suspect as drivers usually failed to qualify a P207 to start in Grands Prix. The two cars lingered in secondary British races, as Jordan-BRMs.

P230 Although it carried a BRM designation, this ground-effects car was built by CTG in 1979, for Derick Betteridge and John Jordan. It was to be used in local

---

continued from p.46

BRP continued into the 1.5litre period as the UDT-Laystall team, and for 1962 bought Lotus 24s, only to find that these were almost immediately outclassed as Colin Chapman introduced the monocoque Lotus 25. So BRP decided to build its own monocoque cars. Tony Robinson's design followed Lotus lines, albeit with a heavier-gauge monocoque. A BRM V8 engine was used, with Colotti-Francis five- or six-speed gearboxes. A second car was completed for 1964.

In 1963 Innes Ireland came fourth in the first BRP in the Dutch and Italian GPs. He won a non-title race at Snetterton in 1964, was fifth in the Austrian and Italian GPs, while team mate Trevor Taylor was sixth in the US GP. These results were good for sixth

and seventh places respectively on the Constructors' Championship tables. BRP built a pair of Indianapolis cars for 1965; a 1966 F1 project was not completed for Grand Prix racing, although the car was used in F5000 and later restored with a BRM V8.

BS

BS Fabrications was a prominent specialist contractor in the British racing car industry, and in 1980 it laid down an F1 car, partly to take up slack capacity. It was a 'Cosworth kit car', to a design by Nigel Stroud. The car was nearing completion when sponsor support was withdrawn and the project was abandoned.

Buc

Bucciali Frères are recalled for their unconventional road cars, and by the standards of some of those their one-off AB6 was mechanically sober. It had low-built sports-car lines, and a 1,490cc sohc straight six. The claimed output was 70bhp, which made it the least powerful Grand Prix car of 1927. It ran in only one Grand Prix, the Spanish race at San Sebastian, where it finished eighth. Bucciali never built another racing car, the company closing down in 1933.

Bugatti

See pp.52–56.

Buc driven by Bucciali, 1925.

Buick

Bob Burman started a Buick 50-based car in the 1908 Grand Prize at Savannah, which was contested by several major European Grand Prix teams. It completed only two out of the sixteen laps before retiring. The Marquette he drove with more success in the 1910 Grand Prize was sometimes referred to as a Buick.

BUGATTI

Bugatti is a difficult subject. Mythology has it that Bugatti was one of the outstanding Grand Prix constructors. Facts contradict this – in the Grand Prix world, Bugatti was a lightweight, in achievement as well as in innovation. But for ten years from 1924 Bugatti built cars that looked simply beautiful, and those aesthetic qualities often seemed all-important. Ettore Bugatti's reported attitudes do not always help his cause – he sometimes steps out of the pages of history as one of racing's great poseurs – and there was always that failure to keep pace in technical matters.

In compiling this book, the pre-First World War American races that closely matched the Grands Prix have not been excluded, and in that respect the Bugatti that ran in the 1915 Grand Prize has to be mentioned in passing (whereas the second place in the 1911 Grand Prix de France could be overlooked, since that event was so disreputable). Johnnie Marquis started one of the 5litre Bugattis then being raced in the USA in the Grand Prix at San Francisco, retiring with ignition problems on a very wet day, but earning a note in the history of the marque in top-flight racing.

The marque entered Grand Prix racing in 1922, and in that season Bugattis were runners-up to the dominant Fiats in the two Grands Prix. In 1924 the Type 35 was unveiled with a flourish, and this is the one Grand Prix Bugatti that deserves the adulation sometimes accorded to any and every Bugatti. It was the prettiest car of its generation, and while it was seldom competitive in top-line racing so long as other works teams were active, the importance of the T35 and its derivatives through the period when racing suffered with the Depression cannot be overstated. Without these cars, Grand Prix racing would have been pathetic, in some cases there would just not have been Grands Prix.

As relative prosperity returned, Bugattis could generally no more live with Alfa Romeos in the early 1930s than they could with Alfas, Fiats and Delages in the mid-1920s. Then came the German onslaught, and Bugatti was to all intents and purposes swept away. An attempt to revive Bugatti as a Grand Prix marque in the mid-1950s had to be taken seriously, as few were then privileged to glimpse behind the scenes. After one race appearance, that programme was abandoned.

From 1922 until 1938, when Bugatti contested the Grands Prix that would nowadays have World Championship status, its cars won seventeen of the eighty-seven races, most of them in 1928–31 against negligible opposition. Happily, the essence of Grand Prix racing is not to be found in results and statistics, and Bugatti is best remembered for supremely elegant little cars in the 1920s, the types that grace modern historic events.

Type 30 The T30 designation was also applied to a sporting car, and this first purpose-built Grand Prix Bugatti was the forerunner of that model (a 5.2litre car had been run in the Grand Prize in 1915, incidentally). The T30 chassis derived from the T22 Brescia, with typical suspension, comprising semi-elliptic front springs and reversed quarter-elliptic rear springs. The 1,989cc straight eight, an sohc three-valves-per-cylinder unit, produced 86bhp in 1922, more than most contenders in the Strasbourg race, but considerably less than the Fiat 804. The brakes, hydraulic at the front and cable-operated at the rear, proved unsatisfactory. Late in the day changes were made to the bodies, as cowled noses (the tops of the trade mark horseshoe radiators coyly poking out) and long tapered tails enclosing the exhausts were added.

The Fiats seemed set to run away with the race, but near the end two were eliminated; de Vizcaya inherited second place for Bugatti, finishing almost 58min behind Nazzaro's winning Fiat, while Marco's Bugatti was the only other car classified (more than half an hour behind de Vizcaya, in an 802km (498 miles) race).

Just one T30 joined the grid for the Italian GP. De Vizcaya drove to a distant third place. Two of the 1922 Grand Prix cars, and three new ones, were taken to Indianapolis in 1923, when one finished ninth in the 500.

Type 32   The 1923 car looked odd, and behaved oddly. Contemporaries referred to it as the tortoise, the dishcover and the beetle, all more descriptive than 'tank', which stuck. The body has been called aerodynamic, but in side elevation it was almost a segment of a circle on a flat bottom – a product of art rather than science. It was carried on a pressed-steel platform, and that may have contributed to chassis rigidity. Drivers complained that they could not see their front wheels, but that only added to problems they already had, notably with handling, stemming from a wheelbase of 200cm and a track of 102cm. The straight eight was a little more sophisticated (with some roller bearings in place of plain bearings), but the claimed output of 100bhp was still not enough.

Friedrich finished the French GP in a Bugatti, behind two Sunbeams. Three T32s retired, the 'tanks' did not appear in the Italian GP, and Bugatti turned to orthodox bodies.

Type 35   For many enthusiasts, this was the typical racing Bugatti. Any variant –

Bugatti T30, de Viscaya driving at the French GP 1922.

Bugatti Type 32 'Tank' of 1923.

more than 200 cars were built, in nine versions – is most attractive, and the Grand Prix cars amongst them were the marque's most important in this category.

The chassis harked back to the T22, in dimensions as well as make-up, and it was clothed in slender two-seat bodywork that was absolutely 'right' overall and in detail.

(Above) Bugatti T35 – first time out, 1924 French GP.

(Below) Bugatti T35B, driven by 'Williams', Monaco GP 1929.

The engine was the straight eight, refined and more robust; in its first T35 1,991cc form it gave 90bhp (again not enough to give Bugatti drivers a fair chance against their rivals with supercharged engines). Attractive cast-alloy eight-spoke wheels incorporated ribbed brake drums (cable-operated front and rear), while the suspension followed tried and tested lines.

First time out, for the 1924 French GP, Bugatti ran five cars. Two retired, one was flagged off, Chassagne and Friedrich were seventh and eighth (last!). Bugatti complained of rear tyres throwing treads, but it seems that he influenced Dunlop in their design. His stalwart drivers Costantini and de Vizcaya then drove T35s to second and fifth places in the Spanish GP.

In the 1925 Grands Prix, T35s with engines giving up to 105bhp were again outrun, Costantini's third place in Italy and fourth in France being the best placings.

Meanwhile, production cars were in demand, notably the T35A with a detuned engine, and the 2.3litre T35T (Targa).

Type T35B/Type 35C These were the 2.3litre and 2litre supercharged models respectively, with engines producing

140bhp and 125bhp in 1928–30, Grand Prix racing's nadir years. Chronologically, they followed the T39/T39A, which were T35 variations.

Only one race was run to the Grand Prix regulations in 1928, and that Monza event was won by Chiron, with Nuvolari third in another Bugatti. In 1929 there was a fuel consumption formula, ignored by the AC de Monaco for its first Grand Prix which was won by 'Williams' in a T35B. He also won the French GP, a fuel-consumption affair, while Chiron won in Spain. Only the Grand Prix de l'Europe was run to fuel-consumption rules in 1930, when Chiron led a Bugatti 1-2-3. That year Dreyfus won at Monaco and Etancelin drove a T35B to win a ragbag *formule libre* French GP.

Type 39 For 1926 Bugatti turned to supercharged engines, first in a 1.1litre T35 then a 1.5litre unit for the new Grand Prix regulations. This produced some 100bhp in the T39A, which like the normally aspirated T39 was a T35 derivative.

The French GP was the infamous Maramas farce: the field comprised three T39As, Goux drove one to win, Costantini was flagged off, fifteen laps down, de Vizcaya retired. Jules Goux then scored a worthy victory in the European GP, with Costantini third, and (in reverse order) this pair was first and second in the Spanish GP. Malcolm Campbell was runner-up in the first RAC British GP in his own T39A (which looked odd with wire wheels). Then there was a Bugatti 1-2 in the Italian GP, Charavel winning.

Delage swept the board in 1927. At the last moment – on race day! – Ettore Bugatti withdrew his team from the French GP as the prospect of another defeat was unpalatable, and he did not send cars to Italy. That left the Spanish race, when Conelli was second, and the British event, when Chiron was fifth in the only Bugatti to finish (six started).

Type 52 In the T50 touring car, Bugatti introduced a twin-cam engine, long overdue in his racing cars. In 1930 he had acquired two Miller 91s from Leon Duray, taken their engines apart, and copied the block and valve gear for a straight eight, which otherwise followed established Bugatti lines. In 2.3litre form in the 1931–32 T51 it developed 180bhp. The rest of the T51 was in a line of evolution from the T35, and it was a well-balanced car which gained a similar reputation for good handling. It was the last catalogued Bugatti car, and production reached forty. Its debut came in the 1931 Tunis GP at Carthage, when Varzi drove one to victory, then in main-line races that year Chiron won the Monaco and French GPs (sharing a car in the 10-hour Montlhéry

Bugatti T53, 4.9litre engine and four-wheel drive, 1932.

Bugatti T57S45, 1939.

race with Varzi). In 1932 Alfa Romeo was on top, and the Czech GP was the only major race to fall to a Bugatti. The T51s served on through 1933, and beyond, with independent teams; Varzi's win at Monaco was the last in a major race for a T51.

Type 53 Bugatti could never have been responsible for the external lines of this cumbersome four-wheel drive car. It was conceived by Giulio Cappa and its detail design was in the hands of Antonio Pichetto. Bugatti adopted it, and built two in 1932. A 5litre supercharged engine was used, with drive to front and rear via a transfer gearbox and differentials offset to the left. It was run in practice for one Grand Prix, at Monaco in 1932, when it quickly exhausted Albert Divo and was set aside. Some good hillclimb times were set in T53s.

Bugatti T59, French GP 1934, Robert Benoist driving.

Bugatti T251, transverse 8-cylinder engine, raced only once, at the French GP of 1956.

Type 54 Track racing called for lower weight above all, so the T54 was created using a T45 chassis and the supercharged straight eight credited with 300bhp. Save for a 1-2 in the 1933 Avusrennen, it proved unsatisfactory in *formule libre* events and its odd Grand Prix appearances.

Type 59 There was a return to elegance in this car, but in other respects even diehard apologists can find little in its favour. It had 'offset single-seater' body lines, made more attractive by wire wheels (although a back plate coped with most loads). It appeared late in 1933 with a 2,820cc straight eight, but from 1934 a 3,257cc version was used, giving some 250bhp. It was reported that 3.8litre engines were used in 1936. There was a measure of independence in the front suspension with a 'divided axle', but most of the specification was familiar, even to cable-operated brakes.

In 1934, Dreyfus and Brivio were first and second in the Belgian GP in T59s, there were some third placings, and Wimille won the secondary Algiers GP. Hoped-for sales did not materialize (half of the six built found their way to Britain).

A T59 chassis was used in a central-cockpit single-seater, which was fitted with a 4.7litre T50B engine. It was run in practice in 1936, but not in the race; Wimille then drove it to finish second in the poorly supported Vanderbilt Cup, and won the first post-Second World War race meeting with it. A second car with a 3litre engine was seldom seen, but its single lap in the 1939 French GP was the last for a works Bugatti in this race until 1956.

Type 73C Production components were used in this car, and the basic layout was that of the 1930s, or even the 1920s. It has been suggested that preliminary design work started in the late 1930s, as Bugatti envisaged an entry into *voiturette* racing, following the Italian lead. A supercharged 1,488cc four-cylinder engine had a claimed output of 250bhp; its capacity was within the Formula 1 limit, but if it had ever been raced, this car's drivers would have carried the same sort of handicap that T51 drivers had as they faced P3 Alfa Romeos. A dumpy little car, the single T73C was built in 1947, but never developed.

Type 251 René Bolloré, who married Ettore Bugatti's widow, was behind this Grand Prix venture for the 2.5litre formula, Roland Bugatti controlled the programme, and Gioacchino Colombo undertook the adventurous design. The T251 emerged as a space-frame car with de Dion suspension front and rear, and a straight eight mounted transversely behind the cockpit. This 2,430cc unit comprised two blocks, with the power take-off and twin overhead camshaft drive between them. Output was reckoned to be around 230bhp. The car was hardly developed when prestige demanded that the two cars built be present at the French GP meeting in 1956. The second car had a longer wheelbase, as efforts were made to overcome handling problems experienced in the first tests, and disc brakes. Maurice Trintignant started in the Grand Prix in the first year despite his misgivings, only to retire after eighteen laps on the Reims circuit.

M. Bolloré lost interest, Bugatti's income from military work dried up as the Indo-China conflict ended, and this last Bugatti Grand Prix programme was abandoned.

Calthorpe

Another company that produced cars of Grand Prix status only by virtue of the classification of the 1912 French race – not that Calthorpe of Birmingham actually featured in the final classification, as its three cars retired from the Grand Prix, two before quarter distance.

Before 1912 Calthorpe entered cars in *voiturette* races, and it built light cars in the Vintage period, so its 1912 *Coupe de l'Auto* cars were its largest racing machines. The 2,971cc side-valve engines gave almost 70bhp, and were carried in stolidly conventional chassis, with bodies distinguished only by the vee radiators. One climbed to eleventh overall by half distance of the 1,540km (957 mile) Grand Prix, before its engine failed. With it, Calthorpe's international ventures ended.

Cegga-Maserati

The 1.5litre Formula 1 that came for 1961 seemed to offer opportunities for fringe constructors to enter Grand Prix racing, although as far as amateurs were concerned that was to prove illusory.

Cegga was an acronym deriving from the name of Swiss brothers Claude and George Gachnang, and their base at Aigle. They had built one-off sports cars using Bristol, Ferrari and Maserati engines, and approached Formula 1 with a car on similar lines. Their car had a space frame, wishbone and coil-spring independent suspension all round, and a neatly finished body. A second-hand Maserati 150S four-cylinder engine mounted behind the cockpit drove through a Maserati five-speed gearbox.

Maurice Caillet failed to qualify the car for the grids of two early 1961 non-championship races, and after that the Cegga-Maserati was only seen in hill climbs.

Chadwick

The Great Six 11.6litre touring car introduced in 1907 was soon followed by a short-wheelbase version that ran in 'stripped' form in US hill climbs, notably driven by Willia Haupt. He was effective-

Chadwick Six – a stripped-down racer in the USA in 1907/1908.

ly the works driver, king of events like the Giant's Despair hill climb, and a search for more spring-event power led to the first supercharged racing car, in 1907.

Outwardly this was a typical large racing car of the period, with a stout chassis and minimal bodywork terminating in a bolster tank and spare tyres. The three exhausts on the left pointed to a straight six. Haupt lured Lee S. Chadwick into producing tuned versions of this 11.6litre unit. One involved using three carburettors, and then a method of compressing mixture fed to the cylinders was devised. This involved belt-driven centrifugal compressors – supercharger in all but name, and in the plural because at one stage there was one per carburettor. The device was known as the 'blower', and that term passed into the language of motoring.

Haupt led the 1908 Vanderbilt Cup for some 70 miles in this car, before retiring with ignition failure. His run in the 1908 Grand Prize was less impressive – the best Chadwick lap was almost two minutes off the 21:36 best – and it ended on the fifth lap with unspecified bearing failure. In 1909 he broke the 10-mile record with this

car. Incidentally, Len Zengle, who took Haupt's place and was no less skilled in the hill-climb arts, won a 10-mile race at the first Indianapolis meeting in 1909 with a Chadwick.

Lee Chadwick left his company in 1911, and it did not long survive that. Fifteen years after that 1908 Grand Prize, the supercharger reappeared in Grand Prix racing.

Challenger

Reg Parnell initiated this project in 1939, anticipating a 1.5litre Grand Prix formula in 1941, but as the car only competed in a 1939 hill climb and a secondary 1947 race it was really another 'might-have-been' in Grand Prix terms. The tubular chassis was completed, together with its wishbone and coil-spring front suspension and de Dion-type rear layout, and attractive body. But the straight six dohc engine, which was to have a two-stage Roots-type supercharger, was never installed. Challenger ran with an ERA engine in 1939 and with a Delage straight eight in 1947, unsuccessfully. Then the car disappeared.

Chevron

Derek Bennett's single-seaters for secondary categories and his elegant sports-racing cars gained a high reputation for his little Chevron company, and a move towards Formula 1 in the 1970s seemed a natural progression. The design of the B41 F1 car was straightforward, and it promised to be a practical DFV-powered machine. However, the only one to be built took shape slowly, and Bennett died in a hang-glider accident in 1978 before it was completed. By that time the concept was obsolescent, for it was not a ground-effects car. The B41 was run in a British national F1 series in 1979, without making an impact.

Chiribiri

In the early 1920s, Antonio Chiribiri's Fiat-inspired cars promised to become a real force in *voiturette* racing, and although they had 1.5litre engines they were run in some Grands Prix in the 2litre period. These were conventional machines, with dohc engines, and handsome bodies behind their bluff radiators.

Chiribiri earned a niche in history as Tazio Nuvolari drove his first Grand Prix, and his first race outside Italy, in a Tipo Monza 1500, taking fifth place in the 1923 Penya Rhin GP in Spain (he had earlier raced in an Ansaldo in lesser events).

Pairs of cars were run in the 1924–25 Italian GPs, outclassed by 2litre cars. There was one on the twelve-car grid at Monza in 1926, when it might have stood a better chance in 1.5litre company, but it caught fire. By that time the Chiribiri company was facing closure, which came in the following year.

Christie

John Walter Christie built the largest Grand Prix engine, and moreover this monstrous 19,891cc four-cylinder power unit drove through the front wheels of his 1907 car.

In that, it followed the New York inventor/manufacturer's preceding cars, after a 1905 effort with one engine driving the front wheels and another the rear wheels. That car was then run with the rear engine removed, and its speed in American short-track events must have encouraged further front-wheel drive experiments.

Christie's patents involved a simple system, with each front wheel driven directly from the ends of the crankshaft, with a cone clutch for each, to give the effect of a differential. The transverse V4 had its front pair of cylinders almost upright and exposed to view, while the rear pair were laid back under the open-fronted bonnet. Bore and stroke of this 'square' unit were 18 × 185 – that's 7.25in × 7.25in! It was a three main-bearing engine, with overhead valves. There was a channel-section frame, the coil-spring front suspension (and drive) was neatly enclosed, and there were semi-elliptics at the rear. The transverse engine installations in the nose meant that the car was the most compact entry for the 1907 Grand Prix, with a 225cm wheelbase, and it was also the lightest, at 810kg (1,786lb). Away from the material aspects, the noise must have been quite exceptional, and the physical effort involved in driving the thing beggars imagination.

In the Grand Prix, it was reported to have a 'curious longitudinal rocking motion', and its best lap for the 77km (48 mile) circuit was 48min 49sec, almost 11 minutes slower than the best time. It completed only four laps, with a tyre parting from its rim on lap 1, one of the clutches misbehaving, and a stuck exhaust valve blamed for its retirement

After that Christie's racing cars appeared on short American tracks, where their front-wheel drive could be shown off as they showered loose track surface material, and that suited Barney Oldfield (Christie gave up racing after driving his car in that 1907 French GP, and for a while turned to front-wheel-drive taxis).

Cisitalia

The Cisitalia company was formed in 1946 by Piero Dusio and Piero Taruffi, and if business sense had ruled it might have gone on to great things. Its first product was a pretty little single-seater, primarily intended for a one-model series, and an even prettier road-going coupe, also using Fiat components, came a little later. By 1947 Cisitalia was involved in an advanced Grand Prix car project. Dusio approached the Porsche Büro, at that time effectively run by Karl Rabe (an associate of Ferdinand Porsche from their Austro-Daimler days, and chief engineer of the Büro when it was set up) for an F1 design. It proved complex and costly, but construction went ahead. This wildly overstretched the little company's resources, and when the first car was rolled out, incomplete, in 1948, Cisitalia was in crisis, nearing failure. Its Grand Prix car project was picked up by Autocar, but the car never ran in a race.

D46 This single-seater was normally run in 1,100cc form, although late cars did have larger engines. It had a space-frame chassis that was advanced by late-1940s standards,

Chevron-Ford B41 of 1979, raced only in the UK.

with Fiat suspension and engines tuned to give up to 70bhp. Seven were completed to be raced late in 1946, and in 1947 Dusio organised a 'circus' of fifteen cars to provide supporting races at major events. Some of these cars were used for many years, and were even the basis for odd Formula Junior cars at the end of the 1950s. Meanwhile, two with 1.3litre engines and increased fuel capacity were by no means outclassed in the first post-war Monaco GP (Taruffi was fifth when, like team mate Nuvolari, he retired).

Typ 360 Carrying this Büro designation, this car proved complex and original, and for its time, unrealistic. It had a space frame with torsion bar independent suspension all round, the engine was an over-square 1,493cc flat 12 with two superchargers in parallel (with a target output of 300bhp), and two- or four-wheel drive options for its driver to match track conditions.

When Cisitalia was collapsing, and one car was almost complete, Dusio persuaded the Argentine President Juan Peron to settle his debts and adopt the Typ 360. As the Autocar that first car was completed, and eventually run in a local record attempt in 1953. A company like Porsche might have been able to make it raceworthy (it seems unlikely that Cisitalia could have managed this) and had it been developed as Rabe, Dusio and others envisaged, the his-tory of Grand Prix racing could have been very different.

Clément-Bayard

Adolphe Clément sold the right to use his name as a marque title when he sold Clément et Cie in 1903, and he hyphenated his name and that of a sixteenth-century hero for his later cars, as Bayard-Clément while change-of-name legalities were sorted out then as Clément-Bayard. So much for semantics. The new company entered racing, with *voiturettes*, in the year it was created and then ran cars in the Gordon Bennett trials and Vanderbilt Cup in 1904 (Adolphe's son Albert was second in the American race). The next year was barren, but Clément-Bayard entered three-car teams in the first three Grands Prix.

The 1906–07 cars were essentially conventional, with bi-bloc four-cylinder engines (160 × 160mm, 12,868cc units), and massive frames. Two of the 1906 cars had wood-spoked artillery wheels with detachable rims – ironically, the car that finished third in that first Grand Prix did not, and Albert Clément was thought to have made a mistake when he rejected the *jante amovible* on his car, for he led into the final stages before tyre changes cost him dear. The other two cars retired.

The death of Albert in a pre-race test accident before the 1907 Grand Prix was a grave setback, but the team went ahead and ran its 12,868cc cars. Garcet and Shepard finished eighth and ninth. Clément-Bayard brought a new car designed by Sabarthié to Dieppe for the 1908 Grand Prix. This had a 13,963cc four-cylinder engine, a long-stroke unit (155 × 185mm) with pushrod-operated inclined overhead valves in hemispherical heads. They were reckoned to be the only engines to match Benz and Mercedes units in power output that year (135bhp was claimed), and this was borne out in the race, when Rigal's Clément-Bayard was the only French car in the first seven, the others all being German. Despite nineteen tyre changes, Rigal was fourth, Gabriel was twelfth, the other team car retired.

When bruised French pride allowed a resumption of Grand Prix racing, in 1912, Clément-Bayard had turned away from motor sport.

Coloni

Enzo Coloni took the big step from Formula 3 driver – and Italian champion – to entrant in Formula 1 in 1987. Formula 1 was not kind to under-resourced teams in the last quarter of the twentieth century,

Clément-Bayard, at the French GP 1906.

Coloni-Ford C3 of 1989, Roberto Moreno driving.

and the Coloni team did not have adequate finance or particularly talented personnel.

Coloni's cars generally had attractive lines, at least for the first three years, when they were powered by Cosworth engines, and just occasionally a driver qualified one to join a Grand Prix grid. An exclusive engine deal for 1990 seemed to promise better results, but the 'Subaru' flat 12 was actually built by Motori Moderni and that had a mediocre record – at best! Coloni failed to get a Subaru-engined car to a grid, and Subaru recognized the futility of the partnership. Predictably, nothing came of reports that Subaru would buy Coloni, and the Motori Moderni V12 did not appear. The 1990 car was quicker when a Cosworth DFR replaced the flat 12.

Coloni struggled on in 1991, with a machine that attracted no admirers but astonishingly did attract a buyer, Andrea Sassetti, who saw this going concern (sic) as a basis for his Andrea Moda Formula (AMF) team. This attempted to run Coloni C4s in the first two Grands Prix of 1992, but as these could not be shown to be original AMF chassis they were excluded and Andrea Moda had to build its own cars. And that AMF story really is pathetic.

FC187 This wholly conventional car made its debut at the Italian GP meeting late in the 1987 season, when the letters DNQ first appeared against Coloni's name on the qualifying time sheets. The design was by Roberto Ori. There was a carbon-fibre/Kevlar monocoque, with double wishbone suspension all round. The Cosworth DFR drove though a Coloni-modified Hewland six-speed gearbox. Nicola Larini qualified the FC187 for the last race of 1987, but retired soon after the start.

FC188 A slightly revised FC187, this car was to undergo further modification in mid-season, when the body was revised with shorter sidepods and repositioned radiators, and new wings, and it was redesignated FC188B.

Gabriele Tarquini failed to pre-qualify seven times, then failed to qualify once, thus starting a Coloni in half the season's Grands Prix. He finished four times, to give Coloni a 25 per cent finishing record. His best placing was eighth, in Canada. That was a Coloni high point.

Two of the three cars were lightly revised for the opening races in 1989, when Moreno and Raphanel each started one race, and each retired (otherwise Moreno's record was a consistent NQ, Raphanel's a consistent NPQ).

C3 Two of these new cars came in the early summer of 1989. Designed by Christian Vanderpleyn, they proved to have some FC188 features, but they were slimmer. Cosworth DFR or DFZ engines were used. Moreno qualified one just once (recording another race retirement), while Bertaggia took Raphanel's place for the last six Grands Prix, and failed to get to a grid.

The C3 chassis was adapted to carry the Subaru flat 12 and transverse six-speed gearbox in 1990. The car was designated C3B, was overweight and appeared cumbersome. The claimed output of the flat 12 was 600bhp, so it was the least powerful F1 engine of the year, as well as the heaviest.

Bertrand Gachot failed to pre-qualify the car for the first eight Grands Prix, Subaru lost faith, and for the ninth race the car had a Cosworth DFR. After recording two more 'NPQ' entries, Gachot at least got a Coloni to full timed practice for the last six races, although he failed to qualify to join a grid.

C4 This car was similar to the C3, the design being attributed to Coloni technicians, with some input by the University of Perugia. It retained pushrod double wishbone suspension, a chassis that might have been carried over, and used DFR engines. Funds were desperately short, and Enzo Coloni was team manager and race engineer. Pedro Chaves failed to pre-qualify in thirteen attempts, Naoki Hattori once.

Andrea Moda Formula (q.v.) attempted to run C4s in the first races of 1992, but the entries were not accepted.

Connaught

This little British constructor came close to Grand Prix success in the 1950s, before it lost its backer and closed its doors in 1957. It had been formed by Rodney

Clarke, who was the designer, soon joined by engineer Mike Oliver, and it gained a reputation for thoroughly engineered cars. Less worthy outfits have achieved less and lasted longer in the age of sponsorship.

The first Connaughts were sports cars, and one was raced by Kenneth McAlpine, who commissioned the first Connaught single-seater, for Formula 2 racing, and was to back the Grand Prix effort.

The first F2 car was completed in 1951, and it was followed by eight more built to a 'production specification'. These were generally owned and raced by amateurs and made no impression on the World Championship races run for F2 cars; beyond that Connaught never had competitive engines, and these A-types had Lea Francis-based power units.

For the 2.5litre Formula 1 from 1954, Connaught built new cars to serve an interim role, as it was anticipated that the Coventry-Climax 'Godiva' V8 would become available; as that was abandoned, Connaught had to use Alta engines that just did not deliver enough power. The cars were painstakingly engineered – it has been suggested that the main Connaught weakness was its policy of working slowly and carefully, and failing to respond to developments quickly, or instinctively.

There was success, notably a victory for a car driven by Tony Brooks at the end of 1955, in a non-championship race in Sicily, but against front-rank Italian cars. In 1956 the team had to concentrate on home races, venturing further afield only when good start money was on offer.

Resources were always thin, and McAlpine withdrew his support in 1957. An advanced rear-engined monocoque project intended for the 'Godiva' engine was discontinued, and fall-back plans for a rear-engined space-frame car were also abandoned. In autumn 1957 the Connaught F1 equipment was sold by auction, when two of the cars were bought by Bernie Ecclestone, who entered them in a few early-1958 races. The Connaughts which were familiar on historic grids are a constant reminder of what might have been.

A-type The first F2 Connaughts had an orthodox tubular chassis, with wishbone and torsion bar suspension all round, but the design was modified with a de Dion rear end in 1951. The Lea Francis engine initially developed 135bhp, but for championship racing in 1952–53 it gained some 30bhp, with fuel injection and bored out to give a capacity of 1,960cc (that enlargement came at some cost in reliability). Apart from a power handicap, the cars gained a good reputation for their all-round qualities.

A score of drivers raced them in F2 events, mostly in British races. Highlights were fourth (Poore) and fifth (Thompson) finishes in the 1952 British GP, and when the high-speed nature of the circuit is taken into account Moss's ninth in the Italian GP also stands out. There were six wins in secondary 1952 races, and in that

Connaught A-type, driven by Dennis Poore at Silverstone in 1953.

activity the record was better in 1953. But the cars were outrun in 1953 World Championship races, with no Connaught drivers scoring points.

Michael Young installed a 2.5litre Alta engine in his A-type, claiming 215bhp for it. Entered in non-championship races in 1955, it made no impact, and was soon abandoned.

B-type The 1954 F1 car had a similar chassis, with wishbone and coil spring independent front suspension and the de Dion rear end. The 2,470cc Alta dohc engine was good for some 240bhp, and was regarded as a stopgap. It drove through a pre-selector gearbox, as on the A-type. Connaught was ahead of the game in using a wind tunnel and an aerodynamicist, and the first B-type had a 'streamlined' one-piece upper body. This was difficult to handle, and was vulnerable, so it was discarded in favour of another stubby body, and open wheels. The third car was to be rebodied as the distinctive 'toothpaste tube' Connaught in 1957.

The team entered British races in 1955, until the end of the season, when Brooks scored that notable Syracuse victory. In 1956 the cars again performed well in Britain, and Fairman was fourth in the Grand Prix. The Italian GP brought an even better result, as Flockhart and Fairman finished third and fifth. Early in the 1957 season, Lewis-Evans was fourth at Monaco in the 'toothpaste tube' car. That was the team's last race.

C-type Completed by Paul Emery after the Connaught team sale, this car had a space frame, B-type front suspension and a revised de Dion rear with inboard brakes. Its only Grand Prix start was in the 1959 United States GP at Sebring, when driver Bob Said was last on the grid and first to retire, crashing on lap 1. A supercharger was later added to the engine, and a hopeful (and fruitless) attempt was made to qualify for the Indianapolis 500.

Connew

This was a brave one-off Formula 1 car, at the beginning of the 1980s when such a venture was possible. By no means the least of Peter Connew's problems was a chronic lack of finance. He had worked for Team Surtees as a draughtsman and designed his PC1 on simple lines, for it was to be built with friends' help in a lock-up garage. There was a bath-tub monocoque, double wishbone suspension with inboard springs/dampers, a DFV engine and Hewland DG300 gearbox, and clean body lines (as far back as the exposed engine).

François Migault brought enough sponsorship for Connew to run the car. In its only British GP practice sessions before a suspension failure he failed to qualify it. Migault did start in the Austrian GP, from the back of the grid, and retired with rear suspension failure. Its last appearance in F1 guise came in practice for a non-championship race at Brands Hatch late in 1972, when David Purley did not complete the warm-up lap because of electrical problems. The Connew was later run in F5000 form.

Conrero

Italian tuning specialist Virgilio Conrero was reported to have a Formula 1 car under construction for 1961. Unlike his unsuccessful F Junior car of 1959, this was a rear-engined design, and was apparently to use a power unit based on the Alfa Romeo Giulietta engine – admirable though that was in its own sphere, and useful though it was in a South African F1 series, it was hardly likely to provide competitive power in Europe.

Cooper

See pp.64–69.

Copersucar

The Copersucar cooperative of Brazilian sugar producers backed the first Fittipaldi Grand Prix cars that therefore carried its name. They are covered in one Fittipaldi sequence (see pp.85, 101–102).

Corre

Corre was very active in early twentieth-century light-car racing, as it was to be with the la Licorne marque name through to the 1920s. It entered Grand Prix racing once, with a single car in 1907. This was low-built but otherwise undistinguished, with a square (150 × 150mm) 10,603cc engine and shaft drive, in common with half the Grand Prix entry.

It was sadly off the pace in the race at Dieppe, Joseph Collomb managing only three of the ten laps in under an hour, when the leaders usually broke 40 minutes. The Corre was twenty-second (of twenty-

Connaught B-type at the Syracuse GP of 1955, Tony Brooks winning the race.

Connaught B-type 'toothpaste tube' style at the Monaco GP of 1957, Stuart Lewis-Evans driving.

Connew-Ford PC1 of 1972, David Purley driving.

were the same front and rear, and brakes were inboard all round. The car was entered for the 1969 British GP, to be driven by Trevor Taylor (who had undertaken much of the test work), but it was withdrawn before the meeting. Keith Duckworth considered uprating the design, but Herd left and in any case costly development would have been needed, for example in a front limited-slip differential (wheelspin on the lightly loaded inside tyre in corners meant unacceptable wear rates, while there was heavy understeer). The project was abandoned, and the completed car became an exhibit in the Donington Collection.

Cote

This short-lived French manufacturer specialized in two-strokes, and ran a team in the 3litre *Coupe de l'Auto* races in 1911–12. As one of its Coupe cars was classified in the concurrent Grand Prix in 1912, Cote achieved the rare distinction of fielding a two-stroke finisher in a Grand Prix. The car did not stand out for its lines in the very mixed 1912 field, nor apparently did its 2,986cc four-cylinder engine endow it with great speed.

Veteran Fernand Gabriel, winner of the notorious 1903 Paris–Madrid race, completed lap 1 in an hour (precisely) when the fastest race lap was put in by Fiat driver Bruce-Brown in 36min 32sec. Gabriel retired with transmission failure on the next lap. His team mate de Vere ran last for most of the race and finished in that position, thirteenth overall.

seven) at half distance and sixteenth (of seventeen) at the end, some 3.5 *hours* behind the winning Fiat.

Cosworth

One of the most original cars of the 3litre Formula 1 years, the Cosworth was advanced in many respects, but also showed up fallacies in the late-1960s case put by four-wheel drive protagonists. It was designed by Robin Herd, extensively tested, but never raced.

Herd chose to use sponsons between the wheels on each side, linked by a stressed floor and bulkheads, effectively making up a broad monocoque hull. The bodywork was intended to contribute aerodynamic downforce, in conjunction with the aerofoils that were tried, although in this respect the car was overtaken by 'wings' during its design and development period.

Most of the tests were run with normal DFVs, but a special lightweight magnesium-block DFV was made up for the car, and this went some way to compensate for the weight of the transmission system. The V8 was reversed in the chassis, and drove via a Cosworth/Hewland gearbox behind the cockpit and a centre differential to shafts offset to the right. Wheels and tyres

Cromard

This Formula 2 one-off marginally qualifies for inclusion among Grand Prix cars as it did run in a 1952 race in company with championship contenders, although that event was not a title race. That year it was in its revised 1951 form, with a tubular chassis in place of the modified Amilcar frame it had in 1949, swing-axle rear suspension and VW front suspension, and a Lea-Francis 1,750cc engine developing around 125bhp.

It was built by Bob Spikins of Laystall, and run by him as the Laystall Cromard Special. After his death it was bought by Peter Clarke, and tested in the 1952 Silverstone International trophy by Joyce Howard, who later raced it in Ireland.

Cosworth-Ford four-wheel-drive car, tested 1969 but never raced.

Many constructors have grown from modest origins, but none has grown to influence Grand Prix racing and racing car design as much as Cooper. And to the end, modesty was a Cooper hallmark. Cooper cars were built for less than a quarter of a century and actually won only sixteen World Championship races, but for ten consecutive years the marque was in the top five of the Constructors' Championships, and it won the title twice.

Charles Cooper owned a garage in a South London suburb, and from his work in the 1930s was known as a race car preparation expert. He was therefore a most practical father figure when his son John, with Eric Brandon, laid down a car for the new 500cc category after the Second World War. A second car was built in 1947, then in 1948 the Cooper Car Company was formed to produce these little cars to meet a demand. They were simple machines, but innovative with a rear-engined layout, for immediate practical reasons rather than theory or precedent. A dozen years on from the first car, Coopers that followed the same lines were in the forefront of Grand Prix racing.

The 500cc category that became Formula 3 gave a new generation of drivers opportunities to compete at International level, and most of them drove Coopers. Therein was Cooper's second great contribution to the sport, and to British racing in particular.

Cooper's cars lent themselves to adaptation, and the 500cc chassis could accommodate larger engines. One of these, Harry Schell's T12 with an 1,100cc JAP engine, was the first Cooper to start in a Grand Prix, at Monaco in 1950.

The front-engined Formula 2 cars in 1952–53 were more important, for these were the years when World Championship races were run to F2 regulations. The Coopers were simple, usually with Bristol engines that were hardly competitive in power output terms. But some of their drivers scored points, and Mike Hawthorn made his name in them.

This front-engined interlude passed, and the next move towards Grand Prix cars came with a sports car modified by Jack Brabham, before Cooper committed to a new Formula 2. Their cars were sometimes run in F1 races, and led to full Grand Prix cars – and to championships.

Every other constructor followed the Cooper lead, some leap-frogged ahead and through the years of the 1.5litre Grand Prix formula, Cooper fortunes slipped. The approach was conservative, and the works team operated on ludicrously low budgets. During that period there was just one Grand Prix victory, in 1962, but there seemed to be a recovery in the first 3litre seasons that was not entirely illusory, but the decline that set in through 1968 proved to be terminal.

Cooper's last points-scoring finishes came in 1968, the last season for the marque in racing. It was wound up in 1969, ending a remarkable story of racing-car production and Grand Prix endeavour.

T20 The first Formula 2 Cooper came in 1952, and was immediately competitive in second-level races, although usually outrun by Ferraris with much more powerful engines in major events. John Cooper arranged to use Bristol (née BMW) straight-six 1,971cc engines that were good for 125–130bhp and were tall. They were mounted ahead of the cockpit in a simple box-section chassis frame, with wishbone and leaf spring suspension following established Cooper lines, that derived in turn from the Fiat 500. Wheels and integral drum brakes were common with Cooper's rear-engined cars.

The cars were light and nimble, although not to the extent that Italian power advantages were offset. Alan Brown placed one of the quasi-works Ecurie Richmond cars fifth in the 1952 Swiss GP, becoming the first Cooper driver to score World Championship points. Overshadowing that, Mike Hawthorn in Bob Chase's T20 was third in the British GP, fourth in the Belgian and Dutch GPs, and earned a Ferrari contract for 1953. Nitrofuel additives helped at the end of the year.

T23 The MkII Cooper-Bristol had a lighter tubular chassis, with the same suspension, but clothed in a smoother body and with the driver seated lower in it as the transmission was dropped to the hypoid rear axle. There were larger wheels, with separate brake drums. A car modified for Stirling Moss had de Dion rear suspension and disc brakes.

The normal production cars were no more powerful than the T20s, so relatively Coopers lost ground. Moss's car had an Alta engine, and on occasion it was fast, but in 1953 no Cooper drivers scored championship points. Another independent conversion had an Alfa Romeo 1900 engine, and was a failure.

The main Cooper concern was still production cars – these F2 cars were just part of that business – and for a while the name appeared in top-flight racing only as the 1952–53 cars were run in *formule libre* events or filled grids in 2.5litre F1 races (notably, Bob Gerard ran one with his 2.3litre version of the Bristol engine).

Cooper-Bristol T20 of 1952, Mike Hawthorn at Goodwood.

T24 A pair of Alta-engined T23s carried this designation.

T40 The 'bobtail' was a clever adaptation of a production T39 sports-racing car by Jack Brabham – really it was a 'Brabham special'. Its chassis was extended by 5cm to accommodate a 1,971cc Bristol engine in place of the four-cylinder Coventry-Climax unit, and it was hoped that lightweight and streamlined bodywork would go some way to compensate for the modest power output.

Brabham started the car in the 1955 British GP, was handicapped from the start with a broken throttle, and failed to finish. Once the car was bedded in, it showed promise in secondary races, and Brabham drove it to win the Australian GP.

T43 Introduced as a production Formula 2 car powered by the Coventry-Climax FPF twin-cam engine, this 'grew' beyond that category early in 1957 as a 1,960cc version of the engine became available, and entrant Rob Walker had a T43 fitted with it, and larger fuel tanks, to run in Formula 1 races.

The T43 had a tubular chassis, Cooper's transverse leaf independent suspension, and the FPF drove through a Citroen-based gearbox. In Formula 2 form it was a spindly little car, and Walker's first 1.9litre version hardly looked like an F1 car in Ferrari, Maserati and Vanwall company.

It appeared in practice for the 1957 Monaco GP, when Brabham crashed. Its engine was transferred to Walker's F2 T43, and Brabham got it up to fifth place at half distance. Despite a fuel stop, he was third in the closing phase, when the fuel pump mounting broke. He pushed across the line, to be classified sixth.

With hindsight, that first Grand Prix result for a Cooper-Climax was historic. Later in the season Roy Salvadori scored two points in the British GP, the first for a Cooper-Climax driver, and then there was a Grand Prix victory.

Walker's T43 with its FPF adapted to run on the AvGas fuel that had become obligatory was entered for the opening race of 1958, the Argentine GP. Stirling Moss's skill, backed by cunning team work, brought a victory that must have seemed improbable.

Alejandro de Tomaso installed an OSCA 2litre engine in a T43 and entered it hopefully for the 1959 United States GP. Its grid time was almost 23sec off pole

Cooper-Climax T43 at the Monaco GP of 1957, Jack Brabham driving.

Cooper-Climax T43 at the Argentine GP of 1958, Stirling Moss winning Cooper's first Grand Prix.

time, but there were five slower cars on the 19-car grid! It failed to complete the race. Another OSCA-engined T43 appeared as late as 1962, was qualified to start once in three attempts and lasted just two laps of that non-title race at Enna.

T44 A type number was given to a T43 modified by Bob Gerard, which was fitted with an enlarged Bristol straight six. It was not competitive.

T45 Laid down to serve F1 or F2 roles, this car had a similar tubular chassis to the 1957 type, but with wishbone and coil-spring front suspension. At the rear the transverse leaf arrangement soon gave way to wishbones and coil springs, with lateral links. The works F1 cars had 2.2litre FPF engines, rated at 194bhp in 1958, driving through ZF 'boxes. Alf Francis produced a 2,015cc FPF for Rob Walker.

Maurice Trintignant scored a sensational victory in Walker's car in the Monaco GP. Salvadori in a works car was second in the German GP, and third in the British GP. He was fourth in the drivers' championship (Trintignant was seventh and Brabham seventeenth); Cooper took third place in the first Constructors' Championship.

T46 A streamlined one-off, the T46 was run only in practice for the 1959 French GP. Basically, it was a T51 with a body enclosing the wheels. It was tested only

Cooper-Climax T45 (Stirling Moss) leading Cooper-Climax T51 (Jack Brabham), Monaco GP, 1959.

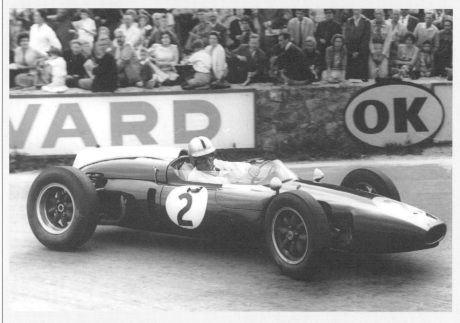

Cooper-Climax T53 of 1960, driven by Jack Brabham in the Belgian GP.

briefly before it appeared at Reims, where it proved fast on straights but unstable as lift developed at high speeds. It was set aside.

T51 The major change in the Formula 1 version of this 1959 car was in the engine, with full 2.5litre units used. Nor-

mally these were Coventry-Climax FPFs, although two independent teams used Maserati 250S engines while Rob Walker indulged Alf Francis's interest in improvement (in this case with a BRM engine and Colotti transaxle), while in 1960 Scuderia Castellotti fitted Ferrari engines into T51s. The BRM-powered car was raced only once, but the Walker team persisted with Colotti gearboxes (it was felt that they would stand up to the torque loads of 2.5litre engines better than the Citroen-ERSA type, but the poor Italian build quality undermined this).

In short, Cooper-Climax cars won five of the eight championship Grands Prix in 1958, Brabham winning in Monaco and Britain, Moss in Portugal and Italy, Bruce McLaren in the USA. Cooper won the manufacturers' championship from Ferrari by a handsome margin – a remarkable achievement for the little British constructor.

T51s continued into 1960, with the works team for the first race (McLaren won that), then in independent hands through the year. There were as many as nine on a grid (at Silverstone), while Gendebien achieved a second place and a third, and Brooks scored top five placings, while

Cabianca was fourth with a Ferrari-engined car at Monza.

T53 The 'low line' Cooper was designed and built quickly, in response to the performance of the rear-engined Lotus 18 in the first Grand Prix in 1960. A little lower and slimmer than T51, it looked really purposeful. Chassis and suspension followed T51 lines, but the FPF (rated at 240–250bhp that year) drove through the Cooper-Knight CS5 gearbox/transaxle. This Cooper could match rivals in speed on fast circuits, but perhaps gave some-thing away to Lotus in corners. Brabham gave the T52 its first Grand Prix victory in Holland, then won the Belgian, French, British and Portugese GPs in succession. He was World Champion, and team mate Bruce McLaren was runner-up, while Cooper headed Lotus in the Constructors' Championship. There were also successes in non-title races.

T53s were sold on into 1961, when 1.5litre FPFs were the usual power units but two Italian teams fitted Maserati engines and a car was run in South Africa with one of the Alfa Romeo engines popular in that country. And late in 1960 Jack Brabham had driven a T53 in trials at Indianapolis, lapping at a very comfortable qualifying pace in this 2.5litre car – its lap speeds would have placed it eighth in the start line-up for that year's '500'.

T55 An interim car with the 1.5litre FPF engine, giving some 150bhp, while the team waited for the Coventry-Climax FWMV V8. This car was similar to the T53 in most respects, but lower and slimmer, with a six-speed gearbox. In championship races, McLaren's third in Italy was the best result, and through 1961 there was a scattering of top six finishes (McLaren, seventh on the table, outscored Brabham, while Cooper slipped to fifth in the manufacturers' championship). T55s were used by the team in early-1962 non-title races.

T58 A T55 was modified for the Coventry-Climax FWMV – Cooper had the first of these engines, as reigning champions. The V8 gave 181bhp, and Brabham qualified the T58 second at its debut racing appearance, only to crash on the first lap at the Nürburgring. He led the 1961 US GP in the car, before retiring. Then he left the team, where he had played vital roles for most of his (and the team's) Formula 1 career.

Incidentally, in 1961 a Cooper with a heavily modified one-time Butterworth flat-four engine, known as the Cooper-Arden, hovered off-stage, but never did appear in an F1 race.

T59 This was actually the 1962 Formula Junior Cooper, but two appeared in F1 guise. One was heavily modified as the Aiden-Cooper (qv); the other was a straight T59 owned by Bob Gerard and fitted with a Ford engine in 1963 and a Cosworth MAE in 1964, when it performed respectably in non-championship races in Britain.

T60 Purpose-designed by Owen Maddock around the Coventry-Climax FWMV V8, this was a workmanlike car, with a tubular chassis that was stiffer and shown by the car's slender outward lines to be narrower. There was a new Cooper-Knight six-speed gearbox.

McLaren won the 1962 Monaco GP in a T60, and that proved to be Cooper's only championship race victory in the five years of 1.5litre Grand Prix racing.

Cooper-Climax V8 T60 of 1962, Bruce McLaren driving.

Cooper-Climax V8 T66 of 1963, Bruce McLaren driving.

Other good placings saw the New Zealander third in the Drivers' Championship, while Cooper took third place in the 1962 Constructors' Championship.

The cars were used early in 1963, when one went to the Walker team to be driven by Jo Bonnier. Another was sold to Honda, as a test vehicle.

T66 A derivative of the T60, with modified suspension and slightly finer lines, achieved as the fuel tanks were modified. The Cooper team no longer enjoyed the status it had in the opening seasons of the formula, and in 1963 it was run by Ken Tyrrell, while John Cooper recovered from a road accident.

Bruce McLaren and Tony Maggs each finished second in a championship race, and there were third and fourth placings, but even with the four points contributed by Bonnier in a Walker Cooper the marque slipped to fifth in the Constructors' Championship. The cars were used into the spring of 1964.

T69 Owen Maddock's last Cooper design, this monocoque car was abandoned some way short of completion.

T73 The 1964 Grand Prix car had much in common with Cooper's F3 single-seater, with obvious differences such as the engine and fuel capacity. There was inboard rocker arm suspension at the front, a wishbone/transverse link/radius arm arrangement at the rear. The Climax engine contributed some chassis stiffening.

Bruce McLaren twice finished second in championship races (but signalled his intention to set up on his own when he ran a pair of cars in the first Tasman series). Cooper was at the foot of the 1964 manufacturers' list, fifth with sixteen points.

Towards the end of the year, Charles Cooper had a fatal heart attack, and John Cooper started to look for a buyer for Cooper; early in 1965 the Chipstead Motor Group took over, and Roy Salvadori became team manager.

McLaren was fifth in a T73 in the 1965 South African GP. One of the cars survived to race once in 1966 with a Ferrari sports car V12 installed.

T77 The final 1.5litre F1 Coopers were T77s, although they might as well have carried a T73 sub-mark designation. The main difference was in a wider track at the front.

The team had an appropriately subdued season with a pair of cars, highlights being McLaren's third place in Belgium and F1 novice Jochen Rindt's fourth in Germany. The season's points brought fifth place for Cooper.

An ATS V8 was hopefully installed in one of these cars in 1966. Its owner entered it for the French GP, when it proved slow (almost 20sec off pole pace) and driver Bonnier transferred to a Brabham.

T80 The chassis for the Coventry-Climax flat-16 engine was economically used when that engine failed to materialize (as far as installation in a racing car was concerned) as a test chassis for the Maserati

Cooper-Maserati V12 T81 of 1966, John Surtees driving.

V12 that was to power F1 Coopers in 1966. It was never raced by the works, but it was loaned to Rob Walker for a secondary event, while his T81 was completed.

T81 The change of ownership was most obvious as the Cooper team was run from a new base in Byfleet as the 3litre Formula 1 period opened. In that it was a full 3litre F1 car running before other British constructors' types, it was also ahead of the game. It was Cooper's first monocoque F1 car, designed by Derrick White, appearing a bulky piece of racing machinery as he had to match it to the very bulky Maserati 60-degree V12. The chassis comprised boxed side members linked by the floor and bulkheads, with mountings for the

engine and rear suspension extending back from the rear bulkhead. The front suspension members were inboard, with disc brakes proud of the insides of the wheels in the cooling airstream, while rear coil springs/dampers were mounted outboard. Giulio Alfieri revised the engines for this F1 role, and the V12 was rated at 360bhp. It drove through a ZF gearbox

Drivers battled with handling problems early in 1966, but John Surtees's mid-season defection from Ferrari was a bonus for Cooper, in car development as well as racing skills terms. He won the last championship race of 1966, the Mexican GP, and with other good placings to add to his Ferrari score from one victory, he was second in the championship. Team mate Rindt was third, with a second place his best race result. Three Coopers were run by independents, Siffert scoring three points in Rob Walker's car, Bonnier one in his T81. The Walker car was to be run until the first Grand Prix of 1968. Meanwhile Cooper was third in the 1966 Constructors' Championship, with a gross points score higher than second-placed Ferrari.

Pedro Rodriguez won the opening race of 1967 in a T81, and that South African victory proved to be the last for a Cooper F1 car. The lighter T81B came during the European season, when Rindt and Rodriguez accumulated a few points, and Cooper was a distant third in the championship. In this car, the V12 was revised, and it drove through a Hewland gearbox. But it showed that there was no development potential in the basic design.

T86 This came as an attempt to produce a second-generation Maserati-powered car. It was lighter but still overweight, with the 2,998cc V12 that was by no means state-of-the-art in 1967, when it was rated at 385bhp. The body was a little more compact, but far from handsome.

These cars were little used, and Cooper's 1967 points (twenty-eight, for third place in the championship) were scored with T81s. A T86 was run in non-championship races early in 1969 by Colin Crabbe's Antique Automobile Racing, and was driven to seventh (and last) place in the Monaco GP by Vic Elford.

The T86B warranted its own type number, for although White followed the existing pattern, even to 'semi-inboard' front brakes, this car was powered by the BRM 2,999cc V12. On paper, its 365bhp was less than the Maserati V12 produced, but the cross-section that defined the car's lines meant that the T86B could be slimmer.

For much of the year, the team relied on stand-in drivers (Elford and Bianchi), who took the places of Redman and Scarfiotti.

There was a third place at Monaco, and a fourth in Spain, then Elford's fifth place in the Canadian GP was the last points-scoring finish for a Cooper in World Championship racing. That year, 1968, the Cooper team was sixth-equal with Honda in the championship.

A T86 with an Alfa Romeo engine was not completed.

The T90 F5000 car based on the T86 was the last Cooper racing car to be built, as the projected T91 Cosworth-powered F1 car for 1969 was abandoned before construction started. That brought an illustrious story to a quiet end.

CTA-Arsenal

One of the most notorious cars conceived to win national prestige on the Grand Prix circuits, the CTA-Arsenal was commissioned by the Centre d'Etudes Techniques de l'Automobile et du Cycles (CTA), funded by a French-government grant, and built at the former State arsenal at Chatillon – hence CTA-Arsenal. The designer was Albert Lory, whose reputation largely derived from his 1926–27 Grand Prix Delage.

Lory's 1947 chassis was hardly of the moment, comprising box-section side members cross-braced by curved tubes, and the odd suspension was independent all round, with vertical slide mountings at the wheels, located and sprung by transverse links and torsion bars. The engine was a 1,482cc 90-degree V8 with two-stage supercharging; claimed output was 260bhp in the first tests, and 266bhp when the car was presented for the 1947 French GP. It was installed at an angle, to run the transmission beside the driver and to allow for a lower seat, to a compact four-speed gearbox and final drive.

The car's track behaviour was capricious, and it was little tested, let alone developed, before practice for its first race. Only one of the two entries was run, its shortcomings only too obvious as it was announced that its appearance was part of the test programme. Raymond Sommer's best time was nearly half a minute off pole time, and (perhaps mercifully) the transmission failed as the race was started. The two cars that had been built were entered for the 1948 French GP, but were withdrawn after the first day of practice at Reims, 'unready for racing'.

Antonio Lago bought them, seemingly did nothing with them, and they eventually became museum exhibits – 'how not to do it' exhibits presumably, for they certainly did not restore glory to French racing.

CTA-Arsenal of 1947–48, tested and practised but never raced.

Dallara

Giampaolo Dallara had wide experience as an engineer and designer in the Italian high-performance car industry, with Maserati, Ferrari, Lamborghini and de Tomaso, before his name first appeared in a racing car title, on the Wolf-Dallara WD1 Formula 3 car in 1978. That did not have an outstanding record. Dallara became a constructor in his own right in the 1980s, and in the second part of that decade the Dallaras were highly rated in Formula 3, and they came to dominate the category in the 1990s, almost to the exclusion of other makes.

Meanwhile, Dallara's entry into Formula 3000 in 1987 brought mediocre results, but perhaps development attention was diverted as the constructor prepared for its first Formula 1 season. It built Grand Prix cars that were to be entered by Scuderia Italia with backing from steel magnate 'Beppe' Lucchini, who took on an active role with the team. A single-car team was run in 1988, then a two-car team for the next four years. The cars were generally competent, and that level was reflected in attainment: Dallaras were entered in seventy-eight Grands Prix; the cars were seldom among the non-qualifiers, but only fifteen points were won.

Scuderia Italia transferred its allegiance (and Lucchini's backing) to Lola for 1993, and Dallara withdrew from Formula 1. Its F3 cars continued to enjoy near-monopolistic success, and it built cars for the Indy Racing League in the USA; this series was overshadowed by CART, and the Indianapolis 500 was its star event, where Dallara's name was added to the list of winners in 1998. Beyond that, Dallara built F1 test chassis for Honda, as the Japanese company prepared for its return to Grand Prix racing.

Bms 188 Designed by Sergio Rinland, the first F1 Dallara was wholly conventional, with a carbon-fibre monocoque double wishbone pullrod suspension and a Cosworth DFZ with a Dallara/Hewland six-speed gearbox. It looked long and low (in fact, only two other 1988 F1 cars were longer). Three were built.

Alex Caffi started in fourteen Grands Prix, achieving a 50 per cent finishing record with a highest race placing of seventh in the Portugese GP.

Bms 189 Marco Tolentino and Giampaolo Dallara reworked the design for 1989, and this showed in refined outward lines. Mader-prepared Cosworth DFR engines were used, and the main changes through the year were in aerodynamic appendages.

In 1989 Dallara reaped rewards for its first 'bedding-in' F1 season, and this was to be its best year in many ways – Caffi scored the marque's first point at Monaco, de Cesaris finished third in the Canadian GP, and with both drivers scoring four points the Constructors' Championship position was equal eighth (with Brabham).

Bms 190 This was another derivative car, attributed to Dallara and Christian Vanderpleyn, still DFR-powered and with the specification of its predecessors. As if to make the point that something more than a gentle progression was called for in 1990, the competitive edge was lost (the continuing use of Pirelli tyres could have contributed).

Neither driver (de Cesaris and Pirro) scored a point – the best race placings were tenth, for each driver – and although there was only one failure to qualify, there were only five finishes.

191 A new car designed by Dallara and Nigel Couperthwaite brought a return to respectability in 1991. The approach was still orthodox, with minor changes in the suspension (pushrod double wishbones all round, instead of the pushrod front, pull-rod rear, of the Bms 190) and a transverse Dallara/Hewland gearbox. For this year, Dallara turned to the Judd 72-degree V10. This was lightweight, compact and straightforward; early in 1991 it was rated at 660bhp, late that year at just over 700bhp. The car was another Dallara with neat body lines, and the fashionable high nose carrying an underslung front aerofoil.

J.J. Lehto joined Pirro, and scored points just once – but that was third place in the San Marino GP (he managed only four other finishes). Pirro scored a single point at Monaco. The pair managed fourteen

Dallara-Ford Bms 189 of 1989, Andrea de Cesaris driving.

finishes, and Dallara was eighth in the Constructors' Championship.

192 Dallara took over the customer Ferrari engine deal from Minardi for 1992, presumably in the knowledge that it would not be supplied with late-specification V12s, but with the assumption that a Ferrari engine would be better than a bought-in power unit from a small British company.

The car was developed from the 191, naturally adapted for the Ferrari V12 and the necessarily larger fuel cell. Through to the summer, Dallara made numerous aerodynamic and suspension changes, as the car's track behaviour was never good, or consistent.

The team's finishing record was over 50 per cent, but its only points were scored by Pierluigi Martini with two sixth places. J.J. Lehto was a reliable top-ten finisher, but his best race placing was seventh. By the summer the drivers had decided to move on, and Lucchini had committed his backing to Lola, and that spelled the end for the Dallara Grand Prix team.

DAMS

The Driot Arnoux Motor Sport team was very successful in Formula 3000 and looked to move up to Formula 1 in 1996. To that end it needed its own car, and extended its mid-1990s association with Reynard, in an F1 car that was a Reynard with DAMS input in most respects. The straightforward design attributed to Barry Ward and other Reynard associates took shape in 1995, and a car ran initial tests with a Cosworth ED V8 engine. However, adequate sponsorship was not found, and rather than attempt a development and race programme without full resources, the team was professional enough to draw a line under the project.

Darracq

Darracq was a pioneering racing marque, especially with light cars at the very beginning of the twentieth century, before it turned to big cars. Some were very big, such as a 22.5litre V8 sprint car in 1905. It entered the first French GP, in company with many leading French manufacturers, for one of the objectives of the race was to demonstrate the superiority of the French automobile.

The 1906 GP Darracq sat squarely on a substantial frame, and stood out for two reasons – behind pointed radiators the engines were exposed (and the crews had even less protection than most), and wire wheels were fitted, whereas all save one of the other teams had wood-spoked artillery wheels. The engine was a 12,711cc four-cylinder unit – only two other teams in that 1906 race used smaller engines – and there was a three-speed gearbox and shaft drive. The driver line-up was strong, but Hanriot's engine failed on the first lap, Wagner's on the second lap, and Hémery's on the seventh lap.

The team was back in 1907, with the same cars fitted with 15,268cc engines. This time only Hanriot retired, Victor

(Above) Darracq of 1906 driven by Louis Wagner.

(Below) Darracq (Talbot) of 1921, André Boillot driving.

Rigal finished fifth and Gustav Caillois sixth, both a long way behind Nazzaro's winning FIAT.

Darracq was merged with Sunbeam and Talbot in 1920, and the combine entered seven cars for the 1921 French GP, two as Talbot-Darracqs (Talbot in this case taking a French pronunciation, whereas the two Talbots were British). These cars had 2,973cc twin ohc straight eights giving just under 110bhp, but alongside the Duesenbergs and Ballots they appeared mildly old-fashioned. André Boillot was fifth in one of the Talbot-Darracqs in the Grand Prix.

When French Talbots next ran in the race, in 1927, there was no Darracq link. The name just disappeared from the Grands Prix.

DB

Charles Deutsch and René Bonnet formed a balanced partnership – flair balancing engineering pragmatism – to build competition cars for half a century, almost invariably front-wheel-drive cars. From sports car specials at the end of the 1930s they looked to the 500cc Formula 3 for a move into single-seaters, and to Panhard for their major components – engine, transmission and suspension. They also built 750cc F2 cars, which were modestly successful in minor French events, and even tried a four-wheel-drive machine with a Panhard engine and transmission at each end. Predictably, this was discarded, unraced.

DB was behind the *Monomill* category, in a series where drivers paid a fee to a race organizer, drew a car from a pool, and raced it. Then the 750cc supercharged alternative to the 2.5litre normally aspirated engines offered by the Formula 1 that came into force in 1954 seemed to offer an opportunity to enter top-flight racing

The DB Formula 1 car used the simple *Monomill* box-section frame, with the wishbone/transverse leaf spring independent front suspension and trailing arm/torsion bar independent front suspension, with disc brakes at the front and drums at the light rear end. The engine was the 746cc air-cooled unit, with a supercharger driven from the front of the crankshaft. This raised power output from a numbing 50bhp to 85bhp – less than half the output of contemporary normally aspirated engines, and with torque that was equally miserable. It was too much to hope that the light weight of the DBs would compensate. Two cars were entered for the 1955 Pau GP, where they were outclassed; Claude Storez retired after fifteen of the 110 laps, and although Paul Armagnac finished, he was lapped eighteen times.

Deutsch and Bonnet recognized the futility of this Formula 1 attempt, and turned back to the *Monomill*, tried Formula Junior with similar cars, and then concentrated on their successful sports-racing cars. Their F1 effort had two distinctions: it was one of only two to use a 750cc supercharged engine, and the only front-wheel-drive F1 car to race in the years of formula racing.

DB F1 car of 1955, with a supercharged 750cc engine and front-wheel drive, Paul Armagnac driving.

Delage

Louis Delage set up his company in 1905 and within a year committed it to *voiturette* racing, moving on to contest the 3litre *Coupe de l'Auto* in 1911. Delage ignored the 1912 event in that series, but entered the 1913 Grand Prix, and with better luck Albert Guyot could have won it. Perhaps the victory for one of the 1913 cars in the 1914 Indianapolis 500 was some compensation.

After the First World War, Delage built some large-engined sprint cars, but the expected 2litre Grand Prix car failed to appear and the return to the Grands Prix came with a magnificently complex car in 1923. These V12 cars were developed until they were almost a match for the Alfa Romeo P2, but did not win Grands Prix until 1925.

They were followed by another outstanding Delage, the 1.5litre straight eight which was flawed when it appeared in 1926 but was absolutely dominant by 1927. These cars were raced on into the mid-1930s, Chiron placing one seventh at Indianapolis in 1929, Lord Howe racing one with distinction in early-1930s *voiturette* events, and Richard Seaman winning International races with a much-modified 1926 Delage in 1936.

By that time, Louis Delage's company had been merged with Delahaye. The flamboyant Frenchman had over-extended his firm's resources in the mid-1920s, and turned away from racing in 1928. The two Grand Prix types of the 1920s were outstanding, in any company.

Type Y The first Delage Grand Prix car was developed from the 1911 *Coupe de l'Auto* 3litre car, by Arthur Michelat. For a fuel consumption/car weight formula, he used a four-cylinder 7,032cc engine, with four overhead valves per cylinder that developed some 130bhp. It drove through a five-speed gearbox (a Delage speciality). In other respects, the cars were conventional, and comfortably within weight limits. With rounded noses, they looked the part, and showed great potential in the 1913 Grand Prix at Amiens. Paul Bablot set the fastest lap in one of the two Delages, and finished fourth. Guyot in the other car led at half-distance, but then had to stop to change two tyres. Then a third tyre failed, and as Guyot slowed down his riding mechanic jumped out … and was run over by his own car. Guyot had to change the wheel single-handed, get the mechanic back in the cockpit, and drive carefully to the pits. He finished fifth.

Later that year, Bablot and Guyot finished 1-2 in the confusingly entitled Grand Prix de France at Le Mans. In 1914 René Thomas drove one to win at Indianapolis, while Guyot was third in the 500.

Type S Michelat's 1914 Grand Prix car looked old-fashioned but was an advanced machine by contemporary standards. It was also unsuccessful.

The 4,441cc engine had two carburettors and twin overhead camshafts with desmodronic valve operation, and it drove through a five-speed gearbox. In common with three other entrants in the 1914 Grand Prix, Delage used four-wheel brakes and a transmission brake – superior braking should have given advantages on the tortuous Lyons circuit.

In fact, the Delages were never in the hunt, and there was even a suspicion that the retirement of Bablot and Guyot late in the race (put down to engine failures) could have been to avoid the embarrassment of lowly final placings. Duray was eighth in the surviving Delage.

V12 The Delage for the 1923 French GP was designed in haste, and getting one to the grid at Tours was a remarkable achievement (a good result would have been even more remarkable, for the car was hardly developed). Charles Planchon

Delage, V12-engined of 1924, René Thomas driving.

laid out a 60-degree dohc V12, with the camshafts gear-driven from the rear of the engine. Like other French designers, Planchon rejected supercharging, but unlike them he could look to generous piston area and high engine speed for advantages. In its first form, this 1,984cc engine developed 105bhp, some 25bhp less than the supercharged Fiat 805 engine. The Delage had a normal channel-section frame, with a rigid axle and semi-elliptics at the front, a live axle and semi-elliptics at the rear, with friction shock absorbers all round. The 1923 body was undistinguished.

René Thomas briefly kept the car in touch with the 1923 Grand Prix leaders, but completed little more than a quarter of the race before stopping with the engine severely overheated. The designer carried the can.

Albert Lory took Planchon's place, experimenting with a twin-supercharged V12 early in 1924 but decided to race the cars with engines largely in their 1923 form, running them at higher revs to gain a modest improvement to a 118bhp output. Smoother bodies were fitted. In this form, the Delages were second and third (Divo and Benoist) in the French GP, and third and fourth in the Spanish GP.

With two Roots-type superchargers in 1925 the V12 gave over 190bhp (some French sources claim over 200bhp) and although weight increased these cars were quick.

All four retired from the first race of the season, the European GP at Spa (one crashed, one had a split tank, the other had 'plug trouble'). The French GP saw a

Delage straight-eight of 1927.

Delage 1-2 (Benoist and Wagner) after the Alfa team withdrew, and the Delage V12's career ended with a 1-2-3 in the Spanish GP, Divo heading Benoist and Thomas.

15S-8 Lory designed a completely new car for the 1926–27 1.5litre formula. It was low-slung and sleek, with no novelties in chassis, suspension or brakes, but with an outstanding straight eight. This was long and heavy, but carefully detailed, for example in the extensive use of ball and roller bearings to reduce internal friction. It was a 1,488cc dohc unit, with twin shaft-driven Roots-type superchargers on the left. It revved to 8,000rpm, and produced 170bhp. No other cars came near that in 1926, but a flaw in the Delage meant that it won only one of the season's major races.

The exhaust ran by the drivers' feet and made the cockpits impossibly hot, to the extent that in the first race, on an already hot day in Spain, one driver had to be taken to hospital with burns and the others needed medical treatment. The only win for the best car of the year came when Robert Sénéchal, relieved by Wagner, won the first British GP. For 1927, Lory reversed the engine in the chassis, so that the exhaust ran on the left (and a single supercharger had to be used, mounted behind the radiator). The straight eight gave a little more power. With the cars in this form, Delage contested odd minor French events and won all four of the season's major races, with 1-2-3 finishes in the French and British Grands Prix.

The cars were then sold. As well as the successes already mentioned, de Rovin placed one of them third in the first Monaco GP, in 1929. Lory of Delage was persuaded to make an independent front suspension conversion as late as 1937, although Prince Chula had little success with this. Two of these old Delages were revitalized by Reg Parnell and raced in the late 1940s. One was then acquired by Rob Walker, fitted with a 1.5litre twin-supercharged ERA engine and run in British *formule libre* and Formula 1 events in the early 1950s. Meanwhile, Delage had been active in sports-car racing in the late 1930s and odd cars from that period, together with some built in the second half of the 1940s, were run in 'stripped' open-wheel offset single-seater form in some racing car events, notable achievements being the sixth place finishes by Trintignant and Louveau in, respectively, the 1947 Belgian and Swiss Grands Prix.

Delahaye

This old-established French company's cars were run in nineteenth-century city-to-city races, but the marque was not successful in main-line circuit racing until the 1930s, generally with the 3.6litre Type 135 in sports car events (including a Le Mans victory in 1938).

Delahaye's success in the French 'Race for a Million' (francs) competition run to encourage the development of French GP contenders led to its entry into the premier class with the Type 145 in 1938. This used the 135 chassis with a pushrod ohv 4,490cc V12 engine and it was intended to be a dual-purpose design, for sports car and Grand Prix racing, and predictably this

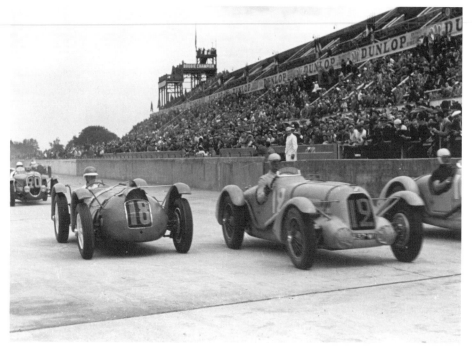

Delahaye 4.5litre of 1937, driven by René Dreyfus in the French GP (for sports cars) of 1937. These cars could be stripped for GP racing.

Delahaye 4.5litre single-seater of 1938.

economy approach was doomed in advance when dedicated German teams ruled in the Grands Prix. However, there was a sensational debut, when Dreyfus beat the only Mercedes-Benz entered for the early-season Pau GP. For the rest of the year the Delahayes were hopelessly outclassed. The Type 155 *monoplace* appeared fleetingly and unimpressively in mid-1938. It used the chassis of the Type 145, with transverse leaf spring independent front suspension and a de Dion rear axle, and the V12 giving some 235bhp and driving through a Cotal four-speed gearbox.

Delahaye's best result in a full Grand Prix was scored at the Nürburgring in 1939, when most of the German cars fell out and reliability saw the Type 145 'offset single-seaters' of Ecurie Laury Schell through to fourth and fifth places in the German GP, with a stripped Type 135 finishing sixth.

Naturally, 135s were brought out again after the Second World War (a few more were built, too), and several were raced; disregarding sports car races, these were generally run in French regional events, with a few excursions to Belgium and Italy. Paul Vallée's Ecurie France ran Type 135 *Course Spéciales*, but faced the inevitable when it acquired Talbot 26Cs in 1948. Ecurie Leutitia, set up by drivers Eugène Chabaud and Charles Pozzi, ran 135s and created a single-seater in 1948 on the basis of a Type 175, with its 4,455cc straight six developing some 185bhp.

In full Grands Prix, Pozzi's fifth place in the 1947 French GP was the best result for a Delahaye while Chaboud was sixth in the 1949 Grand Prix de France (the ACF classic was a sports car race that year) and he was also fourth in the Grand Prix des Nations in 1948. He was the last driver to start in a Grand Prix in a Delahaye, in Italy in 1949, when he retired.

Derrington-Francis

Vic Derrington and Alf Francis gave their names to a car that drew heavily on the remnants of the hapless ATS 163 Formula 1 cars. Francis was a widely experienced and essentially pragmatic engineer – usually recalled as a racing mechanic – best known for his work on Rob Walker and Stirling Moss cars, who was working with Colotti in Italy in the early 1960s. He laid out a new space frame, 15cm (6in) shorter than the original ATS chassis, which was clothed in simple bodywork. ATS mechanical parts were used.

There was some backing from Mario Cabral, and he drove the car in its only Grand Prix, at Monza in 1964; he qualified for the last row of the grid, and retired after twenty-five laps with ignition problems. The car was not raced again.

De Tomaso

Alejandro de Tomaso, an Argentine who based his automotive businesses in Italy, built his first racing car in 1960, using the name Isis for a Formula Junior car on Cooper lines. Later that year he used his own name for a Formula 2 car that crashed in practice for its first race. It reappeared as a Formula 1 car in 1961, and five more cars were built with similar strong Cooper resemblances in 1961, and proved largely ineffectual. In 1962 de Tomaso built a flat-eight F1 engine that provided insufficient power for one car in one race. He also announced an ambitious F1 car which was to have a cast light-alloy monocoque and a V12 engine. This did not proceed beyond an early planning stage.

Formula 3 and Formula 2 cars followed, then Giampaolo Dallara was commissioned to build a Formula 1 car to be run by Frank Williams in 1970. This was an unconvincing machine, and the task of making a success of it might have been beyond Williams and his talented driver Piers Courage. His fatal accident in the Dutch GP spelled the end for this enterprise, although the team ran a single car in most of the remaining races in the 1970 season.

1.5litre cars These cars had space frames following Isis, and therefore Cooper, lines, with double wishbone and coil-springs suspension all round, and bodies that closely resembled late-1950s Coopers. The erstwhile F2 car and one of the 1961 quintet had Conrero-developed Alfa Romeo engines, four had OSCA engines. De Tomaso five-speed gearboxes were used.

The first race for de Tomaso F1 cars was the 1961 Naples GP, when Roberto Bussinello finished fifth in one of the OSCA-engined pair that started. He was later fourth in the Coppa Italia at Vallelunga in an Alfa-powered car. Other appearances were marked by ignominious grid positions, and race retirements. The 1962 record was dismal – a DNQ and an unclassified finish.

De Tomaso's dohc 1,488cc flat-eight engine was presented at the 1962 Italian GP. Even if it had delivered the claimed 170bhp, it would not have matched contemporary V8s. It was installed in the 801 (the first de Tomaso single-seater to be identified by a designation). This car had a space frame and rocker arm inboard suspension on the lines of a 1948 Massimino design for single-seater Maseratis (Ing Massimino worked for de Tomaso in the 1960s). Estefano Nasif failed to qualify it for the grid at Monza.

Various engines then appeared in the existing de Tomaso chassis – as well as the 801, the entry for the Rome GP in spring 1963 included an original OSCA-powered car, two with Maserati 150S engines, one with an Alfa engine and one with a Holbay-Ford engine. Late that year one car was run with a Ferrari Dino 156 V6, and Lippi twice failed to qualify this for races.

308 De Tomaso ignored the early 3litre Formula 1 years, then the Dallara-designed 308 came for 1970. It was a bulky monocoque car with double wishbones and coil springs all round, with a DFV engine driving through a Hewland gearbox. The first car was substantially overweight, the second was at least lighter, but development seemed sluggish. That first car was destroyed in an accident at Jarama, but Courage was third in its replacement in its first race, the Silverstone International Trophy. He failed to finish in a Grand Prix before his Dutch GP accident.

The only Grand Prix finish in the rest of that unhappy season was Tim Schenken's unclassified (but 'eleventh') position in Canada after a long pit stop. De Tomaso's Grand Prix participation ended with a retirement at Watkins Glen.

Diatto

In the early 1920s Turin manufacturer Diatto followed up its First World War aero-engine association with Bugatti and built a handful of Brescia models with 16-valve engine under licence. It moved on from this to build its own overhead camshaft engine that was developed by its engineer and works racing driver Alfieri Maserati. He then worked on the Tipo 20S, a sporting car with a dohc 2litre engine powering a touring-car-based chassis. This was to gain a useful competitions record (Maserati drove one in the 1922 Italian GP, and was apparently 'let down' by his tyres).

Duesenberg of 1921, driven by Jimmy Murphy, winner of the French GP.

The 20S encouraged Diatto to authorize a proper 2litre Grand Prix car in 1924. It made its debut in the 1925 Italian GP. Outwardly, it recalled the Alfa Romeo P2, while the channel-section chassis and suspension by semi-elliptics all round followed normal 1920s practice, and the engine was a supercharged 2litre straight eight. It was not race-ready for the 1925 race at Monza, and Emilio Materassi retired it early when supercharger bolts failed.

By that time Diatto's financial difficulties were severe, and it abandoned its racing programme. However, Alfieri Maserati was allowed to take over the Grand Prix car design. Modified in detail, and with a 1.5litre version of the straight eight, this became the first Maserati car, the Tipo 26 in 1926.

Dome

The Dome Motor Company of Kyoto was known for its sleek sports-racing cars from the late 1970s, and a decade later it became an entrant in the flourishing Japanese F3000 series, before building its first single-seater, F102, for this category. The evolutionary F103 came for 1992, but it was hardly competitive, with Cosworth DFV or Mugen engines.

Dome built the F105 Formula 1 car in 1996. It used Mugen (Honda) engines, and at one stage a formal association with Honda seemed possible. But funding for a race programme failed to materialize, and the Mugen-powered F105 was used as a test and development vehicle. Plans to enter World Championship with the F106 in 1998 failed for the same reason. The development was not entirely wasted, as it was fed into the planned Honda F1 venture and in to work with the Dallara test chassis.

Dommartin

The French Grand Prix challenger unveiled by the Dommartin engine company in 1948 turned out to be the hapless SEFAC of the 1930s (qv), hardly reborn, as it was still overweight and under-powered, if less unlovely with a new body. It retained the 'parallel eight' engine (that was to prove such a challenge to a 1990s

restorer in Britain), bored out to increase the capacity of 3,619cc and naturally without a supercharger to conform with Formula 1 regulations. In this form an output of 200bhp was claimed, and that modest power was to propel a machine that lived up to its SEFAC past in one respect – at 920kg (2,029lb) it was the heaviest Grand Prix car around in 1948. Dommartin's funds were exhausted before there was an attempt to race the car.

Duesenberg

The Duesenberg brothers, Frederick and August, entered cars for only one Grand Prix, but they did so with a sound record in American racing behind them, with aero engine work that included efforts to sort out a Bugatti 16-cylinder design, and then their own race-winning eight-cylinder engine. The Grand Prix was the 1921 French race, still the Grand Prix to those unwilling to recognize the status of the earlier American Grand Prize and in any case soon to lose its exclusivity as the Italian GP was first run. For 1920–22 the

American capacity limit – 183cu in or 3litre – coincided with the Grand Prix formula. Duesenberg's first straight eight had met Ballots with similar engines at Indianapolis in 1919, and that contest was to be renewed at Le Mans in 1921.

The Duesenberg 183cu in engine was a scaled-down version of the 1919 300cu in unit. It had a single overhead camshaft operating one inlet valve and two exhaust valves per cylinder. The crankcase and block were cast in one, and there was a three-bearing built-up crankshaft. Its 1921 rating was 115bhp. The car's frame and suspension followed normal lines, but this Duesenberg became the first Grand Prix car with hydraulic brakes, to all four wheels. The white cars had handsome bodies, with a bluff nose, nicely cowled cockpit and long elegant tail.

The Duesenberg entry for the French race was late, made after the normal entry fee deadline; the fees were paid by the Champion spark plug company, and its involvement meant that a fourth car was entered. The quartet was ready in good time, but during tests Jimmy Murphy crashed when a brake locked. The team's fourth driver, Louis Inghibert, was injured in the accident, and his place had to be taken by André Dubonnet.

As the Grand Prix settled, the Ballots and Duesenbergs seemed well matched, Chassagne leading for the French team, Murphy and Boyer in Duesenbergs. Chassagne retired, so did Boyer. Murphy led for most of the second half, but his victory was in doubt toward the end, because of punctures on the very rough circuit, and a damaged radiator. But he won, team mate Guyot lost second place with just over a lap to go and finished sixth, while Dubonnet was fourth.

The Duesenbergs did not race in another Grand Prix, but their cars were prominent in the USA through the 1920s. There would not be another victory for an American driver in the French GP for forty-one years, and there has never been another victory for an American-built car.

Dufaux-Marchand

Geneva-based brothers Frédéric and Charles Dufaux built sprint and racing cars for four years from 1904, usually with large straight-eight engines (but including one with a 26.4litre four-cylinder power unit!). Their one-off to be driven in the 1907 French GP by Frédéric was one of three straight-eight cars in the race, and with a capacity of 14,726cc it was one of the smaller engines in the Dieppe line-up. The claimed output was 100bhp. Chain transmission was used, with a three-speed gearbox, and in other respects the car was equally orthodox. Weighing in at 1,080kg (2,381lb), it was the second heaviest car in the 1907 Grand Prix.

At half-distance in the race, Dufaux was solidly last with a misfiring engine, and his race ended two laps later. So did the racing career of this obscure Swiss marque, and its modest touring car production did not last out the year.

◆ E ◆

Eagle

Dan Gurney and Carroll Shelby, widely respected and experienced American drivers, set up All-American Racers in 1965 with Goodyear backing, to launch an assault on Firestone's Indianapolis 500 domination. While a base was being established near Los Angeles, Gurney also looked to a Formula 1 venture, and as Shelby went his own way, a parallel Anglo-American Racers operation was set up with its base at Rye in Sussex, alongside the intended machine supplier, Weslake. AAR initially applied to both activities, of course, but the cars were to be known as Eagles.

Len Terry was commissioned to design a dual-purpose car, and this involved surprisingly few compromises, despite very different engines – the track cars were to have several types (Gurney Weslake Ford V8s in the first team cars) and a Weslake V12 powered the F1 version. Both were to bring success to Eagle. However, there were problems with the F1 engine which led to a split from Weslake.

In America, sponsorship and car sales meant that more resources were available: there were seven Eagles at Indianapolis in 1967, when the best-placed finisher was fourth, the Ford-powered 'City of Daytona Beach Special' driven by Denny Hulme. In 1968 Bobby Unser scored Eagle's first Indianapolis victory, in an Offenhauser-powered 'Rislone Special', while Gurney was second and Hulme fourth in Olsonite Eagles.

There were two victories for the Formula 1 Eagle, but in 1968 this programme was run down. It ended as the European season closed, and Dan Gurney drove an AAR-entered McLaren in the final races of the year. Tony Southgate had started designing a second-generation car that was to be lighter and probably costly, and this was set aside. The Indianapolis cars were successful through to the mid-1970s, but then Gurney had to turn away from the single-seaters.

T1G Above all, Terry's design took shape as a most handsome car. Generally, it followed the lines of the Lotus 38 he had designed, with a full monocoque in aluminium and symmetrical wishbone and coil-springs suspension all round for both track and road circuit cars. Coventry-Climax 2.75litre FPF engines were used while the V12 for the F1 car was completed driving through a Hewland gearbox.

The V12 was commissioned in 1965 and designed by Aubrey Woods. It was a 60-degree dohc 2,997cc unit that had a paper rating of 415bhp at 10,000rpm when it came into service late in 1966. A little later 'over 400bhp' was quoted. These engines were inconsistent, reflecting build quality problems, and there were tiny variations from unit to unit – the V12 was just not engineered for reproduction, let alone production. In 1968 Gurney took control of the engine programme.

The first cars were above the formula weight (but only a little above the average weight of 1966–67 F1 cars), and in the fourth example there was a determined effort to save weight, with some use of magnesium and titanium.

The Formula 1 Eagles started in twenty-five Grands Prix. The first was the 1966 Belgian GP, and in the next race Gurney scored points for his marque, when he was fifth in

Eagle V12 in 1967; Dan Gurney winning the 1967 Belgian GP.

the French GP. Fifth place in the Mexican GP added points to bring Eagle sixth place in the Constructors' Championship. In 1967 a second car was run for Richie Ginther in the early races, then once for Bruce McLaren and once for Ludovicio Scarfiotti. In overall terms, the finishing record was poor again, but Gurney drove one of his cars to win the Race of Champions at Brands Hatch and then the Belgian GP. He was third in the Canadian GP. Eagle was seventh in that year's championship (but with thirteen points compared with the four that earned sixth place in 1966).

The Eagles were run in only five Grands Prix in 1968, the last at Monza, and no points were scored. A 1966 car with an FPF engine was entered in the 1969 Canadian GP by John Maryon. Al Pease qualified it seventeenth (of twenty), and was running last when he was black-flagged, in a sad little postscript to the Eagle Formula 1 story.

Eifelland

Named for backer Gunther Henerici's Eifelland caravan company, this was no more than a March 721 with flamboyant bodywork designed by Luigi (Lutz) Colani. March-Cosworth chassis, suspension and mechanical parts were retained, and the only justification for the Eifelland Typ 21 designation was the body. And despite Colani's claims to aerodynamic expertise this proved ineffectual. A March nose cone was used after the first race, an engine cover-cum-rear aerofoil gave way to a conventional rear wing, a central 'periscope' rear-view mirror was discarded – eventually only the cockpit surround remained of Colani's work.

Rolf Stommelen started the Typ 21 in eight Grands Prix in 1972 and was classified five times; his best placings were tenth at Monaco and Brands Hatch. In Austria, where the Type 21 was entered by Team Stommelen, it was running at the end of the Grand Prix but too far back to be classified. Then Bernie Ecclestone bought the team, for its DFV engines, and the car was sold on to Hexagon. Fitted with a normal March body, it was driven by John Watson to sixth place in a late-season non-championship race at Brands Hatch (Watson also drove it to win a *formule libre* race at Phoenix Park).

Eigenbau

Eigenbau was a hopeful Leipzig constructor, building competition cars around production components in the early 1950s. In Formula 2 guise, its 2litre car had a nose closely resembling the Alfa Romeo 158; it also appeared with enclosed wheels, as a centre-cockpit sports car. The 1971cc straight six was the EMW version of the late-1930s BMW engine. An Eigenbau entered for the 1952 German GP failed to start, but in 1953 Krause qualified one twenty-sixth fastest that lasted the Grand Prix to finish fourteenth, two laps down on the winning Ferrari.

Eldridge Special

One of Ernest Eldridge's Specials appeared fleetingly in the Italian and San Sebastian (Spanish) Grands Prix in 1925, albeit in the *vetturette* class at Monza. Eldridge was based in Paris at the time, and he drove his own cars.

This third Special had an underslung chassis frame, with smooth bodywork extended to enclose the semi-elliptic springs front and rear. The offset cockpit made for a low driving position. The basic engine was a 1.5litre four-cylinder Anzani unit, with Eldridge's twin overhead camshaft conversion and a Roots-type supercharger.

Eldridge failed to finish in a Grand Prix, and after an abortive entry in the 1926 Indianapolis 500 (he retired the dohc

Special with steering failure after forty-five laps), he turned to a Miller.

Elios

This car's one appearance in a Formula 1 race came about as the Coppa Italia was organized at Vallelunga late in 1961 to ensure that sufficient qualifying events were run in the Italian championship, and that Giancarlo Baghetti started in the required number of races – he did, and he clinched the title at Vallelunga. The organizers welcomed any entries, and Gianni Cancellieri suggests that the scrutineers were perhaps prepared to overlook 'details' such as the capacity of the engine in the Elios.

Entered by Mario Pandolfo, this 'Formula 1 car' was no more and no less than a Formula Junior de Sanctis, still with its Fiat engine. Pandolfo qualified it last, of ten entries, and failed to complete either heat.

Emeryson

The Emerys, father and son, were essentially garage-based 'special builders' in a tradition that lingers in some club categories but reached into the premier formula into the 1960s. George, a race car preparation specialist in the 1930s, was ambitious to enter Formula 1 as soon as it began, and to build a car for his son Paul to race. As it was built,

Paul became the leading figure in the business. Other, often ingenious, cars, for lesser classes followed, and in an echo of Emerson's 1930s roots there were conversions, through to the 1959 Cooper-Connaught.

The company moved into the one-time Connaught works in 1960, and for a while there was a prospect that a line of cars would be built. But control passed to Hugh Powell in 1962, and although its last Formula 1 car showed some promise, Emeryson became the basis of the Scirocco team, which had a brief life in 1963–64. Paul Emery's enthusiasm was still strong, and although his proposed monocoque car had to be set aside in 1962 and his ideas for a four-wheel-drive F1 car with a turbocharged-rallycross car, and with the oval-racing midget cars he built and raced – he was British champion five times in this field.

Emeryson Special This one-off started life with a Lagonda engine, reduced to 1,087cc and with a 'government surplus' supercharger, mounted in a ladder-frame chassis, with independent front suspension deriving from a Singer and an Alta-type independent rear suspension (Paul Emery had served part of his engineering apprenticeship with Alta). It was hired out to Eric Winterbottom, who raced it with little success after a win at the second British post-war race meeting, at Gransden Lodge.

A project to build an air-cooled flat twelve for it called for resources that were

quite beyond Emeryson, but a 4.5litre straight eight from a Duesenberg was fitted (the chassis had to be lengthened for it) and this made it a Formula 1 car. It ran in a few British races, driven by Bobby Baird. Emery reckoned that the engine gave as much as 400bhp, but whatever the output it was too much for the ENV gearboxes used.

F2/F1 car (1953–57) For the last year of the 2litre Formula 2, Paul Emery built a car that was also to serve as a 2.5litre F1 car, making occasional race appearances until 1957. The chassis layout of the Emeryson 500cc F3 car was scaled up, and there was double wishbone and coil spring independent front suspension with a de Dion rear end. A second-hand (and substandard) Aston Martin engine linered down to 2litres was used, with an Aston gearbox.

The car was woefully uncompetitive in this form, but had one race that stands out in retrospect: Colin Chapman drove his only Formula 1 race in it, finishing twelfth and last in a heat of the 1952 Silverstone International Trophy, then too far back to be classified in the final.

An Alta engine bored out to 2,471cc and an ENV pre-selector gearbox replaced the Aston components, and in this form Emery drove it to finish second to Stirling Moss (Maserati 250F) in a 1956 Crystal Palace race – that must have been the high point in Emeryson history. That year Emery also qualified it twentieth fastest (of twenty-four) for the British GP; in the race it was the fourth car to retire.

With a dry sump, fuel-injected Jaguar engine, the car was run in one secondary race in 1957, then used in hill climbs before it was sold and converted into a sports car. A second car had meanwhile to be completed with a supercharged 2.5litre Alta engine for an American customer.

F2/F1 cars (1960–62) Former Cooper F1 driver Alan Brown, with Dick Clayton and Cecil Libouity, backed an Emeryson plan to build a range of rear-engined F Junior and F2/F1 cars for the 1960s, and the first appeared in F2 form in the summer of 1960. It was promising, and that led Ecurie National Belge to order three F1 cars for 1961.

Space frames built by Lister were used, with double wishbones and coil-spring front suspension and reversed lower wishbones, radius rods and coil-springs at the rear. Maserati 150S 1,484cc engines – the choice of several hopeful 1.5litre F1

Eldridge Special of 1925, Enzo Ferrari at the wheel.

entrants at this time – were fitted in these ENB cars.

The ENB programme proved fruitless. Two cars were crashed in their first race, at Pau, and they were entered for only one championship race (failing to qualify for the Monaco grid). Then they usually failed to arrive at meetings. Fourth place in the Brussels GP was all ENB had to show. André Pilette bought one car, fitted with a Coventry-Climax FPF, and ran it through the non-title 1961 Austrian GP to finish last. Mike Spence made his promising F1 debut in an Emeryson-Climax at Solitude, and finished second in a strong field in a race at Brands Hatch late that year.

Emery built the Mk 3 for Hugh Powell's two-car team in 1962. He envisaged a fibre-glass monocoque for this car, but the compact Mk 3 emerged with no more than a stressed-skin stiffening at mid-section, around pannier fuel tanks. The nose radiator was near-horizontal, with air drawn up from beneath the car. John Campbell-Jones drove one to eleventh place in the Belgian and British GPs, and to finish sixth in a non-championship race at Aintree.

Paul Emery parted company with Powell before the end of the 1962 season, and the team continued as Scirocco (qv).

EMW

EMW picked up the BMW car production threads in 1945, as the Eisenach plant fell in the Soviet Zone of Germany. It also seemed to inherit the old BMW company's interest in motor sport, which was generally expressed in its effective sports-racing cars. But odd single-seaters were built, largely for East European events. Leading driver Edgar Barth made a rare excursion to a single-seater race in West Germany in 1953, with a rather cumbersome EMW Formula 2 car for the German GP. In its main features, especially the 1,997cc straight-six engine, this harked back to BMW, and in mainline F2 company it proved less competitive than the slippery EMW sports-racers. Barth qualified it twenty-fourth on the 34-car grid, but failed to finish in the marque's only Grand Prix appearance.

ENB

Equipe National Belge ran a team of Formula 1 Emerysons with Maserati 150S engines in 1961, without success – but with several accidents – and rebuilt one of them for 1962 as an ENB-Maserati. The space frame and suspension were retained, and so was the sports-car engine into a year when the dominant British teams used purpose-designed V8s. The body had a mongrel appearance, with a 'nostril' nose aping the 1961 Ferrari.

Lucien Bianchi drove the car in the 1962 Brussels GP (retired), at Pau (crashed), and in the German GP (ran last, and finished sixteenth and last). The car was then sold for hill-climb use.

Ensign

There was much to admire in Morris (Mo) Nunn's Ensign team of the 1970s, and perhaps there was an inevitability in its decline early in the next decade. Nunn was a competent Formula 3 driver in the 1960s, and became a constructor as he built an F3 car in 1970. In that it was built in a lock-up garage it was a throwback, but in all other respects it was professional, and attracted orders for replicas in 1971. There was an F2 version in 1973, but more importantly a satisfied F3 Ensign customer Rikki von Opel underwrote the design and construction of a Formula 1 car, and commissioned Nunn to run it for him in 1973.

Von Opel left at the end of that year (to prove with a Brabham that he was not a great driver), and he passed his investment in Ensign over to Nunn. He was thus able to continue in Formula 1, and he found some backing for 1974 from Teddy Yip, a colourful Far Eastern entrepreneur. Moreover, Dave Baldwin joined Ensign as designer, for five years. Enough sponsorship was usually found to keep the team in F1 racing, and it scored Constructors' Championship points. Then there was the enormous setback of Clay Regazzoni's crippling accident at Long Beach in 1980.

Yip supported Ensign again in the early 1980s, but by 1982 the impetus was fading and in 1983 the team was amalgamated with Yip's Theodore Racing. This combination brought no success, so Yip and Nunn turned to CART racing, where the Midlander was to become a highly successful race engineer.

Confusingly, Ensign cars were known by type numbers (N prefix) and chassis numbers (MN prefix).

N173–174 Distinctive on 1973 grids, with individualistic body lines complemented by its dark green and yellow pinstripe colour scheme, N173 (or MN01) was an uncomplicated Cosworth-engined car. The suspension, double wishbones at the front, upper and lower links at the rear, had outboard springs. The DFV drove through a Hewland FGA400 gearbox. A deep cockpit surround meant that the body stood out, there was a functional engine air intake, a low full-width front aerofoil and a rear wing carried on swept-back end plates. N174 in 1974 had less striking body work. Ensign's Grand Prix debut came in the 1973 French race, when von Opel finished fifteenth. The inexperience of the team as well as the driver showed through the rest of that year, when five more starts brought a placing thirteenth in Britain, an unclassified finish in Canada, and three retirements.

The cars were used 1974, with modest results. Vern Schuppan drove in N174 to fifteenth in the Belgian GP, but failed to qualify twice, and was disqualified twice, and retired once. Mike Wilds was entered in the first car in four late races, achieving nothing, and almost incidentally Brian Redman was eighth in the Silverstone International Trophy, in N174.

That second car was driven in two 1975 races by Roelof Wunderink, Gijs van Lennep took tenth place in the Dutch GP with it, then Wunderink managed a non-classified finish in Australia. It was nominally uprated to serve while N176 was completed early in 1976. Chris Amon drove it in two GPs, finishing eighth at Long Beach, and in two non-title races.

N175 Baldwin's first Ensign was first raced in the 1975 French GP. It was conventional, although compared with the first Ensigns it had rising-rate double-wishbone front suspension with 'semi-inboard' springs, and inboard front brakes. Outwardly, there were prominent hip radiators and a tall engine airbox. Van Lennep scored Ensign's first point with it when he finished sixth in the German GP; the less accomplished Wunderink failed to qualify it in Britain, retired in the USA.

It served on in 1976 as the Boro (q.v.).

N176 Another one off, this car followed N175 closely, with suspension arrangements modified (and at the rear to be changed again) and outboard brakes. Chris Amon drove it to fifth place in its debut race in Spain, but then recorded only one more finish in five starts (crashing twice, when components failed). Neve was eighteenth in the French GP, Binder retired in Austria, Ickx took a tenth and a thirteenth place in later races, and retired twice and the car was destroyed when he crashed at Watkins Glen.

N177 MN06–MN08 gave Ensign its best season. The fact that three were built made it unusual among Nunn's cars, and there were two cars on grids through the second half of the season. In design terms it was evolutionary, with the sharp nose and large hip radiators of its predecessor, and inboard suspension all round. Clay Regazzoni drove for Ensign all season, scoring a point in the first race and two each in Italy and the USA, with two other finishes to set against two DNQs and nine retirements. Patrick Tambay drove the second car in the last eight races, finishing fifth twice and sixth once. Ten points brought Ensign tenth place in the Constructors Championship – and exceeded its combined total for its other Formula 1 seasons.

The cars were little changed for 1978, and drivers who brought funds to the team were welcomed. Derek Daly was the only driver to score a point (in the year's last race), from three finishes in six starts. Ertl managed one finish in four attempts, Ickx finished one race, Leoni started once in four attempts, Lees, Lunger and Piquet had single drives.

One car was adapted as a wing car for 1979, for the Spanish and Belgian GPs.

N178 Work on MN10 started, but was abandoned.

N179 In its first form, MN11 was notable for an extraordinary front end, with radiator extending from the nose to the scuttle. Otherwise it was conventional. After three races, it was converted to a normal side-radiator layout, and it was made into a 'wing' car.

It was never an effective Grand Prix car. Daly managed three starts and two finishes in five attempts; Gaillard qualified for two starts (one finish) in five attempts; Surer started twice in three attempts. Daly's eleventh in the first race was the best placing.

N180 Ralph Bellamy and Nigel Bennett designed this car very much on Williams FW07 lines. The aluminium monocoque had some honeycomb strengthening, there was double wishbone suspension with inboard springs, and outboard brakes. It was a compact car, with smooth attractive body lines.

Regazzoni drove for Ensign again, and the car seemed promising in his hands. But in his 132nd Grand Prix his front-line career was ended in that Long Beach crash. None of the other drivers who raced Ensigns that year made an impact, Lammers's twelfth at Watkins Glen the best finish (after Regga's eighth and ninth places). Lees and Needell each recorded a DNQ and a retirement.

MN174 was uprated to B specification for 1981. Marc Surer scored three points in Brazil and one at Monaco, before Eliseo Salazar brought money into the team (and

he did contribute one more point, in Holland); there were six retirements and two 'unclassified' finishes in the 1981 tally, with only one DNQ.

Five points meant Ensign was eleventh in the Constructors' Championship, the marque's last appearance on that listing. The N180B entered in the first race of 1982 for Roberto Guerrero was withdrawn.

N181 Only one of the planned pair of Bennett-designed N181s was completed, following general Brabham lines. It was the only Ensign to have an extensive carbon-fibre content, in the upper front of the monocoque and the side pods. There were no other novelties, and in the turbo age a DFV was still used. Guerrero drove, and failed to qualify only four times (the Imola entry was withdrawn). But he was placed just once, eighth in the German Grand Prix.

Ensign was absorbed into the Theodore team, and the N181 reappeared in 1983 as the Theodore N183.

ERA

See pp.82–83.

Eurobrun

Walter Brun and Paulo Pavanello formed a partnership to enter Formula 1 for three seasons from 1988. On paper this was promising: Brun was a successful businessman, so offered acumen in that sphere as well as a solid record with Brun Motorsport as a sports-car entrant at the highest level, while Pavenello has a racing team base at Senago and his Euroracing experience as a Formula 1 entrant with Alfa Romeos a few years earlier.

Paper promise as not fulfilled. The cars were pedestrian and more often than not failed to get past the qualification hurdle – in 1990 the hapless Claudio Langes failed to pre-qualify fourteen times in fourteen attempts, while Roberto Moreno wasted his talents in Eurobrun cockpits for too long in the same season. The Eurobrun entries for the last two races of that season were withdrawn, and so the team did not quite complete its three-season programme. Nobody missed it, for it contributed no noticeable cars to Grand Prix grids; its best race placing was eleventh, in 1988, it scored no points and saw its cars start in just fourteen races out of a possible forty-six.

Ensign-Ford N177, 1977, driven by Patrick Tambay.

continued on p.84

English Racing Automobiles was formed in 1934 by Raymond Mays and Peter Berthon with backing from Humphrey T. Cook, initially to produce a single-seater on the lines of Mays's famous 'White Riley', for *voiturette* racing. A base was established at Bourne (Mays was unwilling to leave his home there), and seventeen cars were laid down between 1934 and 1937.

With engines in three sizes (1.1, 1.5 and 2 litres), the A-, B- and C-type ERAs were essentially sensible cars for independent entrants. They became familiar on the circuits of Europe, and were very successful until 1936 when more-sophisticated Maseratis and later Alfa Romeos took over *voiturette* racing. Meanwhile, ERAs had appeared alongside Grand Prix cars, from 1935 when Bira finished fifth in his 1.5 litre car in the Donington GP and Mays' 2 litre car ran in the German GP (and retired). Extravagantly outpaced by German heavy metal, and beginning to look antique, early-type ERAs were seen in Grands Prix through to the end of the 1930s. Some were brought out again after the Second World War, when they conformed to the 1.5 litre supercharged engine category of Formula 1 from 1947. It is perhaps a reflection on racing in that recovery period that some of them were by no means disgraced in major races through to the early 1950s.

Meanwhile there had been a determined effort to catch up, in the technology of the E-type. The first was completed in 1939, in difficult circumstances as

ERA of the mid-1930s, 'B. Bira' driving.

Cook took full control of ERA and moved it from Bourne. In chassis and suspension terms, this car was up to the minute, but through the summer its entries for races were withdrawn, and its debut came in France in July.

Cook's interest faded, and the two E-types were sold. They were raced in the late 1940s, with very modest results. The one-off G-type was built when ERA was owned by Leslie Johnson and based at Dunstable, and run in three Formula 2 Grand Prix, but only showed a hint of promise in secondary races in 1952.

The team proposed for 1953 failed to materialize, and Johnson sold the entire project to the British Aeroplane Company. The G-type was used as the basis for the Bristol 450 coupes run at Le Mans, talk of a 2.5 litre ERA came to nothing, and there have been no more single-seater ERAs.

A-, B-, C-types Reid Railton laid out a straightforward channel-section chassis frame for the original ERAs, with rigid front axle and live rear axle carried on semi-elliptic springs (B-types modified to C-type specification could be fitted with Porsche-pattern independent front suspension from 1937). There were friction dampers. Through the production period, minor improvements were to be introduced, for example to the springs. The body was simple and shapely, with a fuel tank forming the tail.

The engine was a pushrod ohv straight six, laid down by Berthon on Riley lines, with Roots-type supercharger by T. Murray-Jamieson (later Zoller superchargers were used). The 1.5 litre version with the original supercharger arrangement gave some 150bhp; Zoller-supercharged engines gave as much as the chassis and suspension could comfortably handle. Preselector gearboxes were customarily fitted.

Race histories are largely of *voiturette* events, but as well as the 1935 GP appearances mentioned, two of the four ERAs in the 1937 Donington GP finished, and three in the 1938 race were placed 6-7-8, albeit lapped several times by German cars.

ERA C-type, visually modified in the late 1940s by Cuth Harrison.

Bob Gerard finished third in the 1948 British GP, when other ERAs were sixth and seventh. A year earlier, Whitehead and Connell had driven the 1936 R10B to seventh place in the 1947 French GP (in 1948 the French organizers ruled after practice that these pre-war ERAs were not suitable cars for a modern Grand Prix!). The cars were most often seen in secondary F1 races, but featured in the British GP until 1951 (notably Gerard's R14B, a late car that he modified and drove – as well as his third place in 1948, he was second in 1949, and then he was sixth at Monaco as well as Silverstone in 1950!). Most of these ERAs, together with two made up from spare parts, are still used in historic events.

E-type Some of the preliminary work on this 1939 *voiturette* was apparently done with 'R4D', the development car used by Mays in the second half of the 1930s. It had a tubular chassis, with trailing-arm independent front suspension and de Dion rear suspension, with torsion bar springing. The Zoller-supercharged 1,488cc straight six had a shorter stroke than previous ERA engines, and an output up to 230bhp was claimed for it. The preselector gearbox gave way to an all-synchromesh four-speed one.

Two were built, and they looked up-to-the-minute. They conformed to Formula 1, and became Grand Prix cars. Performances were disappointing, with few finishes to offset numerous retirements.

G-type Apart from the three-ringed badge, there was little to connect this car with earlier ERAs. It was designed by David Hodkin around a dry-sump version of the 1,971cc Bristol straight six. There was a ladder-type chassis in magnesium, with large oval-section main members, which was reasonably light and very rigid, with wishbone and coil spring front suspension and a de Dion system at the rear. The transmission ran to the left of the off-set cockpit to a four-speed gearbox in unit with the final drive. This advanced car was dogged by component failures, and the development that might have been expected if a second car had been built and if there had been the encouragement of racing successes never materialized. Stirling Moss drove it, from the time that engine failure led to an accident in its debut race (the 1952 Belgian GP) to its eighth and last race, and a fourth place at Charterhall. Its best finish was third in a secondary race at Boreham. Then it was sold.

ERA E-type, as raced in the French GP of 1947.

ERA-Bristol G-type of 1952, Stirling Moss driving.

continued from p.81

ER188 This design by Mario Tolentino and Bruno Zava was totally conventional – not necessarily a bad thing in itself, but in this case coupled with a lack of the inspiration that might have brought rewards. There was a low monocoque, double wishbone pushrod suspension all round, and Mader-prepared Cosworth DFZ engines that drove through Eurobrun-Hewland six-speed gearboxes.

Eurobrun's first season turned out to be its best. Stefano Modena finished five times from nine starts (eleventh in Hungary being the best result), while Oscar Larrauri managed two finishes. Moreno's car was twice excluded for aerofoil dimension infringements and the pair recorded a dozen failures to pre-qualify or qualify.

Despite this dismal showing, two new interim cars designated ER188B were built for 1989, and one of the three 1988 cars was modified to this standard. Judd CV 90-degree V8s were used (giving some 20bhp more than the 1988 DFZs), while body revisions made the cars look a little less bulky and there was a new rear suspension designed by George Ryton.

The single-driver effort in 1989 had a hopeless record. Gregor Foitek got an ER188B past the pre-qualification stage once, and then failed to qualify it to start.

ER189 The 1989 car appeared too late in the season, certainly for a team that seemed to undertake little development work. It was not wholly raceworthy for its GP debut, and was actually set aside in favour of an ER188B for a later race. Designed by Ryton, it had double wishbone pushrod suspension which did not follow the earlier layout in all respects, and was not necessarily an advance as the ER188B suspension was reintroduced. Naturally Judd engines were still used. One car was later reported to have been adapted for the Neotech V12 that was intended for a 1990 Eurobrun.

The ER189 failed in Foitek's hands, and when he left the team late in the summer Larrauri returned, and failed to get a Eurobrun to a grid.

With new rear suspension the cars reappeared in 1990, and served on through the season as the ER190 failed to materialize. Moreno achieved two starts and one finish (thirteenth in the USA). Langes's miserable record has already been mentioned. The team did not travel to the distant late-season races.

Excelsior

This Belgian manufacturer entered a car in the Grand Prix when it was revived by the ACF in 1912, and with only two years' racing experience achieved a satisfactory result, sixth overall. It was a production-based car, sent into a race contested by companies such as Fiat and Peugeot with specialized racing machines. The Excelsior matched the Fiats in its 'traditional' size, and at 1,600kg (3,528lb) it equalled the heaviest (a Lorraine-Dietrich) in weight. Behind a bluff nose, its smooth body was better proportioned – less archaic – than the Fiat or Lorraine, but it certainly did not belong to the new generation represented by Peugeot. The engine had the company's long-stroke side-valve straight six, which had been around since 1907. While it was therefore reliable, with a capacity of 9,138cc it could hardly be expected to match the 14litre Fiat or 15litre Lorraine-Dietrich in terms of power. The Excelsior was the only 1912 Grand Prix car with a five-speed gearbox. Joseph Christiaens steadily lost ground to the leaders through the race, and at half distance was behind several *Coupe de l'Auto* 3litre cars. By three-quarter distance he was up to sixth, and he finished in that position.

In 1907 Excelsior used the straight six in 6,107cc form, and the two Grand Prix cars were considerably smaller and lighter. Except for their bolster fuel tanks they were smooth and handsome. Again they were outclassed, finishing eighth and eleventh in the Grand Prix. Christiaens drove the best placed Excelsior in the Grand Prix, and one of the cars was run with slightly modified bodywork and apparently 7.3litre engine in the 1914 Indianapolis 500. Christiaens led the first 50 miles, before finishing sixth.

In the 1920s Excelsiors were modestly successful in sports-car races.

Eurobrun-Ford E188 of 1988, Oscar Larrauri driving.

◆ F ◆

Ferguson-Climax P99 four-wheel drive of 1961, Jack Fairman driving.

Ferguson

The Harry Ferguson Research Company built a one-off racing car to demonstrate its four-wheel-drive system in 1960, too late for the 2.5litre Formula 1. However, it was raced with a 1.5litre engine in 1961, when Stirling Moss drove it to a convincing victory in the Oulton Park Gold Cup, scoring the only win for a four-wheel-drive car in an F1 race.

The P99 had a conventional space frame, the Coventry-Climax engine was canted to keep down frontal area, and the driver's seat was offset to the right; the transmission was to the left of centre. Drive was through a five-speed Ferguson-Colotti gearbox to a central differential and then to front and rear differentials. The front/rear power split could be varied, but the four-wheel-drive arrangement was permanent. Coil springs and double wishbones were used all round in the suspension, and brakes were mounted inboard (Dunlop Maxaret anti-lock brakes were tested, but not used in races).

The power of the 2.5litre FPF engine was adequate, but weight and the sapping demands of the transmission told against the P99 when it was run as a 1.5litre F1 car. It started in only one Grand Prix, when Jack Fairman drove it through the opening phase of the 1961 British event, and when Stirling Moss took over he demonstrated its qualities on a wet track (the car was disqualified, as

Fairman had had a push start). Moss then won on a damp track at Oulton Park.

The P99 was driven by Graham Hill and Innes Ireland in the 1963 Tasman series, with modest success, Indianapolis tests for Andy Granatelli led to the P104 Novi, and then Peter Westbury used the P99 in hill climbs, winning the 1964 British Championship.

Ferrari

See pp.86–98.

F.I.A.T./Fiat

See pp.99–101.

First

A single First 189 Formula 1 car was completed late in 1988, but it never started in a Grand Prix, as a First in 1989 or later as a Life in 1990. The 189 was designed by Richard Divila on orthodox lines, and was powered by a Judd V8. However, team patron Leoni Lombardi had an agreement with March for F3000 which apparently precluded an entry into Formula 1 (and as with several marginal Italian ventures at this time, resources were less than adequate).

The chassis was bought by Life Racing Engines, to be used as a test vehicle for its W12 engine but later modified and entered as a Life in 1990 Grands Prix.

Fittipaldi

The Fittipaldi brothers, Wilson and Emerson, turned dreams of a Brazilian Grand Prix team into reality in the 1970s, although they never realized dreams of a successful Brazilian GP team, and in the second half of the decade the 1972 and 1974 World Champion sacrificed his career as a top-line F1 driver to race Fittipaldi cars. While he was still driving for McLaren, Emerson was active behind the scenes; Wilson was the front man, and the team's first driver. Substantial backing was obtained from a Brazilian sugar cooperative, hence the name Copersucar, which disappeared at the end of the 1970s.

Wilson Fittipaldi took on Jo Ramirez to run the team, and the first designer was Richard Divila. The earliest cars were built at Sao Paulo, before reality led to a British base for construction work and operations – the cars were Cosworth-Hewland kit cars (there had to be a Brazilian content, but the quality of these was not always of the highest order).

Several designers were responsible for the Copersucar Fittipaldi cars, and when Fittipaldi took over the Wolf team and its equipment in 1980 it also gained the services of Harvey Postlethwaite and team manager Peter Warr. But the promise of that influx of experience and success was not to be fulfilled – there was a new major sponsor, but that lasted for a year, and the team scratched for finance. The brothers had never mastered the art of finding it.

The team's best season was 1978, when 17 Constructors' Championship points were scored. Emerson's last season as a Grand Prix driver, 1980, was also reasonably successful (eleven points achieving seventh place in the Constructors' Championship again), but there were no points in 1981 and just one in 1982. That turned out to be the Fittipaldi team's last season, and it ended early, at the final European race. It had entered 104 Grand Prix, and scored forty-four points in its eight seasons of endeavour.

continued on p.101

FERRARI

No name in recent Grand Prix racing has commanded more attention, and more respect, than Ferrari. Throughout the second half of the twentieth century, Enzo Ferrari (and, after his death, his successors) presided over teams of scarlet cars that carried his name, brought great prestige to Italy and its engineering industry, and a tingle to generations of race car enthusiasts.

For much of that time Ferrari himself exercised control from a distance, for he rarely attended the races themselves. Fiat might have taken a tighter control of the Ferrari company, there might have been discord among his lieutenants, but for more than forty years this was exclusively one man's team. It is the only team to have contested the official World F1 Championship in every season since its inception.

Ferrari cars were often competitive, sometimes embarrassingly falling short of the top standards, and were occasionally outclassed, yet it is greatly to Ferrari's credit that a team was always fielded, or at worst a single-car team. Vitally, until late in the 1990s the team was always more important than its personalities.

Ferrari himself had raced in the 1920s, had formed Scuderia Ferrari in 1929 to run Alfa Romeos, and effectively became the quasi-works Alfa team of the 1930s. After 1938 that arrangement was dissolved, after which Ferrari looked to start running his own cars. The first such car ran, as a sports car, in the 1940 Mille Miglia.

Immediately after the Second World War, and relocated in Maranello, Ferrari began building his own cars, high-performance sports cars at first and – soon – single-seater Grand Prix machinery. The first of these came in the autumn of 1948, and from the following year the marque became well-known throughout Europe.

The first cars had supercharged V12 engines, which reflected Ferrari's obsession with that format, but the first truly competitive Ferraris had larger capacity unsupercharged engines, and the Championship first fell to the 2litre four-cylinder cars of 1952 and 1953. The following years were dismal, but the near-collapse of another Italian concern, Lancia, led to their machinery being donated to Ferrari to use in 1956 and beyond. In the late 1950s the team ran the world's last truly effective front-engined Grand Prix cars.

The old Ferrari belief that engine power was all-important, meant that his technically obsolete cars almost kept up with the new wave of British constructors who had first-generation rear-engined cars, but he lost out badly in the second year of the 1.5litre formula as chassis development moved ahead by leaps and bounds. Later in the 1960s there were distractions, notably the defection of key personnel, but after a proposed Ferrari–Ford merger fell through, Fiat became more closely involved, and took a controlling financial interest at the end of the decade.

The 3litre years promised better times, but after the arrival of the Ford-Cosworth DFV, and its availability to many concerns, up to the mid-1970s Ferrari sometimes won races, but not at all regularly, nor convincingly. At least this concentrated their minds, one result being that wasteful distractions like F2 and sports-car racing were abandoned.

Ferrari was slow to accept technical novelties like rear-engined layouts, and monocoque construction, and it also hesitated before adopting others such as the honeycomb sandwich. In the mid-1970s the classic 312T family put Ferrari back on top, but ground effects technology then caused another downturn (Ferrari's flat-twelve engine got in the way of aerodynamic tunnels), but then came turbocharging, of which Ferrari himself approved, and his designers appreciated. The team began to win championships again, and the Constructors' Championship was the one which Ferrari particularly valued.

Through to the late 1980s the team's fortunes gradually ebbed away once again. There were schisms, particularly as Ferrari finally bowed to pressure and brought in outsiders, while an advanced design centre (GTO Ltd – Guildford Technical Office) was set up in the UK, a long way from Maranello. As Enzo's health deteriorated, so did his control of the team, and immediately after his death in 1988 Fiat instigated a serious shake-out.

This did not always work and, because of the Italians' love of infighting and intrigue, was often counter-productive. Cesare Fiorio (who had achieved great things with the Lancia rally team) was brought in to run the F1 team, and Nigel Mansell won the first race of the 1989 season, in a radical car designed by John Barnard (ex-McLaren), at GTO. This car was an effective challenger to McLaren in 1989, but the team was never settled, and Barnard left the organization before the end of the season.

For the next three years, Maranello was then in comic-opera turmoil, with faces coming and going, able men's opinions being ignored, and a great marque's reputation being sullied. Nigel Mansell predictably left, Alain Prost engineered the dismissal of team-manager Fiorio, then was himself sacked after two seasons when he told the truth about the awful 643, this being a time when a managing 'committee-of-three' made more shambolic errors than one personality could possibly have done.

In 1992 the much-hyped F92A was a technical disaster, so Luca Di Montezemolo finally came back as Ferrari's boss. But change, even with a $160 million budget, would take time. When new-signing Gerhard Berger made his first test runs early in 1993 he was so far off the pace that he found this a great joke. But with his huge retainer (according to the stories that circulated) maybe he could afford to smile?

The fight back then began – slowly at first. John Barnard returned as technical chief (though still operating from the UK), the Frenchman Jean Todt (ex-Peugeot) arrived in 1994, as team manager, to inject logic into the operation, Ferrari took advice from Honda and reverted to four-valve (instead of five-valve) engine operation, and victories began to flow once again.

Then, in 1996, came the truly big upheaval. Di Montezemolo raided a bank (Marlboro's probably) to attract twice world-Champion Michael Schumacher from Benetton, brought a new V10 engine (Ferrari's first-ever) into service, and then began to build a new team around the German.

Within months this had become 'Team Schumacher', evidenced by the arrival of technical director Ross Brawn and chief designer Rory Byrne, both from Benetton, and by Eddie Irvine as a compliant driver who was not as fast as Schumacher, but would do his bidding.

Schumacher's assertive driving behaviour made many enemies – his attempt to drive Villeneuve's Williams off the track at Jerez in 1997 cost him all his Championship points that season, and he later clashed several times with David Coulthard – but there was no gainsaying his driving talents. Year after year, Ferrari fortunes improved – Schumacher won three times in 1996, five times in 1997, and six times in 1998 – and in 1999 the team finally won the Constructors' Championship, which they had not held since 1983.

In that season, unhappily, Schumacher broke his leg in mid-season (after brake failure on the first lap of the British GP), so he personally had to wait until 2000 when he finally won the Drivers' series – his third, and his first with Ferrari. The team's joy was unconfined, especially as it won the Constructors' crown for the second consecutive year.

125 This was the very first Grand Prix Ferrari – though it should be noted that the first Ferrari to start a *grande epreuve* was a stripped-out sports 166, that Prince Igor Troubetzkoy started in the Monaco GP of 1948.

Gioacchino Colombo designed the single-seater 125, which made its debut in the 1948 Italian GP. Its heart was an over-square (55 × 52.5mm, 1,496.7cc) 60-degree V12, with a single-stage Roots-type supercharger, for which 225bhp was claimed. The tubular chassis was straightforward, and a double wishbone and transverse leaf spring independent front suspension was used, with a torsion bar swing axle arrangement at the rear.

For 1950 Lampredi substantially improved the design. With a two-stage supercharger and other improvements, engine power rose to 280bhp; a four-speed gearbox in unit with the final drive unit replaced the original, which had been a five-speed box mounted in unit with the engine. A De Dion rear suspension arrangement took the place of the swing axle. Wheelbase and track were both enlarged – for the original 125 had had a reputation for tricky handling.

Sommer placed one of the works trio of cars third in the 125's first race, and late in 1948 Farina scored the first victory for a 125, in a secondary race at Garda, Italy. A first *grande epreuve* victory was recorded, in the 1949 Swiss GP, by Alberto Ascari.

In 1949, several 125s were sold to independent entrants, most notably to Peter Whitehead, who came close to victory in the French GP, and who won the Czech GP at the end of the year; he ran an ex-works 1950 model during 1951, continuing in F1 and later using his car in F2 guise with a later 2litre engine. A short-wheelbase car became the first Vandervell-entered Thin Wall Special (q.v.), while a 1950 longer-wheelbase car with two-stage supercharging was the

second Thin Wall. A 2,560cc engine was also used in a development programme for the unblown cars.

275/340/375 When Aurelio Lampredi took over from Colombo as Ferrari's design chief, he was a disciple of the unsupercharged (4.5litre) alternative offered by F1 regulations in this period, reasoning that it would make for simpler and lighter, less stressed, more reliable and more fuel-efficient cars. This view was shared by Ferrari himself, and so a 60-degree single overhead cam V12 on these lines was laid down for 1950.

A full-capacity version was reached in three stages – 72 × 68mm, 3,322cc, 80 × 68mm, 4,101cc, and finally 80 × 74.5mm, 4,494cc. The maximum power outputs of these 275, 340 and 375 models were, respectively, 280bhp, 320bhp and 380bhp. The 275 model had an old-type chassis, but for the 340 and 375 types a new chassis with rectangular main tubes was designed, along with double wishbone and transverse leaf spring front suspension, and a de Dion rear suspension with a single transverse leaf spring.

The 275 first appeared in the 1950 Belgian GP, but was clearly underpowered. The 340 confirmed the unblown policy, however, and in the Italian GP of that year Ascari challenged the all-conquering Alfa Romeo 159s with a 4.5litre 375. In 1951 these Ferraris ended the long reign of Alfa success, the real turning point coming when Gonzalez won the British GP in mid-season. A wrong tyre choice at the last Grand Prix of the season cost the team's driver the Championship.

In 1952 the Grands Prix were run for F2 cars, but the 375s were still run in *formule libre* races, and three cars were sold to independents, while one was progressively modified and improved as the third Thin Wall Special. Ironically, the only successes for those cars modified for Indianapolis 500 events were scored on road circuits.

500 To replace the V12 engines in F2, Lampredi designed a simple new four-cylinder-engined car, that evolved very rapidly in 1951, and appeared in 2litre and 2.5litre form. The larger engine actually appeared first, running as a forerunner of the definitive 625 for the 1954 season.

The 500 dominated two seasons of (F2) World Championship racing in 1952 and 1953, though it had already appeared in 1951 when it made its debut at Modena.

In their first European F2 race of 1952, the Syracuse GP, the 500s were placed 1-2-3-4, giving a good idea of what was to come.

In 2litre form the engine was a straightforward dohc unit (90 × 78mm, 1,984cc), that produced 165bhp in 1952, and up to 180bhp in 1953, although cars sold to private owners seemed to have lower peak rev limits, and were reckoned to be distinctly less powerful than the 'works' machines – this being something for which Ferrari was notorious at the time. The engine was set well back in the tubular chassis, making it a well-balanced car, and the suspension followed the successful 375-style pattern.

In two years of World Championship racing, the 500 was beaten only once (at Monza in 1953), and was seldom challenged in secondary races either, although the independent drivers had a tougher time.

The 500 gave Alberto Ascari his two Championships, and Mike Hawthorn drove one to his first-ever Grand Prix victory, the dramatic 1953 French GP race.

625 These were rebuilds of the 1953-style 500s, for use in the new 2.5litre F1, with a 2,498cc (94 × 90mm) version of the well-proven four-cylinder engine, which was rated at 210bhp early in 1954, and 245bhp later in the season. The 553 engine (*see* below) was also used in this chassis. Six cars were retained by the works team as back-up for the later 553, but in fact were preferred to it by the drivers. Other 625s were sold off to independents.

A 625 was driven to Grand Prix victory in 1954 (Gonzalez at Silverstone), and the cars were competitive in secondary races during 1954. They served on into 1955, but were only occasionally placed in the top six, in a season that was bleak for Ferrari, save for Trintignant's lucky victory at Monaco.

553/555 This was the first Ferrari with anything approaching a space frame, and it had lines which led to it being dubbed 'Squalo' ('shark') – which was rather odd, as its midriff bulge around the fuel tanks was most unsharklike. It first appeared as an F2-sized car in the 1953 Italian GP, with a 1,997cc four-cylinder engine, and was then brought out again in 1954 with a full 2,497cc (100 × 79.5mm) version of the same engine, for which 240bhp was claimed.

Ferrari 625 of 1954, Mike Hawthorn driving.

been retained as a consultant) was always at odds with Ferrari staff led by Bellentani.

In came a 'traditional' tail-mounted fuel tank, the panniers were faired into the main bodywork (and, therefore, ceased to be panniers), while the engine was no longer used as a stressed chassis member. The engine itself was modified by Jano and Bazzi, to become more oversquare (76 × 58.5mm, 2,487cc), and to give 265bhp.

Contractual problems were avoided, but on-circuit problems were probably invited, as Ferrari ran the cars on Englebert rather than Pirelli tyres. In 1956 the team had driving strength in great depth, headed by Juan-Manuel Fangio, who rewarded them by winning the World Championship. His Grand Prix victories came in Argentina, Britain and Germany, while Peter Collins won in Belgium and France.

More modifications for 1957 included another version of the engine (80 × 62mm, 2,495cc) to give 275bhp, while suspension revisions included the use of a Supersqualo front set-up. All this led to a designation change – from D50 to 801 – but not to more Championship race victories. In the whole year, only three secondary events fell to the Ferrari F1 team.

Drivers did not like its handling, and changes to the engine position (within very restricted possibilities) did not help. However, a change to coil spring front suspension late in 1954 certainly helped, and Hawthorn drove this revised version to win the Spanish GP.

For 1955, with a new frame, and modified rear suspension, repositioned radiator and lower body lines, it became the Type 555 Supersqualo. That was the year in which many races were cancelled, and the 555s started only fourteen times, recording nine finishes, with best placings being third in Belgium and Italy. The D50/801

types (erstwhile Lancias, see below) were preferred in 1956, although 555s (one of them actually using a Lancia V8 engine) were run in early-season Argentine races.

D50/801 Given cars that were potential worldbeaters – for the complete team of Lancia D50 cars was handed over to him at the end of 1955 – Ferrari set about transforming them into his own image. In part this was because his drivers wanted to change their handling characteristics.

Originally these were Lancia-Ferraris, but became ever-more different derivatives, for original designer Jano (who had

Dino 156/246 Originally conceived in 1956/1957, as an F2 car, fitted with a Jano-inspired dohc 65-degree V6 engine (the name came in honour of Ferrari's only legitimate son, Alfredino, who died at about the same time), this car had a chassis on 555 lines, the 1.5litre engine producing a claimed 190bhp on AvGas fuel, which would be compulsory in F1 in 1958.

Ferrari (-Lancia) D50/801 of 1956, Fangio driving.

Ferrari 156, mid-engined in 1961, Giancarlo Baghetti driving.

As an F2 car it was heavy but successful, and towards the end of the year it was run with engines of 2,195cc and 2,417cc, these effectively being 'field trials' for Ferrari's strategy for the 1958 F1 season.

The definitive 246, still a traditional front-engine/rear-drive car, appeared in 1958, with the 2,417cc (85 × 71mm) engine, in a derivative and smoothed-out version of the 156 – but it was already obsolescent, as in its first race, victory went to a rear-engined British car!

Dino 246s were successful on fast circuits in 1958, and Mike Hawthorn won the World Championship, even though he only won one race (France). Unhappily both Luigi Musso and Peter Collins were killed in Dino accidents in Grands Prix.

For 1959, several changes and improvements were made under Carlo Chiti (when the driving team was completely different). The lines were sleeker, while disc brakes (originally tried at Mike Hawthorn's insistence in 1958) were finally standardized. A 2,474cc (86 × 71mm) engine with 290bhp became available (the 256), and at the end of the

year a wishbone/coil-spring type of rear suspension was used. The car's advantage on fast circuits was almost whittled away, though Tony Brooks won the Grands Prix at Rheims and Avus (Germany).

In 1960 independent suspension all round was standard, the engine was moved back in the chassis, and side-mounted fuel tanks were adopted to preserve the balance. This was desperation, however, signalled more clearly at Monaco where the prototype rear-engined Ferrari first raced.

There was one last victory for the front-engined Dino – in the Italian GP of 1960, at Monza, where British teams did not contest a race that included the rough banked track for the last time. This was the last-ever Grand Prix victory for a front-engined car.

246P Stung by the success of small rear-engined British cars like the Cooper-Climax and Lotus-Climax types, Ferrari hastily designed its first rear-engined car, that was powered by a Dino 246 V6 engine. Dubbed the 246P, it had a tubular frame, independent suspension on 1960

front-engined Dino lines, and most unassuming styling.

It appeared only once, in the 1960 Monaco GP where, driven by Richie Ginther, it finished sixth. In almost every way it was the real ancestor of the Dino 156 types which were to follow in 1961.

Dino 156 Although carrying the same 'Dino' name as its predecessors and a development of the V6 engine, this was an entirely different type of Grand Prix car. Not only was it a rear-engined machine, but it was built specifically for the new 1.5litre Formula, which came into force in 1961.

This was the 'shark-nose' car of 1961, where the power of the V6 engines quite made up for chassis deficiencies. The team dominated the World Championship in the first season. Carlo Chiti was in charge of design. The 65-degree V6 was further developed, and later a 120-degree dohc V6 (73 × 58.8mm, 1,476cc) was also introduced. This was lighter, allowed a lower centre of gravity, and gave a reliable 190bhp. Mauro Forghieri, who was to be responsible for many Ferrari racing cars in the next quarter of a century, worked on its development. The rest of the car followed 246P lines, with a chassis built up around four large tubes.

The car was a winner from the very start, when young Baghetti won the Syracuse GP, and later he sensationally won the French GP in an independently run car. That apart, the 'works' team was beaten only twice in 1961 – by Stirling Moss at his brilliant best.

Von Trips won his first Grands Prix (in Holland and Britain) and seemed set for the Drivers' Championship, but was killed in an Italian GP accident. This then gifted the title to Phil Hill, winner of the Belgian and Italian races.

During the close season that followed, several key Ferrari executives left the company (joining ATS), and the team

started to use monocoques), retained the original front suspension but introduced a new single top link/lower wishbone/twin radius arm arrangement at the rear. Fuel injected versions of the V6 reputedly gave 200bhp. Towards the end of this season this engine was also used as a semi-stressed unit in a Forghieri-designed semi-monocoque intended to take a new V8 (it was dubbed Aero 156), which was used intermittently through 1964.

158 Apart from the Lancia-donated units of 1955, a V8 was a rare engine in the Ferrari repertoire. This particular 1.5litre unit appeared later than planned, with John Surtees driving a 158 to a debut win in the 1964 Syracuse GP.

The engine was a dohc 90-degree unit (64 × 57.8mm, 1,487cc) for which 210bhp

1512 With this car, Ferrari returned to using a twelve-cylinder engine, though this time a flat-twelve (56 × 50.4mm, 1,489cc) rather than a V12. Its maximum power was 220bhp, but it was temperamental until the closing races of the 1.5litre formula. It fitted in the 158 chassis, and was first raced towards the end of 1964. Surtees often preferred to race a 158 instead of a 1512, and the best Grand Prix placing for a 1512 was Bandini's second at Monaco in 1965.

246T Originally intended as a one-off for John Surtees to use in the 1966 Tasman series, it was not used for that purpose. However, as it was based around the 158 chassis, and had a useful 280/290bhp, it was a useful second string at the start of the new 3litre season in 1966 – Bandini placing it second at Monaco.

312 For the new 3litre formula, which bowed in for 1966, pundits proclaimed a return to power, but at first this was not borne out. Ferrari returned happily to using a development of its phenomenal V12 engine, then squandered its head start as team manager Dragoni was allowed to bluster Surtees out of the team.

In any case, approaching economies meant that the engine was not developed from scratch but was derived from a sportscar unit – an arena in which Ferrari had always excelled. This was a heavy 60-degree unit (77 × 53.5mm, 2,989cc), for which 360bhp was claimed, but 300bhp was more honest for its original outings.

Cylinder-head work soon brought improvements, and late in 1966 a three-valve version was introduced that did, indeed, deliver in the order of 360bhp. Chassis design and suspension layout of the first 312 cars was effectively carried over from the late 1.5litre cars. In a season in which much had been expected, very little was achieved. One Championship race was won by Surtees (before his sacking), and another by Scarfiotti.

The monocoque was revised for 1967, weight was pared off, and the engine was uprated to 390bhp. Parkes drove his own personal 'long-chassis' 312 to victory in the International Trophy, then enjoyed a dead heat with Scarfiotti in the Syracuse event. Then Bandini died after a ghastly accident at Monaco, Parkes retired after a serious accident in Belgium, and the season fell apart.

By the time of the Italian GP, Forghieri and Rocchi had completed a 48-valve

Ferrari 156, much changed by 1963, John Surtees driving in Monaco GP.

went into 1962 with the cars revised but still deficient in handling terms, and with the V6 now matched by the new generation of British (BRM and Coventry-Climax) V8s in the power race. That year, Ferrari's only F1 victories came in three secondary races.

The 1963-type 156 was only regarded as an interim car, to serve while new engines were completed. Forghieri laid out a lighter space frame (though Lotus had already

was claimed. The chassis was that which had already been seen in the Aero 156, and was only lightly modified. Apart from a second placing at Zandvoort (Holland), failures in minor components meant that Surtees did not start scoring consistently until the second half of the season, when with victories in the German and Italian GPs, and several second placings, he secured the Drivers' Championship. The 158 was also used in early-1965 races.

lightweight V12, which was good for 390bhp, although it was not for another year that this unit could equal the amazing new Ford-Cosworth DFV. For that year, too, the chassis was updated – and the 312s were once again competitive.

In Belgium the 312s ran with an aerofoil above their engine covers (mounted to the chassis) and with front nose trim tabs. Then, in the French GP, Jacky Ickx became the first F1 driver to win a race in a car fitted with 'wing' aerofoil devices. That was Ferrari's first Grand Prix win for almost two years, while second and third in the British GP looked good too – but after that there was only a third and a fourth in Championship races.

Ferrari came up with an adjustable rear aerofoil (automatic or driver-actuated) in late 1968, but the team's advantages were not exploited, in part because they were obliged to make economies, this leading to more support from Fiat.

In 1969, just one car was run in most of the season's races. The 312 chassis was slightly modified, and the engine developed to give 430bhp in testbed conditions, but there was low reliability on the tracks. Amon retired five times from seven starts, and walked out of the team; Pedro Rodriguez stepped in, and in the last race for a 312, in his home Grand Prix in Mexico City, finished seventh.

312B1 This new car marked the end of a bleak period for Ferrari. A 1969 agreement with Fiat was to safeguard the future of the team, and while its race effort that year (with the last of the 312s) might have

Ferrari Dino 246T, V6-engined, 1966, Lorenzo Bandini driving.

suffered from the absence of Forghieri, he was at least working on an all-new car that was to be a winner, though this seemed unlikely as its engine suffered persistent and prolonged teething troubles through the summer of 1969.

This was a compact flat-twelve ('B' in the designation of the car denoted 'Boxer' for the engine layout), the claimed output of this 2,991cc (78.5 × 51.5mm) engine in 1970 being 460bhp. It was

mounted under a rearward extension of the chassis, that was built on familiar Ferrari sheet alloy and tube lines.

The car was first tried with one of the old V12s fitted, but for 1970 the team was fully committed to the flat-twelve-engined type. It all came good in the second half of the season, with Jacky Ickx winning three Grands Prix, and Regazzoni the one that Ferrari really needed – the Italian GP at Monza.

312B2 A modified version of the 312B – though not necessarily for the better – the B2 had smoother lines, inboard rear suspension and a modified type of flat-twelve (80 × 49.6mm, 2,992cc) for which 485bhp was claimed.

Like other teams at this time, Ferrari had handling problems that stemmed from the latest tyres. Regazzoni gave the B2 a debut victory in the Race of Champions (Brands Hatch) in 1971, and Ickx won the Dutch GP in one, but overall the 1971 season was a disappointment for Ferrari. Despite constant revisions, to engine and suspension, 1972 was also just as disappointing, with just one Grand Prix victory for the B2, when driven by Ickx at the Nürburgring. The cars were used early into 1973, until deformable structure regulations made them instantly obsolete.

Ferrari 312 V12 of 1968, Jacky Ickx driving.

Ferrari 312B1 flat-twelve of 1971, Jacky Ickx driving.

Ferrari 312T flat-twelve of 1975, Clay Regazzoni driving.

312B3 This is the story of a transformation. The first car to carry the 'B3' designation was an ugly short-wheelbase machine, that was tested in 1973, but never raced. The second was the first true monocoque Ferrari – a construction forced on the team in order to meet new regulations.

Design was controlled by Sandro Colombo, as Forghieri was suffering from one of his periods of banishment from the F1 team.

Construction of three chassis was subcontracted to John Thompson's TC Prototypes, a British specialist concern. The car emerged with angular lines, initially smooth, that changed throughout 1973. It was run, for example, with side radiators or nose radiators, but to little good effect until Forghieri was recalled late in the summer.

For 1974 the lines became less angular, the cockpit was moved forward, and the engine was revised to give up to 495bhp. The team was also properly organized for

the first time in years (under Luca Montezemolo), with political intrigue quite ruled out, while Niki Lauda and Clay Regazzoni made a good driving duo. Lauda won two Grands Prix, Regga one, and the Ferrari team seemed to be solidly back in business.

312T In 1975 the team finally had a car that gave it a real edge, the 312 Trasversale, taking its 'T' designation from the gearbox that was installed across the car, instead of in an in-line position, and ahead of the rear axle line. This made for a responsive car, well-suited to Lauda's driving, and Ferrari also had a small power advantage over the DFV-powered runners.

Lauda won with a 312T in its first race in Europe (the International Trophy), won the third Grand Prix in which it was entered (at Monaco), and three further Grands Prix that season, while Regazzoni won two races (including the Italian, again).

Both Championships fell, deservedly, to the team, for the first time since 1964, the same pair of drivers won the first three Grands Prix of the 1976 season – and then the T2 arrived.

312T2 Because high air boxes had been outlawed, the appearance of Grand Prix cars had to change for 1976, and on the 312T this meant that neat air intakes and trunking were installed on each side of the high-sided cockpit. In the off-season a de Dion rear suspension was tested, but this was never used in racing.

The 1976 season saw 'nuts-and-bolts' aspects quite overwhelmed by dramatic events at the circuits, which was very unfortunate for new team manager Daniele Audetto. There were disqualifications (and reinstatements) as Lauda and McLaren driver James Hunt battled for the title, there was Lauda's terrible fiery accident at the Nürburgring, and his equally dramatic return at Monza. Lauda won three Grands Prix in T2s during that year, and while he did not win the Drivers' title these victories helped to ensure that Ferrari took the Constructors' title yet again.

The T2s served on until early-1978 races, with slightly more powerful flat-twelve engines, and minor revisions, and in 1977 they became very reliable. Lauda won three Championship races, and with points piled up from other good placings he became World Champion. He quit the team before the last two races of the season. For these Carlos Reutemann (who was fourth in the Championship) was joined by the young Gilles Villeneuve. Ferrari again dominated the Constructors' Championship.

312T3 New less-rounded body lines, a new monocoque and a new type of front suspension, largely designed to suit the Michelin radial-ply tyres now adopted by Ferrari for 1978, distinguished this car. Reutemann won three races in the season, in T3s, and Villeneuve scored his maiden victory in Montreal, on the circuit later to be named after him. During the off-season, Ferrari had to experiment with ground effects, running T3s with skirts. Despite shortcomings, these were used in the two opening races of the 1979 season.

ending to the 1970–80 story of the illustrious flat-twelve power unit.

126CK Ferrari's first turbocharged F1 car appeared in the summer of 1980, and was run in practice for that year's Italian GP. Its first race start was at Long Beach (USA) early in 1981, and it first finished a race at Imola later in the year.

Throughout the season it underwent a sometimes difficult process of development, as the chassis and running gear all called for refinement. In mid-1981, Ferrari hired Harvey Postlethwaite to design a new monocoque, hoping at least to get on terms with the British constructors.

Ferrari designers, however, had a very sure touch with the new engine, for the car was powered by a 120-degree V6 (81

coil spring/damper suspension broadly carried over from the 126CK, and the V6 with turbocharger modifications aimed at further reducing throttle response lag, driving through the transverse gearbox.

Through the year the engine was improved and pullrod suspension was introduced, but mechanical developments were overshadowed. Pironi snatched victory in the Imola race from Villeneuve, and at the very next GP meeting (Belgium) the Canadian was killed in an accident during practice. Patrick Tambay took his place, and after Pironi had been seriously injured in a Hockenheim (Germany) practice accident in rain and poor visibility, he won that German race.

Mario Andretti then returned to Ferrari for the two late season races. Out of

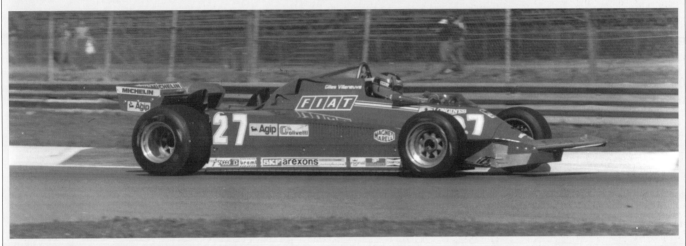

Ferrari 126CK (turbo V6), 1981, with Gilles Villeneuve driving.

312T4/312T5 The T4 served for most of the 1979 season – very effectively so, for its drivers, Scheckter and Villeneuve, were first and second in the Drivers' Championship, while the team clearly won the Constructors' Championship.

It was a ground effects car, built around a narrow monocoque, but with the built-in handicap of the flat-twelve engine intruding into the area important in ground effects terms. Suspension was tucked out of the undercar airflow, and upper body surfaces were broad and flat.

The cars were rebuilt as T5s for 1980, with revised suspension, bodies and aerodynamics, and while it was not to be expected that the 1978 tally of six victories could be repeated, a wretched failure was a real surprise. Ferrari was tenth in the Constructors' Championship, in a sad

× 48.4mm, 1,496cc) that was to serve the team well. It was tested both with a Brown-Boveri Comprex supercharger, and with twin KKK turbochargers.

Learning from all this, Ferrari chose to race with the turbocharged engine, despite its initial poor throttle response and high thirst, and tried to sort out the chassis race by race, for in ground effects terms it was never more than mediocre. Villeneuve was the man to drive over, and around, such problems, and he did so to such good effect that in the face of all probability he won the Monaco and Spanish GPs of 1981. The next best placing for the team was his third place, in Canada.

126C2 For his first Ferrari chassis design, in 1982 Postlethwaite used a honeycomb monocoque, with the rocker arm/inboard

the year's dramas and tragedies came success, for Ferrari won the Constructors' Championship.

In a 'B' flat-bottom version, the same but modified cars served through the first half of 1983, when a revised rear suspension arrangement was introduced. There were two more Grand Prix victories (at Imola and Montreal) before the C3 was introduced.

126C3–C4 Although outwardly similar to the final 126C2B, the C3 had Ferrari's first in-house carbon-fibre monocoque, which was combined with the earlier car's suspension, and of course with the turbo V6 that had around 625bhp available. The cars were first raced in the 1983 British GP, and Arnoux won the German and Dutch GPs in the same year, to help clinch another Constructors' Championship for Ferrari.

As the C4, the design was further developed for 1984, with up to 660bhp regularly on tap, but with two types of engine management system tried as the 220litre fuel tank size limit was a worrying new factor. As the year went by, though, this was not the only worry, for although the cars were constantly being revised they were only spasmodically competitive. Michele Alboreto – the first Italian to drive a Ferrari Grand Prix car since 1975 – won the Belgian Grand Prix, but as runners-up in the Constructors' Championship, Ferrari did not remotely challenge the dominant McLaren-TAG team.

156/85 There were upheavals on the personality side in 1984. Forghieri was once again removed from the racing side of Ferrari, this time permanently, and soon took himself off to do what he knew best – to design new racing engines.

Ildo Renzetti from Fiat took on engine development, to face the uphill task of attempting to combat the TAG-Porsche power supremacy, in this turning to a new alloy-block version of the existing turbo V6.

Postlethwaite designed a new chassis, and outwardly the car was sleeker than before. The whole ensemble was subject to revision through the season, when the engine did not produce enough power, and was markedly fragile when attempts were made to remedy the deficiency by increasing the boost.

That state of affairs led to a compromise in aerodynamic settings that were intended to reduce drag, but these also reduced grip. Alboreto managed to win two Grands Prix, however, in Canada and Germany, and Ferrari was once again runner-up in the Constructors' Championship.

F186 In effect the 1986 car was a substantial redesign of the 1985 model, and there was a return to an iron-block engine, which was more reliable and allowed even more power to be delivered. Garrett turbos took the place of KKK units throughout the year. There were some handling problems, and traction was poor on some circuits. Fortunes slumped, too – no Grand Prix victories, and only fourth place in the Constructors' Championship.

F187 and **F187/88C** This was time for a new start. Gustav Brunner was briefly

Ferrari F186 of 1986, driven by Stefan Johansson.

very prominent in the chassis design team, there was some input (suspension, particularly) from John Barnard/GTO in the UK, and some ex-Renault expertise was also brought in. A pullrod double wishbone arrangement was used, and there was yet another new engine, a 90-degree V6 (for which the same internal dimensions were quoted), and for which 880bhp was claimed, driving through a new longitudinal six-speed gearbox.

The car looked a winner from the start, but it was not a consistent winner on the circuits until the end of the season, when Gerhard Berger won the Japanese and Australian GPs. Ferrari's efforts were, perhaps, distracted by an Indycar project at this time – but such a car was never completed, or tested.

The 1987 design was reworked for 1988 as the F187/88C, this being a year when Enzo Ferrari himself died and when there was turmoil in the team as executive and technical personnel went, and – less frequently – came. The car was a little slimmer, the aerofoils were revised, fuel consumption was improved (which it had to be, to align with the new maximum fuel allowance of 150 litres), though the car never challenged McLaren over a complete race distance. There was one lucky win, at Monza, when the McLaren effort failed. Some detail development work was carried

through in the (2.5 Bar) twilight year of turbocharged cars.

640 (F189) Here was the start of a new era for Ferrari – and for Grand Prix racing. As turbocharged engines were henceforth banned, this was the first normally aspirated Ferrari F1 car since 1980, and the first of a whole series of V12 and V10-engined machines to be campaigned before the end of the century.

A normally aspirated development car, the 639, was extensively tested in 1988, but never raced. Later that year, and ready for 1989, came the 640 (or F189, a title mentioned but not used), which was the second complete Ferrari designed by the John Barnard team.

A sharp-nosed car, it had a narrow monocoque but bulging flanks that housed the radiators for the new 65-degree V12 engine, and the bodywork tailed back to a sharply nipped-in rear. Effective aerodynamic performance was essential, as only 600bhp was claimed for the V12 at the start of the campaign, this not being sufficient to match the Honda engines that powered McLaren at the time. A double wishbone pushrod suspension system used torsion bars.

Although there was opposition from Fiat, Barnard also insisted on the use of an electro-hydraulic gear change, which was the 640's most radical feature. Although there were teething problems, its value was soon proved. Like many such systems that followed, the driver only needed a clutch pedal to start from rest. Two levers behind the steering wheel looked after upward and downward changes, there being seven forward ratios. There was no gear-linkage in the conventional sense, for operation of clutch and gearbox was by electronically actuated valves.

The 640 was clever and sleek, and also very strong (as Berger's early-season high-speed accident proved). Nigel Mansell, new to the team, drove the 640 to a Brazilian GP debut victory, won in Hungary, was twice second and twice third, while Berger won in Portugal and was second in two other races.

Ferrari was third in the Constructors' Championship, which all looked very promising for the future.

641 There were high hopes for Ferrari's new 1990 contender, not merely because John Barnard had inspired the 641 before he moved out to Benetton, but because Alain Prost had joined Nigel Mansell in the driving team, and ex-Lancia team boss Cesare Fiorio was now to run the cars at the circuit.

As ever, there was bound to be plenty of power from the V12 engine, the budget was higher than anyone else's, and excellence was expected. If it had not been for Ayrton Senna's bullish behaviour at Suzuka, where he rammed his McLaren into the back of Prost's Ferrari after the start, the Frenchman could so easily have been World Champion in his first year with Ferrari.

Steve Nichols had arrived from McLaren to engineer the car, Enrique Scalabroni had arrived from Williams, both the drivers urged improvements to the V12 engine (that duly arrived), and the 641s improved significantly throughout the year. The most significant car problems, throughout the year, were engine failure, and the transmission and its delicate controls that were on paddles behind the steering wheel.

In this, his second season with Ferrari, Mansell's problem was that he did not like being out-driven by Prost, he was regularly upset, occasionally parked perfectly healthy cars, and had decided to leave well before the end of the year. Prost was as smooth and analytical as usual.

The results speak for themselves: Prost seventy-one points (including five wins),

Mansell thirty-seven points (but only one victory and, importantly, nine retirements). At this point Ferrari's fortunes seemed to be on the up.

642 New from the very start of the 1991 season, with Alain Prost now partnered by Jean Alesi, great things were expected of the 642 – but rarely realized. Was the 642 a disappointment? Let's just point out that the *next* new Ferrari F1 car – 643 – would appear within six months – and that, according to team-leader Alain Prost, he had had his worst season so far.

Personnel upheavals (nothing new at Ferrari) caused all manner of car problems. Enrique Scalabroni had wanted to design an all-new car for 1991, but left precipitately, so Steve Nichols and Jean Claude Migeot (ex-Tyrrell) had no option but to rejig the 641 to 'take advantage' of new and tighter aerofoil regulations. Except that it did not.

Team-leader Alain Prost was so disappointed in the car that an urgent redesign followed, the result being the launch of the 643 (the 642 with more bells and whistles) in July 1991.

643 Although early-1991 experience showed that Ferrari needed a new car – and quickly – to match McLaren and Williams, this was not practically possible. The 643 was really 642 plus a Tyrrell 019-clone high nose. First appearing in the French GP in mid-1991, it was no more successful than its predecessor.

In 1991 Prost and Alesi did not record a single win, but could raise only three seconds and five thirds between them. Not only that, but of thirty-two car starts, there would be crashes or retirements in sixteen of them – seven due to a fragile V12 engine.

For a natural 'mid-field' team this might have been acceptable, but for Ferrari it lined up as a national disaster and disgrace. Well before the end of the year Prost had lost all patience with a shambolic effort, said so in public and (typical, this, from Ferrari) was sacked before the season's last race – Australia – for telling the truth. His replacement, Gianni Morbidelli, was simply not in the same class.

F92A The previous season having been described as a shambles by many observers, it was thought that the 1992 Ferrari programme had to be more successful. Wrong. From thirty-two car starts during the year,

the hapless F92A only struggled to the finish eleven times, the team celebrating just two podium positions.

One should have inevitably sensed doom when Ferrari said they would be governed by a committee of three in 1991, rather than one strong man. That, uninspired drivers, and an awful car, duly delivered Ferrari's worst season for many years. Steve Nichols left in disgust and not even the return of Luca di Montezemolo and Dr Harvey Postlethwaite could change that at once.

As a racing car the F92A simply didn't work. Gorgeous, and apparently aerodynamically sleek, it used a much-vaunted 'twin floor' underside that proved to be ineffective. Mechanical grip and road-holding were lacking, the active suspension took ages to settle and – of all things – the V12 engine didn't seem to be competitive. And, if a Ferrari wasn't the most powerful of all, it was surely nothing?

Nice man though he was, Ivan Capelli eventually stretched Ferrari's patience too far, for in fourteen races he crashed the car six times: his late-season replacement, Nicola Larina was just … slow.

F93A Another poor car, and another poor F1 season for Ferrari, and because they now had two top-class drivers (Alesi and Berger) there was no viable excuse for any of it. The latest V12 engine was now struggling against its opposition (it couldn't match the Renault V10 or Ford-Cosworth's fully matured HB V8) and if Ferrari couldn't produce class-leading engines, they would always be lost.

The team, at least, struggled hard, threw money at the problem, and even took advice from Honda on engine developments – who recommended that five-valve technology should be dropped in favour of a well-proven four-valve layout, which worked immediately.

But it wasn't easy. Even so, like other well-funded F1 cars of the day, the F93A had all the toys, including semi-automatic transmission, traction control and active suspension.

The new car was designed by ex-Tyrrell engineer George Ryton, who abandoned the disastrous twin-floor arrangement of the F92A, but it was still only thought of as an 'interim' machine before the hoped-for Barnard-designed machine took over in 1994.

The result? Only twenty-eight points in the entire season – sixteen of them for

Ferrari F93A (V12) of 1993, Gerhard Berger at the wheel.

Alesi. If Gerhard Berger had not been cushioned by a huge salary, he might have been even more depressed.

All change again for 1994?

412T1 Except that here was yet another way of describing a Ferrari F1 car by type number, for 1994, it seemed, there was going to be a fair amount of stability *and* continuity in the Maranello. The team, no question about it, was on the way back, for with new team director Jean Todt (ex-Peugeot) now in charge, they clawed their way up to a solid third in the Constructors' Championship.

Still with a 775bhp/65-degree V12 engine (for which Engineer Osamu Goto,

ex-Honda, took much of the credit), the Barnard-designed 412T1 was a gorgeous-looking creation, but proved rather difficult to drive. With gizmos like semi-automatic transmission, traction control and active ride suspension now banned, this was perforce a simpler car, though Barnard turned it into a miracle of packaging (the V12 was bulky), particularly around the front suspension, where everything was neatly packaged above and ahead of the driver's feet. Detail innovations in the front suspension included what was known as 'knife-edge' pick-up points for the suspension inner joints.

It was less gorgeous, but more effective, after the later engine required bulges

around its extremities for, from Hockenheim, a new-generation 75-degree V12 (supposedly with 820bhp) took over.

Gerhard Berger won once, and added two second places and three thirds, while Alesi added a second and three third places, and (while Alesi recovered from injury) even stand-in driver Nicola Larini managed one second place too: not bad for a year in which the latest Williams and Schumacher's Benetton-Ford spent most of the year disputing victory.

412T2 After the thwarted resurgence of 1994, much was expected of the 412T2 model, new for the 1995 season, when all engines were limited to 3litres. With

Ferrari 412T2 of 1995, V12-engined, Gerhard Berger driving.

John Barnard overseeing design, with Jean Todt directing the team on-track, and with excellent drivers, was there really any excuse for failure to win every crown?

No excuse, perhaps, though many were made. 'Next year' became a familiar Ferrari refrain through the late 1990s, this year being no different. In the end the 412T2 was good enough to deliver third in the Constructors' Championship, yet there was only one race victory – Alesi in Canada, and that quite unexpected.

Distinguished by its low nose (when rivals were mostly following Benetton's original high-nose approach), at a casual glance the T2 looked like a logical advance over the T1. Although all components had been reworked, the fuel tank was much smaller; indeed the whole car was smaller. Suspension mountings were back to uniball types, after one season with knife-edge pick-ups. The latest engine was still a V12 (neither power nor internal dimensions were quoted), but with a steel instead of iron block, and 10kg (22lb) had been saved: a V10, it seemed, was already being designed: other weight-saving came from the use of a carbon-fibre transmission bellhousing. The cockpit was now a two-pedal layout, with the clutch operated by a paddle under the steering wheel.

F310 This was the first year in which Luca di Montezemolo's philosophy became clear. He would spend whatever it took to make Ferrari into consistent World Champions again, and (to quote Fiat's Gianni Agnelli) 'if Ferrari doesn't win with Michael Schumacher, it will be our fault'.

From the previous year to this, it was a major clear-out, with a new car, a new V10 engine, and new drivers. On balance, better but not yet good enough. Michael Schumacher won three races, finished second three times and third twice. Eddie Irvine, by comparison, trailed. The Barnard-designed F310 helped Ferrari take second in the Constructors' series. Not good enough, but a start.

Still with a low nose until mid-season, the F310 was a rather bulky-looking Ferrari, the first-ever car from Maranello to use a four-valve V10 engine – though not at all reliable at first. It had taken time for Ferrari to wean themselves away from their beloved V12, but in packaging, fuel efficiency and power terms the V10 eventually seemed to be the best solution.

According to designer Barnard, who had spent a lot of Ferrari's money in wind-tunnel testing, it was more aerodynamically efficient than before – but humble pie was then eaten when a high-nose layout was adopted partway through the year.

This was the year, too, when Ferrari tired of having cars designed in the UK, by a personality who never visited the races. In 1997 it would be different – Schumacher saw to that.

Ferrari F310 of 1996, Ferrari's first V10-engined car.

F310B Better than in 1996, more effective, and producing more victories than before, the new F310B's team performance was quite spoiled when Michael Schumacher tried to drive Villeneuve's Williams off the road in the Spanish GP, failed, and then had his entire season's points (and victories) removed.

Although Benetton's dynamic duo – Ross Brawn and Rory Byrne – both joined Ferrari for the 1997 season, they did not influence the design of the F310B that they had to campaign; this had been conceived by John Barnard's FDD organization before he parted with the Italian concern early in 1997.

As its title suggests, the 1997 contender was a revision and update on the 1996 machine. Broadly satisfied with what had been achieved in 1996, Barnard's team designed the F310B to improve on all that. The V10 engine was

an uprated version of the 1996 unit (that, itself, had been brand-new), the gearbox, bellhousing and entire rear suspension all being the same as before, while the torsion bar front suspension and some aerodynamic features all nodded to what Williams had already been doing.

Many detailed packaging and aerodynamic changes were made to accord with the latest rules on cockpit dimensions and rollover safety. If the F310B had a fundamental problem, it seemed to be in its handling, for the centre of gravity was said to be too high.

In spite of Schumacher's reckless tendencies, Ferrari kept all its manufacturers' points, finishing a close second behind Williams. Schumacher, pre-Spain, finished first five times, but had all those victories annulled. Irvine, self-admittedly not as talented, had five podium finishes.

F300 The first, and extremely effective F1 Ferrari from the Brawn/Byrne design partnership ran through 1998, a good car but not a great car – unless, of course, you discount the McLaren MP4-13s which regularly beat it.

Although it had to comply with the latest regulations, the F300 was evolved from the F310B in every way, and was almost infinitely adjustable. Seven different front wings and five different rears were used during the year, the wheelbase could be longer or shorter, and the front-suspension was capable of speedy adjustment at pit stops.

From mid-season, the engine exhaust was redirected through the top of the side-pods: this reduced the temperature of the gearbox, and proved not to have any aerodynamic disadvantages. 'X' wings, those horrid little add-ons tacked on to side-pod pillars, were used in mid-season, but swiftly banned.

Because the entire team was built around Schumacher, Eddie Irvine had to make do with what was provided, but seemed to like this car much better than in previous years. Although no match for Schumacher, he still notched up forty-seven points, with eight podium positions (but no victory).

Helped along by the adulation of team-manager Jean Todt, Schumacher was just Schumacher, and almost capable of matching the McLarens: in sixteen races he won six times – Argentina, Canada, France, Britain, Hungary and Italy – and also took five other podium finishes. Even so, he could only take second place in the Drivers' series, as could Ferrari themselves in the Constructors'.

This, no question, was the most effective Ferrari for some years, and there were high hopes for 1999.

F399 This was breakthrough time for Ferrari, but only in one respect. After many barren years, the team won the Constructors' Championship, but Michael Schumacher's own series was spoilt by a first-lap British GP crash (the brakes had failed) that broke his leg, and kept him out of the next six races too. For once, it seemed, the season could not unfold to Bernie's script.

Even though the newly imposed four-groove tyres made handling a bit more knife-edge, both the drivers seemed to enjoy the F399, described by observers as a 'benign', easy-to-drive machine. Even so, its aerodynamic performance was not ideal, for it didn't seem to be as slippery as the latest McLaren.

The major technical innovation was to the rear suspension, which used horizontal torsion bars located above the gearbox, these being speedily adjustable at track side, as was the suspension ride height.

The team's major disaster was the loss of Schumacher during the season, for Irvine was never quite as fast, and Mika Salo no more than a competent stand-in. Schumacher won three times before his Silverstone shunt, and Irvine four times throughout the season, but in Japan, where it mattered, Eddie could not match Hakkinen's McLaren. By this time, in any case, he had revealed his 2000 plans – which were to be with Jaguar.

F1-2000 Claimed to have made a huge aerodynamic advance compared with the 1999 car, the new-for-2000 Ferrari looked evolutionary in almost every respect. Yet under the similar-but-not-the-same looks was a new-generation Type 049 V10 engine (this time with a 90-degree instead of an 80-degree angle), a physically smaller, but seven-speed, gearbox, and torsion bar suspensions containing mostly carbon components.

Recognizably from the same pedigree as before, the new car had a typically high nose, large and effective barge boards, the latest fashionable 'periscope' exhaust system (aircraft had this well over 50 years earlier, by the way), and the same stunning Marlboro-with-scarlet colour scheme.

Although the technical team – Brawn + Byrne + Todt – was as before, there was one major driving change. With Schumacher's leg fully recovered, the German was now to be partnered by Rubens Barrichello (ex-Stewart), for Eddie Irvine had moved to Jaguar (ex-Stewart) in his place. The 2000 campaign was a triumph, with Schumacher becoming World Champion (including a record number of race victories), Barrichello winning his first-ever Grand Prix – and Ferrari winning its second consecutive Constructors' Championship.

Unless the team was to win every race it started, there was no way that it could improve on this – or was there?

Ferrari F300 of 1998, V10-engined, Michael Schumacher as lead driver.

The great Italian company entered racing in the first year of the twentieth century and was still heavily involved in its last year, in the name of one of its companies, Ferrari. It enjoyed golden periods in Grand Prix racing, first with typically large cars in the Edwardian era, then in the first half of the 1920s with sophisticated cars that set a pattern that was to be widely followed. Fiat then withdrew from Grand Prix racing. However, in 1955 Gianni Agnelli arranged for the cars and equipment of the Lancia racing department to be taken over by Ferrari, together with a Fiat subsidy to ensure that the D50 cars were raced, to uphold the honour of Italian automotive technology. From the early 1960s Fiat's role in ensuring the survival of Ferrari was much stronger, and from the late 1970s the name Fiat was prominent on the engine covers of F1 Ferraris. Following the death of Enzo Ferrari, the team that had so faithfully mirrored his character increasingly became Fiat's Formula 1 racing arm.

Those first F.I.A.T. Grand Prix cars may have looked typical 'giant' racers of the period, but they had advanced engines with pushrod-operated overhead valves. In 1907, when the name 'Fiat' was generally used, similar Fiats won the season's four major races.

Big chain-drive cars were raced through to 1912, new Grand Prix types failed in 1914 and did not shine in 1921, but a neat new car was a winner in 1922 and then Fiat introduced the supercharger to Grand Prix racing in 1923. The company generally withdrew from racing in 1925, but continued to build experimental racing engines and then raced a car with a complex 12-cylinder engine just once. A win for that Tipo 806 in the Milan GP was the last for a Fiat Grand Prix car. Sadly that car, and all those built from 1922 to 1925, then disappeared. Only faithful scale replicas made by Fiat apprentices remind us of a glorious period.

As Fiat turned away from the Grands Prix, its major international competitions effort was directed to the Schneider Trophy contest for aircraft. At least the company became a major provider of competitive small sports cars.

'100hp' This 1906 Grand Prix car was developed from the 1905 Gordon type, when two of the three cars finished second and third. In their massive frames the three cars entered for the 1906 Grand Prix were conventional, the four-cylinder

Fiat Taunus of 1907, Felice Nazzaro driving.

ohv engines were in 16,286cc form, giving 110bhp at 1,200rpm, and chain drive was used (in common with four other Grand Prix types). The cars were within a kilo of the 1,007kg (2,220lb) maximum weight limit. These were the only cars in the race at Le Mans to have artillery wheels with detachable rims all round that gave worthwhile advantages when tyre failures were frequent.

Much was expected of the team, but Felice Nazzaro in its leading car was out of touch in third place at half distance. He eventually finished second, more than half an hour behind the winning Renault, while Lancia was fifth in another F.I.A.T. and Weillschott crashed the third car of the team.

'130hp' The 1907 cars followed closely similar lines, but were slightly heavier while the engines developed 130bhp at 1,600rpm. In 1907, Nazzaro convincingly beat the 1906 Grand Prix winner, winning the 477 mile (770km) French race at Dieppe at 70.61mph (114kph), while his team mates Wagner and Lancia retired. However, Wagner won the American

Grand Prize while Nazzaro was third. Nazzaro also won the Targa Florio and the Kaiserpreis with an 8litre engine in the Grand Prix chassis.

SB4 The 1908 Grand Prix was run to regulations (the 'Ostend Formula') that imposed a minimum weight limit of 1,100kg (2,425lb) and limited the cylinder bore to 155mm for four-cylinder engines or 127mm for sixes. Fiat stayed with the overhead-valve four-cylinder format, with a 12,045cc engine producing some 100bhp. This also incorporated production components, and in the Grand Prix engine-failures accounted for two Fiats (Nazzaro's after he had led the opening phase) and Lancia's. Wagner also led but retired. His victory in the American Grand Prize was some compensation for Fiat, especially as Nazzaro was third.

The ACF did not run a Grand Prix again until 1912, but the SB4s were still raced. Seemingly, Vincenzo Lancia drove one of these cars when he won the 1909 Targa Florio, while it is assumed that Ed Parker was driving one when he took second place in the Vanderbilt Cup.

Fiat S74 of 1911, David Bruce-Brown driving.

However, both cars could have been S61s. This was a limited production machine on general SB4 lines, best described using a later term as a sports-racing car. None of the three cars in the 1910 American Grand Prize finished, and there was little real glory in Victor Hémery's win in the 1911 Grand Prix de France, for that was dubbed the Grand Prix des Vieux Tacots – 'old crocks' race!

S74 This was the least effective Grand Prix car of the first generation, a big car with a thumping 14,137cc four-cylinder engine and chain drive. But although the car appeared archaic, that engine was an efficient ohc unit that delivered as much as 190bhp.

David Bruce-Brown drove one to win the 1911 American Grand Prize. In France, for the revived Grand Prize in 1912, these giants met the cars of a new generation, and almost held their own – Bruce-Brown led before being disqualified in the 956 mile (1,540km) race at Dieppe, while Louis Wagner finished second in one of the Fiats. De Palma was also disqualified.

Bragg won the 1912 Grand Prize in an S74, and the larger-than-life Barney Old-field was fourth (he took the place of Bruce-Brown, who was killed in a training accident). The S74s were still raced by independent entrants in 1913–14, although they were not eligible for the Grand Prix.

S57 Fiat's 1914 Grand Prix car appeared up to the minute, with an sohc 4,492cc four-cylinder engine that had a claimed output of 135bhp at 3,000rpm, and four-wheel brakes. However, in the Grand Prix the Fiats did not match the speed of the Mercedes, with an engine giving 115bhp.

Two Fiats retired, leaving Fagnano to finish the French race in a very distant eleventh, and last, place. The S57s were reworked, with enlarged engines, for the 1917 Indianapolis 500. That race was cancelled, and they were not seen in races until 1919–21, when the most notable result was Masetti's win in the 1921 Targa Florio (Antonio Ascari won two minor 1919 events in these Fiats, at the start of his illustrious career).

Tipo 801 Built for the 1920–21 3litre formula, this was first run in an interim form in 1920, and not raced until the following year. In some respects it harked back to the S57, and at first had the 401 dohc four-cylinder engine, with an output of 112bhp.

With the 402 straight eight, these Fiats were ready for the 1921 Gran Premio d'Italia – Grand Prix racing was no longer an exclusively French sport in Europe (that first Italian GP was run at Brescia). The 402 engine gave 115bhp, and at Brescia the Fiats were fastest by a small margin. But Sivocci crashed on the first lap, Bordino led but retired, and that left Wagner to finish third behind two Ballots (the veteran had to make five stops to change tyres).

Tipo 804 For Fiat's 1922 2litre Grand Prix car, Giulio Cesare Cappa headed the design team that included Bazzi, Becchia, Bertarione, Jano and Zerbi – an outstandingly talented group assembled by overall design director Guido Fornaca. They drew on experience, particularly in the 404 straight-six engine, which had the same bore as the 402. The capacity of this dohc unit was 1,991cc; for its first race it gave 95bhp, but later in 1922 it was rated at 112bhp. Following Fiat practice, there was a four-speed gearbox in unit with the engine. The car was compact and neat, weighing in at 662kg (1,455lb), slightly above the minimum permitted weight. The Tipo 804 proved fastest on every sector of the Strasbourg circuit when the car made its debut in the 1922 French GP. Felice Nazzaro soon outpaced the field, and won by an outrageous margin – the Bugatti placed second was almost an hour behind. However, Nazzaro's nephew

Fiat 801 of 1921, Pietro Bordino at the wheel.

Fiat 804 of 1922, Nazzaro at the wheel.

supercharger intakes of the three Fiat 805s were not shielded, and road debris caused them to fail on all three team cars.

For the next race, the Italian GP, Roots-type superchargers were fitted, power was up to 140bhp, and Salamano and Nazzaro were comfortably first and second. That was the first Grand Prix victory for a supercharged car. The cars were refined for 1924, when the engines developed 145bhp, a little more than the Alfa Romeo P2 designed by Jano and Bazzi on Fiat lines. A P2 won the French GP, and all three Fiats retired. There were no Fiats at Monza for the Italian GP: Agnelli was not pleased to see his cars beaten by cars designed by ex-Fiat men, and withdrew the Fiat team from racing. One 805 was raced in America by Bordino in 1925, and he placed it twelfth at Indianapolis.

Tipo 806   In 1926, a Fiat opposed-piston two-stroke 1.5litre engine designed by Zerbi was tested, but failed to deliver competitive power and was never run in a Grand Prix car. But it was followed by the twin-six 406 engine, in the low-slung Tipo 806. The Roots-type supercharged engine had three overhead camshafts, the central one operating the inlet valves, and twin crankshafts. By the time it was raced, it delivered 187bhp, more than enough for Bordino to see off second-line opposition in the 1927 Milan GP. That was the last Grand Prix Fiat to race.

Biagio was killed when the back axle of his Fiat failed, and Bordino was eliminated with a similar fault. Brodino and Nazzaro then finished first and second in the Italian GP. Bertarione was the first member of the design team to defect, to design the 1923 GP Sunbeam that followed the 804 in general and in many details.

Tipo 805   For 1923 Fiat produced a car as neat as the Tipo 804, and with a supercharged 1,979cc straight eight. This dohc power unit was introduced with a Wittig low-pressure supercharger, which for its first race gave 130bhp at 5,500rpm, an average of at least 15bhp over the best of the rest in a glittering French GP field.

Bordino was almost out of sight of the rest at the end of the first lap of that 1923 French GP, and at three laps only a Sunbeam broke into the Fiat procession. But a 'Fiat in green paint' was to win, for the

continued from p.85

FD01   The first Fittipaldi car – which almost inevitably was first shown in Brasilia – was mechanically conventional and eye-catching with lines that were rounded beside the monocoque, angular at the nose, and with squared-off aerofoils. Double wishbone and outboard coil-springs suspension was used at the front, with upper and lower links, radius rods and outboard springs at the rear. Inevitably, Cosworth DFV engines and Hewland gearboxes were used. The water radiator was in the tail, and seemingly ineffectual as for the car's second race conventional radiators flanked the engine. At the same time the rear suspension was revised for the first time. The car was troublesome, and the first FD01 spun wildly out of its first race. In any case, Wilson Fittipaldi was not a development driver, or a top-rate race driver. He finished six Grand Prix in 1975, for a best placing of tenth (in the USA); when he was injured, Merzario took his place for the Italian GP, was slowest in practice and

eleventh in the race. The third (of three) cars built was driven by Ingo Hoffman in the first race of 1976.

FD04   Divila's second Fittipaldi design was to serve through 1976 and on into 1977. Early in the first of those seasons a two-car team was run, before the effort was sensibly concentrated on the number one driver, Emerson Fittipaldi. Outwardly, FD04 was a nicely balanced car, with a chisel nose, neat body lines, and large side radiators. Components such as the suspension followed FD01 lines. Two of the quartet were built in Britain but little development was undertaken.

Emerson Fittipaldi scored the team's first point at Long Beach, but the season was disappointing. He finished eight races (with two more sixth placings, at Monaco and Silverstone), but his inexperienced team mate Hoffman failed to qualify an FD04 in his three attempts.

In 1977 Fittipaldi scored in three of the first four races with the revised cars that were used for eight races. Fourth places fell to him in Argentina and Brazil, and fifth at Long Beach. Hoffman was sixth in Brazil, but he only drove in the South American races.

F5   Dave Baldwin designed this car, which resembled his last Ensign, and he moved on again before it was raced, which cannot have helped F5 development. In specification, this was another orthodox Cosworth-Hewland kit car, outwardly similar to the last Divila car in all save its side pods. The F5 was not competitive, and in particular there were handling shortcomings. To set against one scoring finish (fourth in Holland), Fittipaldi, twice failed to qualify.

Giacomo Caliri's Fly Studio revised the F5 as a ground effects car for 1978, notably with new suspension and long side pods.

This F5A proved to be the most successful Fittipaldi in points-scoring terms. Emerson's second place in Brazil was a high point – the high point in the teams history – and it was backed up by two fourth places, two fifths and a sixth for that seventh place in the Constructors' Championship.

The cars were uprated for use in 1979, and served through to the British GP because of shortcomings in the replacement

for a two-car team was run. Fittipaldi and Keke Rosberg enjoyed some success with F7s, each taking a third place, while Emerson was also sixth once (his third place at Long Beach was his last podium finish in a Grand Prix).

F8 Postlethwaite followed a Wolf line of evolution in the F8, notably in its honeycomb monocoque and suspension, and outwardly in the long side pods and short nose.

and he finished only three races, scoring Fittipaldi's last point in the Belgian GP.

F9 This was a one-off, driven by Serra at six meetings, when he reached the grids three times and finished each of those races, with a best placing seventh in Austria (the last effective runner). The car was attributed to Divila and Tim Wright, and followed the same lines as the F8, with the cockpit well forward. It looked purposeful, but it was a DFV-powered car in the turbo age, and it was outclassed. The Italian GP proved to be the last for the team, as Serra failed to qualify to start in the US GP.

Fomet

This name lasted for just one season, 1991, before giving way to the logical Fondmetal title – Gabriele Rumi owned the Fondmetal wheels company that had previously backed Osella and in effect took over that team as a basis for his own. He moved the assets to a new home, and the design responsibility was taken on by Fomet 1 in England, and two cars were to be built (an Osella was used early in the season). It proved an inauspicious first year for the little team that effectively reappeared as Fondmetal in 1992.

F1 The first Fomet F1 appeared at the third race of 1991. Designed by Tino Belli and Tim Holloway of Fomet 1, it was a straightforward Cosworth DFR-powered machine that proved far from competitive despite some refinement contributed by Richard Divila.

Olivier Grouillard was the driver at thirteen meetings, but he failed to pre-qualify eight times, and he finished only one race (tenth in Belgium). Gabriele Tarquini took his place for the last three Grands Prix of 1991, and he finished in two (twelfth and eleventh).

Two revised cars, named Fondmetal and designated GR01, were run in the first six races of 1992, unsuccessfully.

Fittipaldi-Ford F9 of 1982, Chico Serra driving.

car. Fittipaldi scored his only point of the year with F5A/2 in the Argentine GP.

F6 Journeyman designer Ralph Bellamy was responsible for the 1979 car, a full ground effects machine that looked the part. However, it was not effective in ground effects terms, and when Caliri reworked it as the F6A to overcome that failing some outright speed was lost. The DFV was still used, with Hewland gearboxes. The two cars built were set aside at the end of the season.

F7 Wolf WR8–9 were modified as the Fittipaldi F7s for the first half of the 1980 season, while a new car designed by Postlethwaite was built. A new impression of strength extended beyond the machines,

This car seemed to have great promise, but the only scoring finish for an F8 in 1980 was Rosberg's fifth in the Italian GP.

Three were built, and one was modified to F8C specification for 1981 while two new cars were built. The designer had left for Ferrari, and Gary Thomas was responsible for the revisions. The cars first appeared with no sign of sponsorship, and that was reflected in budget economies. Rosberg's best finish was ninth, while Chico Serra was seventh in the opening race; between them they managed only five finishes, and failed to qualify fourteen times.

The two F8Ds available for the one-car 1982 team were rebuilt 1981 cars, and were used by Serra until the summer. He failed to pre-qualify once, then did not qualify twice,

Fondmetal

Gabriele Rumi took his team into its second Grand Prix season under the Fondmetal name. As with Fomet in 1991 resources were still thin, but in 1992 a two-car team was run. An updated version of the Fomet F1 designated GR01 was used in the first

Fondmetal-Ford GR01, 1992, Gabriele Tarquini at the wheel.

races, before a new car was introduced at the seventh race. However, this GR02 was used for only seven races, for the team was withdrawn after the Italian GP.

GR01 The great advance over the Fomet 1 was the Ford HB engine, giving around 100bhp more than DFR – this showed in qualifying, when the drivers never failed to pre-qualify (although 'NQ' appeared against Andrea Chiesa's name seven times in ten attempts, perhaps reflecting his abilities rather than the car's qualities). Gabriele Tarquini started each of his six races in these cars, but failed to record a finish.

GR02 This was a new design by Sergio Rinland, thoroughly conventional with double wishbones and pushrods suspension all round, the Ford HB, and a six-speed transverse gearbox. Little development was put into it – the team seemed more concerned to preserve the cars. Tarquini invariably qualified a GR02, but finished only one race (fourteenth in Britain). Eric van der Poele replaced Chiesa for the team's last three races, and scored its best finish (tenth at Spa).

Footwork

In the second half of the 1980s, Watara Ohashi aspired to enter top-flight racing, and used his multinational and multi-activity Ohashi Group to back the Footwork Sports Racing Team, initially using the car name 'Mooncraft'. Footwork Formula was set up in 1988, and Formula 3000 cars were built as a sensible lead-in to an F1 car for 1990. In the event, this was set aside as Ohashi acquired a major shareholding in Arrows. That constructor's cars were run as Footwork Arrows from 1991 until 1993, and the 'FA' car designation lasted until 1996. The cars are covered in the Arrows sequence (*see* pp.19–23).

Forti

Guido Forti's team took the giant step into Formula 1 in 1995, on the back of experience in F3000. Although surviving as an F1 constructor was far removed from winning races with an F3000 Reynard, it did, however, start with adequate resources and there was promise in its first season. In 1995 Pedro Diniz achieved a 50 per cent finishing record, and was seventh in the last Grand Prix of the year.

That promise was not carried over to 1996. Diniz and his backing were lost to Ligier. Forti struggled with inadequate resources and had quibbled with backers, the new cars were late, and they ran for the last time in practice for the British GP. Neither driver qualified to start in that race, completing only a few practice laps, as a dark shadow of debt hung over the little team. Its cars were at the next race, but did not reach the track – ownership was in dispute, Cosworth was no longer prepared to be a benefactor, and 'no-show' penalties would have been incurred if the team had tried to continue but failed to appear.

The Forti team entered twenty-three Grands Prix, achieved fifteen finishes, scored no points.

FG01 This wholly conventional car was designed by Giorgio Stirano, with some help from the more experienced Sergio Rinland. It used a Ford ED customer V8 and Hewland gearbox, with double wishbones and push-rods suspension all round. The FG01 was overweight, and the redesign of parts such as the side pods took priority over reducing that handicap. Pedro Diniz, who brought much financial backing to Forti Grand Prix, gained in confidence through the year, out-qualifying his more experienced team mate Robert Moreno by mid-season (and finishing more races – eight to four).

The cars were run in the first four races in 1996, with a 'B' designation and Ford Zetec-R engines. Badoer and Montermini each qualified an FG01B twice in four attempts, and the latter recorded his only finish of the year with one, tenth in Austria.

FG03 Designed by George Ryton, this 1996 car followed the general lines of FG01, with a Zetec-R engine and Hewland transverse gearbox. This time there seemed to be substance to claims that weight had been saved. Badoer recorded one race finish (tenth at Imola), to set against three retirements and two DNQs, while Montermini's record was two retirements, three DNQs and a DNS.

Frazer Nash

AFN found a customer for a single-seater version of its Le Mans Replica sports car in 1952, and the first Frazer Nash Formula 2 car appeared that year. Peter Bell ran this car in a handful of World Championship and non-title events for Ken Wharton; two others followed, but these only appeared in national races.

The Frazer Nash had a twin-tube ladder chassis, transverse leaf spring and lower wishbone front suspension and a live rear axle. The Bristol 1,971cc straight six gave some 140bhp and drove through a four-speed gearbox. The car was heavy, handicapped with its outmoded suspension, and not very pretty. Wharton placed it sixth in its debut race, a heat of the Silverstone International Trophy, and seventh in the final. He then scored World Championship points with a fourth place in the Swiss GP, and was third in the non-championship Eifelrennen. That was the last finish for the F2 Frazer Nash, for Wharton crashed in the Belgian GP, retired from the Dutch GP and failed to finish its final race, a minor event at Turnberry.

Germain

This Belgian manufacturer built cars under licence from 1897, then to its own designs from 1903. These cars tended to be advanced, with a performance potential sometimes shown in races and trials, and an entry in the 1907 Grand Prix must have seemed logical. However, the three cars prepared for it were based on production models, even to Germain's distinctive round radiator. With T-head four-cylinder engines of only 5,123cc, they were the smallest cars in the field at Dieppe. The Germains weighed in at 940kg (2,072lb) and only three other cars were lighter. All the Germains finished, the best being in fourteenth place three hours after the winner, and the others fifteenth and seventeenth.

A lesson seemed to be learned, for the 1908 Germain Grand Prix car was a racing car, with a 12,443cc engine and a reversion to chain final drive. These were handsome cars, with crews seated relatively low behind

pronounced scuttles. They were regarded as outsiders, but while one fell out early in the Grand Prix, Perpère made his way up the order, to fifteenth by halfway and to tenth at the end. Degrais finished twenty-second (of twenty-three) in the other Germain.

That was the last Grand Prix for the company, and until production ceased at the start of the First World War its racing activities were in any case limited.

Giaur

The Formula 1 regulations that came into force in 1954 allowed for a 750cc supercharged engine alternative to the 2.5litre normally aspirated engines that became the norm. Two minor constructors were tempted to try 750cc supercharged engines, largely because they were already working with power units in that capacity. In Italy Domenico Giannini and Bernardo Taraschi, engine and chassis men respec-

tively, took their Italian F3 car as a basis. This had a simple ladder-frame chassis, independent front suspension and a live rear axle, and a dohc development of a Fiat engine. The F1 version proved as uncompetitive as the DB supercharged F1 car in France, and like that car appeared in only one race. Taraschi drove the Giaur in the Maserati-dominated 1954 Rome Grand Prix, and into obscurity.

Gilby

Sid Greene raced cars until the early 1950s, then entered cars in the name of his Gilby Engineering Company, running F1 and sports Maseratis and a Lotus before he became a constructor at a very modest level with the first Gilby, a Coventry-Climax-powered sports-racing car campaigned in 1960. That led to a Formula 1 car. Designed by Len Terry, this was an orthodox space frame with a Coventry-Climax FPF engine driving through a Colotti gearbox, double wishbone suspension all round and a distinctive aluminium body.

Keith, Sid Greene's son, drove the car in six secondary races and the British GP in 1961 (he was fifteenth in the Grand Prix). It was run with the FPF engine, but a six-speed gearbox in place of the five-speed unit, early in 1962, again in secondary events, with a third in the Naples GP Greene's best placing. A modified space frame was introduced for a BRM V8, and this version was hardly an improvement – Greene finished once, seventh in the Mediterranean GP, in three attempts. Gilby Engineering was then taken over, and this car was sold to Ian Raby, who raced it in 1963 (best placing third in the Rome GP) before selling it, without its engine so that it was adapted for use in a minor sport.

Glas

In 1989 Mexican businessman, Fernando Gonzalez Luna, announced an agreement with Lamborghini, to build cars for his GLAS team (Gonzalez Luna Associates). Perhaps predictably, this 'Mexican' project was stillborn, but it did foreshadow Lamborghini's F1 engine programme, and its later entry into Grand Prix racing.

Gilby-Climax of 1961, Keith Greene driving.

Gleed

An enthusiastic but misguided attempt to create a 750cc supercharged F1 car towards the end of the seven-year period when the regulations permitted this form of power unit, the Gleed was actually completed in 1958, but was never seen at a race meeting. Peter Gleed stretched a Mk IV F3 Cooper chassis to accommodate a supercharged MG R dohc engine, claiming a scarcely credible 180bhp, behind the cockpit. The Cooper suspension was used, and so apparently was the chain final drive. Photographs show no signs of adequate fuel tankage for a two-hour Grand Prix, so perhaps the objective was shorter non-championship events.

Gobron-Brillié

By later racing car standards this car was old when it came to the line at Le Mans, as the seventh starter in the first Grand Prix, for it dated from 1903. It was also unusual in two respects, its light tubular chassis and its 13,547cc four-cylinder opposed-piston engine. Before 1906, these Gobron-Brilliés had a particularly solid record of achievement in sprint events.

In the first Grand Prix, Louis Rigolly kept it in mid-field into the second half, eventually retiring when the radiator was damaged. It started in the 1907 Grand Prix, and when Rigolly retired on the half-distance lap he had already lost an hour to the race leader and was in eighteenth place (out of twenty-seven). New regulations meant that its proposed entry in the 1908 Grand Prix was ruled out.

Gordini

Amedeo Gordini learned his craft in his native Italy, notably with Isotta-Fraschini, before moving to Paris in the 1920s and taking French nationality, and a French version of his forename, Amédée. The foundation for his later work was his tuning skills, above all with Fiat engines, and from its formation in 1934 with Simca that manufactured Fiats under licence. Gordini's association with Simca lasted until 1951, and from 1946 he built simple, light and nimble Simca-Gordini single-seaters.

These were *voiturettes*, then a 1,430cc engine, still using Simca components, came in 1948 and powered cars run in the then-new Formula 2, accepting a handicap because of the 2litre limit for that category. Moreover, with the addition of a supercharger the four-cylinder unit would be transformed into Formula 1.

The Simca-Gordini relationship was not always harmonious, and while Simca did agree to a substantially reworked engine with new heads and crankshaft, it would not sanction the 'proper' Grand Prix car that Gordini was anxious to build. This envisaged using a 4.5litre V12 developed with OSCA, and therefore following Maserati lines (it took shape as the OSCA F1 engine).

In supercharged Formula 1 guise, Gordini's little cars were really fragile (they lacked stamina in lesser categories). In 1950 there was just one scoring finish in a *grande epreuve* (Manzon's fourth place in the French GP), and in 1951 there were none. Car preparation suffered as Gordini contested F1, F2 and sports-car races, and failure after failure contributed substantially to the loss of Simca support.

The 1952–53 Formula 2 World Championship races appeared ideal for Gordini. He had built his own new four-cylinder engine for 1950, and then went ahead with a straight six that was a full 2litre F2 engine. The F2 cars were modestly successful in the 1952 Grands Prix, but were marginalized in 1953. With a 2.5litre version of the engine, the simple cars served on into the new Formula 1 years, with very few finishes to encourage the little equipe.

Gordini struggled on until 1957. A new F1 car with a new straight eight came late in 1955, but it was never competitive. The team faded away in 1957, and Amédée Gordini accepted a consultancy role with Renault, where his name was to be associated with the Régie's high-performance cars. A tendency to admire the plucky underdog has distracted attention from the Gordini marque's race record, which was very poor.

T15 These cars are generally recalled in *voiturette* or Formula 2 contexts, but when a Wade supercharger was fitted to the 1,430cc four-cylinder engine in 1950–51 they could be run as full Grand Prix cars. They had a simple and light ladder frame, Simca-originated front suspension (lower wishbones, transverse links and coil springs) and rigid rear axles with torsion bars. An intake on the right of the bonnet showed when a supercharger was fitted (or sometimes had been), and in this form with modest *compresseur* boost the pushrod inclined-valve engine produced some 115bhp. Oddly, the best results came on fast 'power' circuits – third at Albi and fourth in the French GP at Reims in 1950. In the next season, F1 Gordinis were outclassed in championship races – none of the three drivers scored – and the only success came in the Albi GP, which Trintignant won, with Simon and Behra fourth and sixth.

T16 For the 1952 championship season under F2 rules, Gordini had a new engine, a straight six that appeared in 1,498cc 155bhp form and was to be developed as a 1,988cc 175bhp unit. There was a new chassis, on similar tubular lines, and torsion bars were used all round. The cars looked neat and unpretentious, and had the Gordini virtues of lightness and nimble handling.

In 1952 Gordini was the only French marque active in World Championship racing, yet it attracted little patriotic support. First showings were promising – Behra and Manzon respectively were third in the Swiss and Belgian GPs (Behra drove his brand-new car from Paris to Berne for the Swiss race!). After that there was a single fourth place and three fifth placings, but there was success in non-championship races, none greater than Behra's triumph in the Reims GP, when he beat the best that the Italians could field.

The team survived 1953 on a hand-to-mouth basis, with no development work undertaken, inadequate preparation and cars that in any case were worn out. There were minor race successes, but in championship events Trintignant's fifth places in Belgium and Italy were the only points-scoring finishes.

The same chassis were used with a 2.5litre engine for the new F1 from 1954 (but the engine was hardly new, being the six with new cylinder liners and crankshaft to increase bore and stroke and give a capacity of 2,473cc – a variant already used in a sports car). Up to 220bhp was claimed, but that was significantly less than Italian and German engines, and an increase to maybe 230bhp in 1955 hardly helped. There were two scoring finishes in 1954 (Bayol and Pilette in the first two Grands Prix) and none in 1955, although there were successes in minor French provincial events.

The cars served on through 1956 and 1957. Da Silva Ramos was the last Gordini driver to score in the World Championship, with fifth place at Monaco in 1956, and Manzon won the non-championship

Naples GP. After that there were the crumbs of placings in minor events.

T32 Meanwhile, Gordini had built an all-new car, the uncharacteristically bulky and heavy T32. This had a ladder-type tubular chassis, but with independent suspension all round, and Messier disc brakes (inboard at the rear). The engine was a dohc 2,474cc straight eight; its claimed 256bhp might have been achieved in static tests, but 230–240bhp was more realistic. There was a five-speed gearbox.

Two cars were completed, and although they were modified as the little team sought to make the T32 competitive, radical development was called for. Sixth places in two British non-championship events in 1956 were its best showings, with seventh place in Monaco that year. Drivers preferred the old sixes.

Graf

This one-off was an adaptation of a 1924 La Perle sports car by Jean Graf in 1925. He gave it his name and ran it without distinction in the Rome and San Sebastian Grands Prix that year, and at San Sebastian again in 1926. It was, of course, an offset single-seater, retaining La Perle's cowled radiator and sohc 1.5litre engine.

Grégoire

A Grégoire was the smallest car to start in the first Grand Prix, and it was also one of the three cars that failed to complete a lap in that historic event. Its make-up was orthodox, with a channel section frame, artillery wheels, a four-cylinder engine and shaft drive. It was the lightest car at Le Mans, weighing in at 886kg (1,953lb) when most entries were close to the 1,007kg (2,220lb) limit, but it also had by far the smallest engine, a 7,433cc unit. Civelli de Bosch retired it with a broken radiator (incidentally, a second Grégoire failed to appear).

There were four Grégoires in the 1912 Grand Prix, albeit these were in the concurrent *Coupe de l'Auto* for 3litre cars. These were low-slung in the new fashion, with T-head 2,944cc engines mounted well back in the chassis and two-speed back axles giving six speeds. Only two of the cars reached half distance, and they were then withdrawn.

Gordini of 1954, Jean Behra at the wheel.

Greifzu

Paul Greifzu was an accomplished East German driver – he won the 1951 Avusrennen in a BMW-powered Eigenbau – who turned constructor and built his own promising Formula 2 car that marginally qualifies here as it would have been eligible for the 1952–53 World Championship races. He was fatally injured racing it in a minor East German event early in 1952, but the Greifzu-BMW was little damaged and his widow continued to enter it in local events.

Guérin

In 1946 the Société Guérin, a contractor to Air Industrie, built a one-off racing car designed by Enguerrand de Coucy on the same 'supplier' basis. With the 1.5litre supercharged engine intended for it, this would have been a Grand Prix car, and as such promised better than any contemporary French efforts. But apparently resources were slender, for chassis and engine never came together, although both were run.

De Coucy's design featured a ladder-frame chassis, with independent suspension front and rear, the 1,487cc dohc two-stage supercharged straight eight (255bhp at 8,200rpm was claimed for this), a semi-automatic four-speed transmission, and an odd body that was low from nose to cockpit but had a disproportionately high and bulky tail. The car was run with an 1,100cc engine in 1947, while the engine was used in another French car, but never in a Grand Prix.

Guyot

Albert Guyot had an active front-line racing career from 1907 until 1923, when he was a member of the Rolland-Pilain team. Two years later he built the first Guyot Spéciale, using a Rolland-Pilain chassis and a 1,986cc sleeve-valve straight six giving some 125bhp. Only the Bugatti T35 of the 1925 regulars was less powerful, and the Guyot was not competitive (in any case, it was retired from its two 1925 Grands Prix, in Spain and Italy). Those were the only Grand Prix appearances for a Guyot, but Albert Guyot drove one of his cars, in 1.5litre form, at Indianapolis in 1926, when it lasted just eight laps (two other Guyots run as Schmidt Specials lasted forty-one and forty-four laps). Guyots also appeared in late-1920s *formule libre* races, and a sleeve-valve-engined car was run as a Bucciali.

Halford Special

Major Frank Halford's one-off special was one of the more enterprising of the breed between the World Wars, not least because of its 1,496cc dohc engine designed by Halford. Completed in 1925, the car had an Aston Martin chassis with semi-elliptic suspension front and rear and an attractive no-nonsense body. At first an exhaust-driven turbocharger with an inter-cooler was fitted (in Grand Prix car specification terms that seems to be half-a-century ahead of its time!), but a more conventional Roots-type supercharger was used in racing. An output of 96bhp was claimed, which apparently tended to over-stress the Aston Martin gearbox. This car seemed to have development potential, but rather than exploit that Halford turned to a V12 project (this did not take shape).

Halford had some success with the car at Brooklands, but retired on the eighty-second lap of the 110-lap 1926 British GP at the track, when a transmission U/J failed. After 1926, the Halford Special was raced by George Eyston, who was flagged off when he had completed three-quarters of the 1927 French GP but achieved placings in minor events.

HAR

Horace Richards had this straightforward and good-looking car built in his own engineering works, primarily for his own enjoyment, although sales of replicas were envisaged (one was built to carry the name Woden, but it was not raced in single-seater form and was completed as a sports car). The HAR had a simple tubular frame and independent suspension all round, by unequal-length wishbones and torsion bars. When the car was run in F2 form, the engine was basically a straight-six 2litre Riley unit. In well thought-through detail, spur gears allowed for the transmission to run low under the driver's seat, and also made for easy ratio changes.

Richards entered the car in several categories, with appropriate engines, including British F2 races, but not in the 1952 and 1953 British GPs – he presumably recognized his limits – and even in 2.5litre F1 races in 1954 and 1955. The car had an active career stretching from 1952 until 1960, but never featured in race results (perhaps the driver's ability showed in its 1954 runs in important non-title races, when it was 20sec off pole time at Goodwood and 32sec off the fastest race lap time in the Silverstone International Trophy.

Heck

Ernst Klodwick entered and raced BMW-powered single-seaters during the period when German racing was re-established after the Second World War, using a twin-cylinder motorcycle unit in a 750cc rear-engined car and then a 328-derived 1,971cc straight six in a Formula 2 car that started in two World Championship German GPs. This F2 car was also rear-engined, and in performance terms was seriously outclassed: Klodwig started from the back of the 1952 grid, and although two Veritas were slower in 1953 his qualifying time was 2min 25sec off pole time at the Nürburgring. He retired in 1952, but was placed fifteenth in the 1953 German GP. The Heck was primarily a car for German national events (Klodwig was eighth in the 1952 Avusrennen).

Heim

One-time Benz engineer Franz Heim launched his road-car line in 1921, and optimistically built a pair of cars for the 1922 Italian GP, the first to be run at Monza and, unlike the French race, open to German entrants that year. The Heim was basically a sports car, and for the Grand Prix had a straight six in 1,995cc form, rated at 80bhp. This made it one of the least powerful cars at Monza, where its top speed was more than 20kmh (14mph) slower than the dominant Fiat 804. The Heim were rated outsiders, Franz Heim and Reinhold Stahl made no impression in the race, and both retired.

Heron

The prototype for a proposed run of Formula Junior cars (that did not come to pass) was bought by Tony Maggs and fitted with an Alfa Romeo engine for the local South African F1 series in 1961. Designed by Les Redmond, it was a wholly conventional rear-engine space-frame car on Cooper lines. In 1961 Ernest Pieterse started four races in the Heron. He finished sixth in the Rand GP and eighth in the Cape GP, albeit laps down on the winning Lotus in each case; Pieterse failed to finish the South African and Natal GPs.

The car appeared again in the Rand GP in 1964, driven by David Hume; it was running at the finish, but not classified in the overall results.

Hesketh

In the mid-1970s the Hesketh team fascinated a wide audience outside racing and was very much in the spirit of a period that now seems long past. Lord Alexander Fermor-Hesketh came into racing as an entrant in 1972, and ended his involvement with the team that carried his name in 1975, although his continuing interest in the sport meant that he would become prominent in the affairs of the British Racing Drivers Club, and Silverstone circuit.

From the outset, with Dastle cars in Formula 3, the team had a playboy image that in the end may well have damaged its prospects. However, it was always a serious professional effort. Hesketh entered Formula 1 in 1973, when Dr Harvey Postlethwaite re-engineered its March 731, and James Hunt drove to score fourteen championship points. In 1974 Hesketh became a constructor, with cars that were quick in Hunt's hands, if not always reliable.

A high point came when Hunt won the Dutch GP in 1975, and that year Hesketh was fourth in the Constructors' Championship – no small achievement for a team in its first year with its own cars.

The budget to run a team at this level called for sponsorship income that could not be found. Cars were leased, or sold to other entrants, but that helped only a little. Hesketh withdrew, and the 1975 cars were sold to Walter Wolf (Postlethwaite and some team members also joined Wolf's venture). Hesketh's team manager Anthony 'Bubbles' Horsley kept the Grand Prix effort alive for a while, running cars for paying drivers, taking on Cosworth preparation and

Hesketh-Ford 308 of 1974, driven by James Hunt.

Hesketh-Ford 308E of 1978.

other specialist work, and even building five new cars in 1977. But as a Grand Prix force, Hesketh was spent, and it faded away with a few whispers in 1978.

308 Postlethwaite's first design was a sensible Cosworth-engined car, with simple but efficient wedge lines. The suspension was orthodox, double wishbones at the front, upper and lower links with radius arms at the rear, and outboard springs all round, until late in 1974 rubber was introduced as the springing medium at the front. A nose radiator soon gave way to radiators flanking the engine. A Hewland gearbox was almost an automatic choice.

The car was competitive for its first race start, from pole position in a non-title race at Brands Hatch. Hunt drove it to win the International Trophy race at Silverstone in 1974, and to third places in the Swedish, Austrian and US Grands Prix; Hesketh was sixth in the Constructors' Championship.

The car was revised for 1975, when both rubber and normal coil springs were used. Hunt scored that memorable victory at Zandvoort, was second in championship races in Argentina, France and Austria, fourth in Britain and Canada; none of the drivers in other Hesketh cars that had been sold or leased scored, so Hunt's thirty-three points was Hesketh's total, placing the team fourth between Brabham and Tyrrell in the Championship.

The design was uprated for 1976, as the 308D, and the cars run by Horsley on a 'rent-a-drive' basis. Edwards, Ertl, Ribeiro and Stommelen drove 308Ds; Ertl was the only one to finish races in the top ten.

308C This distinctive car appeared towards the end of the 1975 European season, and was to become the Wolf FW05 in the following year. Postlethwaite sought to reduce frontal area and drag, but the shallow monocoque that contributed to this was insufficiently rigid at first and had to be strengthened to provide acceptable handling. The first of the three cars had a narrow track, and that too was to be revised. Suspension members were inboard, and rubber or coil springs were used. The Cosworth/Hewland combination was retained.

This was a difficult car, but Hunt drove it to fifth in the Italian GP and fourth in the USA.

308E Frank Dernie laid out a car for Horsley's 1977 team that had to be straightforward and economic, and therefore was an orthodox DFV-powered design. The tapering outward lines were attractive, and it was unfortunate that the 308E was never properly developed.

Only Keegan and Ertl managed top-ten placings in 1977 (a seventh and a ninth respectively), and in seven 1978 attempts only one driver, Eddie Cheever, even managed to qualify for a grid. Odd Heskeths then languished in a British national series.

Hill

Former World Champion Graham Hill launched the Embassy Racing Team in 1973 with a Shadow DN1 and then ran a pair of Lola T370s in the smart red and white colours in 1974, for himself and Rolf Stommelen. A development of this car was commissioned for 1975; this appeared as the Lola T371, but was soon renamed as the first Hill, and redesignated GH1.

Graham Hill continued to drive into 1975, making his last Grand Prix start in Brazil and sadly failing to qualify at Monaco, so that his last actual race was in the Silverstone International Trophy (his drive in the second GH1 seemed lacklustre, and he finished eleventh). The team ran five other drivers that year, notably Rolf Stommelen, until he crashed heavily in Spain, Alan Jones and Tony Brise, who scored championship points. The year ended abruptly, as Hill's aircraft crashed in poor conditions (on the approach to Elstree airfield on 29 November), after new car tests at the Paul Ricard circuit. Hill, Brise, designer Andy Smallman, and other team members died instantly.

GH1   This was a car on typical Lola lines. The design work was carried through by Andy Smallman, who was then seconded to Hill's base near London Airport to oversee development. Four monocoques were built by TC Prototypes. The overall make-up was conventional, with double wishbone front suspension, upper and lower links at the rear, and outboard springs all round, with a Cosworth DFV driving through a Hewland gearbox.

Stommelen placed the first car seventh in its debut race, in South Africa, and he then led the Spanish GP before an experimental carbon-fibre wing support failed. Migault drove Hills twice and Schuppan once, but Alan Jones with one scoring finish (in Germany) in four starts and Tony

Hill-Ford GH2, 1976, completed but never raced. Here driven by Tony Brise on a test session.

Brise with a sixth place in his nine starts seemed to set the team on the road to success. It was eleventh in the Constructors' Championship (or twelfth if the two points scored by Donohue in a March are attributed to Penske).

GH2   Smallman designed a neat little car with distinctive pyramid lines for 1976. There were 'new car' problems in its first runs at Silverstone and le Castellet, but there was time to correct shortcomings before the season opened. The car was set aside as the team was wound up following Hill's fatal accident, but it survives.

Honda

Soichiro Honda was a racing enthusiast, who had built and raced a one-off aero-engined special in the 1920s and Ford-engined cars in the 1930s, and seen the company he founded in 1945 grow to dominate top-level motorcycle racing by the early 1960s. By that time, Honda was poised to enter world car markets, and the company's first Formula 1 programme was to play a promotional role in this. A Cooper was tested to provide experience, and Honda looked to a collaboration with Brabham or Lotus, but the only outcome of that was to be an F2 engine partnership with Brabham. Honda's own first prototype

F1 car was tested in 1963. That RA270 was never raced, but led to the RA271 that was run in three exploratory Grands Prix in 1964. Eight of the eleven 1965 Grands Prix were contested, and Honda did win the last of the 1.5litre Formula, at the end of that season, before committing to 3litre cars that were no more than modestly successful in 1966–68. In 1967 F1 racing manager Yoshio Nakamura shifted the development and racing base to England, where Honda Racing was set up in tandem with Team Surtees. John Surtee's driving ability, technical pragmatism and relationship with Honda meant that progress was made, and there was a Grand Prix victory. But the company then withdrew, and returned to Formula 1 as an engine supplier in 1983.

Its turbo engines started winning races in 1984, with Williams, and the normally-aspirated units that followed were equally successful – Honda-powered cars won sixty-nine World Championships races, 1984–92, and there were to be more victories with engines labelled Mugen, in the late 1990s.

The next return was to be as a full constructor in 2000, and to this end an extensive (and expensive) development programme was initiated, with a test car run from a British R&D base. Jos Verstappen set competitive times in this from its first 'open' test runs through the spring of 1999. Then late in May Honda shelved its team plan, backing away from the cost of development and racing, and entering into a collaboration with the well-funded BAR team. That was to extend beyond the supply of engines, for example into chassis development, and allowed for the continuing use of Mugen-Honda engines by the Jordan team. It seemed an odd U-turn, that could perhaps best be explained by the company's accountants.

RA271 The space-frame RA270 was developed into this 1964 race car that had a monocoque centre section with tubular subframes in place of the full space frame. The front suspension was by upper wishbones and lower radius arms, with inboard coil springs/dampers. Reversed wishbones with top links and twin trailing arms at the rear were mounted to the subframe

Honda V12 RA273 of 1967, John Surtees driving.

that in turn mounted the engine that was thus a stressed member. At that stage, the Honda car did not impress F1 regulars when it appeared for the German GP in August 1964; however, the engine did impress. It was a 60-degree dohc 1,495cc V12, fed by six carburettors, and mounted transversely with a central power take-off to a six-speed gearbox. The V12 gave some 220bhp in its first form; fuel injection replaced carburettors in the second car, run in the last two 1964 races. At the Nürburgring there were comments about motorcycle practices and 'miniaturizations' (and John Cooper's, 'There you are – I told you they did it sideways').

The RA271 was driven by Ronnie Bucknum, a little-known American West Coast sports-car driver, in its first exploratory races. He retired in Germany, but doubts about the engine were dispelled when he ran as high as fifth in Italy before retiring, and the engine let him down in the USA.

RA272 The 1965 car looked similar, but had an extended monocoque and changes to the suspension, and it was lighter. The developed V12 was the most powerful engine of the 1.5litre formula, with an output of 230–240bhp, and it would run to a then phenomenal 14,000rpm. However, the effective revs range was narrow, and the engine tended to lose power as it became hot. Experienced Richie Ginther was the number-one driver and scored the team's first championship points in Belgium. He was also sixth in the British GP and at the end of the season won the Mexican GP. Bucknum started in only six races and was fifth in Mexico. Honda was sixth in the Constructor's Championship.

RA273 Perhaps too much was expected; the first 3litre Honda was late – its debut came in Italy in 1966 – conventional and so much overweight that the power advantage given by its V12 was squandered. The 90-degree 2,992cc engine gave almost 400bhp when it first appeared, but the dry weight of the car was 743kg (1,638lb), almost 50 per cent above the formula minimum. The car

had a full monocoque, lower wishbone/upper radius arm suspension front and rear with outboard springs/dampers. It looked bulky. Ginther crashed out of the car's first race. He was joined by Bucknum for the last two Grands Prix of 1966; neither finished in the USA, but they were fourth and eighth in Mexico.

Two of the three RA273s built served on in 1967, and Surtees was third in the year's first Grand Prix; he also placed fourth in Germany and third in Britain, before a replacement car came into service.

RA300 John Surtees arranged for Lola to build this lighter one-off in 1967, and it expediently followed the T190 Indianapolis car very closely, with an adapted monocoque and suspension units (it even had a Lola designation, T130). This 'Hondola' was lighter by more than 100kg (220lb), and consequently less fuel had to be carried. With almost 400bhp it was competitive. Surtees proved this when he drove it to win its first race, the Italian GP. He retired in the USA and was fourth in Mexico. Honda was fourth in the Constructors' Championship, ahead of Ferrari.

The car was run in the 1968 South African GP, when fuel injection faults meant that Surtees was eighth.

RA301 A pair of cars was built for 1968, with a revised engine notable for its convoluted exhausts in the vee, a reworked gearbox and suspension. The claimed output was 430bhp, but weight was up again. Surtees drove one to second place in the French GP, third in the USA and sixth in Britain, while Jo Bonnier was fifth in Mexico in the second car. But Honda slipped to sixth in the Championship.

RA302 After the first tests, Surtees judged that this innovative car needed development before an attempt to race it, and an accident in its presumably premature debut appearance cost the life of Jo Schlesser in 1968. The RA302 had an air-cooled 120-degree V8, which gave 385bhp in its early form. It was hung from a backbone extending from the rear of the short monocoque, and drove through a new five-speed gearbox. The suspension was conventional.

Soichiro Honda was in France for the launch of the N360 saloon, and it seemed important to run the RA302 to support this, and to put a French driver in the cockpit. A separate Honda team turned up at Rouen to run the car – to Surtees's astonishment. Schlesser qualified it for the back row of the grid, and on the third lap of the race lost control as the engine cut out, and died as the near-full tanks and magnesium skin of the monocoque were ingredients in the fierce fire.

Honda lost heart. The second RA302 was never raced, and the company withdrew from Grand Prix racing at the end of the year. Its proposed return was confirmed in March 1998, a test chassis was completed by Dallara, first runs promised much, then that single-seater with a Honda badge on the nose was set aside.

Hotchkiss

The French company entered a team of three cars in the first Grand Prix, but complete failure in that race and the 1906 Vanderbilt Cup led it to turn away from the premier racing category. The Type HH followed on from very large cars built for the 1904–05 Gordon Bennett races, with an engine that was slightly smaller than those giants, at 16,286cc. Shaft drive was used, and for the Grand Prix wire wheels were fitted. The only other outward distinguishing feature was the 'trade mark' Hotchkiss round radiator.

In that Shepard had one car in fourth place at half-distance in the Grand Prix, the Hotchkiss was not outclassed, but

Honda V8 RA302 with air-cooled engine in 1968.

wheel failures led to retirements on laps 2, 4 and 7 of the 12-lap race. Shepard also retired in the Vanderbilt Cup, when running sixth in the second half of the race.

Hotchkiss HH of 1906.

HRG

The misguided enthusiasm that lay behind several British racing ventures led Peter Clarke to commission an F2 car on the basis of a sports HRG in 1948. The simple fact that it retained the beam front axle and live rear axle of a bygone era should have consigned the project to the bin, but it went ahead. A modified Standard Vanguard engine provided possibly 115bhp and drove through a Standard three-speed gearbox. The body was built by Coopers. After a few unimpressive outings in 1949 the car was left to gather dust, but it was brought out again in 1952. It never got to a World Championship status entry list, but Mike Keen raced it at Goodwood and failed to qualify it for that year's International Trophy at Silverstone.

Hume

This British 'special' was a conversion of driver Chris Bristow's Cooper T39 sports-racing car by John Hume, whose name it carried in entry lists. It was intended for Formula 2 at the end of the 1950s, and still with a Coventry-Climax FPF engine it became a Formula 1 car in 1961. It was hopefully started in three non-championship races and was predictably far from competitive in 'real' F1 company – its best finish being last.

HWM

Racing drivers John Heath and George Abecassis set up Hersham and Walton Motors in 1946, and their second HWM car was a dual-purpose sports/Formula 2 car, which was the forerunner of 'proper' F2 cars. These were offset single-seaters, but they performed creditably in Europe and led to central cockpit F2 cars in 1951. Meanwhile, HWMs had appeared in Formula 1 company, a notable result coming when Stirling Moss finished third behind two Alfa Romeo 158s in the 1950 Bari GP (admittedly he was lapped twice).

Formula 2 HWMs were, of course, eligible for the World Championship Grands Prix in 1952–53, but they were seldom competitive, outpowered by Italian rivals. A 2.5litre version for the opening season of the seven-year formula was unsuccessful.

Formula 2 cars The 1951 cars had a chassis of two main tubes, with many suspension parts bought in, to achieve a double-wishbone independent front suspension with a de Dion rear end. The Alta engine was uprated during 1951, to give up to 130bhp, and pre-selector gearboxes were used. These were useful cars, with some victories in minor events and good placings in main-line F2 races.

The 1952 cars had lighter tubular chassis, with torsion bars in place of the quarter-elliptic springs at the rear, where the brakes were inboard. Pannier fuel tanks made the cars look more substantial than their 1951 counterparts. The Alta engine was still used, modified to give 140–145bhp, and a little more in 1953 – perhaps 155bhp.

There was encouragement when Paul Frère scored points with fifth place in his home Grand Prix, at Spa in 1952, and when Macklin and Rolt finished first and second in the International Trophy at Silverstone. But generally these cars were off the pace in 1952–53, and reliability was suspect. In the second year of F2 Grands Prix there were no worthwhile placings in championship races, and Yves Giraud-Cabantous's fifteenth place in the Italian GP was the last for an HWM in a title race. In secondary events,

second and third places scored by Frère and Collins in the 1953 Eifelrennen stand out.

For 1954 a 2.5litre version of the 1952–53 cars had a 2,464cc Alta engine, bored and stroked by HWM in a necessary economy product, and one had fuel injection. This produced some 200bhp that was quite inadequate in a season when Mercedes-Benz returned to the Grands Prix and Formula 1 became serious again. The last World Championship race for an HWM was the 1954 French GP, when Lance Macklin was running last in the works car when its engine failed. Very little was achieved in secondary British events, as HWM faded from the Grand Prix scene.

HWM-Alta of 1950, Stirling Moss behind the wheel.

HWM-Alta, 1953, driven by 'B. Bira'.

Iso

Frank Williams's cars were named Iso-Marlboro in 1973–74, and until his new cars meeting the 'deformable structure' regulation that came into force in spring 1973 were ready, the erstwhile Politoys FX3s were used. Through the rest of 1973 and in 1974 the team was associated with Iso-Rivolta and backed by Marlboro, but it still battled for survival rather than success, on very mean budgets. The IR cars from this period became the first to be entered as Williams, with an FW designation, in 1975.

FX3B One of the cars run in the first Grands Prix of 1973 was the original FX3, uprated to the FX3B specification of a new car. The best placing in that period was in a non-title race, when Tony Trimmer was fourth at Brands Hatch. In the three Grands Prix where the cars were entered, Howden Ganley was seventh in Brazil; he was also tenth once, while Galli was ninth in Brazil.

IR John Clarke's design to meet the 'deformable structure' rules was the straightforward Cosworth-powered IR, and four were built. Suspension was by double wishbones at the front, upper and lower links at the rear, with outboard springs all round. Giampaolo Dallara was called in to rework the rear suspension during 1973. Save for the cockpit surround, the body lines were angular to the point of being austere.

The cars gained a reputation for good handling, perhaps the most important quality as no fewer than eight drivers occupied their cockpits during the season. Ganley was the regular driver, and he scored one point (in Canada); of the rest, only Gijs van Lennep scored a point (in Holland). In 1974 the cars were modestly revised and Arturo Merzario was the regular driver. He was sixth in South Africa and fourth in Italy, but five other drivers contributed no points to the Iso total, and Frank Williams's team was tenth in the Constructors' Championship.

Ray Stokoe carried through another update for 1975, when the cars still served, alongside the new FW04.

Itala

Very soon after Fabbrica Automobili Itala was established in 1904 its founders, Guido Bigio and Matteo Ceirano, looked to racing, and in 1905 Giovanni Batista Raggio drove one of its 15.5litre cars to win the Coppa Florio. It entered a team in the first Grand Prix, and the 1908 and 1913 races, but its cars were never front-runners and achieved only two modest finishes from nine starts in those Grands Prix (the best result for the Itala team at this level was ninth in the 1908 Grand Prize at Savannah).

1906 Alberto Balocco followed his 1905 design in the 1906 Grand Prix car, broadly a typical 'giant racer'. There was a ladder frame with channel section main members, unforgiving non-independent suspension with semi-elliptic springs to the beam front axle and live rear axle, and artillery wheels for the race. Detachable rims were to be used, but these pushed the cars over the 1,007kg (2,220lb) limit. The engine was a 16,666cc four-cylinder inlet-over-exhaust unit. There was a four-speed gearbox and, unlike most Italian high-performance cars of the period, the Itala had shaft drive. Wheel failures put two cars out on the second lap of the 1906 Grand Prix; Alessandro Cagno completed two laps in the third car, before retiring with a broken radiator. A pair of cars made no impression in the Vanderbilt Cup race.

1908 As the famous '1907 GP car' never ran in a Grand Prix, Itala took a one-year sabbatical. Its 1908 car was the heaviest in the Grand Prix field, the lightest of the three weighing in at 1,414kg (3,118lb) – 414kg (913lb) above the minimum! Like most entries, the Itala engine was close to the maximum permitted bore, 155mm, but the capacity of 12,045cc was slightly below average.

Piacenza's Itala retired early, and the other two were outpaced. Cagno had dropped almost an hour to the leader at half distance (when team mate Fournier was another 20 minutes back). Cagno lost less time in the second half, and pulled back to finish eleventh while Fournier was tenth.

The same trio drove the solidly handsome cars at Savannah, where they were still outclassed, Fournier salvaging a little with ninth place. The cars were then seen in minor events.

1913 The third Grand Prix Itala did not look quite up-to-the-minute alongside some of the 1913 cars, and that impression was borne out as two of the three were right on the 1,100kg (2,425lb) maximum weight limit. At 8,325cc the Itala engines were the largest in the field, and the one novelty was rotary valves. In chassis and running gear respects the cars were wholly conventional. Once again an Itala retired on the second lap of the Grand Prix, the great Felice Nazzaro was never in the running and retired before half distance, as did team mate Moriondo (who had rolled his car at the end of the first lap, righted it with the

Iso-Marlboro, Ford V8-engined for 1973, driven by Howden Ganley.

Itala of 1913, Felice Nazzaro driving.

help of his riding mechanic, Foresti, and restarted). These 1913 cars were raced after the Grand Prix, and one was placed second in the 1919 Targa Florio.

Tipo 15 Giulio Cesare Cappa, another of those ex-Fiat engineers who played significant roles in the 1920s, laid down this remarkable design for the 1.5litre Formula that was to come into force in 1926. It was also to be eligible for 1,100cc *voiturette* racing, in Tipo 11 form.

Cappa started with a clean sheet of paper, and laid out a low front-wheel-drive car with a very light frame, independent suspension by top transverse leaf springs in streamlined fairings and lower links, a supercharged V12 with drive shafts allowing for lateral steering and vertical wheel movements, and a single-seater cockpit on the centre line.

Itala was battling to survive – rather ineffectually, as the Italian government Reconstruction Finance Agency was to take it on in 1929 – and only one *voiturette* Tipo 11 was built. There was no spare cash to build or develop the Tipo 15 in 1926. And surely much development would have been needed with such a radical car at that time? It remains a great 'might-have-been' of racing history.

◆ J ◆

Jaguar

Cynics immediately called this an exercise in 'badge-engineering', for the Ford-owned Coventry car builder was not technically involved, neither were the new F1 cars to be based there. Indeed, there was no more than a little light re-branding, and a great deal of marketing hype behind the change from 'Stewart' to 'Jaguar' at the end of the 1999 season.

Following their purchase of the Stewart Grand Prix operation, it had not taken Ford long to decide on such a change, so the new 'Jaguar' team took over the modern 'Stewart' HQ in Milton Keynes. Initially, Jackie Stewart remained as chief executive, with his son Paul continuing as chief operating officer, while Ford's Neil Ressler became chairman in January 2000. Unhappily, early in the season Paul Stewart also had to step down because of a serious illness, which left Ressler in total control.

Naturally, Ford instructed Jaguar Racing to look to another newly-won subsidiary, Cosworth Racing, for its V10 engines. Well before the end of 1999 (even before 'Stew-

art' ceased to exist) a Stewart SF-3, re-painted in provisional 'Jaguar green' livery, was exhibited at the Frankfurt Motor Show.

This, though, was an over-hyped entry in F1 – not as irritating as that of BAR had been, but still over-the-top – and the team struggled even to match what Stewart had achieved in 1999. Ford, however, was not about to throw away its investment, and promised better things for the future.

R1 For Stewart SF-4, read Jaguar R1, for the reality of this new team was that the car which appeared as a gorgeously-liveried new 'Jaguar' was originally designed by technical director Gary Anderson (ex-Jordan) as a new Stewart.

A direct descendant of the surprisingly effective Stewart SF-3, it was claimed to use many McLaren-like aerodynamic details (but not enough, clearly, for it to behave like those cars), and also used the revised Ford-Cosworth CR2 V10 engine, which was supposedly even more powerful (820bhp?) than the CR1 of 1999 – but failed to prove this during the coming season. This, too, was the first 'Stewart' to use power-assisted steering.

This was a season of disappointment throughout, as the cars were never at the top of the pecking order, usually qualifying in or around eighth to tenth position on the grid. According to the pundits, they were neither fast enough in a straight line (defective aerodynamics were usually blamed), nor as fast as the top teams on twisty circuits. Eddie Irvine, amazingly, kept his lip thoroughly buttoned, and said only nice things about his car, while Johnny Herbert, the hero of Stewart in 1999, simply lost heart, and headed off, out of F1, at the end of the year.

In balance, the R1 was a competent, but unreliable car – and its successors will have to be much better designed and built if they are to shine in future years.

JBW

Brian Naylor campaigned sports-racing cars widely in British and Continental secondary events in the second half of the 1950s, and the first JBW built by his mechanic Fred Wilkinson was a Maserati-engined sports car. This stimulated ambition.

continued on p.117

When Eddie Jordan made the leap from Formula 3000 to Formula 1 in 1991 many pundits did not expect his team to survive, despite his record in lesser categories. But it enjoyed an impressive first season, then proved to have stamina as it got through poor years and then scored well through the second half of the 1990s. At the end of the decade, it was a leading 'best of the rest' contender behind the two dominant teams.

Eddie Jordan Racing was set up to support his racing – his career stretched from karts in 1970 to a Formula 2 car in 1979 – but he gave up driving and from 1981 ran a Formula 3 team. His flair as a talent spotter was amply demonstrated – he gave Ayrton Senna his first opportunity to test an F3 car, and his team drivers included future F1 drivers such as Brundle, Donnelly, Herbert and Johansson. From 1988 an F3000 team was run. This dominated the 1989 season (Alesi was European Champion driving Jordan's cars), then in 1990 two of the drivers were Irvine and Frentzen. That year Jordan Grand Prix was formed.

In Formula 1 Jordan faced familiar problems, but for the 1991 season sponsorship was at least adequate (if not abundant); Gary Anderson laid out a handsome and effective car, with the reliable Ford HB engine, and among the five drivers that year were Michael Schumacher and Alessandro Zanardi, both having their first F1 drives in the green and blue cars.

The team did not have the best of engines through the next three seasons, and budgets were still constricting. But the cars were highly rated, and Jordan does not give up easily. There was some encouragement as a first Jordan podium finish fell to Rubens Barrichello in Japan. Meanwhile, a purpose-built headquarters

had been set up hard by Silverstone circuit, and this was to be expanded in 1996.

By that time the team had a major new sponsor and was into its second season with a 'works-level' relationship with Peugeot. There were more resources for R&D work, and for testing. Peugeot took its engines to Prost in 1998, and the outlook for Jordan seemed less promising, as for almost half the season it struggled with problems such as seemingly incompatible electronics and Mugen-Honda engines. Then in a summer downpour, Damon Hill scored Jordan's first Grand Prix victory. Moreover, it was a team 1-2, for Ralf Schumacher followed him past the flag at Spa.

Eddie Jordan's optimism was fully justified at last, although his team's fortunes were again mixed in 1999: while Heinz-Harald Frentzen's career blossomed in the Jordan 199, Damon Hill's withered, and extraordinarily this successful team saw the Honda works engines it sought for 2000 committed to a new and unproven team.

The result, by comparison with the team's sparkling late-1990s form, was a disappointing year, with no victories. Williams, already defeated by Jordan in 1999, climbed back over them with their unproven BMW-engined cars, so Jordan could only look ahead, hopefully, for more success in the future.

191 The first car of the new marque was convincing. Gary Anderson did not have an outstanding CV as a designer – his single-seaters had been the F3 Anson and a Reynard F3000 car – but he had been senior mechanic and then chief engineer with leading teams. The 191 was his first F1 car and was to confirm Jordan's assessment of his ability; he was to design F1 Jordans through to the last year of the century.

The 191 was a neat and economical design, conventional and little changed through the 1991 season. It followed that there was a carbon-fibre monocoque, and with pushrod unequal-length wishbones suspension all round the car gained a reputation for good handling, especially in fast corners. The Ford HB was rated at 730bhp, and as a 'known' power unit was ideal for a new team in its first season, some friction (over finance) with Cosworth notwithstanding. A Jordan transverse six-speed gearbox (with Hewland gears) was used. The upper surface lines of the car flowed attractively, an carried evidence of apparently adequate sponsorship.

Unexpectedly, there were problems with drivers. Andrea de Cesaris drove through the year, and scored Jordan's first points when he was fourth in the Canadian GP. Gachot was his team mate until the summer. Michael Schumacher took his place, but was lost to Benetton after one race. Moreno joined for two races, Zanardi for the last two. Despite this turmoil, Jordan was fifth in the Constructors' Championship at the end of its first Grand Prix season.

192 The switch to the Yamaha OX99 70-degree in the essentially evolutionary 192 seemed a step forward, but was to prove a setback, so this partnership lasted for just one season. The engine was no more powerful than the HB, once sacrifices had been made in a search for reliability. The seven-speed gearbox was also troublesome early in the season. In terms of results, that was bleak: in the last race, Stefano Modena scored the team's only point (to set against four failures to qualify, and eight retirements), while Maurizio Gugelmin's best placing was seventh and he retired eleven times.

193 Based on the 192, the 1993 Jordan was powered by a Hart V10, which proved basically reliable if not enormously powerful. However, minor problems afflicted ancillaries, the semi-automatic six-speed transverse gearbox, and the traction control. A full active suspension system was beyond Jordan's resources, but there was ride height control at the front. Rubens Barrichello showed great promise, but scored just two points (in Japan) and recorded eight retirements. Boutsen finished in five races, Capelli, Apicella and Naspetti each had a fruitless outing, then at the end of the season Eddie Irvine made

Jordan-Ford 191, Andrea de Cesaris driving in 1991.

his Grand Prix debut in a Jordan in Japan, and scored a point.

194 Steve Nichols joined as technical director in 1994, to strengthen that side of the operation, and that year Jordan got back on course after its two poor seasons. The car was again evolutionary, with a revised Hart V10 giving a little more power.

Barrichello started the season with a fourth place and a third, was fourth in four more races, and recorded Jordan's first F1 pole position, in Belgium. Irvine scored three times, but suffered a three-race ban after a televised 'incident' in Brazil. De Cesaris stood in twice, was fourth at Monaco; Suzuki's single drive was ineffectual. Jordan claimed fifth place in the championship, with twenty-eight points.

195 Hart engines were set aside in 1995 in favour of an association with Peugeot that, coupled with the driver pairing of Barrichello and Irvine, promised much. But there was a major challenge, as the team had to learn how to work with a major manufacturer. The car followed familiar lines, although it was a completely new design to complement the Peugeot A10E 72-degree V10. This drove through a Jordan semi-automatic seven-speed longitudinal gearbox. Much of the technical effort had to be directed to achieving reliability.

Barrichello finished eight races, scoring in four with a best finish second in Canada; Irvine recorded ten finishes, and his best was third in Canada (thus there were two Jordan drivers on that podium). Their twenty-one points gave Jordan a disappointing sixth place in the Constructors' Championship.

196 The 1996 cars carried the dominant livery of a single major sponsor, and the relationship with Peugeot should have settled down. There was potential, but there were also weaknesses, and Jordan still did not threaten the major teams. The high-nose configuration was adopted, partly as a convenient means of meeting a cross-section requirement expected to come in 1996, to improve safety (in the event, this was deferred to 1997). More attention was paid to achieving mechanical grip, in suspension aspects and weight distribution, and power steering was adopted. The Peugeot A12 was developed from the A10, and was expected to be more reliable as well as more powerful.

Jordan-Hart 194 driven by Rubens Barrichello.   *(Below)* **Jordan-Peugeot 195, Eddie Irvine driving.**

Barrichello and Brundle seldom qualified well, and coincidentally both retired seven times. The Brazilian was fourth in Argentina and Britain, and scored fourteen points; Brundle's best result was fourth place in Italy, and he scored eight points. Jordan was fifth in the championship, again.

197 Changes in the 1997 car did not appear to be significant – outwardly, there were shorter side pods, and a different engine air intake and cover – but there was substantial aerodynamic refinement (by this time Jordan had its own wind tunnel). Detail aerodynamic work led to a longitudinal gearbox (the in-house seven-speed sequential 'box). The A14 engine was lighter and smaller than the previous Peugeot V10, and more powerful. That year Jordan's design and engineering staff was doubled, to twenty at the start of the season, and for the first time Anderson was in a position to carry on development through a year.

Two young drivers took the places of experienced men: Giancarlo Fisichella scored his first points, with a fourth place at Imola, and went on to two podium

finishes and a total score of twenty points; Ralf Schumacher was third in Argentina, fifth in four races and scored thirteen points. The retirement rate was acceptable (fourteen in seventeen races), but Jordan still did not win a Grand Prix and was again fifth in the championship.

198 Changed regulations meant a new car for 1998, although strong 'family characteristics' were carried through, and there was a change to the Mugen Honda MF301HC 70-degree V10 engine. Push rods and unequal-length wishbones were used in a suspension layout intended to suit the obligatory grooved tyres; an extension to the wheelbase improved handling after the early races. There were numerous detail modifications aimed at aerodynamic efficiency. The engine, too, was to be uprated during the year. Its torque characteristics meant that a six-speed longitudinal gearbox was used. Early-season tests were frustrating, and so was a lack of competitiveness in the first races.

By midsummer the car was a front runner, and Damon Hill scored points in five of the last six races – fourth in Germany and Hungary, then that overdue victory in Belgium, and a season's total of twenty points (Jordan was the first new constructor name in a list of Grand Prix winners since 1986, when a Benetton first won a Grand Prix). Ralf Schumacher first scored in Britain (a single point), was second in Belgium and third in Italy, and contributed fourteen points to Jordan's total. That gave the team fourth place in the championship.

199 Well-financed, and boosted by a maiden victory in the previous year, Jordan looked for great things from the new 199 in 1999. There would be joy, and two victories for Frentzen, but sorrow as Damon Hill's season sank away into misery and disillusionment.

With a settled car/team/engine combination, the 199 was expected to perform well, and in Frentzen's hands it usually did. Mike Gascoyne's team produced a good-looking, strikingly liveried, and competitive machine, whose MF 301HD Mugen-Honda V10 power was better than in 1998. Both the drivers caused surprises – Frentzen by his obvious pace, and relish in his new team (in a driver swop, he had replaced Ralf Schumacher, who travelled to Williams in his place), and Damon Hill by the way his performance trailed away.

Frentzen complemented his car – two victories and four other podium finishes, to take third in the Drivers' series – while Damon Hill just got slower and slower. Never finishing higher than fourth, his last two points, for sixth place each time, were in Hungary and Belgium. Having

announced his decision to retire well before the end of the season, he even toyed with throwing away his helmet before the end of the year: on reflection, it would have been better if he had.

Jordan, though, had one consolation – that they finished third in the Constructors' Championship.

EJ10 There was a real air of confidence, and novelty, about Jordan's programme for the year 2000, if only because it had a new type number – EJ10 – which confirmed that the ebullient Irishman had now been in F1 for a decade.

Technical director Mike Gascoyne claimed that EJ10 was a big step forward in aerodynamic and mechanical terms,

though he said little about the Mugen-Honda V10, which was now seen as struggling to stay on terms with its rivals. Lighter than the previous 199, it was optimistically claimed to have 810bhp, and was allied to a new in-line six-speed gearbox. Suspension, front and rear, was merely an evolution of that found in the 199.

Much was made of new-signing Jarno Trulli's youth (Damon Hill, after all, had been thirty-nine when he retired), and there was no doubting the zest in early-season testing, but none of this was turned into success on the race track. In 2000, as in the mid-1990s, Jordan was back to the mid-field struggle, with a car that was neither fast enough nor reliable enough to make the front end of the grid.

Jordan-Mugen-Honda 199, Damon Hill driving.

continued from p.114

The first single-seater JBW was a Formula 1 car, very much on mid-engined Cooper lines, with a Maserati 250S sports-car engine driving through a five-speed gearbox. It was entered in three events in 1959, retiring from the International Trophy and the British GP, and failing to start in the Oulton Park Gold Cup. In 1960 Naylor again qualified well for the British GP (fifteenth of twenty-four), and finished thirteenth.

A 1.5litre car followed, on similar lines and initially with a Maserati 150S engine and Colotti gearbox. For its second race a Coventry-Climax FPF engine was fitted. This car was first run in a secondary Brands Hatch race, and perhaps over-ambitiously was entered for the Italian GP; it started

from the back of the Monza grid and Naylor retired it after six race laps. Two more runs in second-level British races served to show that Naylor and Wilkinson were perhaps out of their depth – this JBW retired once and its only finish was in a distant ninth place in the 1961 Gold Cup.

Jennings

South African Bill Jennings built this one-off F1 car for 1961, using a Porsche flat-four engine. He ran it in four local races, including the Grand Prix in that year before it became a World Championship event, placing twelfth and outpaced by the dominant works Lotus 21s. Jennings' best

finish was ninth in the Natal GP, another race won by Jim Clark.

Jicey

This marginal French constructor built a pair of Formula 2 cars on very conventional lines at the end of the 1940s, using BMW engines. They were still being raced in secondary events during the F2 Grands Prix period, but they never appeared in a World Championship event.

Jordan

See pp.115–117.

Kauhsen

Willibald Kauhsen entered and raced sports cars with little distinction before he set up a single-seater team, to run the erstwhile Elf 2J F2 cars under his name in 1977. In 1976 these had been driven by the European F2 champion; modified as the Kauhsen-Renault for 1977 they were hopeless, despite the services of drivers including Leclère and Prost. Nevertheless, Kauhsen went ahead with a Formula 1 programme for 1978. This proved an inept, and presumably costly, exercise: Kauhsen claimed that five cars were built and two were actually seen at two race meetings, when they failed to qualify by wide margins. Kauhsen turned his back on Formula 1, and Arturo Merzario acquired some of the material for his own hapless team.

Klaus Kapitza designed the car that carried Kauhsen's initials on Lotus 78 ground effects lines, with input from an impressive trio of academics who collectively failed to appreciate all aspects of wing-car aerodynamics. Cosworth DFV engines and Hewland gearboxes were used. The WKs seen in practice for the Spanish and Belgian GPs differed in details such as the fuel tank arrangements. Kauhsen's protégé Gianfranco Brancatelli was almost nine seconds off pole time at Jarama, and thirteen seconds off at Zolder.

Kieft

The Formula 3 cars produced by Kieft Cars Ltd enjoyed mixed reputations, but Cyril Kieft looked to move on to more ambitious projects, to abortive Formula 2 proposals and to a 1954 design for a Formula 1 car to be powered by the Coventry-Climax Godiva 2.5litre V8.

Two tubular chassis designed by Gordon Bedson were actually made, and one of these was mounted on the coil spring and wishbone independent front suspension and wishbones and transverse leaf spring rear suspension. Outboard disc brakes were to be used all round, and the intention was to fit a Wilson-type preselector gearbox. The incomplete car had a smooth and rather bulky body that quite possibly would have had intakes and outlets cut in

it ... if a real engine had been installed, rather than a dummy V8 provided by Coventry-Climax.

Klodwig

Ernst Klodwig first caught attention with a neat mid-engined single-seater for a German national class, powered by a 750cc BMW boxer engine. His 1952 Formula 2 car appeared cumbersome, but was also mid-engined (it was referred to as a 'BMW-Heck' in the 1952 German GP entry list, Heck simply meaning stern or rear). The power unit had that familiar 1,971cc capacity that identified it as a straight-six BMW unit.

Klodwig started from the ninth row of the thirty-car Grand Prix grid at the Nürburgring, and completed fourteen of the eighteen race laps. In 1953 his one-off was the slowest timed car on the grid (thirty-second, almost 2.5min off the pace), but this time he was classified in the German GP, fifteenth and lapped three times.

Kojima

The Kojima Engineering company of Kyoto, Japan, built cars for Japanese categories in the early 1970s, and ran March cars in the important local Formula 2 championship later in that decade. Matsuhisa Kojima then moved on up to Formula 1, adopting a tentative approach with apparently competent Cosworth-engined cars that were only entered in the 1976 and 1977 Japanese GPs. Nothing came of a rumoured Honda-engined Kojima for 1978, or the proposal that the German entrant Willibald Kauhsen would run a Kojima in the World Championship series. Either approach could have led to the development that these cars obviously needed, and probably deserved.

KE007 Designer Masao Ono used as many Japanese components as possible in the first F1 Kojima, but had to turn to Cosworth for engines, Hewland for gearboxes, and European specialists such as Hardy-Spicer, Lockheed and Ferodo for other components. There was an aluminium

monocoque, double wishbone-front suspension, with upper and lower links and radius rods at the rear, and outboard springs all round (the damper could be adjusted from the cockpit). Outwardly, the car featured a full-width nose, but side radiators, and a deep cockpit surround flanked by engine air intakes.

Masahino Hasemi qualified the car for the fifth row of the 1976 Japanese GP grid (alongside Ronnie Peterson, no less), but made two pit stops in the rain-saturated race, finishing eleventh and last. But after his second stop he set the fastest race lap – qualifying tyres were fitted and an historical footnote salvaged!

KE009 Ono revised the design for the 1977 car, increased the Japanese content among minor components, and cleaned up the body lines. Two cars were entered for the Japanese GP, a white works car contrasting with the sombre black of the 1976 car (and Japanese symbols that presumably indicated sponsorship) and a second more obviously sponsored car in the name of Heros Racing. Kazuyoshi Hoshino finished eleventh in the works car, lapped twice, while Noritake Takahara crashed the Heros car in the opening phase.

Kurtis

Kurtis Kraft never built a Formula 1 car, but its 1.7litre short-oval midget cars complied with the Grand Prix car regulations in the late 1950s, and 1959 Indianapolis 500 winner Rodger Ward entered one for that year's US GP at Sebring, encouraged by his success in a road-race meeting at Lime Rock.

The Kurtis had a tubular chassis, with solid axles and torsion bars front and rear, and simple disc brakes. There was a dohc Offenhauser four-cylinder engine, and a two-speed gearbox.

At Sebring, Ward soon found that mainstream Formula 1 was a very different proposition from US amateur competition, and the Kurtis was hopelessly outclassed in practice and the race. It was retired after twenty laps when its clutch failed. In a detail, the car carried modest signs of sponsorship.

Lamborghini

Lamborghini's modest entry in Formula 1 in 1988 seemed to some to signal the arrival of a major new player, especially as Chrysler was in the background. Lamborghini Engineering was largely funded by Chrysler, and set up in Modena, away from Lamborghini's Sant'Agata factory, with Mauro Forghieri, Ferrari's volatile engineering supremo from the early 1960s to the 1980s in charge of the technical side. Sadly, he seemed to have lost his touch, or to be out of touch as a traditional drawing-board man.

Even at that early stage, Forghieri wanted to build a complete F1 car to take on the might of Ferrari, but his associates from business manager Daniele Audetto to Chrysler executives were against this.

In 1990, funding for a Lamborghini F1 programme promised by Gonzales Luna failed to materialize, before the car even ran. The programme was saved by Carlo Petrucco, who effectively became a Lamborghini customer as he siezed the chance to take his Modena team into F1. The cars were named Lambo Formula. The financial backing was hardly adequate, and this was reflected in sluggish development; the Doi Group's late contribution led to the team being renamed Central Park Team Modena.

It lasted for just one season. The Lambo 291 was not a competitive car, and in any case Chrysler backed away – indeed, it was prevented from closing Lamborghini Engineering down on the spot only by Italian labour laws. After that, Lamborghini V12s were supplied to two minor teams in 1992 and 1993, but the heart had gone out of the organization.

It might have been so different if McLaren had gone ahead with a plan to use the V12 – which was impressive during tests – but Ron Dennis preferred the Peugeot alternative (and perhaps the financial deal that came with it?).

Lambo 291 Design of the 291 was attributed to Forghieri, with contributions from Mario Tollentino and Peter Wyss. It was wholly conventional, and generally was the heaviest car of the 1991 series. The basis was a triangular-section monocoque, with straightforward double-wishbone pushrod suspension front and rear. The heavy 3512

Lamborghini 291 of 1991, driven by Eric van der Poele.

V12 engine was rated at 700bhp, and it drove through a Lamborghini six-speed gearbox. Handling and grip shortcomings were never overcome, and modest development during the summer failed to produce competitive performances.

Lambo 291 qualified for only six Grands Prix, although the first outing had seemed encouraging as Nicola Larini finished seventh in the US GP. Eric van de Poele ran as high as fifth in the San Marino GP before retiring on the last lap (that was the only time he qualified in sixteen attempts). Larini drove a 291 to sixteenth places in Hungary and Italy, then the cars faded away, although a pair survived, to be offered at auction later in the 1990s.

Lancia

Vincenzo Lancia was a leading driver in the first decade of the century – he drove for FIAT in the first Grands Prix – but his racing career ended in 1908 as he concentrated on his own infant company. Its cars were generally of the highest quality, and Lancia was often regarded as a sporting marque, yet through to his death in 1937 he carefully steered it away from main-line motor sport. His son Gianni had different ideas, and had an ally in Vincenzo's widow Adele. In the early 1950s Lancia entered top-level sports-car racing, as a prelude to an entry into the Grands Prix.

A design team under the highly respected Vittorio Jano laid out an original and promising car, the D50. However, Fabbrica Automobili Lancia e Ca was a fragile company, and Lancia Corse proved one burden too many. The death of its leading driver Alberto Ascari in an unofficial test run in a Ferrari sports car seemed to be a final blow, and Lancia was pitched into insolvency. Eventually it fell into Fiat's hands, and much later was to become its rally arm, but immediately its Grand Prix team and equipment was handed to Ferrari, whose 1955 cars were desperately uncompetitive.

The D50 owed little to conventional thinking, was relatively small and light, and was intended to have good handling and traction qualities. Under Jano, Ettore Mina laid out a 2,489cc 90-degree V8, a high-revving unit that soon produced 260bhp. It served as a stressed member, and was mounted at an angle to give an offset prop shaft to the transaxle. There was a wishbone and coil-springs front suspension, and a de Dion rear end. Sponsons between the wheels were intended to improve the airflow and carried fuel and oil tanks, so that weight distribution

Lancia D50 of 1955, driven by Alberto Ascari at Monaco.

1952 – and would have added variety to the routine grids of similar cars, for its engine was mounted behind the cockpit in a substantial space frame. The suspension, sliding pillars at the front and transverse leaf spring at the rear, came from the Lancia Aurelia, and so did the transaxle. However, no more than 130bhp was claimed for the tuned Aurelia 1,991cc engine, and that was not a competitive F2 output in 1953. In another oddity, the front brakes were outside the wheels, for effective cooling (there were inboard brakes at the rear).

Tests only proved that the car was seriously underpowered, and apparently its handling called for development work. It was set aside, unraced.

Larrousse

As the 1990s opened, one-time Renault F1 manager Gerard Larrousse was involved with a team running Lola cars, with Lamborghini engines in 1990 and Cosworth engines in 1991 – a season made difficult as a Japanese partner withdrew, making for financial embarrassment, and there was a disagreement with FISA (*see* Lola). Larrousse found support to continue, primarily from Central Park and the small French specialist car manufacturer Venturi, whose name was applied to the 1992 Larrousse cars. The Fomet design studio was commissioned to lay out and construct cars, in the process becoming Venturi-Larrousse UK. Lamborghini engines were secured for two seasons. The Venturi association lasted for just one year – that company was experiencing its own cash-flow problems.

The team struggled on slender budgets, but at least Larrousse kept it in being through 1992, when in aspects such as pit-lane appearance it looked good enough to be the leading French team he hoped it might become. That year it was equal eleventh in the Constructors Championship, when Ligier was seventh. In terms of points, 1993 was better, then it slipped from three points to two in 1994. There were new sponsors that year, but the team's financial state was precarious, little or no development work was done, drivers who could contribute cash were welcome – six men drove for Larrousse during the season – and fortunes slipped. Without realistic new financial backing for 1995 the situation was hopeless, and the Larrousse team became a tiny footnote to the Grand Prix history of the 1990s.

remained near-constant as these loads were reduced through a race. As Lancias, these cars gained a reputation for tricky handling.

The D50 was first raced at the end of 1954, showing speed if not stamina in the Spanish GP, while in the Argentine GP early in 1955 both cars left the track. There were two minor race victories, and a second, then Castellotti took second place at Monaco after Ascari's plunge into the harbour, and D50s were also fifth and sixth. Castellotti was then allowed to run a D50 'independently' in the Belgian GP before Ferrari took over. The cars appeared again in late summer with 'prancing horse' badges. Jano was retained as a consultant, but Ferrari engineers started to modify the cars to a 'conventional' format, for example, with the sponsons faired into the bonnet.

In 1956 Fangio drove these Lancia-Ferrari D50As to win the World Championship, while Peter Collins was third. The cars were driven to five Grand Prix victories that year, sometimes in shared drives. They were then developed still further from their Lancia origins.

As a footnote, Lancia production engines were used in other cars, and in a conceit common during the period the name of the engine manufacturer sometimes appeared ahead of the chassis constructor, hence Lancia-Marino and Lancia-Nardi, which might

have had some appeal in race entry terms but were as odd as, say, Mercedes-McLaren would have appeared in the 1990s.

Lancia-Marino

This obscure Formula 1 special by Marino Brandolfi made just one race appearance, slowly and for only a few laps before it retired, in the 1957 Naples GP. Broadly, it comprised Lancia Aurelia components, and as Ferrari had discarded the Lancia name (if not all the origins of its cars) that year, this marginal one-off saw the last use of the great marque's name on an F1 car.

Lancia-Nardi

Enrico Nardi is recalled for specialist components and for his involvement with Ferrari's first car, the Auto Avio 815 of 1940, and the name is now associated above all with steering wheels. It should also be known for some of its post-war sports cars, notable the elegant and potent Nardi-Alfa Romeo of the late 1940s.

Lancia supported a Nardi Formula 2 project, for a car that could have been raced in the second year of the 2litre World Championships – it was built in the summer of

LC92 This car was designed quickly by Tino Belli and Tim Holloway, with some guidance from Robin Herd, and a pair was ready for the first race of the season. The LC92 was quite conventional, some work was carried over from previous Fomet 1 designs, and major components (such as the monocoques) were made by outside suppliers. There was double-wishbone suspension, pushrod at the front, pullrod at the rear. The Lamborghini 3512 V12 was rated at 730bhp (but was inconsistent), and it drove through a Lamborghini six-speed transverse gearbox.

As the series got under way, the LC92 began to appear competitive, but the single point scored by Gachot at Monaco turned out to be the only one of the year. He recorded only two other finishes; Ukyo Katayama finished five races, but also failed to qualify to start in two.

LH93 The 1993 car followed similar economic lines, with a specification that was almost interchangeable – the budget simply would not allow for novel or advanced features such as active suspension. The V12 was no more powerful, and little development work was put into it, as Lamborghini Engineering was also underfunded. In those circumstances, the promising pair of drivers did well to score three points, Philippe Alliot with fifth place at Imola and Erik Comas with sixth at Monza. Alliot retired five times, Comas seven times (the former had to stand down

for the last two races in favour of Toshio Suzuki, who brought money to the team).

LH94 Once again the existing design was modified, but more substantially as Ford (Cosworth) HB V8s were used. These drove through a Benetton six-speed semi-automatic transverse gearbox. Further modifications had to be made as mid-season rule changes were precipitately made following accidents. Together with too many engine failures, this stretched the budget and ruled out car development.

Comas scored the team's only points, with sixth places in the Pacific and German GPs, and he drove in all save one of the season's sixteen races. Olivier Beretta started in ten, with his best placing seventh in Germany. Noda started in three, Dalmas in two, Deletraz and Alliot in one each, and between them scraped one finish (Dalmas's fourteenth place in Portugal).

The Larrousse team's 48-race career ended miserably with two retirements in the last race, and eleventh place in the 1994 Constructors' Championship.

LDS

L.D. 'Doug' Serrurier was the leading South African single-seater constructor from the mid-1950s to the mid-1960s, generally building Cooper- or Brabham-inspired cars that usually qualified for For-

mula 1 events. Most were intended for the then-flourishing Gold Star and International F1 series that came to attract some leading European teams during the northern hemisphere off-season. Some LDS runners were by no means disgraced in their company, although they seldom ran with race leaders and did not feature high on the results lists when top teams were present.

The first LDS was a front-engined car, but the second followed Cooper T45 lines and became an F1 car when it was run by Sam Tingle. He used the locally popular Alfa Romeo Giulietta engine, naturally in a tuned state and driving through a Cooper transaxle. Tingle raced this LDS2 for five years, qualifying well for the first South African GP with World Championship status (1962), but retired in the race; in 1963 he was classified eleventh in this race, but was lapped seven times by Clark, and then slumped to last on the 1965 grid and thirteenth in the race (but six other local drivers, including Serrurier in one of his own cars, failed to qualify for the grid).

Similar cars had Coventry-Climax engines, and highly rated John Love raced the fourth LDS with a Porsche flat-four engine.

The sixth and seventh cars were based on the Cooper T53, and an LDS7 with an Alfa Romeo engine driving through a Hewland gearbox was moderately competitive in Serrurier's hands. Two more similar cars were seen in local events. LDS10, or the Mk3, was an authorized copy of a Brabham BT11, with a 2.7litre Coventry-Climax FPF. Tingle qualified it fourteenth fastest for the 1967 South African GP and approaching half-distance in the race climbed as high as eighth, only to crash at three-quarter distance (this was the race Love sensationally led in an elderly Cooper).

The next car, LDS11, followed the lines of the tenth, but with a smaller FPF. It was driven by Serrurier in local events, and effectively was the last LDS that could be described as an F1 car. It was followed by two more on Brabham BT16 lines, one with a 2litre FPF, that were the last of Serrurier's baker's dozen.

LEC

The LEC one-car team was a brave venture, initiated for a brave man. It was financed by Charlie Purley for his son

Larrousse-Lola-Ford of 1987.

David, and named for his LEC refrigeration equipment company. David was an accomplished and experienced driver, and clear winner of the European F5000 championship in 1976, the year before the LEC CRP1 appeared.

This distinctive car was designed by Mike Pilbeam (hence the third initial in the designation), invariably in the mid-1970s around a Cosworth DFV engine and Hewland gearbox. It had a riveted aluminium monocoque, double wishbone suspension with inboard springs, with upper and lower links and radius rods at the rear. The dark blue body was neat, with side radiators. Various nose aerofoils were tried as the little team bedded in.

Purley finished sixth in the car's debut race, the 1977 Race of Champions, failed to qualify at a first Grand Prix attempt (in Spain), then placed the LEC thirteenth in Belgium and fourteenth in Sweden. During practice for the British GP, Purley crashed heavily when the throttle slides struck open, and suffered extensive leg injuries. When these had been repaired, he drove a second LEC in the British national series, but soon turned away from motor racing.

Leyton House

Leyton House Racing Limited was formed in 1989 by Japanese real estate entrepreneur Akiri Akagi in the name of the company's leisure division and that year it purchased March Racing, the constructor's Formula 1 team (which Leyton House had sponsored, 1987–89). In 1990 the March name was discarded, but it reappeared late in 1991, as the Leyton House group retreated, as one consequence of financial crises in Japan. The 1990–91 cars are described in the March sequence (*see* pp.147–148).

Life

Pre-qualification was a daunting requirement for lesser Formula 1 teams as the 1990s opened, and the Life drivers never did manage to leap that hurdle. Gary Brabham and Bruno Giacomelli were perfectly competent but their car was hopeless.

Franco Rocchi designed a W12 engine for Life Racing Engines, and the chassis built for the First team in 1988 (but not raced in 1989) was acquired, to be used as a running test bed. It was then adapted by Ernesto Vita's team, becoming the Life F190 for the 1990 Grand Prix season.

The conventional car was revised to meet the 1990 crash test requirements, as well as accept the W12 in place of a Judd V8. Seemingly, it was little tested with Signor Rocchi's complicated engine, for when it appeared at circuits it sometimes refused to function, and when it did, cynical observers commented that it was usually with fewer than twelve cylinders contributing to the power output.

Gary Brabham could do nothing with it in pre-qualifying for the first two Grands Prix, then Bruno Giacomelli stuck with it through ten attempts ('NPQ' every time). a Judd V8 was installed for the last two Grands Prix in Europe; in Portugal it refused to run, In Spain Giacomelli completed just two laps, the best some 25 seconds off the pole position time. The Life team did not appear for the Japanese and Australian GP preliminaries.

Ligier

See pp.123–126.

Leyton House-Judd (March) CG891 of 1989–90.

LIGIER

Guy Ligier was a successful businessman in the heavy construction industry – and he looked the part – and in the French manner he had powerful connections. He was to exploit these in the twenty-one years that a Grand Prix team carried his name, and that often carried the burden of French expectations of glory. Before he became a constructor, Ligier had played Rugby at international level, and in those distant days when independent entrants were welcome in the Grands Prix had been good enough to score a World Championship point.

He gave up driving when his close friend Jo Schlesser was killed in a 1968 French GP accident (all Ligier cars carried a 'JS' designation in his memory). By that time, Automobiles Ligier had started work on the JS1 coupe that appeared in 1969. Other production coupes and sports-racing cars followed, before the first Formula 1 Ligier came in 1976.

The team continued as Ligier until 1996, although by that time Guy Ligier's interest was reduced to 15 per cent, at the end of a very uncertain period when Flavio Briatore controlled the team and Tom Walkinshaw ran it. The Scot's hopes of buying control from Briatore foundered when Ligier refused to countenance 'his' team losing its French basis. That awful possibility receded as Alain Prost took over for 1997, and it seemed that France had a national team again.

Ligier's record was not brilliant, and its cars were hardly innovative. It contested 326 Grands Prix, yielding nine victories and 388 points. There were runner-up and third places in the Constructors' Championship, in 1980 and 1979 respectively, but there were also seasons when no points were scored.

JS5 In some ways Ligier picked up where Matra left off, as the patron exploited his connections in high places and the State tobacco company that was the major sponsor. First and foremost, he obtained the Matra V12, while Matra engine specialists continued development work. The design team was controlled by a former Matra manager Gérard Ducarouge and included Matra chassis designer Michel Beaujon and Paul Carillo.

The body lines by SERA aerodynamicist Robert Choulet were curvaceous, with a short nose and initially a very large engine airbox, and the car looked bulky (the wheelbase was actually relatively short, but the track was fairly wide). A revised version that came later in 1976 appeared slimmer. Under the skin the make-up was conventional, with double wishbone front suspension and upper and lower links with radius rods at the rear. The V12 was rated at 520bhp and it drove through a Hewland gearbox.

A one-car team was run, and Jacques Laffite scored its first points in its third

Grand Prix, finishing fourth at Long Beach. His best finish, second, came in Austria and there were third places in Belgium and Italy. Encouragingly, at the end of the year Ligier was equal fifth in the Constructors Championship with twenty points.

JS7 The 1978 car was in a direct line of evolution from the first F1 Ligier, most differences being due to the new MS76 engine. This was lower, and called for changes to the rear suspension and ancillaries. This V12 proved no more powerful than the MS73, and for a while it was troublesome. The outward lines of the car were still distinctive, smooth but still bulky, and with a full-width nose aerofoil; a narrow-track version appeared in mid-summer and gave a significant reduction in frontal area.

For half a season, Laffite failed to score, then he won the Swedish GP. Luck played a part, and that race was noted for fluke results, but it was a first championship race victory for Ligier. The team then went off the boil, and there were just three more scoring finishes (second in Holland, fifth in Japan and sixth in Britain) so that it slipped to eighth in the championship.

The JS7 was uprated for the opening races of 1978, primarily with a Hewland FGA six-speed gearbox. Laffite was fifth in two Grands Prix later in this car, and achieved a similar result with 'JS7/9' (in the French GP).

JS9 In most respects this was another evolutionary car that was to be developed through the year, primarily in the suspension. The MS76 still had a quoted output of 520bhp, but the effective revs band was broader (it was expected to be the final season for this engine, although it was to be brought out again in 1981). Laffite drove JS9s to third places in Spain and Germany, fourth in Italy and fifth in Austria, his nineteen points scored with JS7s and JS9s gaining sixth place in the championship for Ligier.

JS11 In 1979 Ligier ran a two-car team and became a real force in Formula 1 with the handsome JS11 ground-effects car designed by Beaujon and Ducarouge. This proved to be as tough as it looked, and its prominent side pods flanked an adequately stiff monocoque. For power units, Ligier turned to Cosworth and the DFV. Unfortunately, the team was to break with its

Ligier-Matra V12 Type JS5 of 1976, Jacques Laffite driving.

established wind-tunnel associate in mid-season, and continuity was lost; at the same time the suspension (basically, lower wishbones and top rocker arms front and rear) was modified, to no advantage.

In a strong start to the year, Laffite won the Argentine and Brazilian GPs, and was second in Belgium, while Patrick Depailler was second in Brazil and won in Spain. Injury then put him out of racing early in the European season and Ickx took his place (the Belgian was past his F1 best, but he did speak French!). In the summer Laffite was third in three Grands Prix, and Ickx scored three points, to give Ligier sixty-one points and third place in the Constructors' Championship.

JS11/15   The 1980 car was built around the JS11 monocoque, with revised rear suspension, aerodynamics broadly in 'fast' and 'slow' configurations (outwardly with a front wing used only on slow tracks), DFV engines and attractive bodywork.

Laffite and Didier Pironi each won a Grand Prix (in Germany and Belgium respectively), but some observers felt that they should have won more, if the team had been more focused. Between them they also scored three second places, four third places, two fourths and three fifths. Their sixty-six points meant that Ligier was runner-up in the championship, the highest placing in its history.

JS17   There were echoes of the Cosworth-engined cars in the lines of the 1981 Ligier, but much was different. The cars were entered as Talbot-Ligiers, and that association was a reason for a return to the Matra V12, in MS81 form, but no more powerful in absolute terms

Ligier-Matra V12 Type JS17 (sometimes called Talbot-Ligier) of 1981.

(although its rev limit was higher, and so was the decibel output). In most other respects, this last Ligier design in which Ducarouge had a hand followed earlier types, but Ligier started the year with 'legal' suspension and did not develop a hydropneumatic system to circumvent the sliding skirt ban until the European season was under way.

Laffite drove through the year, and scored all of Ligier's points. He won the Austrian and Canadian GPs, was second twice, third three times and sixth twice, to secure fourth place in the championship for the team. Jarier (two races), Jabouille (six) and Tambay (eight) failed to score.

The JS17s were mildly revised for the early-1982 races, when the only notable

result was Eddie Cheever's second place in the USA East GP at Detroit.

JS19   Michel Beaujon's 1982 car looked original, with the cockpit well forward in the wheelbase and a long engine deck behind it. The ground-effects skirt was also very long, and scrutineers objected. Eventually Ligier had to give way, the skirts and pods were shortened, and much of the calculated ground effects downforce was lost. So was the team impetus, until the summer. Moreover, the turbo V6 that Matra was to supply (with Talbot labels) never did materialize, so although the old V12 was outclassed it had to serve through the season.

Third places at Zolder and Las Vegas (both scored by Cheever) were the best

(Talbot) Ligier-Matra JS19 of 1982, Eddie Cheever driving.

finishes for JS19s, and Ligier slipped to eighth in the championship.

JS21 In a downbeat 1983 season, Ligier failed to score any points. Beaujon and Claude Galopin used JS19 monocoques as the basis for two JS21s, and one new car was built to this specification. But in the turbo age, the team had to fall back on Cosworth customer engines. Boesel and Jarier each finished six races, and each had a best placing just outside the points.

JS23 This was one of the ugliest cars of a period not noted for elegant Grand Prix machines, as turbo engines allowed them to drag outsize aerofoils around circuits. The turbo engine behind the cockpit of the car designed by Beaujon and Galopin

moved to Ligier, and chassis expert Michel Tétu went with him. They inherited the JS25, which Tétu was to develop. It had a new monocoque and pushrod suspension, the Renault engines were to give up to 800bhp in their EF15 form, and they drove through Hewland gearboxes. Tétu's first target was to lose excess weight on the car.

Laffite returned to Ligier, scored a point in the first race, was third in the British and German GPs, and second in the final race in Australia. De Cesaris contributed three points, but retired eight times in eleven starts, and was sacked after the last of those, which had ended in a lurid accident. Philippe Streiff started in four Grands Prix, and finished third in the last of those. Ligier was sixth in the 1985 championship, with twenty-three points.

JS29 Tétu designed this car for the Alfa Romeo 415T engine (that never raced) then had to hastily rework it for the Megatron (née BMW) unit – Arnoux was indiscreet in public and the Italian engine was withdrawn from the team (this probably suited Alfa Romeo and its new owner, Fiat). The Megatron engine was heavier and bulkier, and that upset the balance of the pretty JS29. This had to be developed during the season, eventually seeing the year out as the JS29C.

The engine problems meant that the team missed the first race. After that, which both drivers recorded nine retirements, and each had a DNS against his name; Arnoux scored just one point, Ghinzani none.

Ligier-turbo Renault JS23 of 1984, driven by Andrea de Cesaris.

was the Renault V6. The carbon-fibre monocoque and pushrod suspension were straightforward, and during the year were to be modified in the JS23B.

Andrea de Cesaris scored just three points (two in South Africa and one at Imola), and his 1984 team mate, newcomer François Hesnault failed to score. They recorded nineteen retirements, and Ligier was eleventh in the championship.

JS25 Ligier's failure was not the only one to afflict French teams in 1984, and Renault Sport's slump meant that its director, Gerard Larrousse, was 'released'. He

JS27 Tétu reworked the JS25 design for 1986, when Ligier negotiated a government grant to obtain Renault engines again, albeit these were Mecachrome customer units rather than full works engines.

Laffite started in eight races before a British GP accident ended his racing career. His value to Ligier had been underlined as he scored five times (with second place at Detroit his best finish). René Arnoux also contributed fourteen points, while Alliot was brought in to replace Laffite and contributed just one point to Ligier's total, which was good for fifth place in the championship.

JS31 Ligier was equal eleventh in the 1987 Constructors' Championship, and it did not feature at all in 1988 – Tétu's car lived up to its odd layout and appearance. In its overall lines, it resembled the hapless 1986 Brabham BT55 'low line' car, and it certainly had a low frontal area. But it was complex, with a fuel tank between engine and gearbox and another in each flank, with the driver able to control the use of fuel from each to retain optimum weight distribution and handling (that was just one area where the car was deficient). Double wishbone suspension was used, pushrod at the front, pullrod at the rear. Power steering was tried, and abandoned. A Judd CV engine provided the power.

Arnoux finished only five races, and his best placing was tenth. Stefan Johannson finished only three races, and was ninth in the first and last races of the year. Ligier hit rock bottom again.

JS33 Beaujon laid down the 1989 Ligier, and Richard Divila was brought in to complete the job. They produced a wholly conventional car that used Cosworth DFR engines.

It gave Ligier a recovery period, with points against the name again – two scored by Arnoux in Canada in one of his six finishes, and one scored by Olivier Grouillard in France (he finished five races). Ligier was thirteenth in the championship.

The cars were uprated as JS33Bs for 1990, with new front suspension on the same lines (adopted by virtually every designer) and some weight saved. Philippe Alliot and Nicola Larini drove, but neither scored a point – Larini's seventh places in Spain and Japan were Ligier's best finishes in another very poor season.

JS35 The 1991 car was put in hand as the team was changing its approach, its engine supplier, its drivers, and soon its designers. In its first form, the JS35 was the work of Beaujon, Galopin and Divila, but before it raced Frank Dernie had been brought in, and he modified the car to JS35B form. By mid-season this was showing promise. It was conventional in most respects, but for this season the Lamborghini 3512 V12 was used, in the expectation that a Renault V10 would become available in 1992. An Xtrac transverse gearbox was used.

Thierry Boutsen and Erik Comas drove throughout the season, and the record was dismal, although at least reliability was good as the pair recorded eleven retirements. But Comas failed to qualify three times, and the best race placing was seventh, achieved twice by Boutsen, and that hardly supported assertions that Ligier was a top-rate team.

JS37 Ligier had its Renault engines for 1992, Dernie was backed up by Ducarouge, Alain Prost tested the car, finance seemed adequate. Yet the end product was half a dozen championship points.

The engine was the competitive Mecachrome-supplied and maintained RS3B/3C, which gave up to 770bhp and

was generally reliable, and it drove through the Xtrac/Ligier six-speed gearbox. The car looked good, but appearances seemingly deceived as far as aerodynamics were concerned. The suspension also had to be revised.

Comas scored three times (a fifth and two sixth places) in mid-season, Boutsen was fifth in the final race, and the retirement rate was back up to 50 per cent. Equal seventh place in the championship was probably less than France expected, and certainly less than Guy Ligier expected. He backed away, passing control to businessman Cyril de Rouvre, who had presided over AGS, 1989–91, and so knew about life at the end of pits rows where poor teams lived. His reign was short, and Flavio Briatore was to take control in 1994.

JS39 Reorganization came under the new team president, and Ligier fortunes improved. Ducarouge and John Davis designed a new car, the Renault engines were retained, and Williams semi-automatic gearboxes were available (together with quiet support), while the team pulled together to give its pair of British drivers a fair chance. There was nothing startling in the car. It did not have active suspension, which was a handicap, and aerodynamics had to be refined during the year.

Martin Brundle and Mark Blundell restored Ligier's middle-rank status, and on the end-of-season table it was not far behind Ferrari, in fifth place. Brundle scored in seven races (thirteen points), with his best finish third in the San Marino GP, while Blundell was third in South Africa and Germany, and scored ten points.

Cyril de Rouvre's financial problems meant that funds were frozen, and the team lived a hand-to-mouth existence early in 1994. When Briatore took control he brought in Frank Dernie from his Benetton team, to overhaul the car as the JS39B. Adequate power was available, in the RS6 Renault V10s, but aerodynamic shortcomings had to be sorted out.

Driver pairings fluctuated. Olivier Panis was entered in all sixteen races, retired only once, and scored nine points with a best of second in Germany; Eric Bernard drove thirteen races for the team, with one scoring finish (third in Germany); Franck Lagorce made no impression in two races; Johnny Herbert started the European GP in a Ligier, and then was drafted to Benetton. Ligier slipped one place in the championship, to sixth with thirteen points.

JS41 The team management was changed again for 1995. Tom Walkinshaw, whose organization had a Ligier role in 1994, was brought in to head the team, while Tony Dowe replaced Cesare Fiorio as team manager. One-time Ligier stalwart Jacques Laffite, who had scored 196 points driving Ligiers (more than half of the team's total), returned in a managerial role, lending a French presence to the only French team.

Dernie designed a new car, for the Mugen Honda MF301 V10. Close similarities to the Benetton B195 were remarked at the time, and indeed some components were common to both cars. The Renault engines had gone to Benetton and the Mugens seemed less powerful, for the disparity in speeds could not be completely put down to aerodynamic differences.

Panis retired from six races, but more importantly he scored in six, with his highest placing second in Australia to back up two fourth places. Aguri Suzuki and Martin Brundle were his team mates (six and eleven times, respectively); the Japanese driver scored a point in Germany, while Brundle was third in Belgium and fourth in France. Ligier was fifth in the championship.

JS43 A promising effort was undermined by yet more management changes, inadequate funding, and uncertainty. Frank Dernie designed a car on JS41 lines, still using Mugen V10s driving through a Benetton-type transverse gearbox. As he left, Loic Bigois and André de Cortanze took over the technical side, and Fiorio returned as team manager.

As the season wore on prospects seemed to improve, especially after Panis won the Monaco GP. But that was a high point, never to be repeated. Panis had just two more scoring finishes, sixth in Brazil and fifth in Hungary, and while Pedro Diniz brought financial backing he was still a relative novice, who scored his first points (two) in his year with Ligier. The team also saw its cars retire seventeen times.

There was some expectation that a rejuvenated Ligier team could become a force in Grand Prix racing in 1997. The JS45 was built and tested, but the team that entered it for the first Grand Prix of the new season was Prost Gauloises Blondes, and at the end of the year that team was to take the sixth place in the Constructors' Championship, as Ligier had done in 1996.

Locomobile

Oddly, Locomobile did not contest the first Grand Prize race, for in 1908 George Robertson scored a famous victory for the marque in the Vanderbilt Cup, up to that year America's equivalent to the Grand Prix. His car, to become known as 'No 16', was a typical large racing car of the period, designed by A.L. Riker, with a 16litre engine. It was built in 1906, and that year Joe Tracy won the Vanderbilt Eliminating Trials, but retired on the ninth of ten laps in the Cup race (however, in a field that included leading European Grand Prix cars and drivers, he set the fastest lap).

A dispute in 1908 meant that the European teams concentrated on the Grand Prize, so Robertson faced a field of American cars and Grand Prix cars run by independents in the Vanderbilt Cup. He won by less than two minutes from an Isotta – a close finish in those days – with Jim Florida third in another Locomobile. Then the company lost interest in racing, although its cars ran in some stock events, and 'No 16' did the rounds of showrooms. That car is now remembered for the first American victory in a major international race.

Lola

See pp.128–130.

Lorraine-Dietrich

De Dietrich cars were seen in competition in the final years of the nineteenth century, and as the next decade opened the company developed typical large racing cars that, save for a good team result in the 1905 Coppa Florio, generally had modest records. Entries for the first Grands Prix unsurprisingly followed, for the first in 1906 under the marque name Lorraine-Dietrich (to make the point that this was a French company).

The 1906 Grand Prix car was typical, bluff-nosed with wide-open cockpit, channel-section frame and wood-spoked artillery wheels, with spare tyres stacked above a bolster tank at the tail, a thumping great four-cylinder engine (of 18,146cc) and chain final drive. The trio at Le Mans for the first Grand Prix were at the 1,007kg (2,220lb) weight limit, or close to it. Gabriel, Rougier and Duray were the team's regular drivers throughout this period. Only Duray survived the

1,238km (769 mile) race, finishing eighth, more than three hours after the winning Renault. Gabriel completed only one lap, Rougier ran last until he retired with two laps to go.

Duray then finished third behind Wagner (Darracq) and Lancia (Fiat) in the Vanderbilt Cup race. He also started in the 1911 Grand Prix de France at Le Mans in one of the 1906 cars – this was after all the race dubbed Grand Prix des Vieux Tacots (old crocks) – and led the race but retired.

The 1907 Grand Prix Lorraine-Dietrich had a slightly smaller engine (17,304cc –

only one car in that Grand Prix had a larger power unit) and a specification following 1906 lines, save for the use of detachable-rim wheels. The car was quick, in the official practice period, and in the race when Duray set the fastest lap. He led for half the race, but his engine failed near the end. Rougier also retired with engine failure, leaving Gabriel to finish fourth, losing time in the closing laps as he was cautious in this fuel-consumption event.

The 1908 engine had to be smaller, as 155mm maximum cylinder bore regulations were in force, but Lorraine-Dietrich made their four-cylinder unit as large as possible, and at 13,586cc it was the largest in the field. In other respects, the car fol-

lowed its Grand Prix predecessors. In advance, the Lorraine-Dietrichs were not highly rated, and all three were out by lap three of the race, two with magneto failures, one with clutch failure.

Lorraine-Dietrich was back when the Grand Prix was revived in 1912, with a quartet of cars that seemed almost archaic. Once again, a large engine was used (the largest in the race). But at least these 15,095cc four-cylinder units had overhead valves. These were one of only three types in the race with chain drive, and although they were shown off at the Lunéville

Lorraine-Dietrich GP car of 1906.

factory with Rudge Whitworth wire wheels they started the race with artillery wheels. None of them raced for long – Hémery and Heim completed only one lap each before their engines expired, and Bablot's engine lasted only seven laps; Hanriot reached half-distance in this two-day Grand Prix in a reasonable tenth place, but during the night his car caught on fire.

Lorraine-Dietrich sports cars were raced in the 1920s, but the company never returned to the Grands Prix.

Lotus

See pp.130–142.

Eric Broadley set his face against a full Lola Formula 1 works team for four decades, and when he eventually succumbed, the move to all intents and purposes brought down his company. To that time, Lola had sometimes built F1 cars to meet commissions. None of them were particularly successful. Broadley made his name, and firmly established Lola, with brilliant little sports-racing cars in the late 1950s. The first Lola single-seater was a front-engined Formula Junior car introduced for 1960, as constructors were swinging to the rear-engined layout. This was adopted for the Mk 3, another F Junior car (one was fitted with a Ford 109E 1,340cc engine and run in a non-championship F1 race at Brands Hatch late in 1961).

By that time, Reg Parnell and John Surtees had obtained finance company backing for a Grand Prix team, and approached Broadley to build cars for it. These were promising in 1962, well placed in two Grands Prix and with non-title race success, before that effort tailed off. The strong Surtees connection then led to a Lola T90 Indianapolis car design being hastily adapted for Formula 1 as the Honda RA300 in 1967, successfully as Surtees drove it to Honda's only championship race victory in its 3litre F1 venture.

The next F1 cars were built for Graham Hill in 1974, and led to the Hill cars. The Lola connection with the cars known as Beatrice-Lola or Lola-Haas in the mid-1980s was tenuous. The Larrousse-Calmels cars later in that decade scored a few points, in 1990 enough for a sound sixth place in the Constructors' Championship, but the French outfit went into liquidation, leaving Lola financially bruised. A liaison with Beppe Lucchini's Scuderia Italia did not last a full racing year – completing it with wretchedly uncompetitive cars must have seemed pointless.

Then there was the disastrous 1997 venture, based on an ill-conceived method of sponsorship and cars that were not developed to raceworthiness when they had to be entered for the first Grand Prix of the season. They were hopeless. Broadley lost control of his company, Martin Birrane salvaged the remnants to continue to build customer cars, for F3000 and US racing, areas where Lola had done well.

Mk 4   The first F1 Lola was built exclusively for a team that came close to having 'works' status, and possibly the undertaking was too big for a small company – when it appeared, Lola had built no more than seventy-six cars. The Mk 4 had a space frame that lacked rigidity and had to be strengthened with additional tubes; the fourth (and last) car built had some stiffening aluminium panels, and was dubbed Mk 4A (the 'semi-monocoque' description sometimes used was hardly justified). The outboard suspension comprised wishbones, coil springs and long radius arms. The dark blue glass-fibre bodies were smooth and handsome. The Mk 4 was designed for the Coventry-Climax FWMV V8, and as these engines were not available for the first races of

1962 four-cylinder FPF engines were used, with Colotti gearboxes.

Lola's Formula 1 race debut came in the non-championship Brussels GP, and the first with a V8 came at Goodwood a few weeks later. The cars showed promise in several secondary races, and in the summer Surtees drove one to win a Mallory Park race. The first championship races were disappointing, then Surtees was fifth in the Belgian GP and went on to finish second in the British and German GPs. He scored nineteen points that year, and that gave Lola fourth place in the Constructors' Championship (his team mate Roy Salvadori failed to score).

Surtees then used one of these cars with a 2.7litre engine to win the 1963 New Zealand GP. His championship programme that year was with Ferrari, and in any case the first Lola F1 backers had withdrawn. In Formula 1, two of the cars were run by Reg Parnell in 1963, and one by Bob Anderson. The Parnell cars were driven by Chris Amon, who was finding his feet but was seventh in the French and British GPs, and five other drivers. But Anderson did best, in that he won a secondary race (the Rome GP) and was well placed in others.

T130   John Surtees was responsible for the Honda Formula 1 effort in 1967, and as he struggled with the Japanese company's heavy and cumbersome RA273 he obtained approval for Lola to create an RA300 using the powerful V12. Most of the car – monocoque, suspension, etc. – was pure Lola, and it was lighter and simpler than the RA273. It was also a Grand Prix winner first time out, driven by Surtees at Monza. This was a major contribution to Honda's championship score of twenty points that earned it fourth in the table.

T180   This was the Honda RA301, a development of the RA300 by Surtees, Lola and Honda for the 1968 season. Two were built, and the outstanding moment came when Surtees led the Belgian GP before retiring. Second in Britain and third in the USA, plus two fifth places, meant that this car gave Honda sixth place in the 1968 championship. By its nature, the points table did not even allow an honourable mention for Lola.

T370   Graham Hill commissioned this car for his Embassy-backed Formula 1

Lola-Climax Mk 4 of 1962, John Surtees driving.

team in 1973, when he raced a Shadow DN1 in the cigarette company's distinctive white and red colours. The first T370 was tested well before the end of that year, as cars had to be ready for the early-January start to the championship series in Argentina.

The Cosworth T370 was a 'Cosworth kit car', on the broad lines of Lola's successful T330/332 F5000 models, in the monocoque and double wishbone front suspension, with upper and lower links and radius arms at the rear, and outboard springs all round. The DFV drove through a Hewland FGA 400 gearbox. In dimensions such as wheelbase and track, the T370 was the third-largest F1 car of 1974, but the vast engine airbox and rear wing made it appear to be the largest. Hill scored his team's only point when he finished sixth in Sweden. Edwards, Gethin and Stommelen failed to score.

The cars were run in the first three races of 1975, driven by Hill and Stommelen, to a tenth place and three finishes outside the top ten.

T371 Despite the Lola type number, this car was hardly a Lola, and it was raced as the Hill GH1. It was the work of designer Andy Smallman, and had some Lola features.

THL1 The 'L' in this Beatrice designation indicated Lola, and it was useful for Team Haas (USA) to make the connection, as well as list Eric Broadley as a design consultant. But the team was Beatrice, and so were the cars.

LC87 Lola was back in Formula 1 in 1987–91, building cars for a French team run by Gérard Larrousse and backed by Didier Calmels, hence the LC designations. This time Lola's involvement was closer to the operating team.

Designed by Broadley and Ralph Bellamy, the first LC car followed Lola's F3000 type fairly closely, with a carbon-composite monocoque and double wishbone pullrod suspension. A 3.5litre Cosworth DFZ engine drove through a Hewland FGB gearbox. The car was overweight, and was to be logically developed through the year.

At first a single car was run, for Philippe Alliot, who started in fifteen Grands Prix and finished sixth in three of them; Dalmas started in at least three Grands Prix, but did not score. Lola was

Lola-Ford T370 of 1974, driven by Graham Hill.

ninth in the Constructors' Championship, second in a subsidiary championship for teams running normally aspirated cars in the turbo-dominated era.

LC88 Chris Murphy was coupled with Eric Broadley in the design credits for this evolutionary car for 1988, with the only significant changes in the front suspension. Alliot and Dalmas drove, but failed to score a single point.

Two cars were modified for the Lamborghini 3512 V12 for the first race of 1989, when they made no impression, save perhaps when they were weighed.

LC89 Ducarouge added his experience to the design of the definitive Lamborghini-engined car, which also had Lamborghini's transverse gearbox. Necessarily, this was a larger car (by as much as 20cm/8in in the wheelbase) and largely because of its engine it was overweight. Its make-up was conventional. The season was disappointing. Alliot scored the team's single point (in Spain) to give Lola fifteenth place in the championship. Dalmas qualified only once before he was dropped; Bernard started in two mid-season races; vastly experienced Michele Alboreto started in five of the last Grands Prix of the 'European season'.

As LC89B the car was revised in some details for the first races of 1990, and more importantly Forghieri's engine was uprated and a gearbox allowing an automatic option was available. Bernard placed an LC89B eighth in the first race of the season.

LC90 This was a development of the 1989 car, with design attributed to Ducarouge and Murphy (who was soon to depart). It retained the principal features of the LC89, and this time continuity paid off. Eric Bernard was fourth in the British GP, and twice finished races in sixth place, while Aguri Suzuki was third in his home Grand Prix in Japan, and also took two sixth places. There were also seventeen retirements, but Lola was sixth in the championship, its highest placing since 1962.

Unfortunately, Larrousse had been declared to be the constructor, so the points were forfeit, and that could have meant that the team would have to pre-qualify in 1991, with all the sponsorship and problems that that might incur. In the event, the pre-qualification threat was lifted.

The Larrousse team did intend to build its own cars, become a constructor, but in the interim it had to survive. In addition to the FISA actions, it lost ESPO Corporation backing, by the autumn of 1990 it knew that it was to lose the Lamborghini engines to Ligier, and in 1991 it was to see Ducarouge depart to Ligier.

L91 For its last season with Lola, the Larrousse team had to use Cosworth DFR V8s in a holding operation. The L91 was a modified L90, which ran through the season with little or no testing or development, so there was little to cheer about after the single point scored by Suzuki and Bernard in the first half of the year. Beyond that, Larrousse's drivers failed to qualify six times, and recorded twenty-one retirements, and after scoring his point in the first race, Suzuki failed to get to a grid or retired for the rest of the season! If there was consolation, it was in the two championship points (for eleventh place), in a season when the well-financed French rival Ligier failed to score at all.

T93/30 On paper, this Scuderia Italian venture must have seemed promising, for it brought together a Lola chassis and a Ferrari engine. In fact there seemed to be shortcomings in both. Lola's chassis and suspension were conventional, and the Ferrari 65-degree V12 was the 'customer' engine, which, as others have found, generally falls short of works standards.

There was a transverse six-speed gearbox.

Michele Alboreto and Luca Badoer could not drive the car to a competitive level, even Alboreto returning a string of 'DNQ' entries in the records. The cars were actually placed ten times, Badoer's seventh at Imola being the best result (but only nine cars were classified in that San Marino GP, and two of those were not running at the end). At the end of the European season the team was withdrawn.

T97/30 Eric Broadley finally ran a works Formula 1 team, overseeing the design of a straightforward car for the 1997 season. It followed normal practice in components such as its double wishbone pushrod sus-

pension with inboard springs, and it was powered by the Ford Zetec-R 75-degree V8, which drove through a Lola semi-automatic six-speed transverse gearbox.

A novel sponsorship scheme was devised that seemingly allowed for little up-front funding, so cash-flow problems hamstrung the project, and the build programme ran late. In practice for the Australian GP, the slowest qualifier lapped in just under 1min 35sec; Sospiri's time in the quickest Lola was just under 1min 45sec, Rosset's best in the other car was just over 1min 42sec. Reality had to be faced, and the Lola entry for the second Grand Prix of 1997 was withdrawn. Worse still, the company was brought to its knees.

LOTUS

The Lotus Grand Prix story was one of the most important in the history of motor racing. This ran from 1958 until 1994, and at times was complex, and stormy. The bald record of 491 Grands Prix contested and seventy-four won was outstanding, but reveals nothing about the personalities involved with Team Lotus, or the original thinking behind many of its cars. This was very much Colin Chapman's marque, and Team Lotus was his team. His racing-car concepts were sometimes brilliant, sometimes clever but misguided, but there is no doubting his capacity for original thought in this most challenging field. His management methods, at circuits or away from them, might be questionable, but he kept his occasionally precarious companies and team in being and always in the forefront of Grand Prix racing throughout the 1960s and 1970s.

The early Lotus single-seaters made little impact, as for three years Chapman resisted the rear-engined layout for his Formula 1 cars. When he did accept it, he did so with a car that was more sophisticated than most of its rivals, however unlovely or simple that 18 might have appeared. It won races in Formula Junior, Formula 2 and Formula 1 forms, and as the 1960s opened Lotus had to be recognized as a serious single-seater constructor.

Chapman soon brought monocoque construction to Grand Prix racing, and sooner or later every other constructor had to follow that lead. Then he was instrumental in persuading Ford to back

the Cosworth DFV engine that was to be the backbone of Formula 1 for more than a decade. He enthusiastically adopted 'wings' and took the lead in developing that form of automotive aerodynamics – and pushing ahead too fast with it. And on another front he brought the first major sponsors from outside the sport into Grand Prix racing in the 1960s; the establishment might have disapproved, but Chapman had the vision to seek income on the scale that would be needed as Grand Prix racing moved ahead.

In the 1970s, Lotus took a step forward in refined aerodynamic terms in the 72, and then made a giant stride in the 'ground effects' 78 and 79. In between there had been failures, there had been a gas turbine F1 car venture (following Lotus Indianapolis cars with turbine power units). And after the immensely successful 79, Chapman again went too far in his aerodynamic adventures, producing an F1 Lotus 80 that was hopeless, and another that offended the authorities and was never raced.

Lotus suffered three blank seasons, 1979–81, then there was a Grand Prix victory again in 1982. The car was the last Formula 1 Lotus developed before Colin Chapman's death, and at least he did see one of the cars that were so precious to him win another Grand Prix.

Team Lotus continued, of course. Team manager Peter Warr, long a Chapman disciple, took over until 1990, then Tony Rudd briefly controlled the team. It seemed to recover, did in fact recover in that it scored

seven World Championship race victories 1985–1987. However, apart from the innovative 'active suspension' in the late 1980s, its cars were increasingly conventional. Perhaps the trend of technology and race regulations were against fundamental novelties, but there was no presiding genius to find a way round those, or the shortcomings of some of the engines the team had to use, or indeed to persuade an engine builder to produce something special.

Team Lotus survived into the mid-1990s, as memories of its last Grand Prix successes began to recede. In 1990 and 1991 Lotus scored just three Constructors' Championship points, its lowest scores since its first season in Grand Prix racing. Almost unthinkably, its cars were grid-fillers in 1994, as management cracks and severe financial problems began to show up. By autumn of that year Team Lotus was in administration, broken. There was talk of a new American owner reviving the team, but there were no Lotus cars on the 1995 grids. Then, towards the end of the century, there was more optimistic discussion of a reborn Team Lotus. Meanwhile, there was a glorious Grand Prix history to reflect on.

12 It was not unusual for a new Lotus to be shown prematurely in the 1950s – that just typified Chapman's bubbling optimism. The first 12 appeared late in 1956, in Formula 2 form and without an engine, and the 12 was to just grow up as the first Grand Prix Lotus. Incidentally, although it was the first single-seater Lotus, Colin Chapman had already had experience with F1 cars, notably as a consultant to Vanwall and BRM.

The 12 was tightly packaged, and it is still difficult to see how an F1 car with its engine ahead of its cockpit could have been smaller. There was a lightweight space frame, with an undertray contributing to rigidity, effectively a double wishbone front suspension and a de Dion rear end (soon to give way to a new independent arrangement – coil springs/dampers, radius arms and half shafts, mounted to substantial cast hubs, in the 'Chapman strut' suspension). 'Wobbly wheels' appeared for the first time, cast magnesium disc wheels, lighter, stiffer and stronger than the traditional wire wheels that were soon displaced in Formula 1 (save on Ferraris).

The F1 12 came in 1958 with a 1.96litre version of the Coventry-Climax FPF four-cylinder engine. Graham Hill made the first race start in an F1 Lotus, in the Silverstone International Trophy, when he finished eighth (albeit two places behind Cliff Allison's F2 Lotus 12). In the marques World Championship race debut, at Monaco, Hill retired but Allison placed a 2.2litre 12 sixth. He also placed this car fourth on the very fast Spa circuit, was seventh (with a small engine) at Monza, and tenth in the Morocco GP. Lotus finished its first Grand Prix season with sixth place in the Constructors' Championship, although it has to be admitted that that was also last place on the table.

16 In the summer of 1958, the first 16 was run alongside the 12s. On the face of it a derivative, this was substantially a new and more sophisticated design, with outwardly sleek lines that recalled the F1 Vanwall (it came to be dubbed 'mini-Vanwall'). It had another lightweight space frame – Chapman was obsessed with weight-saving to the extent that his tubular chassis tended to be fragile, and so was the aluminium bodywork of the 16. Suspension on 12 lines was used. The Coventry-Climax FPF was inclined as much as 62 degrees at first, but at 17 degrees in the definitive version. The step-down transmission of the 12 was retained, with an offset to allow the transmission to pass to the left of the driver to the rear-mounted gearbox. In 1959 2,495cc FPFs were used, in place of the 1958 1.96 and 2.2litre units. The 16 had a modest racing record,

Lotus 16-Climax, 1959.

Hill's fifth in the Italian GP being the best 1958 result, while in 1959 there were single fourth and fifth places (scored by Ireland) in World Championship races. Lotus's fourth place in the championship was again the last place.

18 Colin Chapman's first rear-engined car was introduced in Formula Junior form at the end of 1959, but within weeks the Formula 1 version led the Argentine GP, eventually finishing that F1 debut race in sixth place. The 18 was to establish Lotus as a leading Grand Prix constructor. A space frame was naturally used, with heavier gauge tubing in the F1 version. There were unequal-length wishbones in the front suspension, lower wishbones and fixed-length driveshafts with radius rods and deep hub carriers at the rear. The Coventry-Climax FPF, driving through a Lotus transaxle, was normal, in 2.5litre form in 1960 then 1.5litre as the F1 regulations changed. Fuel was carried in tanks around the cockpit – most of it above the driver's legs – so that weight distribution remained constant.

Innes Ireland drove 18s to win the important early-season non-title races in 1960, to confirm the promise shown in Argentina. Rob Walker bought a car for Stirling Moss to drive, and at Monaco he scored the first World Championship race

victory for Lotus. Late in the year he won the US GP. Jim Clark drove his first Grand Prix that year, finishing fifth in his second Grand Prix with Team Lotus, at Spa.

In 1960 Lotus was second in the Constructors' Championship, as it was in the first year of the 1.5litre formula, when its cars were sadly underpowered. That success owed much to Moss, who won the Monaco and German GPs in Walker's second 18.

That Walker 18 was converted to take the Coventry-Climax FWMV V8 late that season, and with a Colotti transaxle and Lotus 21 type rear suspension, this car was referred to as an 18/21 – clashing fuel contracts meant that Lotus could not sell a 21 to Walker. Moss's front-line single-seater racing career ended when he crashed at Goodwood in this car.

Aside from the FJ cars, few 18s had alternative engines. In the last year of the 2.5litre Formula, Vanwall fitted one of its engines in a half-hearted experiment as an International Formula car was put in hand, and Centro Sud fitted a Maserati straight six in an 18 that appeared once. This car was later run in Italian secondary races with a 1.5litre Maserati engine, with little success. Borgward 1.5litre engines were used in two BKLs, which seldom qualified to start in minor races in 1963–64, and another 18 with a Borgward engine was run in two 1962 South African F1 races.

21 Once again a Lotus F1 car followed an F Junior car, in this case the 21 deriving from the 20. That Junior was as low and sleek as the 18 had been bluff, and the 21 was an interim F1 spin-off to be powered by the FPF engine while Lotus waited for its Coventry-Climax V8s. In one significant departure, a ZF gearbox was used instead of Lotus's unreliable unit. The space frame followed 18 lines, with fuel in pannier tanks that helped keep the frontal area low. The suspension was different, too, with inboard springs at the front and top links at the rear, which meant that the fixed-length driveshafts had to go.

Team Lotus first used the 21 in the 1961 Monaco GP, but its European successes came in non-championship races. Then in the USA Ireland drove one to the team's first Grand Prix victory – and he was then dismissed by Chapman! Team Lotus had a good South African season with the 21s in 1962, winning all four Springbok races. Later that year, 21s were used by independent entrants, including the Brabham Racing Organization and Rob Walker.

22 One of these FJ cars was modified to F1 standard by Brausch Niemann for use in South Africa, when its enlarged FJ Ford engine meant that it was hardly competitive with main-line F1 cars in 1963–64. Niemann had earlier had a stripped 1.5litre Lotus 7 entry accepted for two local races!

(Top) Lotus 18-Climax of 1960, Stirling Moss driving. *(Above)* Lotus 21-Climax of 1961, Jim Clark leading Innes Ireland.

24 The first Lotus for the Coventry-Climax FWMV broadly resembled the 21. It came early in 1962, and as far as team Lotus was concerned it was to have a short life for, to the consternation of customers, the monocoque 25 followed within three months. The 24 was sleek, and was to be run with Climax or BRM V8s.

The team used it in early-season non-title races, Clark winning two of the four entered, while Trevor Taylor was in a 24 in the Dutch GP. After that, 24s served independent entrants; nine were sold 'new', two team cars were sold on, and Reg Parnell Racing built four more (only one of them was run in Formula 1 races). Five of these 24s had BRM V8s. Several non-title races fell to independent 24s, driven by Brabham, Ireland, Gregory and Siffert.

25 Monocoque construction was not new in 1962, but Colin Chapman brought it to Grand Prix racing with this car. It became the car to beat, and in four seasons Team Lotus won fourteen World Championship races with it, Jim Clark won his first world title driving 25s in 1963 (when he won seven Grands Prix) and that year Lotus won the Constructors' Championship for the first time. By later standards, the open bathtub monocoque of the 25 was simple, comprising two side pontoons that housed the fuel tanks and were linked by the stressed undertray, bulkheads and instrument panel. It was very light, at just under 30kg (66lb). The glass-fibre bodywork formed the top of the cockpit, and overall it gave the little car beautiful lines. While the suspension followed 24 lines, it was more supple – the chassis was very stiff – and this combination gave road-holding benefits. A Coventry-Climax/ZF engine/transmission combination was normal, although some cars that were passed on to independent teams from 1963 were to be fitted with BRM V8s and Hewland gearboxes.

The first 25 raced in the 1962 Dutch GP, and Clark drove one to win the type's third Grand Prix, in Belgium, and later won the British and US GPs. In 1963 the team cars wore the broad fore-and-aft yellow stripe, and were revised in technical detail and aerodynamic refinement, while uprated V8s were used. That year Clark won in Belgium, Holland, France, Britain, Italy, Mexico and South Africa. He was World Champion, and after finishing second in the 1962 Constructors' Championship, Lotus clearly headed that table in 1963.

The 25s left in Team Lotus service were uprated for 1964, anticipating the 33 in areas such as suspension and wide wheels, and these cars were often referred as 25B or 25C. Clark drove one to win the Dutch, Belgian and British GPs, and the French GP in 1965. Apart from good placings in some non-title races, other drivers fared less well in 25s.

33 This was a direct development of the 25, to the extent that the chassis number sequence was continued, R1–R7 being 25s, R8–R14 being 33s. The 25 had put on weight – anathema to Chapman – and effort was put into reducing this. The monocoque was redesigned, as was the suspension (for 13in wheels), while power unit and transmission arrangements were unchanged.

The first 33 was crashed during tests, and in its first race, at Aintree. A 33 did not win until high summer, when the non-championship Solitude GP fell to Clark. His retirement rate was high that year, when he was third in the championship and Lotus fell to third on the constructors' table. Clark and Lotus topped both championships again in 1965, when Jim won the Grands Prix in South Africa, Belgium, France, Holland and Germany in 33s, as well as secondary races at Goodwood and Syracuse. The Lotus 'Number Two', Mike Spence, had a reasonable season, with a third place in a Grand Prix and two fourths, as well as victory in a non-championship race at Brands Hatch. Meanwhile, there had been other non-championship successes, notably when Spence and Stewart (in his only F1 race in a Lotus) won heats of the 1964 Rand GP. BRP and Parnell drivers picked up minor placings in Grands Prix. With 2litre FWMVs (and a 2.1litre BRM V8), 33s had to serve in the first year of the 3-litre Formula 1, and on into 1967 when Graham Hill was second at Monaco in the last race for a Team Lotus 33. In 1966 there had been little reward for effort – Lotus was fifth in the Constructors' Championship, and half of its points were scored when Clark won the US GP in the unloved 43.

39 This was a 33 revised for the Coventry-Climax flat-sixteen engine that was destined never to be raced. The one-off 39 did not run as an F1 car, but it was adapted by Maurice Phillippe to take a 2.5litre FPF engine for Tasman racing.

43 Briefly, the complex, bulky and heavy BRM H16 engine seemed to be the only full 3litre power unit available to Lotus, which turned to it to hold the line while the Ford-Cosworth DFV was agreed, designed and built. Two 43s were built for this engine (the pair started in only one Grand Prix, the 1967 South African race). The car had a full monocoque, with the engine mounted to the rear bulkhead, acting as a stressed member, and carrying the rear suspension. A BRM six-speed gearbox was used, and the transmission proved one of the weak points of the 43.

Lotus 43-BRM H16 of 1966, Jim Clark driving.

The car first appeared in practice for the 1966 Belgian GP, and Peter Arundell made the type's first race start in the French GP. That first 43 was the only one to finish a race, when Clark drove it to win the 1966 US GP. After the 1967 South African race both cars were sold.

49 This was the second really significant Lotus Grand Prix design, a car that was essentially straightforward, but in combination with its DFV engine set the standard for the early years of the 3litre Formula 1. Chapman looked to a simple car, recognizing the importance of the engine: he had been instrumental in persuading Ford to back Keith Duckworth's V8 that was to become so important to Grand Prix racing, and outstandingly successful. In 1967 it was exclusive to Team Lotus.

Hill took pole for the 49's debut, in Holland, handsomely within the Zandvoort lap record, and Clark won the Grand Prix. Pole position was to be taken by 49 drivers in the next eleven races. Clark won three more Grands Prix in that first year; he was third in the Drivers' Championship, and Lotus a disappointing second in the Constructors' Championship.

Jim Clark won his twenty-fifth and last Grand Prix in the 1968 South African GP. He went on to contest the Tasman series in the 2.5litre 49T variant (winning four of the eight he entered). This series saw 49s appear in a sponsor's colours, and one briefly appeared with an extemporized rear wing.

In F1 form, the 49 was revised for the main 1968 season. ZF gearboxes gave way to more practical and sturdier Hewland units. A longer wheelbase, revised suspension geometry, and more weight aft (outwardly with an oil tank above the gearbox) were

In 1969 the 49s had to serve the works team for another full season, and two were involved in accidents that ended the era of high wings. Hill won in Monaco, Rindt in the USA, and there were non-championship successes for the 49B. The type's career had to be extended into 1970, with modifications that hardly justified the 49C designation. There was a third successive Monaco GP victory, this time scored by Rindt, which brought the 49's score in the World Championship races to twelve. In the summer Emerson Fittipaldi drove his first Grands Prix in a 49 – and scored his first points in the German GP – then a 49 raced for the last time in works colours, in Austria.

56B Chronologically, the 63 was Lotus's first successor to the 49, but in the previous year the gas turbine-powered 56 had been run at Indianapolis. The 63 was not successful, there was a spare 56 at Hethel, and Pratt & Whitney provided a gas turbine equivalent to a 3litre piston engine. So a one-off 56B was completed for 1971.

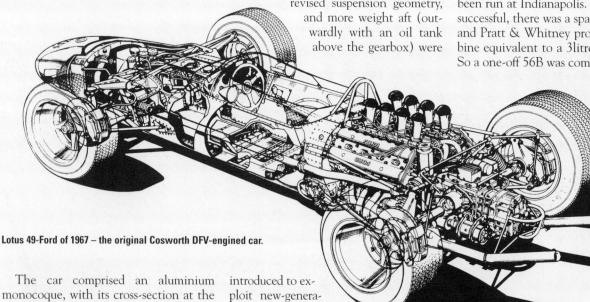

Lotus 49-Ford of 1967 – the original Cosworth DFV-engined car.

The car comprised an aluminium monocoque, with its cross-section at the rear bulkhead determined by the 90-degree V8's proportions. Suspension followed normal Lotus lines, with a rear subframe bolted to the engine block and heads, and twin radius rods to the rear of the monocoque. The DFV served a stressed member role. At the front the coil springs/dampers were mounted inboard.

The first DFVs gave some 400bhp (410bhp later in 1967) – less than the outputs claimed for rival 12-cylinder engines, but in fact quite enough. Compared with other early 3litre F1 engines, the 90-degree V8 looked neat and compact, and while it was not without vices, for example in its excessive vibrations, it was to prove reliable. In the first 49s, it drove through a ZF transaxle. Graham

introduced to exploit new-generation tyres. An engine cover improved the car's appearance. Soon rear suspension-mounted strutted aerofoils were to appear on 49Bs, complemented by modest nose fins to balance aerodynamic forces.

After Jim Clark's death in a Formula 2 race, Graham Hill revived Lotus Grand Prix morale and fortunes with victories in Spain and Monaco in 1968, and his win in the last Grand Prix of the year clinched drivers' and constructors' championships. In the British GP, Jo Siffert drove Rob Walker's borrowed 49B to secure the last Grand Prix victory for an independent entrant (Walker's own 49 had been involved in a garage fire, and was assumed to be destroyed).

It had four-wheel drive and distinctive bodywork with a wedge nose. In early-season British races there were teething problems, as well as the anticipated throttle lag, but nevertheless Fittipaldi took third place with it in a heat of the International Trophy at Silverstone. Dave Walker drove it in the Dutch GP (he crashed), Reine Wisell drove it in the British GP (to retirement), Fittipaldi drove it into eighth place in the Italian GP and then to finish second in a non-title race at Hockenheim.

58 The 57 was a Formula 2 car with a de Dion rear axle, which was built and

Lotus 49B-Ford of 1968, Graham Hill (left) and Jo Siffert (right).

(Above) Lotus 63-Ford four-wheel-drive car of 1969, Jochen Rindt driving.

tested in 1968 but never raced. The 58 design followed similar lines, and was envisaged as a Tasman car, with the DFW V8 and a ZF gearbox. It could have been transformed for F1 but in the event was another stillborn model.

63 Four-wheel drive was widely expected to become universal at the end of the 1960s, and most F1 constructors introduced a 4wd design. Lotus's Type 63 was complex, with features in common with the 64 Indianapolis car. The cockpit was well forward, to the extent that a driver's feet were ahead of the front axle line — one reason why Hill and Rindt were

Lotus 56B of 1971, with a Pratt & Whitney gas-turbine engine and four-wheel drive, Dave Walker driving.

Lotus 72-Ford of 1973, Emerson Fittipaldi driving.

reluctant to have anything to do with the 63. The DFV was reversed, so that the clutch was immediately behind the cockpit with the Hewland gearbox on the left and drive taken to front and rear ZF final drives. Fuel was carried alongside the engine. Two cars were built.

John Miles drove 63s in five Grands Prix in 1969, finishing only once (tenth in the British race); Andretti retired from two Grands Prix, Bonnier from one. Rindt achieved the best placing, second in the Oulton Park Gold Cup, before these heavy and difficult cars were set aside.

72 The 72 was another innovative car, and like the 25/33 and the 49 it was to have a long front-line life, when it was driven to win more Grands Prix than any other Lotus type. Chapman laid down the concept lines in 1969 for Maurice Phillippe to detail. There was no alternative to the DFV engine, so Chapman looked to aerodynamic efficiency – outwardly so obvious in the wedge lines – and minimal pitch to exploit it, low unsprung weight (and indeed minimal overall weight) and light suspension loads to use the then-new soft-compound tyres to best effect. The car emerged with torsion bar suspension, inboard brakes to keep heat away from tyres, a rear oil tank to increase a rearward weight bias, and twin radiators alongside the rear of the cockpit.

Obviously there were to be changes, which sometimes led to sub-designations. The 72B and 72C (1970) had no anti-dive or anti-squat in the suspension; 72D (1971) had revised rear suspension, with twin radius rods and lower links; 72E met

new regulations for 1972 in its deformable structure and reskinned monocoque; 72F in 1975 had coil-spring rear suspension and 'helper' coils at the front. Changes such as the 1973 revisions to suit Goodyear tyres included repositioning the oil tank amidships to shift some weight towards the front tyres, and seemingly did not class for number changes, nor did various rear wings (and mountings) or engine airboxes used.

And, of course, Gold Leaf Team Lotus livery gave way to the John Player Special black and gold in 1972.

The 72 made its Grand Prix debut in Spain in 1970, and that spring there were teething problems to be overcome. But later in the year Rindt won the Dutch, French, British and German GPs in succession. In practice for the Italian GP he was running a 72 without wings, in an experiment, when brake-shaft failure led to his fatal crash. But his World Championship lead, and ultimately the title, was preserved for him as Emerson Fittipaldi won the US GP in a 72. That victory secured the Constructors' Championship for Lotus, too.

Fittipaldi's maiden Grand Prix victory notwithstanding, driver inexperience played a part in Lotus's decline in 1971, when there were no F1 victories (Fittipaldi was second in Austria, and twice placed third, while Wisell was twice fourth). Then from fifth place in the Constructors' Championship that year Lotus moved back to first in 1972, as Fittipaldi won in Spain, Belgium, Britain, Austria and Italy, and was second in two Grands Prix (he also won four non-championship races).

In 1973 the Brazilian was joined by Ronnie Peterson. Fittipaldi won three Grands Prix (Argentina, Brazil and Spain) while Peterson won in France, Austria, Italy and the USA, and the teams' title went to Lotus again.

The 72 had to serve two more front-line seasons, as the 76 failed. Peterson won the Monaco, French and Italian GPs in 1974; apart from a sparkling victory in a non-championship race in the rain at Brands Hatch, his team mate Jacky Ickx's best finish was third in the Brazilian GP. The team slipped to fourth in the championship. The best it could field in 1975 was a 'new' lightweight 72 for Peterson, whose best Grand Prix finish was fourth at Monaco. He garnered just six points; Ickx scored three before he left in midseason, Crawford, Watson and Henton scored none. Lotus slipped to seventh in the championship, as the 72's six-year front-line career ended in the USA. Independent cars were run, notably by Rob Walker in 1970 (when Graham Hill scored seven points for that leading private entrant) and South African Dave Charlton from 1972.

76 The proposition was a refined and lighter 72, with a new monocoque but with similar suspension incorporating torsion bars. The detail design responsibility was Ralph Bellamy's. A novelty was an electric magnetic clutch, operated by a button on the gear knob, and four pedals with the linked central pair allowing for left-foot braking. The system was soon abandoned. The DFV–Hewland combination provided power and its transmission.

The car's slender lines misled, and it was no lighter than a 72. And it just did not work. Increasingly, the 72s were used. Peterson did lead the 1974 International Trophy at Silverstone and the Spanish GP in a 76, but retired from both races. A hybrid, 76 monocoque and 72 rear end, was no more successful. At the end of 1974 the cars were quietly set aside, and few recall that they were officially 'John Player Special Mk 1'.

77 With this experimental car, Lotus moved back towards F1 competitiveness. This time Chapman's ideas were developed by a design team, including Geoff Aldridge (responsible for the monocoque) and Martin Ogilvie (suspension) and later joined by Tony Southgate as chief engineer. Body lines appeared slender and conventional, and the usual Cosworth and Hewland elements were used. But this 'adjustacar' allowed for wheelbase, track and weight distribution variations, drivers could adjust the rear anti-roll bar, and late in the year there were brush 'skirts' to control under-car airflow. Once Len Terry had reworked the front suspension, results began to come.

Peterson quit after the 77's mediocre debut in the South African GP, but then Gunnar Nilsson put in a good performance in the 1976 International Trophy and Mario Andretti joined the team. Third places followed (Nilsson in Spain, Andretti in Holland and Canada) and then Andretti won the last Grand Prix of

the year, in Japan. Lotus was a reasonably respectable fourth in the championship.

78 The skirts on the late version of the 77 introduced another significant development, the F1 'wing car'. Lotus people were not the first to be attracted to under-car aerodynamics, but Chapman's aerodynamics research team headed by Peter Wright brought effective ground-effects techniques to Formula 1, and the 78 (or

JPS Mk III) introduced a trend that every other constructor had to follow.

The 78 had a slim monocoque, incorporating some dural/aluminium sandwich sheets, flanked by wide side pods. These contained radiators and fuel tanks, and their sides extended down to bristle 'skirts' that sealed them to the track (soon more efficient rigid skirts were to be introduced). At the rear, the undersides swept up to create areas of low pressure, so

(Above) Lotus 76-Ford of 1974.
(Below) Lotus 78-Ford of 1977, the first 'ground effect' car, driven by Ronnie Peterson.

that in effect the car was sucked to the track. In the front suspension care was taken to avoid interference with the airflow to the side pods (the suspension comprised lower wishbones at each end, with upper rocking arms at the front and upper links with radius rods at the rear).

In 'ground effects' Chapman found the 'unfair advantage' to offset the power handicap that was beginning to afflict Cosworth DFV-using teams, and Lotus won more Grands Prix than any other team in 1977 (Andretti won at Long Beach, in Spain and France, and in Italy, while Nilsson won the Belgian GP). But the record of minor placings was poor, and meant that Lotus was second in the Constructors' Championship.

The 78s were used in the early 1978 races, when Andretti and Peterson both won a Grand Prix in one, before two of the four built were sold to Mexican entrant/driver Hector Rebaque. The others were retained as team spares, and Ronnie Peterson had fallen back to one of these for the Italian GP, where he was fatally injured.

79 In this refined car, Lotus exploited experience with the 78 and its head start in the ground-effects era, and by no means incidentally produced the most elegant F1 car of the 3litre years. Chap-

man controlled the project, Aldridge and Ogilvie undertook the detail work. In the monocoque, sandwich material was largely set aside, sheet being used for all but the floor, and the tub soon had to be strengthened to cope with ground-effects loadings. There was a single fuel cell between cockpit and engine, so the side pods contained only radiators (water on the right, oil on the left). Rear suspension components were inboard, to give a free airflow exit. A Lotus-Getrag gearbox was fitted, but was soon dropped in favour of the reliable Hewland 'box, to the relief of everybody involved, except Chapman.

The 79 made its Grand Prix race debut in Belgium, when Andretti drove it to victory. He also won in Spain, France, Germany and Holland, while Peterson won in Austria. Lotus dominated the teams' championship table.

The 79s had to be used again in 1979, when they were suddenly almost outclassed. Carlos Reutemann achieved the best results, second in two races, while other scoring finishes produced a modest points total for fourth place in the championship.

80 Lotus's second-generation ground-effects car was a failure, as Chapman was over-ambitious in pushing ahead with a technical development. This car had lit-

tle ground-effects skirts under its nose, but the fundamental flaw was in the extended side pods and skirts curving inside the rear wheels. There were persistent problems with skirts sticking in their slides, leading to unpredictable and unnerving car behaviour as the ground-effects seal was broken and then perhaps re-established as the skirt freed.

Andretti placed an 80 third in the Spanish GP, but the 80 started in only two more races, and practised for two, before it was abandoned.

81 After the 80, this was a simple and sensible car, and hardly a successful one. The monocoque derived from the 80, and the side pods had straight lower edges and straight skirts. In the suspension there were lower wishbones and upper arms front and rear, with inboard springs. New monocoques and a longer wheelbase in mid-season led to an 81B designation.

Newcomer Elio de Angelis was second in Brazil and third in Spain in 1980. Andretti scored just one point and Mansell none in his two races, and Lotus was a very distant fifth in the championship. De Angelis scored points with 81Bs in the 1981 Brazilian and Argentine GPs, while Mansell scored his first World Championship points with third place in the Belgian GP.

86 This one-off F1 research vehicle was never raced, but built and run to test a dual-chassis approach. An 81 monocoque and other components were used, with a second chassis carrying a light but rigid bodywork and aerofoils. Run in autumn 1980, this car was never intended for race use.

87 Lotus's 1981 season was confused. The 87 was its conventional F1 car, sharing many components with the controversial Type 88 (when that car was ruled out, 88 to 87 conversions were made). The monocoque was made up of carbon-composite sheets, suspension was on the same lines as the 81, as were the Cosworth-Hewland arrangements, while the body was neat (and once again in JPS colours by the summer, after starting the year with the gaudy Essex scheme).

The best placings with 87s in 1981 were two fourths, scored by de Angelis (in Italy) and Mansell (in the USA), and with a few lesser placings the 87 contributed thirteen points to Lotus's total of twenty-two that gained it seventh place

Lotus 79-Ford of 1978, driven by Mario Andretti.

Lotus 87-Ford of 1981. Left to right: Nigel Mansell, Colin Chapman and Elio de Angelis.

in the championship. Slightly modified as the 87B, two of the cars were run in the first Grand Prix of 1982.

88 The twin-chassis concept was developed and raceworthy in the 88, and in 1981 this car was at the centre of a wonderful controversy.

The monocoque was conventional, save in its use of carbon composites, but it was referred to as the secondary chassis, which also included the suspension, engine and transmission. The primary chassis comprised the bodywork, with side pods and aerofoils, and could be regarded as a large aerofoil in itself. It was carried on springs acting on the suspension uprights. Thereby considerable downforce was achieved without the stresses involved with the rock-hard suspension called for in normal ground-effects arrangements.

It was all too clever. There were protests as soon as an 88 appeared at a race meeting, when at first it was allowed to practise. As the wrangles continued, Lotus modified the bodywork and entered the car as the 88B in mid-season; The RAC was prepared to accept it for the British GP. But more protests from less ingenious Italian and French constructors won the day – they had been able to copy Brabham's 1981 hydro-pneumatic system,

but might it have been less easy to follow this Lotus? With normal bodies in place of the primary chassis, 88s became 87s.

91 To all intents and purposes, this was a derivative of the 87B, stronger and lighter and, in that it won a Grand Prix in 1982, much better. Carbon fibre-Kevlar sandwich material was used in the tub, and while there were no departures in the suspension, three wheelbase variations were allowed for and there were trials with a pullrod system. Water-cooled brakes, that odd ploy used by teams in the last DFV phase, were also featured. This was another F1 Lotus with handsome lines.

The car was first raced in the Belgian GP, and de Angelis scored minor placings in six races before he won the 1982 Austrian GP – the last Lotus Grand Prix victory that Colin Chapman was to see. Mansell also scored twice, his best being third in Brazil. His place was taken for one race by Geoff Lees. Lotus's sixth place in the Constructors' Championship seemed to point to better times ... but in December Colin Chapman died.

92 Two of the 91s were converted to meet the 'flat bottom' regulations, to serve as stand-in cars while the team waited for its first turbo engines. One was also used

in active-suspension trials late in 1982 and into 1983, before this work was set aside for a while following disappointing performances in two early-season races. Mansell scored one point in a 92, in the US GP – the last scored in an F1 Lotus-powered engine in the DFV/DFY series that had been created for Team Lotus seventeen years earlier.

93T The first turbo Lotus appeared for the first Grand Prix of 1983, unhappily as it was used in practice and then not in the race. The design was attributed to Ogilvie, who again used a folded carbon fibre/Kevlar sheet monocoque, flanked by full-length side pods. The rear suspension was on previous Lotus lines, while a pull-rod arrangement was used at the front. The engine was the KKK-turbocharged Renault EF1, driving through a Lotus-Hewland gearbox. The car proved to be ponderous, and was in no way helped by its Pirelli tyres. De Angelis managed one finish in eight starts in 93Ts; Mansell retired from his only race in a 93T.

94T Gérard Ducarouge was brought in early in the summer of 1983, and his first task was a quick-fix, to devise a competitive turbo car, rather than start on a new ground-up design. He used the 91 as a basis, with revised bulkheads in the tub to suit suspension and engine mountings. The suspension geometry and weight distribution were better suited to Pirelli tyres. Two cars were completed very quickly, for a British GP debut (Mansell took fourth place with one). Although Mansell was third in the late-season European GP, the first promise was not sustained and Lotus was seventh in the championship.

95T At least the 94T gave a breathing space, and Ducarouge could lay down a new car for a welcome return to Goodyear rubber in 1984. In fact the make-up followed familiar lines, save in pullrod suspension all round, and the outward change was in the short side pods. Good handling and sound aerodynamic packages ('fast' and 'slow') went some way to compensate for engines that were not the most powerful of the year.

De Angelis was third in the first race, second in Detroit, and scored points in nine of the first ten races. Mansell was third in two races, and scored in three more. Lotus was third in the Constructors' Championship.

97T Ducarouge refined his first design in this successful 1985 car. It necessarily met changed regulations, for example in its deformable nose box, and was generally rated sound in aerodynamic respects. The Renault engines (EF4 and EF15) were more powerful but less reliable.

Driven by de Angelis and Senna, the 97T brought Lotus back to the forefront. De Angelis won the San Marino GP and scored points in eleven races – every one he finished. Senna scored in fewer races, but he won in Portugal and Belgium. Lotus was equal third with Williams in the championship ... but would never again score as many points (seventy-one) in a season.

99T The 1987 F1 Lotus was in a line of evolution, but there was much that was new about it. There was a reversion, in that the monocoque was formed from sheets again. Beyond that, there was a computer-controlled active suspension, hydraulically activated at each corner (the basic arrangement comprised double wishbones and pullrods). The car was tested with passive suspension, but the active system was used at Senna's insistence. The engine was Honda's turbocharged 80-degree V6, in RA166E and RA167G forms, more powerful than the Renault types and with a wider effective rev band, but prone to excessive vibrations. The

100T The 1988 F1 car was a development of the 99T, but with 'passive' suspension (double wishbones and pushrods all round). The engine was Honda's RA168E, with more power. But seemingly there were aerodynamic shortcomings in this needle-nose car, which changes through the season failed to correct, while variations in track and wheelbase contributed little.

Nelson Piquet led the team and gave it the best results, third in the first two Grands Prix and the last. The Brazilian scored in four other Grands Prix, but Nakajima scored just one point and twice failed to qualify. Lotus slipped one championship place, sharing fourth with Arrows. Gérard Ducarouge left at the end of the season.

101 Frank Dernie took on the design responsibility, and had to produce the 1989 F1 car quickly. As the turbo era ended, the team turned to Judd's CV 90-degree V8, and this drove through the existing six-speed longitudinal gearbox. Double wishbone suspension was used, pullrod at the front, pushrod at the rear. The body lines were distinctive, but in view of Dernie's background and reputation they were doubtless efficient.

In the background, Team Lotus was in turmoil through the height of the season, then Tony Rudd was drafted in as Executive Chairman. A low point came when neither driver qualified for the Belgian GP – an unhappy 'first' in Lotus Grand Prix history.

Piquet managed two fourth places, Nakajima one. Lotus slumped to sixth in the Constructors' Championship, and even that was an achievement in a season of struggles – it even seemed possible that the team would not appear in 1990. Nevertheless, in preparation for the 102 in 1990 a 101 was tested with a Lamborghini V12 late in 1989.

Lotus 97-turbo Renault of 1985, Ayrton Senna recording his first win.

98T While in most respects this car followed on from the 97T, it was the first Lotus to have a moulded carbon composites monocoque and early in 1986 an hydraulic adjustable ride height system was introduced at the rear. The engine was Renault's EF15B, and the variant with pneumatic valve operation was sometimes used. A Lotus-Hewland DGB gearbox was fitted.

Senna won the Spanish GP and the US event on the streets of Detroit in this car, was second in four Grands Prix and scored in four others. His inexperienced team mate Johnny Dumfries scored just one point. Lotus, running its cars in black and gold colours for the last time, was third in the championship – what might have been achieved with two top drivers.

Lotus-Hewland six-speed gearbox was retained.

The cars appeared in bright yellow colours in 1987, when the team was officially Camel Team Lotus Honda. The lines of the car were to change during the year, as efforts were made to overcome aerodynamic shortcomings, especially at the rear.

The 99T was the first car to race with active suspension (in Brazil) and the first to win with it (at Monaco).

Senna won the Monaco GP, and he won in the USA, and in 1987 he also finished second in four Grands Prix and third in two, and scored in three other races. Satoru Nakajima contributed seven points to Lotus's total, and once again the team was third in the championship.

102 In this car Dernie concentrated on developing the 1989 design, with necessary changes to accommodate the engine and its ancillaries such as the larger radiators called for. Lamborghini's 3512 80-degree V12 was designed by Mauro Forghieri, and had shortcomings stemming from a 'traditional' approach and Lamborghini's limited resources – it was bulky and heavy, and there were variations from unit to unit. To complement it there was a Lotus-Lamborghini six-speed gearbox.

(Above) Lotus 101-Judd V8 of 1989, Nelson Piquet driving.

Lotus 107-Ford V8 of 1992, Johnny Herbert driving.

This was another unhappy season. The drivers, Derek Warwick and Martin Donnelly, tried hard with ill-handling cars. Donnelly survived an enormous accident in practice for the Spanish GP, and Herbert took his place for the last two races. Warwick scored the team's only points, with a sixth place and a fifth (three points was Lotus's lowest score since 1958), and the retirement rate was high – eighteen times in sixteen Grands Prix – often with transmission failures.

The 1991 car had a 102B designation, but there was a fundamental change, to the Judd EV 76-degree V8. Gordon Coppuck oversaw many other changes that had to be carried through on a limited budget, for there was no single main sponsor. Much of the bodywork was new, the suspension was revised, the plumbing had to be new.

Mika Hakkinen started his F1 career with Lotus in 1991, failed to qualify only once, retired seven times, and scored two points. In four attempts Julian Bailey qualified once, but scored a point in that race. Michael Bartels failed to qualify in four attempts. Herbert was in the second car for the remaining races, did not qual-

ify once, and finished five times with seventh his best placing. Lotus's score was again three points, and in the championship it slipped one place, to ninth.

As 102Ds, the cars appeared at the first six Grands Prix of 1992, albeit one was raced for the last time in the fifth event. In place of the expected V12 Judds, they had Ford HB V8s. Lotus-Lamborghini gearboxes were still used. Hakkinen and Herbert each scored a point with 102Ds, before the car was superseded.

107 Chris Murphy was design director, with an enlarged staff, responsible for the definitive 1992 car that carried signs of major sponsorship. It was conventional in most respects, although the double wishbone pushrod suspension

incorporated a simple reactive system, based on Lotus road cars (the 107 could be raced with the suspension in active or passive forms). The HB engine drove through a Lotus-Xtrac six-speed transverse gearbox.

Hakkinen was fourth in two races and second in three other Grands Prix, while Herbert scored a single point in a 107. Lotus moved up to fifth in the championship. The 107B was a refined version, but tight finances hampered its development for 1993 – in particular, the traction control that was considered essential in Formula 1 that year was not available until the summer. The improvements came in the fully active suspension, and in details. The HB in Series V form was used. Some development work was put into a semi-automatic gearbox (Chapman would have approved of that!).

Herbert was fourth in three Grands Prix (the Brazilian, European and British races), but then the two points he gained in the Belgian GP were the last scored by a Lotus driver. Zanardi scored a point, was then side-lined after a massive accident at Spa (Lamy took his place for the last four races). Sixth place in the Constructors' Championship seemed encouraging.

The 107C run in the first Grands Prix of 1994 was a stand-in, originally intended for tests with the Honda-Mugen 72-degree V10, basically an old engine. It was heavy, and the car was overweight, and far from competitive. Herbert did manage seventh place in the two opening races of the year, and that was the nearest a Lotus driver came to scoring in 1994. Lamy had a serious test accident, and Zanardi came back but failed to score in a 107C.

109 Although it derived from the 107, the 1994 F1 Lotus was ominously late, making its race debut in the fifth Grand Prix of the season. Later in the year – too late – the new Honda ZA6C engine became available, and it transformed the 109. Lighter and more compact, it improved the behaviour of the 109 in all-round terms. The active suspension was ruled out for 1994, and with the new engine the 109 seemed none the worse for not having it.

By the time the car came, Lotus was on the brink. The one consistent driver, Herbert, was 'released' to Ligier before the end of the season. Zanardi was not a permanent driver, as he could not bring in financial backing, Adams, Bernard and Salo did not impress. In any case, the administrator was in control by the autumn. Perhaps it was for the best that the team did not linger into another year.

Lozier

The Lozier company built road cars of the highest class and went racing in 1907, running stripped reproduction models in 24-hour races on US short tracks, looking for stock car honours and winning them. In 1908 Lozier entered the first Grand Prize race at Savannah, still using a stock chassis but with an enlarged 12litre version of its four-cylinder engine devised by chief engineer John Perrin. In most respects, this appeared to be a typical Grand Prix car of the period, with a channel-section frame, semi-elliptic springs and artillery wheels, and exposed cockpit and bolster tank, and shaft drive in place of the chains used on the 1907 cars.

At Savannah, Lozier faced Grand Prix entries from Benz, Fiat, Clément-Bayard and Itala. Lozier's leading driver through the company's racing history, Ralph Mulford, led on the road at the end of the first lap, but this was illusory because of the interval start, and in any case overheating led to its effective retirement (it did complete a few laps late in the race).

That car was not raced again, but a pair of 8.9litre cars based on the sporting Type 46 were run in the 1910 Grand Prize, outlasting the Grand Prix Fiats and finishing fourth and fifth (Mulford and Horan) behind the victorious Benz team.

The next year was Lozier's last in racing, and once again there was main-line opposition, in the Vanderbilt Cup and the Grand Prize. In the first of these races Mulford beat de Palma in a 1908 Grand Prix Mercedes, and Grant was fourth in the second Lozier. Mulford briefly led the Grand Prize, but retired with transmission failure. The cars did not feature at this level again, although some were run independently after Lozier turned away from motor sport, its capital resources drained by a factory move.

Lyncar

Martin Slater designed and built a handful of Formula Atlantic cars from 1971; one of these (005 in the series) was driven by John Nicholson to win the 1973 Formula Atlantic championship, and 005 was fitted with a Cosworth DFV for hill climbs. Nicholson was McLaren's DFV engine expert, and he commissioned a Lyncar Formula 1 car in 1973.

It emerged as a very straightforward car, following Slater's general Formula Atlantic lines, with an aluminium monocoque, double wishbone front suspension, with lower wishbones, top links and radius rods at the rear. The DFV drove through a Hewland gearbox. The outward lines of the car were unassuming and tidy. Nicholson finished the two British non-championship races in the spring of 1974, qualifying 007 off the pace for both, and classified a modest sixteenth at Brands Hatch and a more interesting sixth in the International Trophy (by no means the last F1 car in that F1/F5000 race). However, he failed to qualify 006 for the British GP.

In 1975 Nicholson again started in the British non-championship races, retiring at Brands Hatch and placing 006 thirteenth at Silverstone. He was the slowest qualifier for the British GP, and was placed seventeenth, although when the race was stopped the Lyncar was one of half-a-dozen cars trapped in the Silverstone catch fences.

It seems that his half-dozen Formula 1 race attempts convinced Nicholson that he was not destined to be a Grand Prix driver, and he turned to power boats. Lyncar 006 was raced in some British national series events by Emilio de Villota in 1976–77.

Lyncar 006-Ford of 1977, Emilio de Villota driving.

◆ M ◆

Maki

This optimistic Japanese entry into Formula 1 was announced as the first phase in an advanced automotive engineering programme that in fact did not progress beyond inept Cosworth-Hewland kit cars in 1974–76. These were designed by Kenji Mimura, with some assistance in 1974 from Masao Ono, who presumably learned from the experience as his Kojima designs later in the decade were more convincing. Maki cars were entered fairly regularly in 1974–75, but actually ran at only seven meetings, plus one in 1976. However, a Maki reached a grid only once, started only once, and finished once … in last place. That seems to sum up the inglorious F1 career of Maki.

F-101 The first car was conventional, made up of bought-in components, and looked smoothly bulky. There was double wishbone front suspension, with upper and lower links at the rear. Maki was to find out that there was more to a 'Cosworth-Hewland kit car' than buying the parts. The car first appeared for British GP practice in 1974, when two of the thirty-four entries were slower although the Maki driver, Howden Ganley, was almost 1.5 seconds off the slowest qualifying time. In practice for the next race, at Nürburgring, he crashed heavily when the rear suspension failed.

A revised version of the car was built for 1975, when it failed to reach a grid for the four championship races entered. Tony Trimmer did qualify it to start in the non-championship Swiss GP at Dijon, and completed the race, finishing thirteenth and last.

F-102A The specification was familiar, but this one-off had less corpulent lines. Although it was not ready to race, it was entered for the Japanese GP (and ran for the first time in practice). Trimmer completed just eight practice laps in it, his best more than 13sec off the slowest qualifier's time at Fuji.

March

See pp.144–148.

Marmon

As far as racing is concerned, this Indianapolis luxury car company is invariably recalled for its victory in the first 500 run at the local Speedway in 1911. However, it also contested the principal US road races of the period, with cars based on its production models.

The Model 32 provided the basis for the straight-six 5.2litre car first raced in 1909, when a company engineer, Ray Harroun, won a short race at the first Indianapolis meeting and also faced European Grand Prix opposition in the Grand Prize, when he finished last. In 1910 Harroun and Joe Dawson placed a Marmon sixth in the Grand Prize, while Dawson was second in the Vanderbilt Cup in a version with an engine from a short-lived four-cylinder stock model. Burman challenged for the lead in the 1911 Vanderbilt Cup in a straight six, while Cyrus Patschke retired his 8.1litre four-cylinder Marmon. Patschke actually led the more important Grand Prize on the same Savannah circuit a few days later, before retiring with engine failure.

After its triumph in the first Indianapolis 500 – its six-cylinder car was the first single-seater in a major race – the Marmon company officially withdrew from racing.

Martini

Tico Martini's little company built its first Formula 3 car for the Winfield Racing Driver's School at Magny Cours in 1968, and generally successful cars for that category and French *ab initio* classes followed, with MW (Martini-Winfield) or MK (Martini-Knight) designations. A move up to Formula 2 in 1975 was rewarded as Jacques Laffite clearly won the European championship in the MK 16, then René Arnoux won the title with the MK 22 in 1977.

A move to Formula 1 must have seemed logical. The one-off Mk 23 built for 1978 was a straightforward 'Cosworth-Hewland kit car', with a monocoque following Williams' lines, front suspension by lower wishbones and top rocker arms, with inboard springs, and rear suspension by parallel links and radius arms. The DFV drove through a Hewland FGA six-speed gearbox.

A single-car team, inadequately sponsored and with a very simple machine, had a very steep hill to climb as the ground effects period opened and major teams' cars were increasingly sophisticated. Arnoux failed to qualify at the little team's first Grand Prix attempt, in South Africa in 1978, and did not pre-qualify at the second attempt. The MK 23 made its race debut at Belgium, when Arnoux finished ninth. He equalled that placing in Austria, and Martini's only other finish was fourteenth in the French GP.

The venture almost brought the company down, and Martini abandoned Formula 1 before the end of the season. It returned to Formula 3, sometimes enjoying success again, but seemingly failed to learn one important lesson from its Formula 1 days, as it returned to Formula 2 in 1983–84 with a single car that was not competitive.

Maserati

See pp.149–154.

Maserati-Platé

Enrico Platé ran a team of independent 4CLT/48s in 1951, when owner/drivers de Gaffenried and Bira achieved nothing. Platé had technical ability, and confidently undertook the conversion of these F1 cars for the Formula 2 World Championship races in 1952.

The superchargers had to be discarded, of course, and new blocks were cast for a 1,995cc version of the Maserati engine that had a claimed output of 140bhp. Rather than just leave a space where the superchargers had been, the chassis was shortened and the wheelbase reduced by some 20cm (8in). The nose lines were revised, and the fuel tank in the tail was naturally smaller.

The cars were too heavy to be competitive in front-line company, and there were persistent braking problems. The cars just made up the numbers on grids for the few championship races contested, but they were useful contenders in the regional Grands Prix that were still common.

continued on p.154

The world of racing was changing as Max Mosley, Alan Rees, Graham Coaker and Robin Herd set up March Engineering at the end of the 1960s, to build single-seater cars on a commercial basis. The market was expanding, as sponsorship became accepted, and the principal specialist components – engines, gearboxes, and so on – were readily available, even at Formula 1 level. Alan Rees, a good driver, is credited with identifying the broad market opportunity; Max Mosley, another driver who had not made it to the highest level, saw Grand Prix possibilities; Graham Coaker, a club driver, was a business and production man; Robin Herd was highly rated as a designer.

'March' was an acronym of their names, and this lamentably under-financed company completed its first car, the 693 for Formula 3, late in 1969. The first two figures in the designation signified the year, the third the category, and this system was to be used through to the 1980s. The F2 and F3 cars of the 1970s were sensible, generally user-friendly, and often successful. Formula 1 was alluring, rather than sensible business, and the March commitment was a major factor leading to Coaker and Rees leaving the company within two years. However, at the outset there were customers for F1 cars, and there was STP backing for a works team.

Jackie Stewart drove one of Tyrrell's March 701s to a World Championship victory in Spain in 1970 – further, his victory in a non-title race and Amon's in the International Trophy meant that March won three of the first four F1 races it entered. A new constructor could hardly have hoped for a better baptism, but in truth the simple 701 was outclassed from its first race. Herd had time to be more original in its successors, although these were not always successful, and when they were competent they were flattered by their drivers. In its first two seasons, March was third in the Constructors' Championship, and it was never to reach such heights again.

March turned its back on Formula 1 after the 1977 season, when Mosley left. The production racing-car business fluctuated, and so did trading results. The name returned to the Grands Prix on a car built for the RAM team in 1981, built by Herd's March engineering company. For the following year, Adrian Reynard designed an F1 car for this separate outfit, and as a 1983 RAM-March did not appear then there was another break.

In 1987 March Racing entered Formula 1 with cars that showed promise, then in 1989 its major sponsor, Leyton House, bought this subsidiary from the March Group (after months of time-wasting negotiation). Briefly, the cars carried the Leyton House name, but then the parent group turned away from racing because of its severe – even scandalous – financial problems in Japan. Meanwhile, and incidentally, Robin Herd had cut his links with March. While Leyton House had its difficulties, there were upheavals in the team. But this survived, and emerged in 1992 as March F1, and that year March scored its last Constructor's Championship points to bring its grand total to 180, scored in 230 Grands Prix – a commendable average, although eighty-two were accumulated in the marque's first two seasons, 1970–71. Hoped-for finance for a 1993 programme did not materialize.

701 The first F1 March was essentially straightforward, built around an aluminium monocoque, with outboard wishbones and coil-springs suspension all round. A Cosworth DFV was bolted to the rear of the tub, and drove through a Hewland DG300 gearbox. This was not a handsome car, but outwardly there was an innovative detail – aerodynamicist Peter Wright collaborated in the design of fuel tank housings on each flank that were shaped as inverted aerofoils, anticipating the coming ground effects age.

March completed cars for Tyrrell and Crabbe as well as the STP works team, and these proved only just competitive, in the hands of Stewart and Amon. The Scot finished third in the 701's debut race, the South African GP, then won the Race of Champions and the Spanish GP, while Amon won the International Trophy. Amon was second in two GPs, Stewart in two, while Cevert contributed an odd point to the March Constructor's Championship total of 48, good enough for third place on the table. Six of the cars built appeared in non-championship races in 1971.

711 The 1971 car was individualistic, with rounded aerodynamic body lines. Frank Costin advised in this area, but some of the bodywork was soon set aside because of overheating problems. The strut-mounted front wing was equally distinctive. There were hip radiators aligned with the rear of the cockpit, and the tendency was to run cars without their fairings. Coil springs were inboard at the front, outboard at the rear. The car was designed with inboard brakes, but after a

March 701-Ford of 1970, driven by Jo Siffert.

March 711-Ford of 1971, driven by Ronnie Peterson.

brake-shaft failure at its first race, outboard front brakes were substituted.

The works cars ran with DFVs and Alfa Romeo V8s (from the T33/3 sports-racing car). Usually these Alfa-engined 711s were run for the Alfa Romeo protégés de Adamich and Galli, but Ronnie Peterson also drove one in odd events. Independent 711 entrants included Frank Williams Racing, Clarke-Mordaunt-Guthrie and Skip Barber.

Peterson scored his first championship points with second place at Monaco, was second in three other Grands Prix, and was runner-up to Stewart in the drivers' championship. The only other March driver to score was Pescarolo, in Williams' car. March was again third in the championship, with thirty-four points. In 1972 Carlos Pace scored his first championship points in a 711, in Spain and Belgium, driving a Williams car.

721 This was an uprated 711, with a chisel nose in place of the strut-mounted wing after the first race. Peterson scored three points in the first two Grands Prix, then persuaded Herd to adopt an Alfa sports-racing-car layout, with the gearbox ahead of the rear axle line (in turn the rear suspension was revised). This variant was designated 721X, and was a disaster – it just could not be made to work with the Goodyear tyres. It recorded three race finishes, in the hands of Peterson and Lauda.

By the summer it had been abandoned in favour of the 721G. This was built around a Formula 2 chassis, and the first was completed in nine days for independent entrant/driver Mike Beuttler. In

effect, a 721 rear end was added to a 722 (F2) chassis, with beefed-up suspension and brakes, and a DFV engine. Its best placing was third, driven by Peterson in Germany. March slumped to sixth in the Constructor's Championship.

Frank Williams's 721 was frequently crashed by Pescarolo. One 721 was oddly modified as the Eifelland, but was returned to March specification and appearance for John Watson to start his F1 career. Two 721s were run in the first

three Grands Prix of 1973, but did not record a single finish.

731 The 721G was modified for 1973, in part to meet new regulations concerning deformable structures. The track was narrower, the wheelbase longer, and deformable side pods coupled with a nose radiator meant that these cars looked very different. But the chassis numbers were carried over to these 731s. It seems that while new tubs were made, no complete new cars were built. A works car was run on a minimal budget for Jean-Pierre Jarier, until his F2 campaign took priority from mid-season. Mike Beuttler continued with his independent car, and David Purley ran his in some races. Roger Williamson started a 731 in two Grands Prix, and in the second was fatally injured at Zandvoort. And Lord Hesketh ran a 731 for James Hunt. James first scored in the French GP (his second Grand Prix in the car), and as the series ended he finished second in the US GP. He scored all fourteen points credited to March in the Constructor's Championship, giving it fifth place. This car was used in early-1974 races.

741 A Formula 2 design was adapted for the 1974 Grand Prix car, with a new monocoque, full-width nose, and radiators

March 731G-Ford, 1973.

angled back alongside the DFV. It was another economy model, useful in terms of scoring points, but not a potential race winner.

Hans Stuck scored his first championship points in a works 741, fifth in South Africa and fourth in Spain, but then his season was accident- and incident-prone. Ganley drove in the first two GPs, then Vittorio Brambilla brought sponsorship, and took over the second drive. He, too, scored a point in his first championship season, in Austria. This shoestring season produced six championship points, and ninth place for March in the championship. The March team used one of these cars in the first Grands Prix of 1975.

and for a works March. In another 'half-points' race, the Spanish GP, Lella Lombardi had scored half a point in the other works car, and she is still the only lady driver to have scored in a World Championship Grand Prix.

The spare works 751 was sold to Stuck, who finished only one of his five races in it (and March could have shot itself in the foot if one of its works pair had been seriously damaged). A new 751 was bought by the Penske team for comparative purposes. Mark Donohue placed it fifth in the British GP (where it was entered as a Penske, so that points were credited to that team), retired it in Germany, then was fatally injured in it in an

race. But unreliability and accidents meant that he scored in only one other race. Brambilla scored just one point, but Stuck, with two fourth places and a fifth, contributed points to the March total of nineteen, which earned seventh place in the championship. Lombardi left after one race, Merzario finished twice in five 1976 races in his 761.

Several independent 761s were run in 1977. Brian Henton got a good result (fourth) in a Brands Hatch non-title race. Patrick Neve drove the Williams Grand Prix Engineering car to six finishes from eight starts, the best seventh at Monza (but he also recorded three DNQs).

Save for the last three Grands Prix, the works cars for 1977 were 761Bs, and three 761s were revised to this specification. The car was shorter, but other improvements were in minor aspects. Alex Ribeiro and Ian Scheckter drove the works cars, but their inexperience meant that development input was negligible, and that handicap was compounded as Herd had to give priority to the March-BMW F2 programme.

March 761-Ford of 1976, Ronnie Peterson driving.

751 The 1975 car followed broadly similar lines. It had a stiffer monocoque, was lighter and outwardly neater. Naturally, a Cosworth-Hewland combination took care of power and its transmission. A narrow front track introduced in mid-season gave advantages.

Brambilla scored well for the team, led the Swedish GP and was leading the Austrian GP when it was stopped because of very heavy rain – that was to count as a 'half-points' victory, but it was a first Grand Prix victory for Brambilla,

accident at the Osterreichring. March was eighth in the championship.

761 Once again an F1 March was an evolutionary car, again stiffer and lighter, with a wider track than the 751 and two wheelbase lengths (used to suit circuits). It proved to be quick, and Ronnie Peterson returned to the team, to exploit its qualities.

The Swede led races, and at Monza scored the only victory for a works March in a full-length World Championship

771 Intended as the definitive 1977 F1 car, this had a new monocoque and a front radiator. There seemed to be no performance advantage, and there was no development work, so a 771 started in only four Grands Prix, Scheckter finishing once (tenth in the Dutch GP).

March scored no championship points in 1977, with 761s, 761Bs or 771s. At the end of the year Mosley, who had managed the team and acted as engineer, left March. Then March was withdrawn from Formula 1, and its FOCA membership was sold to ATS.

'2-4-0' Herd was intrigued by the potential of four-wheel drive, and this led to a six-wheeler, with four close-coupled driven wheels at the rear of a 761 (in fact more than one 761 as the experiment progressed, just a little). The proclaimed intention was that this rear end would be properly designed into the 771. A Hewland transmission was adapted and used as the purpose-designed transmission would have been too costly. There were two sets of lower links and coil springs/dampers in the rear suspension, and each rear wheel had an inboard disc brake.

Circuit tests were driven by Howden Ganley, and the car was then loaned to Roy Lane, who won hill climbs with it.

March 2-4-0-Ford six-wheeler of 1976, tested but not raced.

had to contest the whole series to qualify for future FOCA membership. This car failed to come to the grid for that first 1987 race, after engine failures in practice (in any case, its 130litre/28.6gal fuel tanks meant that it could not have run the Grand Prix distance).

The 871 was designed by Gordon Coppuck, and was closely related to the F3000 car. It was therefore conventional, with a carbon-fibre monocoque and of course F1 fuel capacity, double wishbone suspension (pullrod at the front, pushrod at the rear) and a Cosworth DFZ driving through a March six-speed gearbox. Ivan Capelli and his manager Cesare Gariboldi had been key figures in the Leyton House deal, and the young Italian proved more than competent as the team's only driver, starting every race entered with an 871, finishing six times, and scoring a point in the Monaco GP.

Although it was never raced, it generated enormous publicity for March.

781S The 771 design was revised to meet an order for an F1 car to contest the Aurora AFX Championship, a British series. The car did not have fuel capacity for a full Grand Prix, as Aurora AFX distances were usually just over 100 miles. Guy Edwards won two races in a 781S, and was fourth in the 1978 championship.

811 March Engines was commissioned to build Formula 1 cars for the RAM team in 1981. The 811 was Herd's first ground-effects car design, and to a degree it followed the Williams FW07s that RAM had run in the 1980 Aurora AFX series. The cars carried RAM chassis plates. They were conventional, with lower wishbones/top rocker arms/inboard springs all round, DFV engines and Hewland FGA gearboxes. But this was another low-budget operation, and that showed in the materials used, leading for example to tubs that were not stiff enough. Herd looked to strengthening the cars, but he soon left; Gordon Coppuck and then Adrian Reynard took on the task. The latter devised a short-chassis version that showed promise, and looked ahead to 1982.

In 1981 Derek Daly managed to qualify eight times, and finished in four races, with seventh in the British GP his best placing. Salazar failed to qualify four times, retired

from the only race he started in an 811, then quit for an Ensign drive.

821 Reynard was responsible for this car, really a definitive version of the 811. The team appeared to have healthy sponsorship, but when a major contributor withdrew in the late spring, development virtually ceased. And development was needed, as RAM switched its tyre supplier.

Jochen Mass came close to scoring in the early-season American GP West, with eighth place, then he was demotivated by accidents. Rupert Keegan took his place, failed to qualify twice, retired twice, was once twelfth in his five attempts. Raul Boesel drove through the season, finishing only three races (the best placing was eighth in Belgium). Villota did not qualify once in his five attempts in a car run by Onyx.

871 Although a 1983 car was known as a RAM-March it was a RAM, and the next Formula 1 March did not appear until 1987, with Leyton House backing. The constructor was March Racing. At the end of the turbo era, the new team chose to enter the 'naturally aspirated division', using 3.5litre Cosworth DFZ engines (occasionally 3.3litre DFL sportscar V8s as the supply situation was complicated). A one-car team was run.

For the first race, that car was an adapted F3000 87B, designated 87P, as a team

881 Encouraged by the 1987 season, Leyton House committed a larger budget to the team in 1988, when there was a new technical director, Adrian Newey. His top-flight experience had largely been in CART racing, and that led to a Leyton House car that was highly refined in aerodynamic respects. The 881 was a slender car with a narrow monocoque, long wheelbase and narrow track, outwardly with contoured flanks. There was pushrod suspension all round. For its power unit, March turned to the normally aspirated Judd CV 90-degree V8, and a derivative of the March CART gearbox was used. During the season the team was able to test, and make revisions on a scale seldom possible with earlier March cars.

Mauricio Gugelmin joined Capelli in a two-car team that began to prosper as the cars became reliable. High points came in Japan, when Capelli briefly led the Grand Prix – in a normally aspirated car – in Portugal when he finished second between the McLarens, and in Belgium where he was third. Gugelmin scored points in Britain, with a good fourth place, and in Hungary. March was sixth in the Constructors' Championship, and twenty-two points was its third-highest score.

CG891 The new designation style was a tribute to Gariboldi, and the 1989 March was late, reflecting Group problems (that led to its sale). So 881s had to be used in the opening races (five starts produced four retirements and third place for Gugelmin in the Brazilian GP). The new cars turned out to be disappointing.

Newey followed his 1988 lines, in a more tightly packaged car with the new Judd EV narrow-angle V8, a 76-degree unit that contributed to a reduction in frontal area. There was a new longitudinal six-speed gearbox. Capelli finished only one race in this car (twelfth in Belgium), while Gugelmin finished only four, placing seventh in three. Only his first-race points with the old car gave March a championship place, twelfth.

CG901 As far as race entries were concerned, there was no reference to March in the 1990 cars, but the team was basically the same. The CG901 was a development of the 1989 car, by Newey and Brunner, with revised suspension and aerodynamics, and Judd EV engines.

Pronounced handling problems had to be overcome in the first half of the season. Capelli failed to qualify twice and

Gugelmin failed four times. Each then recorded just one scoring finish: Capelli was second in the French GP, after leading for more than forty laps (and Gugelmin was third when he retired), while Gugelmin was sixth in the Belgian GP. The pair retired sixteen times – a rate of over 50 per cent, once the DNQ efforts are taken into account. March was sixth in the championship.

CG911 The 1991 season started against a background of discord in the team – manage Ian Phillips and Adrian Newey both left – and towards its end the Leyton House financial difficulties threatened its existence. Chris Murphy and Gustav Brunner were credited with the design of the new car, but by midsummer Brunner had assumed control of technical matters, after a fundamental weakness had been discovered in the suspension. An Ilmor V10 was adopted, to drive through a new six-speed transverse gearbox.

Capelli scored the team's only point, in the Hungarian GP, and he managed only two other finishes to set against eleven retirements. Gugelmin finished eight races, with best placings seventh (three times). Mercedes-Benz 'bought' a drive for Karl Wendlinger at the end of the year, when Capelli had to stand down (Wendlinger retired once and was twentieth in the Australian GP).

Under the March name again, the team ran CG911s in 1992 – it could not fund construction of its 921 design, and there was some hope that this might take shape for 1993. Survival was a struggle, and Brunner oversaw little car development before he left late in the season (in any case, the reduced workforce had to concentrate on keeping cars in the field). The reliable Ilmor V10s were still used.

Four drivers occupied March cockpits in 1992, their funds sometimes helping to keep the show on the road. Wendlinger drove in fourteen races, finished six, and scored three points in the Canadian GP. They proved to be the last for a March F1 team, and gave it ninth place in the Constructors' Championship. Paul Belmondo was entered in the first eleven races, qualified to start in five, and finished every time, with ninth in Hungary his best placing. Emanuele Naspetti qualified for all of his five races with the team, and finished in two (twelfth and thirteenth). Jan Lammers was run twice, and his single finish, twelfth in the Australian race, was the last for a March car in a Grand Prix.

As that new design was set aside, the CG911s were reported to be uprated for 1993, but the sad fact was that there were no funds to pay for engines.

(Top) **March 821-Ford of 1982, driven by Raul Boesel.** *(Above)* **March 871-Ford of 1987, driven by Ivan Capelli.**

Officine Alfieri Maserati was established in Bologna in December 1924, but the Maserati marque dates from 1926, as Diatto turned away from racing and three of the six Maserati brothers laid down their first car in their tuning boutique. The second race for that first car was a Grand Prix, and the name did not disappear from Grand Prix racing until the end of the 1960s, albeit the presence was sometimes marginal and in the end Maserati supplied engines to another team.

Five of the brothers were dedicated to engines, cars and motor sport. The oldest, Carlo, designed a motorcycle in 1897, and later became the head of Fiat's test department before he died in 1910. Alfieri and Ettore built and raced their first special in 1913, and with Bindo worked on Isotta aero engines and a racing car. Alfieri then developed Diatto competitions cars, and designed that company's Grand Prix car in 1922. Effectively, his Diatto design was adopted for the first Maserati.

Customers were attracted, for the brothers' cars were practical and generally orthodox, even the *Sedici Cilindri* of 1929, with its engine made up of two straight eights in a search for capacity and power. The normal straight eights were successful in works or quasi-works team hands, as well as with independents, at least until Alfa Romeo and the German teams dominated top-flight racing.

Maserati seemed on the verge of joining this elite company, even supplanting Alfa Romeo, at the end of the 1930s, and a straight eight designed for Grand Prix racing went on to great success in the Indianapolis 500.

By that time industrialist Adolfo Orsi had to all intents and purposes taken over Maserati, mainly it has to be conceded for its spark plug business. The three surviving brothers, Bindo, Ernesto and Ettore, entered into a 10-year contract to continue with 'their' car company from 1938. The base was moved from Bologna to Modena, but the trident badge of Bologna that it had adopted was retained, and remained in use at the end of the century. The brothers honoured their contract, then left to set up Osca; Adolfo Orsi's son Omer controlled Maserati.

Maserati single-seaters remained popular – in truth, there were few cars of this quality available as the 1940s gave way to the 1950s, even if they were outclassed in the *grandes épreuves* by Alfa Romeo. Then they generally raced in the shadow of the equally simple Ferraris through the 2litre World Championship years. In many ways the 2.5litre 250F was also a car of that period, as the racing world was changing, but it proved to be the outstanding Grand Prix Maserati, competitive in 1954 and developed over five years. Once again, this was a Maserati that was an ideal private entrant's car, but Fangio won a World Championship in works 250Fs. In the front line, these cars faded away late in the 1950s, but they were destined to become popular in historic racing. Sports cars almost brought Maserati down, inadvertently, when the entire team of 450s was written off in the Venezuela GP – a costly disaster for the small company. Later sports-racing cars were built to order, then an engine that had been put in hand for the 250F in 1957 was dusted down and used by Cooper in the opening years of the 3litre Formula 1. It powered the British cars to two Grand Prix victories and twice to third place in the Constructors' Championship. A low-key run to seventh place at Monaco in 1969 was the last for a Maserati engine in a Grand Prix.

The company continued its small-volume high-performance road car manufacture, eventually being taken under Fiat control, when ironically Ferrari expertise was brought in to sort out its production activities in the 1990s. The single-seaters with the Trident badge epitomised the Italian racing car over a long period, products of passion and know-how rather than science … often successful and now sought after.

Tipo 26 Seemingly, the designation was owed to the year of the car's introduction, 1926. The first appeared in the Targa Florio, and was driven by Alfieri Maserati to win the 1.5litre class. Later that year, a pair started at the Italian GP at Monza.

The Tipo 26 was a conventional two-seater racing car, with a channel-section chassis, rigid front axle and live rear axle with semi-elliptics, and a dohc supercharged 1,492cc straight eight. The 1,980cc Tipo 26B came in 1928, with an engine rated at 130bhp compared with the first type's 115bhp (some T26s were to be fitted with 2litre engines). Production of the two types amounted to some twenty cars.

At the end of the 1920s, cars of this type tended to be dual-purpose machines, suitable for such races as the Targa Florio as much as Grands Prix – indeed, the Sicilian race was often more highly regarded. There were class successes for the 26/26B, but in 1926–29 second places were the best Maserati results, first in the 1927 Coppa Acerbo, in minor events in 1928–29 and in the 1929 Tripoli GP. 26Bs were fifth and sixth in the 1928 European GP at Monza.

V4 This 1929 one-off had similar exterior lines to the existing Maserati, but a 16-cylinder engine that comprised two 26B straight eights on a common crankcase The right block had reversed porting, so that eight-into-one exhausts appeared on each side of the car. Some 305bhp was claimed for this 3,960cc engine (there was no capacity limit in the Grand Prix regulations, but in any case most races were *formule libre* events).

Like other 'twin-engined' cars of that period, the V4 was fast in a straight line, but reports that handling was 'difficult' are quite credible! It started in seven races, and Borzacchini drove it to Maserati's first outright victory, in the 1930 Tripoli GP. Its only other victory was scored by Alfieri Maserati, in the 1931 Rome GP. In 1929, incidentally, he had set the record for the Monza banked track at 124.2mph (200kph), while at Cremona Borzacchini had covered 10km at 152.9mph (246.2kph) in this machine.

8C This designation was applied to 1100, 1500, 2500 and 2800 cars built in 1929–31, in mildly uprated T26 chassis with supercharged engines that were also reworked. Outwardly, they were distinguished by a sloping radiator. At least a dozen were produced, but some were bodied as sports cars, and there was an 8C-2500 coupe.

The normal 8C-2500 was the first true Maserati Grand Prix car, with a 2,495cc supercharged engine rated at some 185–195bhp. It was first raced in the 1930 Targa Florio and Arcangeli scored the type's first victory in the Monza GP. Later in the year Fagioli won two races and Varzi three, including Maserati's first victory outside Italy, in the Spanish GP (the Tripoli GP was regarded as a 'home' race). 8Cs were less successful in 1931, when high points were Fagioli's wins in a heat and the final of the Monza GP in an 8C-2800. Then Campari won the 1933 French GP in a similar car, heading five Alfas.

V5 Another 16-cylinder one-off *formule libre* car, the V5 of 1932 had a 4.9litre engine made up of two 8C-2500 the 1933 Tunis GP. Then Nuvolari drove one to win the Belgian GP and two secondary races, and finished second in the Italian GP. There were successes through to 1936 when Seaman won the British Empire Trophy at Donington, while Falchetto, Etancelin and Straight won other secondary races in 8CMs.

4C The four-cylinder cars built from 1932 were usually 1100 and 1500 models – and very pretty *voiturettes*, too. However, a 2,482cc supercharged four-cylinder unit was seen in 1934, in a car driven in two Grands Prix by Zehender and at Monaco by Taruffi, who was running fourth when he retired.

6C In 1934 six-cylinder engines were also fitted into 8CM chassis. A 3.3litre version came first, but a 3.7litre was normally seen, and this was rated at 280bhp, perhaps optimistically.

Late that year, Maserati followed the Alfa Romeo example and entrusted its official effort to an independent team, Scuderia Subalpina, which used these 6Cs until the new cars were ready.

Earlier Nuvolari had placed a 6C/34 third behind an Auto Union and a Mercedes in the Czech GP; he was fifth in the Italian GP and won late-summer secondary races at Modena and Naples. In 1935 Etancelin and Zehender finished third in the Tunis and French GPs respectively, and those were Maserati high points in a poor season.

V8R1 This car was a departure, in that it had a V8. This 90-degree Roots-supercharged engine was first run in 4.2litre form but was usually a 4,788cc unit, with an output of no more than 320bhp, despite claims of power outputs that almost matched rival German cars. There was a light channel-section chassis, with transverse links and torsion bars front suspension, and swinging axles and semi-elliptics at the rear – this was the first all-independent Maserati. The body looked up-to-the-minute, with shrouded front suspension; one car was run with a high tail.

Despite teething problems, Etancelin finished second in the V8R1's debut race, a heat of the Marne GP at Reims. These cars were then used spasmodically – little development was undertaken – and unsuccessfully. Farina did lead the 1935 Donington GP in one, but retired. The

Maserati 8C-2500 of 1930, driven by Luigi Fagioli.

units, giving some 330bhp (as much as 360bhp was claimed for it in 'record' form). Fagioli drove it to win the 1932 Rome GP and a Monza GP heat (he was second in the final, as he had been in the Italian GP). Ruggeri was fatally injured when he crashed in a record attempt, and the car was not rebuilt after a second heavy accident, in the 1934 Tripoli GP.

8CM Under Ernesto Maserati – Alfieri had died after an operation in 1932 – the straight eight was further developed for

1933, and in 2,992cc form, initially giving some 220bhp, was used in the first monoposto Maserati. This had a narrow channel-section chassis that proved far from stiff, so that most owners added braces in attempts to improve road-holding to an acceptable standard. This was the first Grand Prix car since the 1921 Duesenberg to have hydraulic brakes, at the front. Fortuitously, the new Maserati came as Alfa Romeo withdrew the Tipo B from racing. Nevertheless, Ferrari's Alfas beat the 8CM into third place in its debut race,

Maserati 8C-3000 of 1934, Whitney Straight driving.

Maserati V8R1 of 1935, Fifi Etancelin driving at Monaco.

only victory in an International race came in the 1936 Pau GP, when Etancelin just beat modest opposition. The cars were then sold, and two ended up in the USA, where they contributed to efforts to keep flickering road racing alive through the early post-Second World War years.

8CTF Built to the 1938 Grand Prix regulations that admitted supercharged engines up to 3litres, this was an Italian Grand Prix car with performance to challenge the ruling German teams. Sadly, this potential was not backed with adequate development, but the model had an

outstanding record at Indianapolis, one of the three built winning the 500 twice, and finishing third twice.

The chassis was on familiar Maserati lines, with torsion bar independent front suspension and a live rear axle with quarter elliptic springs. The dohc 2,992cc straight eight had two Roots-type superchargers at the nose and was first rated at 355bhp. It drove through a four-speed gearbox. Overall, the 8CTF had classic lines.

In Grands Prix it had speed, but not stamina – Trossi set the fastest lap in the type's debut race, the 1938 Tripoli GP, but retired. He also drove an 8CTF to its first finish, fifth in the Italian GP. The Maserati team contested only one Grand Prix in 1939, when Paul Pietsch led the German race and eventually finished third.

The 8CL was an improved version, built in 1940 with a developed 2,978cc engine giving more than 400bhp. Two were completed, but neither ran in a Grand Prix. One was seventh at Indianapolis in 1946, but that failed to live up to Shaw's two 500 victories in the Boyle Special 8CTF in 1939–40, or Horn's third place in the same car in 1946–47.

4CL Maserati was very successful in *voiturette* racing from the mid-1930s, until Alfa Romeo introduced the 158. To match that car, Maserati laid down a four-cylinder type in the winter of 1938–39, and it was ready for racing in 1939. Effectively, the engine was half of the 8CTF unit, a 1,489cc 16-valve straight four with single-stage supercharging. Its 220bhp was not a match for the Alfa engine, but these Maseratis were successful in 1939, and were 1-2 in the last race of the period, the 1940 Targa Florio that was run as a closed-circuit race at Palermo.

These pre-Second World War cars naturally appeared as soon as racing picked up again, in 1946 when Villoresi drove one to win the Nice GP and in 1947 when they became Grand Prix cars under the regulations that restricted supercharged engines to 1.5litres. In those mainstream events contested by Alfa Corse they were outclassed, elsewhere their drivers enjoyed successful seasons. Among them, Nuvolari drove a borrowed 4CL to his last single-seater victory, at Albi in July 1946. The principal cars were run by Scuderia Ambrosiana, and after a South American series expedition early in 1948 two of its cars were bought by the

Argentine Automobile Club, for Fangio and Galvez.

4CLT Before 1948 it was obvious that something more competitive was called for, hence the 4CLT. It was regarded as the first new Maserati after the brothers left, but although the design was attributed to Alberto Massimino and Victor Bellentani, the first tubular chassis had been designed by Enesto Maserati and Massimino. The chassis of the 4CLT (T–Tubolare) used substantial main tubes and cross members, while in the front suspension coil springs took the place of torsion bars. The engine was reworked, notably in the introduction of two-stage supercharging, and power output was increased to some 260bhp. Lists show

(Above) **Maserati 8C of 1938, Luigi Villoresi driving.**

Maserati A6GCS of 1949, Juan-Manuel Fangio driving.

that twenty of these neat and workmanlike cars were built, 1948–50. The new chassis was first seen in 1947, but the 4CLT as such did not come until June 1948. At the San Remo GP, Ascari and Villoresi placed the new cars 1-2 in that race, and its name was adopted for the car. At times 4CLT San Remo drivers challenged the Alfa Romeo team for top three placings, though not for outright victories, and soon they had to face Ferraris (in 1949 leading Ambrosiana drivers Ascari and Villoresi moved to Ferrari).

In 1948 ten top-flight races fell to Maserati, including the Grand Prix des Nations and the Monaco GP (Farina) and the British GP (Villoresi). On paper, this record was equalled in 1949, but the only victory in a major event was de Graffenried's in the British GP. In 1950 the car was no longer competitive, and the only victory of note was Fangio's in the Pau GP.

Scuderia Milano and Enrico Platé attempted to breathe new life into the cars (*see* Maserati-Milano and Maserati-Platé), and there was the 4CLT/50 spin-off with a 1.7litre engine built for South American *formule libre* racing.

A6GCM This Formula 2 car developed from a sports car introduced in 1947, and in 1952–53 it was a World Championship series car. In the chassis and suspension

Massimino followed the 4CLT, but the engine was a new dohc 1,988cc straight six that initially produced 165bhp and gave as much as 190bhp in 1953, in the cars also referred to as A6SSG (a 2litre four-cylinder engine designed by Massimino gave similar power but was never used). Four-speed gearboxes were standard, with the gear lever still positioned between the driver's legs. Cars were sold to prominent independent entrants.

The works cars did not race until June 1952 and were run in only two championship races that year, showing speed to equal the Ferrari 500. Gonzalez's second place in the Italian GP was the best showing in 1952.

The first victories fell to a Platé car driven by de Graffenried in the 1953 Syracuse GP and two short Goodwood races. The works effort was stronger that year and one of its drivers, Fangio, was runner-up in the Drivers' Championship. In the French, British and German GPs he was second, and at the last opportunity, in Italy, he won.

Some cars were uprated with 250F engines for the first season of the 2.5litre Formula 1, and were well placed in secondary races through to the summer.

250F This Maserati was the classic front-engined Formula 1 car of the 2.5litre years, not the most advanced in technical respects and backed by only modest resources, but the one Maserati that was an outstanding Grand Prix car, and aesthetically one of the most attractive of the type. It was actually used throughout the seven-year life of the formula – a 250F started in its first Grand Prix and another in its last – and for four of these years it was a front-line car.

The design was by Gioachino Colombo and Luigi Bellentani, with later development by Giulio Alfieri. There was a multi-tubular chassis, with wishbone and coil-spring front suspension and a de Dion rear axle. The 2,493cc straight six derived from the Formula 2 engine, and at the start produced 240bhp (by 1957 it had a 270bhp rating). The first of the thirty-two cars had four-speed gearboxes, later versions had five-speed units. The total of thirty-two cars is not precise, incidentally, for it includes A6GCM-based cars, the odd chassis, a confusing rebuild, and twenty-seven 'new' ground-up 250Fs.

The first appeared corpulent, then a slimmer and neater body came in 1955 (together with a streamlined car, later rebodied). An offset body came in 1956,

Maserati A6SSG of 1953, Froilan Gonzalez driving.

Maserati 250F of 1957, Juan-Manuel Fangio driving.

allowing for the transmission to the left and a lower cockpit seating position, and these cars had longer noses. A V12 then called for a slightly bulkier body. Finally, in 1958 the lightweight 'Piccolo' variant had a shorter wheelbase and a neater tail (these cars were built in the AvGas era, and therefore less fuel had to be carried and the tail tank could be smaller). In parallel there were development changes, from wheelbase to brakes, some weight was shed and a car owned by the Owen Organization (to give BRM people racing experience!) was fitted with disc brakes. Two types of fuel injection were tried in 1956, then the 2,489cc 60-degree V12 was fitted to two cars in 1957, but not really developed before the works racing effort was wound up (power outputs up to 320bhp were quoted for this power unit).

Fangio drove a 250F to a debut race victory in the 1954 Argentine GP, and won the Belgian GP before Mercedes' cars were ready for him – he could have won the championship driving Maseratis that year; as it was he scored seventeen of his forty-two points in 250Fs. He was to return to Maserati in 1957, when he did win the title with the team (he won outright in Argentina, Monaco, France and Germany).

Two other championship Grands Prix fell to Moss in 1956, the Monaco and Italian races. That gave a total of eight victories in the twenty-eight ranking events run in 1954–57. But the 250F was also the mainstay of racing in the mid-1950s. Moss won fourteen secondary races in 250Fs, and others who won non-championship races with these cars were Behra, Bira, Collins, Gerard, Gould, Hawthorn, Marimon, Musso, Salvadori, Schell and Simon, while Moss and Jensen won New Zealand races. Most drivers of the period seemed to race in these cars, and the last top-three placing of any consequence was scored by Munaron, third in the 1960 Buenos Aires GP. Then 250Fs had a glorious second life, in historic racing.

Independent attempts to keep the car in the forefront were hardly realistic, when Cooper had set such a firm new trend. Temple Buell backed Piccolo cars, and curious noses contrived by Fantuzzi were grafted onto a trio sent to New Zealand in 1959 (lack of success there led Buell to sell the cars). The Tec-Mec (qv) had been put in hand by Maserati as a successor and was built by Colotti at the behest of driver Giorgio Scarlatti. He lost interest (realistically) and when the car was eventually raced it was obsolete.

During the 1.5litre Grand Prix years, Maserati sports-cars engines were used in a few marginal Formula 1 cars, then Alfieri revived the 2.5litre V12 in 3litre form as a power unit for Cooper in the first years of the formula introduced in 1966, when it briefly brought the Maserati name back to main-line racing.

continued from p.143

The best championship race finish was de Graffenried's sixth in Switzerland (that did not score a point then), and he was third in secondary races at Silverstone, Aix-les-Bains and Cadours. Pagani, Cortese, Schell and Crespo had no success in these cars – their potential was perhaps best shown by the seventeenth and nineteenth places achieved by Schell and de Graffenried in the 1952 British GP. The pair run in practice for the Italian GP failed to qualify.

These cars were set aside in 1953, in large part as Maserati sold A6GCMs to independent entrants.

Mathis

Emile Mathis's Strasbourg company was German until 1918, when Alsace-Lorraine became French again, and from 1898 until 1903 it built only one-off cars. It then built production Hermes (designed by Ettore Bugatti), before introducing a catalogued Mathis road car in 1910. In the following year Mathis drove a Stoewer badged as a Mathis in the *Coupe de l'Auto*.

A true Mathis was entered in that contest in 1912, when it was run concurrently with the Grand Prix. The Mathis was the smallest car in the race, with an 1,849cc four-cylinder ohc engine. Esser drove it to twelfth place overall in the Grand Prix (eighth in the Coupe category), and it was reliable, if not exactly quick – Esser finished 220min behind the winner! A similar car with a 1,460cc engine started in the 1913 Grand Prix, when Esser retired early in the race with engine failure.

Mathis was admitted to the 1921 French GP as it was by then a French marque (German entries were not accepted). Once again it was a small car, with a 1.5litre ohc four-cylinder engine, and four-wheel brakes. And again Mathis's objective was to demonstrate reliability, but this was undermined as the engine was very new and little tested, and Mathis retired when it failed after only five laps. However, the engine was later used successfully in touring car races in the 1920s, before Mathis turned from racing.

Matra

See pp.155–157.

MBM

Peter Monteverdi made his name with limited-production high-performance cars from the late 1960s, basing the business at his BMW agency at Basle-Binningen. Earlier he had a modest career as a sports-car driver. In 1961 he had his first brush with Formula 1, as the MBM was introduced (his second involvement was to be in his own name when he took on the Onyx team in 1990).

The first MBM single-seater was a Formula Junior car introduced in 1960, Monteverdi-Basle-Motoren being changed to Monteverdi-Basle-Mantzel for this venture, as DKW engine expert Dieter Mantzel was involved. Monteverdi was not the first constructor to see the possibility of modifying an FJ car for the 1.5litre Formula 1, nor the first to find that this was unwise.

The MBM had a multi-tubular chassis that was modified to take a 1,488cc Porsche RSK air-cooled flat-four engine, for which 150bhp was optimistically claimed. Two of these cars were built for 1961, and Monteverdi competed in hill climbs before qualifying last for the non-championship Solitude GP, and retiring after just two race laps. That car was then written off in an accident at Hockenheim. Monteverdi abandoned this venture, buried the wreckage of the crashed car, and exhibited the other unraced F1 MBM in his showrooms for a while.

McGuire

Australian driver Brian McGuire ran a Williams FW04 in the Shellsport national series in 1976, winning one race, and updated it for 1977 as the McGuire BM1. It was entered for only one Grand Prix, when McGuire failed to qualify it for the British race by a wide margin. He returned to the British series, and was killed in a Brands Hatch accident during practice in BM1.

Matra – Mécanique-Aviation-Traction – was primarily an aerospace company that entered the automotive industry through Matra Sports, a subsidiary that came into existence because of company founder Marcel Chassagny's friendship with René Bonnet. The little Bonnet specialist car company was close to collapse in 1964 – it had struggled for three years after the original DB, Deutsch-Bonnet, partnership had split up. Chassagny took it on, and continued production of the Bonnet Djet sports car, as the Matra Djet.

Jean-Luc Lagardère ran Matra Sports, and set up a competitions department. This led to the construction of the first Matra single-seater, the Formula 3 MS1 built to aerospace standards in 1965. At Reims in high summer, Jean-Pierre Beltoise drove a Matra to win the F3 race in the French GP support programme, and in French newspapers this moment of glory rated coverage than Brabham's Grand Prix victory.

Formula 2 cars soon followed, with Ken Tyrrell playing a pivotal role. He ran Matra cars with BRM F2 engines in 1966 and Cosworth FVA engines in 1967. His principal driver was Jackie Stewart, joined in 1967 by Jacky Ickx, who won the European Championship – a first major title for a Matra driver.

By that time the Elf oil company had agreed to back a Matra Formula 1 effort, and that attracted a government grant of six million francs. Design work on a Matra 3litre V12 started. But that was the year that saw the debut of the Ford-Cosworth DFV and pragmatic Ken Tyrrell saw promise in the combination of a Matra chassis and a DFV. Lagardère was receptive to Tyrrell's approach, recognizing that a twin-track approach increased the chances of success, and agreed that a chassis should be developed for the British V8, to be run alongside the car with the French V12.

The V8-engined cars were highly successful, Stewart winning nine Grands Prix with them, the World Championship for himself and the Constructors' Championship for Matra, both in 1969. This Matra International programme ended that year – a Matra association with Chrysler France meant that a new F1 car with a Ford-labelled engine could not be sanctioned (the existing chassis had been made redundant by changed regulations).

Save for a season when sports cars had overriding priority, Matra persisted with its V12-powered cars until the end of 1972, but never won a Grand Prix. Nevertheless, nine victories from sixty championship races stand to Matra's credit, as do 155 championship points. That record gave French motor sport a boost, and the shrieking V12 did eventually power Grand Prix winners, when it was made available for Ligier in 1976.

MS9 This was a test bed, but it was raced once. A Formula 2 monocoque was modified to accept a DFV engine that served as a stressed member, as it had in the Lotus 49 (the Matra did have a light frame linking the monocoque and rear suspension). The suspension incorporated components from the MS630 sports-racing car. Formula 2 fuel tanks were still used, so the MS9 would not have run a full Grand Prix distance without refuelling. In its only race, the 1968 South African GP, Stewart was running third just after half distance when the engine failed.

MS10 The first purpose-designed Matra-Ford F1 car followed the lines laid down by Bernard Boyer's preceding single-seater. There was another functional monocoque chassis, with side tanks and a fuel cell between the cockpit and the rear bulkhead. Boyer also retained the frame linking the monocoque and the rear suspension. There was wishbone front suspension, with lower wishbones, top links and radius arms at the rear, and the MS10 started life with sports car components in the suspension (early modifications saw lighter parts substituted). The DFV drove through Hewland gearboxes. During the season, the first 'wings' appeared, mounted amidships to the chassis and later to rear suspension uprights.

The race debut came in the Race of Champions, and the Grand Prix debut was in Spain, where Beltoise led but finished fifth. Servoz-Gavin drove the sole MS10 at Monaco, and led before retiring. Stewart was back in racing for the next Grand Prix, and led the Belgian race before a late pit stop dropped him to fourth. In Holland he scored Matra's first Grand Prix victory, and in 1968 he also won in Germany and the USA, as well as the non-title Oulton Park Gold Cup. Matra was third in the Constructors' Championship with forty-five points – an outstanding first-season achievement.

The two MS10s were run early in 1969, carrying large aerofoils. Stewart won the South African GP and the Silverstone International Trophy, before the MS80 came into service.

MS11 There were high hopes for the 'all-French' F1 Matra that was unveiled in March 1968 and made its incredibly noisy race debut at Monaco in 1968. The suspension and chassis were similar to the MS10, save that the box-section members

Matra MS10-Ford of 1968, Jackie Stewart driving.

were run back from the monocoque to carry the V12, which could not be used as a stressed member (that added 60kg/132lb to the dry weight). During the season larger fuel tanks had to be contrived – the V12 was very thirsty – making for a break line in the flanks, and primitive aerofoils were added.

The V12 was designed by a team headed by Georges Martin. It was a 60-degree dohc that had a disappointing output of 390bhp. During 1969 it was to be reworked in a search for competitive power and reliability.

The high point in 1968 came in the third race for the MS11, when Beltoise was second in a wet Dutch GP. After that he scored twice, with a fifth and a sixth. Pescarolo drove an MS11 twice, finishing ninth in Mexico. One MS11 was used as a test hack for a hydraulic transmission for a Caussin-designed four-wheel-drive system, intended to provide drive to the front wheels when it sensed that the rear wheels were losing traction. This project was set aside.

MS80 Boyer built on experience with the MS10 in this F1 Matra that became the best known and most successful car built by the marque. Partly because it was intended to run alongside a four-wheel-drive car (on a 'horses-for-courses' basis)

only two were built, to serve for one season.

The chassis was stiffer than the MS10, and the suspension was modified, partly to suit wider wheels. Outwardly the bulged 'Coke bottle' flanks pointed to location of all the fuel around the centre of gravity, as the cell behind the cockpit had been abandoned. At first a high rear wing was fitted; the aerofoil arrangements after the hasty change in regulations following Lotus's Spanish GP accidents were more attractive. In 1969 the DFV was rated at 430bhp, and the Hewland DG400 gearbox was used.

Stewart drove Matra International MS80s to win the Spanish, Dutch, French, British and Italian GPs, was second in Germany and fourth in Mexico. Beltoise's second place in France was particularly important to the constructor and sponsors, and he scored in five other Grands Prix while Servoz-Gavin scored a point with the four-wheel-drive MS84. Matra clearly won the Constructors' Championship.

MS84 Four-wheel drive was felt to be important as the 1960s ended, to utilize the power of 3litre engines – a presumption that was soon shown to be false. Matra International asked for a four-wheel drive, and Matra obliged with the

space-frame MS84. This had a DFV turned through 180 degrees, with the gearbox positioned ahead of it and a transfer box feeding propeller shafts run fore and aft. Derek Gardner engineered the Ferguson transmission system. Torque split was 25:75 front:rear, but by the end of the year the car was running with power to the rear wheels only. It was complicated and heavy. Servoz-Gavin scored a point with it in the 1969 Canadian GP.

MS120 Circumstances meant that Matra Sport was on its own in Formula 1 in 1970, when there was a chauvinistic welcome for a completely French venture that ignored the continuing use of British components such as gearboxes. The new monocoque of the angular MS120 complemented the V12, revised so that it could be used as a stressed member. The suspension (double wishbones and outboard springs all round) followed MS80 lines. The flat upper surfaces of the car were reckoned to provide some downforce, and wide-chord nose fins and rear aerofoils were usual. As well as its strengthened crankcase, the MS120 V12 had revised heads. In its main features it was identical to Matra's sports-car V12, but as Martin's team sought to match DFV outputs, 'exotic' materials were used (such as titanium con rods), and led to unreliability. That thirst remained, too,

Matra MS80-Ford of 1969, Jackie Stewart driving.

and the fuel load handicapped drivers in the early laps of races.

The team scored three third places in championship races in 1970 (Beltoise in Belgium and Italy, Pescarolo in Monaco), and with a few minor placings Matra was sixth in the championship.

The MS120B had a more rigid mono-coque, generally more rounded but still inelegant, and late in the season the MS71 V12 with revised heads and a higher rev limit came into use. But fortunes declined. Chris Amon scored nine points (third in Spain, twice fifth and once sixth) and, as Beltoise failed to score, these points made up Matra's total, for seventh place in the championship.

The MS120C was a rebuild, two cars being uprated with all-round minor improvements. Amon – the team's only driver in 1972 – scored single points in the Monaco and Belgian GPs, before the MS120D was introduced at the French GP.

This turned out to be the last single-seater Matra. It had new, more rounded, monocoque and was lighter, while as much as 480bhp was claimed for the engine ... but Matra bench outputs were seldom repeated with V12s in cars, and the F1 version of the engine was still unreliable.

MS120-Matra, 1970 version.

Amon led the French GP convincingly in an MS120D fitted with a sports-car V12, was most unlucky to suffer a puncture and finished third. He was fourth in Britain, fifth in Austria and sixth in Canada, and that was the last championship point scored by a Matra driver. Amon's twelve points scored during the season gave Matra eighth place in the championship, and as it ended Matra abandoned Formula 1, in favour of sports cars.

McLAREN

New Zealander Bruce McLaren was already a successful Cooper Grand Prix driver when he set up Bruce McLaren Motor Racing in 1963, with Teddy Mayer, to run Coopers in the Tasman series. He then moved steadily forward to become a manufacturer, first of all with sports cars.

After running the Zerex Special sports-racing car, the first McLaren as such, the M1A sports-racing car appeared in 1964. The M1B followed in 1965, and at the end of that year McLaren broke his links with Cooper, to take his small company into the single-seater field.

The M2A single-seater test car had been built in 1965, and the first McLaren single-seater that actually raced, M2B, was completed before the end of that year, ready for the 1966 F1 season. McLaren's early problem was in finding an engine, and the M2B was not successful.

The V12 BRM-engined cars that followed showed promise, then came Robin Herd's last McLaren design, the Cosworth DFV-powered M7. Bruce drove an M7A to join the exclusive band of driver-constructors who have won races in their own-make cars – in Belgium in 1968. With these handsome orange-liveried cars, McLaren was established as a front-running team in Grand Prix as well as in sports-car racing.

Bruce McLaren's death, while he was testing a racing sports car at Goodwood in 1970, came as an enormous blow to the sport in general. His wife and associates kept the company and its racing teams in the forefront through to the second half of the 1970s.

The sports-car side was abandoned after 1972, but the first half of the 1970s was a golden period for McLaren in top-flight F1 racing. At the same time there were successful Indycar race cars, and this was the period in which John Barnard first made his name as a designer.

The M23, which became a design classic, first appeared in 1973, brought McLaren the Constructors' Championship in 1974, and brought Drivers' Championships to Emerson Fittipaldi (1974) and to James Hunt (1976). The M23 was the first McLaren to carry red-and-white Marlboro (cigarette) colours, this partnership going on to survive until the mid-1990s.

Fortunes declined later in the 1970s, especially as McLaren struggled to master ground-effects technology. The company was then, to all intents and purposes, taken over by Ron Dennis's Project Four team in 1980 – a merger was proclaimed, but it was really a shotgun marriage, with Philip Morris (Marlboro's parent company) behind the shotgun.

The new company was re-formed as McLaren International, but the initial arrangement, which retained Bruce McLaren's erstwhile founding partner Teddy

Mayer as managing director, lasted for no more than two years.

Under Dennis, the company first became Marlboro-McLaren, and then Honda-Marlboro-McLaren, while car designations were changed to reflect the new ownership, and Project Four. John Barnard became technical director, and his innovative MP4s went on to gain an outstanding, long-lasting, record.

All this had to be set against Ron Dennis's vision for the future, and the new standards he imposed. Seeing how F1 ought to evolve, he was determined to keep McLaren at its forefront. The first McLaren base had effectively been a large hut at Feltham, the move to Colnbrook (near Heathrow) coming in 1965. McLaren International's first 1980s base was at Woking, immaculately clean, but still in adapted buildings that became progressively cramped, so in 1988 a short move was made to a brand-new and most impressive purpose-built factory. There the research and development facilities Dennis regarded as essential could really be deployed, and departments from engineering to marketing could all operate efficiently under one roof.

Success was imperative (Marlboro's pressure saw to that), and in that light the bold move in commissioning a turbo-charged engine from Porsche, and the obtaining of financial backing from Techniques d'Avant Garde (TAG) were no less than expected. This succeeded, as planned, and the partnership with Honda that followed was no less fruitful.

A glance at the Constructors' Championship table shows just how well – for although McLaren-TAG-Porsche had won twice, McLaren-Honda would win four times in succession, this in spite of a bewildering number of engine changes from Honda, and an annual chassis re-jig from McLaren itself.

Suddenly, at the end of 1992, everything went belly-up when Honda decided to withdraw its official factory support (and its engines) from F1 racing, one consequence being that McLaren would use three different makes of engine in the next three years.

Ayrton Senna made do, brilliantly, with 'customer' Ford V8s in 1993, but then left to sign for the Rothmans-sponsored Williams team (he was tragically killed at Imola, just three races into that relationship), the team then made a dreadful error in joining forces with Peugeot for 1994 (a 'works' Ford deal was on offer),

started a comeback with Mercedes-Benz (Ilmor) in 1995 – and won no races in 1994, 1995 and 1996.

Predictably (for multinational cigarette companies harbour no sentiment), Marlboro saw this as terminal decline and withdrew their sponsorship at the end of 1996. Nothing daunted, McLaren then signed a new, long-term, deal with West, a European-based cigarette company – and went from strength to strength thereafter!

Steve Nichols and Neil Oatley produced the very competent MP4-12 for 1997, which won three victories in that year, Adrian Newey then joined the team (from Williams) in time to inspire the MP4-13 of 1998, which completely dominated the season and provided World Championship transport both for the team and its lead driver, Mika Hakkinen. In 1999, too, there was another magnificent silver-liveried McLaren for Hakkinen to notch up two in a row, though not even the phlegmatic Finn and his robot-like team could quite repeat the dose in 2000, when both were beaten by Ferrari.

M2 The first McLaren single-seater, M2A, was built as a Firestone test vehicle, designed by Robin Herd, and was built up around a Mallite composite material monocoque (Mallite was a sandwich, of aluminium/wood/aluminium) with inboard suspension. Its engine was a 4.5litre Traco-Oldsmobile V8. Apart from its testing value to the tyre company, it was also useful to prove out the monocoque construction and systems.

M2B was the F1 car that evolved from it, with the light, strong and rigid Mallite monocoque, and with orthodox suspension, with inboard front coil-spring/damper units. For power McLaren first chose a reduced-capacity Ford dohc Indianapolis V8, which was tested in two different 3.0litre forms, but eventually used as a 95.66 × 52.07mm (2,995cc) unit. This was big and heavy, and gave only 300bhp with a narrow effective rev band.

McLaren then turned to a Serenissima V8 – this Italian company having F1 ambitions, which were never fulfilled. This engine was even less powerful, but more compact, and Bruce even scored a point with it in the British GP. Later in the year he reverted to the Ford V8, and with it managed fifth in the US GP. Two cars of the projected three were completed, but a second team entry for Chris Amon never appeared in a race.

M4 The M4 was a simple, all-can-do design by Robin Herd, originally intended for use in F2, F3 and even Formula B guise. It was eventually modified as M4B, as a stop-gap F1 car.

It had a constant-diameter bathtub type of aluminium monocoque (Mallite had been abandoned, not being suitable for series production), with fuel tanks in the sides, plus a seat tank, and with conventional suspension detailing. Even when fitted with a Cosworth FVA engine, it was not outstanding as an F2 car.

Meanwhile, Herd contrived the M4B as a one-off, stand-in, F1 car to use in 1967. This was a conversion of the M4A, powered by an ex-Tasman BRM 2.1litre V8, with additional fuel tanks prominent on each flank. McLaren drove it in five races, to a best finish of fourth at Monaco. It was badly damaged when he crashed it in the Dutch GP, and was later cut up.

M5A This was another F1 one-off/stop-gap car, but at least purpose-built with a 24-valve BRM V12 engine in full 3.0litre capacity. The chassis followed general M4 lines, but the main fuel tanks were not within the side pontoons so that there were no ugly bulges: additional fuel was carried above *and* below the driver's legs, and in the extensions from the monocoque that supported the lengthy V12 engine.

This car was competitive – McLaren challenged for the lead in the Canadian and Italian GPs with it in 1967, but it was placed in the points only once, when Denny Hulme took fifth in the 1968 South African race. After that, it was sold off to Jo Bonnier, who raced it late in 1968, and was sixth in the Italian GP.

M7A–M7D This was the first noteworthy single-seater McLaren that was designed specifically for F1 racing, basically laid out by Robin Herd (before he left to join Cosworth), with the design completed by Bruce McLaren himself, and by Gordon Coppuck.

An open-topped (bathtub) monocoque of riveted and bonded aluminium was used, with suspension comprising lower wishbones and top links at the front, double wishbones with radius arms at the rear, the power, of course, coming from a Ford-Cosworth DFV engine, and a Hewland DG300 gearbox.

It was a winner, first time out, in the two British non-championship races early in 1968, and then at Spa Bruce won

McLaren M7A-Ford of 1968, Bruce McLaren driving.

McLaren M7A-Ford, with wings and extra fuel in 1968, Denny Hulme driving.

the Belgian GP, his first victory in one of his own orange single-seaters. Later that year, Hulme won in Italy, and in Canada.

The cars were modified in detail during the season, for example with two types of little external fuel tanks, and of course with first-generation 'wings', these being odd little things mounted above the DFV and fixed rigidly to the roll-over bar.

The M7As served on through 1969, with a best placing of second place, and also appeared in 1970. In 1968 McLaren, still a new team, finished second in the Constructors' Championship, but in 1969 and 1970 they were only fourth.

One car was reconfigured, to become an M7B, in 1969, with broad sponsons containing fuel tanks, which were faired into the body. Initially this was used by the works team, then sold to Colin Crabbe for Vic Elford to drive, until it was written off in a German GP accident.

M7C was another one-off, which was built up around the hull of an M10 (F5000) car, but with M7A suspension. It was Bruce McLaren's personal car in 1969 (he scored a second and two thirds in it), and was then sold to Team Surtees, and later passed on to Ecurie Bonnier.

In 1970, an M7D appeared, and was around for half a season, although it only raced once. It was a new car, fitted with an Alfa Romeo V8, and was used by Andrea de Adamich until a new Alfa-engined M14 was ready.

M9A This was McLaren's first, and only, four-wheel-drive F1 car, designed by Jo Marquart and, in common with all other four-wheel drive F1 cars at this time, completed before it was realized that four-wheel drive was not an easy way to go forward in F1.

To accommodate the system, the DFV was 'reversed' in the chassis, and the McLaren-derived transmission followed Ferguson lines. Equal-size (small) wheels were used at front and rear. This car started only one race, when it fell out of the 1969 British GP with rear suspension failure.

M14A–M14D This was a derivative of the M7C of 1969, with modifications made to the monocoque to improve the size of the fuel tanks, with suspension and other detail improvements.

In 1970 it was moderately successful (when McLaren tied with Brabham for fourth place in the Constructors' Championship), and was also used into 1971. The first of these seasons was particularly difficult for the team, for Bruce McLaren himself was killed, and Denny Hulme was handicapped while his hands (burned in an Indianapolis accident) healed.

M14D picked up on the Alfa Romeo V8 engine theme, for one car was completed early in the summer of 1970. Its best place was eighth in the Italian GP (when Galli failed to qualify his M7D, otherwise there would have been two Alfa-engined McLarens on the grid).

M19A–M19C This was a new design, by Ralph Bellamy (Gordon Coppuck was committed to Indycar work, and Marquart had moved on). It had an aluminium monocoque with fibreglass bodywork, and novelty was confined to the suspension features – which proved to be the problem area. Rising-rate suspension was devised, with inboard coil-spring/dampers, and it seems that this was not at all compatible with the car's latent aerodynamics, or to changes in tyres.

Outwardly, the M19A had pronounced 'Coke-bottle' lines – it was low, with sides swelling out below the cockpit surround – with neat aerofoils, and later with an engine airbox that sat rather oddly above an otherwise exposed DFV engine. The best 1971 race result was Donohue's third in the Canadian GP, in his first race with the car that Penske had acquired as he looked to enter F1.

M19As were also run early in 1972, with conventional rear suspension. That year the M19C, a slightly refined version, also appeared, and was to be used into 1973, until it was made obsolete by newly imposed deformable-structure regultions.

In 1972 the traditional McLaren orange colour scheme gave way to Yardley (cosmetics) colours. The year started well, as Hulme was second in the opening race in Argentina, and then won the South African GP in an M19A. Later there was a second and third in Austria. McLaren was third in the 1973 Championship.

M23 This became one of the outstanding Grand Prix cars of the 1970s. It was Gordon Coppuck's first full F1 design, with lines deriving from his previously successful M16 Indianapolis cars, and some elements, notably the suspension, that had been carried over from the final M19C layout.

It had a narrow monocoque conforming to the new deformable structure requirements, and the integral side pods which housed radiators also contributed to safety in this respect, as well as providing lateral rigidity. The DFV drove through a Hewland FG400 transmission.

Here was a functional, well-mannered car as far as the drivers were concerned, with no problem areas when it came to setting it up for circuits or different conditions. It was to serve McLaren for more than four seasons, and won sixteen Championship races.

In 1973 the Yardley-liveried cars won three Grands Prix (Hulme winning in Sweden, Revson in Britain and Canada). Marlboro (cigarette) colours arrived the following year – though a Yardley-sponsored car carried on, run separately for Mike Hailwood to drive.

Hulme won in Argentina in 1974, at the start of his last McLaren F1 season, while Emerson Fittipaldi won three Grands Prix and the Drivers' Championship: he won twice in 1975, and was championship runner-up.

In 1976, in a quite extraordinary season, James Hunt joined the team, and narrowly took the drivers' title from Niki Lauda of Ferrari, with victories in Spain, France, Germany, Holland, Canada and the USA.

In the seasons when McLaren was running M23s (1973–77), they finished third, first, third, second and third in the Constructors' Championship (some of the points being contributed by M19Cs and M26s). The cars then served on in second-string racing.

M26 This Coppuck design was a replacement for the long-running and ageing M23, following the proven lines of that car, but lower, lighter, cleaner through the air, with honeycomb monocoque construction and M23 suspension. The first car was completed during the summer of 1976, but it was not allowed to supplant the M23 until the 1977 season was already well under way. During that long gestation period, the radiator positioning problems posed by the ultra-low monocoque were solved by moving the oil radiator into the nose.

Like the M23, this was another forgiving car, but it had only a relatively short competitive life, as Lotus moved all the goalposts by introducing its first ground-effects car (the Z8) in 1977.

James Hunt won three 1977 Grands Prix with M26s (at Silverstone, Watkins Glen and Fuji). In 1978 the team's best placing with an M26 was Hunt's third place in the French GP, and McLaren slipped down from third (in 1977) to eighth in the Constructors' Championship of 1978.

M28 McLaren's first ground-effects car followed the original Lotus example, and was deliberately made as large as current regulations permitted, in a search for maximum control over under-car airflow. To the same end, its suspension was tucked away, inboard, all around.

A honeycomb monocoque formed the basis of the structure, with very broad side pods that contained radiators and a fuel cell (there was also a third cell behind the cockpit). Yet the M28 was insufficiently rigid, lived up to its bulky appearance with a low top speed, and gained a reputation for poor mechanical grip. The car was revised here and there in detail, and the cars were rebuilt, but the only real solution was to replace them – and this could not be done until mid-1979. The best placing was fourth by John Watson at Monaco, with a car designated M28C.

McLaren M23-Ford of 1973, Denny Hulme driving.

McLaren M26-Ford of 1976, Brett Lunger driving.

Watkins Glen later in the year, after starting just three races.

MP4/1–MP4/1C The new designation denoted 'Marlboro-Project Four', and emphasized the origins of the new owners/backers in the new design. In many ways this was still an interim car, as some background work was being done by John Barnard, before McLaren International came into being. Outwardly, this new car was as shapely as its immediate Colnbrook predecessors had been bulky. Carbon fibre was used extensively for many major components, such as the slim monocoque (this 'space age' material had previously only been used for incidental parts in racing cars, but McLaren turned to Hercules Inc, of Salt Lake City, USA, to make the monocoque sections). Carbon fibre was very costly, but in this application it made for a light and very rigid monocoque that also had outstanding impact-resistance qualities. The rest of the design was relatively conventional. From its introduction, early in 1981, Cosworth DFV engines were used, though work had already started on a turbocharged engine, initiated by Ron Dennis, financed by TAG, and being engineered by Porsche.

A first victory for the MP series was scored by John Watson in the British GP, though the next did not come until 1982, when Niki Lauda won at Long Beach (USA). That was in a 'B' car that had been revised in detail in a search for better aerodynamic performance and, with Michelin's help, better mechanical grip. Early MPs were also run on narrower rear tyres than the turbocharged cars, which gave a tiny, but useful, gain in drag.

The MP4/1C was a 'flat-bottom' car, powered by DFV or finally DFY engines,

M29 This replacement for the M28 came commendably quickly (it was sorely needed) once the M28's shortcomings had been accepted. It had a sheet-metal monocoque in place of the honeycomb construction of the M28, a single centrally positioned fuel cell, shorter wheelbase and track dimensions, and later in the 1979 season also had revised rear suspension, under-car aerodynamics and outboard rear brakes. Once again, the best 1979 placing was fourth, by John Watson at Silverstone in its very first race.

The car was revised for 1980, becoming the M29C, with all the late-1979 modifications, and more weight saving.

Development continued up to the point when the M30 appeared in mid-season. In 1979, Watson was fourth with M29s in Long Beach (USA) and Montreal. Two of the cars were used early in 1981.

M30 This was the last of Gordon Coppuck's F1 designs for McLaren, and indeed was the last of the pre-Dennis company's cars. Compared with the M29, which it replaced in 1980, it was stiffer, with brakes outboard all round, and improved aerodynamic performance. It turned out to be a one-off, and a short-term one-off at that. It was first raced in the 1980 Dutch GP, then destroyed in a practice accident at

McLaren M29-Ford of 1979, John Watson driving.

McLaren MP4/1-Ford of 1981, John Watson driving.

which served in 1983 until McLaren's first turbocharged car was ready. McLaren fortunes certainly began to look up under this new regime; the team was sixth in the 1981 Constructors' Championship, and a close second to Ferrari in 1982.

MP4/1D–MP4/1E An adapted, originally Cosworth-engined MP4 was used as a development vehicle ('1D') for the TAG-Porsche turbocharged engine, running tests for the first time at Silverstone in July 1983. MP4/1E was the first true race car with this engine, completed very rapidly for Lauda to drive in the Dutch GP of 1983. It was an adaptation of the existing design, pending the appearance of a true second-generation Barnard F1 McLaren design, but it did not appear like a lash-up, for the V6 and its ancillaries (primarily the twin turbochargers and intercoolers) seemed as if they had been made for the chassis. The brand-new engine was an 80-degree V6 (82×47.3mm, 1,499cc), with two KKK turbochargers, and produced some 750bhp in race trim. These turbo cars made seven race starts in late-1983, and in that bedding-in and development phase, there were no finishes.

MP4/2 In its A, B and C sub-derivatives, the MP4/2 served McLaren through three seasons, taking two Constructors' Championships and three Drivers' Championships. Although this was a new design, in some respects it was merely a major redesign of the MP4/1E, for example in the monocoque, allowing for a shorter engine, and a larger (220-litre) fuel tank. Broad side pods were

retained, with turbochargers mounted further forward than before, and these pods curved in at their rear to completely enclose the engine and gearbox, taking careful regard for aerodynamic realities.

The 1984 car's suspension had lower wishbones with top rocker arms, and of course inboard coil springs/dampers; revisions were to bring a pushrod system front and rear in 1985. There were sixteen championship races in 1984, of which McLaren won twelve (Prost won seven, Lauda five); in 1985 Prost won five Grands Prix, while Lauda won once only, at Zandvoort.

There were more changes for the 'C' version, for example in the subtle aerodynamic reshaping as the fuel-tank allowance was cut to 195litres – and in the rear suspension. There were some fuel consumption problems, which meant that McLaren's season fell just short of being brilliant. Prost won four Grands Prix (and the drivers' title), but his new team mate Keke Rosberg did not score a single victory.

MP4/3 For 1987, this was a new car, and was the last McLaren to use the TAG-Porsche V6 engine. It was designed by Steve Nichols, often by following proven lines which had been laid down by John Barnard (before he left to set up Ferrari's GTO division in the UK). Suspension and transmission were carried over, but there was a new body style that certainly appeared to be more slippery. New for McLaren was the use of side outlets for air that had passed through the radiators, and there were new-type aerofoils. Porsche

McLaren MP4/2C-TAG V8 of 1986, Alain Prost driving.

put much effort into engine development, but the V6 was near the end of its cycle, and because of this a spasm of unreliability set in.

During the season, one chassis was set aside for test-vehicle use with the new Honda engine (that would be used in the MP4/4). Prost won three Grands Prix in 1987, but although McLaren was second in the Constructors' series, it was still a long way behind the Williams team.

MP4/4   This was another totally new car for 1988, with design controlled by technical director Gordon Murray (ex-Brabham), and directly handled by project leader Steve Nichols. Compared with 1987, the major change was the adoption of a Honda engine, the turbocharged RA168-E, which had been redesigned for

Alain Prost – the two accounting for fifteen of the season's Grands Prix. McLaren won the Constructors' Championship with 199 points – the next six teams below them scoring 192 points between them.

Meanwhile, with 1989 in mind, an MP4/4 chassis was used extensively, for testing with Honda's new normally aspirated 3.5-litre V10.

MP4/5 and MP4/5B   Design and development of this new normally aspirated car went ahead very early for 1989, virtually in parallel with that of MP4/4, the design group for this car being led by Neil Oatley.

The monocoque was new, there was double wishbone suspension at front and rear (pullrod at the front, pushrod at the rear), and power was from a Honda RA109-E 72-degree V10 (92 × 52.2mm,

revolution, for the principal change was that Alain Prost had left the team (having come to detest Senna), while Gerhard Berger had joined in his place. Since Berger was considerably larger than Senna (or Prost), it was mid-season before he could become comfortable or completely effective in the MP4/5B.

Before the season started, Senna did no testing (he was in dispute with FISA about his grumpy attitude), but when he deigned to return he found that the Honda V10 had more power (which everyone had expected). Mechanical grip was sometimes a problem, but Honda-power made up for that. The results were conclusive – six victories for Senna (though none, yet, for Berger), and the Constructors' crown for McLaren, for the third consecutive year.

McLaren MP4/5-Honda of 1988, Ayrton Senna driving.

one final season's racing, primarily with a reduced boost (by regulation), and so that it sat lower in the chassis.

There were no innovations in the chassis, except that a smaller (150litre) fuel cell had to be fitted to meet new regulations, this shorter component compensating for the fact that drivers' foot pedals now had to be positioned behind the line of the front wheels to increase safety provisions. Unequal-length wishbone suspension was used, pullrod at the front, pushrod at the rear, with the shock absorbers mounted vertically inside the slender nose bodywork. A new six-speed McLaren gearbox was also specified.

The team had an immensely strong driver line up, for Ayrton Senna had joined

3,490cc), whose unstated power output was thought to be close to 700bhp. It drove through a McLaren six-speed gearbox – longitudinal at first, but with a new transverse design from mid-season.

The McLaren team had problems in 1989, not only with mechanical problems, but due to serious personality clashes between the two superstar drivers. Nevertheless, at the end of the season Prost and Senna took first and second in the Drivers' Championship, with ten victories between them. As in 1988, too, McLaren totally dominated the Constructors' Championship.

For 1990 the design progressed to MP4/5B (Neil Oatley was credited with the rework), an evolution rather than a

MP4/6   So, what if this new V12 Honda-engined chassis was not perfect, it delivered the goods for McLaren. By giving them the Constructors' Championship for the fourth successive season, and by providing Ayrton Senna with his third drivers' crown in four years, it did its job.

With Senna relaxing in Brazil during the British winter, it was down to Berger to do much of the testing, in particular making sure that the new-generation V12 was better than the V10 that it had replaced.

McLaren, it seemed, had taken a long look at Ferrari's 641 of 1990, hired Henri Durand from Ferrari as its new aerodynamicist, picked up on its good points, emphasized all their own existing strengths, plugged in the formidable new V12 power unit – and gave Senna a winning car the moment he returned to work.

After Senna had won the first four races, the season was already effectively 'game over': he added three more wins, three second places and two thirds later in the year. Berger, now in a much more comfortable cockpit than in 1990, was less flamboyant, but still managed a victory in Japan and five podiums. All this, incidentally, in spite of Senna's constant complaints about early-season V12 power – and it was typical of Honda's commitment that they then provided a virtually new type of engine from Hungary!

In case the new MP4/7 didn't work properly straight out of the box, McLaren actually took up-dated MP4/6Bs to early-season events in 1992, racing them in Kyalami and Mexico City – though nothing was likely to beat the new Williams FW14Bs of that period.

MP4/7 Amazingly for McLaren, at first the new-for-1992 MP4/7 didn't work as well as the previous MP4/6, but the team soon made it into a competitive machine – not as successful as the latest Williams-Renault, but in that year, what was?

This time there was a break from evolution, for the MP4/7 was the first truly *new* McLaren for some time. Although the general principles were all the same, every component had been re-thought. Although it was always seen as heavy and over-thirsty, the Honda V12 was approaching its peak (at this point we did not realize that it was starting its last season), there was a new fully-automatic gearbox (with manual override, the whole thing controlled by buttons on the steering wheel), active suspension, electronically sensed traction control and a fly-by-wire throttle.

Yet because it could not compete, head-to-head, with the latest Williams-Renault, driver Ayrton Senna was positively rude about it. Not for the first time, his prima-donna attitudes demeaned a colossal talent: that, and his holier-than-thou attitudes to driving tangles were not worthy of such an amazing driver. Gerhard Berger was more pragmatic, and equally effective.

Even so, in fourteen races during 1992, MP4/7s won five races, and notched up six other podium positions. Aided by the MP4/6B, McLaren took second in the Constructors' Championship.

MP4/8 Amazingly, Ron Dennis's McLaren organization almost tripped up in 1993, and if it had not been for Ayrton's driving genius, they would have had an awful season. With Honda dropping out at the end of 1992, Dennis's attempts to get Renault engine supplies eventually failed, and in the end he was obliged to lease Ford-Cosworth HB 'customer' V8s instead. As Gerhard Berger had defected – to Ferrari – it was set to be a difficult year.

Even so, although Benetton's identically engined B193 handled better (and had Michael Schumacher!) the new MP4/8 was nimble enough, and the HB versatile enough (all in all, this was one of the best, unheralded, engines in F1 history), for Senna to win five races and finish second in the Drivers' Championship. From the start of testing, and with all the well-established electronic gizmos of previous years, it flew, and (unconfirmed) statistics of 700bhp and 13,500rpm were enough to make it competitive: Senna did the rest.

New signing Michael Andretti (Mario's son) did not. Hired because of his searing CART reputation, he never came to terms with F1, didn't know the circuits, didn't test much, and jetted back to the USA after every race. Well before the end of the season his time was up, with 'test driver' Mika Hakkinen taking over, and impressively too. Later in the season, McLaren tested MP4/8s fitted with the latest Lamborghini V12 engine, and although Senna wanted to see this

used in a race, it never happened. Loads of power, according to Senna, were therefore thrown away, this being one of several reasons why he then abandoned the team for 1994.

MP4/9 This was a year in which McLaren was away with the fairies. Senna had jumped ship (tragically to be killed in the Williams he had chosen instead), Ron Dennis had asked for too much before failing to get competitive engines from Ford – and the Peugeot V10 he chose instead was an embarrassment. This partly explains, but not totally so, why his Marlboro-sponsored cars slipped down to fourth in the Constructors' Championship, and his protégé driver, Hakkinen, could only score twenty-six Championship points. Hakkinen was a real find, though we would not properly realize this until 1998.

All signs of previous high-tech had been banished by new regulations, though here was a two-pedal car, with the 'clutch pedal' a hand-operated paddle. The engine was not only down for power, but fragile – the lists showing many DNFs in a cloud of steam, oil, flames or, as at Silverstone with Brundle, all three. It wasn't surprising, therefore, that the much-vaunted Anglo-French tie-up was to be brief.

Glory? With no victories, none really, though Mika and Martin shared two second places and six thirds between them: with Ford Zetec-R power, there might have been victories too.

McLaren MP4/7-Honda of 1992, Ayrton Senna driving.

McLaren MP4/9-Peugeot of 1994, Mika Hakkinen driving.

MP4/10 By McLaren's own exalted standards, this was a rather shambolic campaign. Not only was this the first occasion when a 3litre 'Mercedes-Benz', (Ilmor) V10 engine was used (McLaren's fourth make of engine in four years), the car was ugly (some said, but maybe 'gawky' was a better description, but no-one ever admired it) – and there was the incredibly unwise choice of original drivers. With a high nose, a nasty little wing mounted above the engine cover, and poor handling (a lack of front-end grip) in original form, the MP4/10 was also hampered by an overweight Nigel Mansell to drive it. Mansell was apparently so uncomfortable in the original tub that new tubs had to be evolved, with a more spacious cockpit.

Mansell missed the first two races, complained through the third, and parked a healthy MP4/10 in the fourth – and then retired! Mark Blundell subbed in the first races, then took over on a permanent basis, doing a fine, if unspectacular job. Unlucky, and yet incredibly lucky, Hakkinen suffered a high-speed crash in Australia, broke his skull and so nearly died – but would bounce back remarkably in the following year.

Fourth in the Constructors' Championship, Hakkinen scoring only seventeen points, and just two second places. It is better to draw a veil over the details, perhaps.

MP4/11 Forget all about the traumas of 1995, and the ridiculous Mansell/'undriveable car' saga. 1996, at least, showed a way up, though there were still no victories, which did nothing to satisfy long-term sponsors, Marlboro. The multinational cigarette company therefore dumped them, unceremoniously, at the end of the season – nearly a quarter of a century after McLaren had started delivering the goods.

Mika Hakkinen, still young in F1 experience, made an astonishing recovery from his Adelaide-sustained head injuries, and took fifth in the Drivers' Championship, though McLaren themselves languished in fourth in the Constructors' series. The car (and the drivers' confidence) seemed to improve later in the season, but there were no victories, and only six podium finishes. Amazingly, Alain Prost had even been persuaded to do some test driving, but nothing would then encourage him actually to drive in races.

Neil Oatley's MP4/11, which had a totally new carbon-fibre tub and chassis,

McLaren MP4/10-Mercedes Benz, Mark Blundell driving.

McLaren MP4/11-Mercedes-Benz of 1996, Nick Heidfeld driving.

had no influence on MP4-12, his lengthy 'gardening leave' necessitated by a contract dispute with his old employers. In the meantime Steve Nichols and Neil Oatley, as expected, produced a thoroughly competent car.

Not quite as fast as the latest Williams-Renault (but what was, in 1997?), it still gave its sponsors and drivers a great deal of hope for the future. Fourth in the Constructors' Championship (but only just behind Benetton-Renault), it provided David Coulthard with two victories and Mika Hakkinen one victory to celebrate – they also spanned the first *and* the last races of the year, which was symmetrical, at least – and there were four other podium placings too. On the way back, after the mid-1990s slump? No question of that.

MP4-13 Superb and supreme – that is the only way to describe McLaren's dominant 1998 F1 car. The first McLaren to be totally designed under Adrian Newey's guidance (his 'gardening leave' from Williams was finally over), the first narrow-track MP4 type, and the first of the top team cars to run with Japanese Bridgestone tyres, it got the job done – magnificently.

McLaren won the Constructors' Championship at a canter, Mika Hakkinen took the drivers' crown by a distant fourteen points, while David Coulthard finished third in that series. McLaren won nine of the sixteen races (Hakkinen eight times, Coulthard once), and there were eleven other podium positions. Dominance, or what?

followed established McLaren principles, yet looked much neater, trimmer and more purposeful than the MP4/10 had ever done. The Ilmor/'Mercedes-Benz' V10 seemed to be a big improvement, and the handling was undoubtedly better. It was a start, but by Ron Dennis's and McLaren's standards, it was not enough.

MP4-12 The shock of seeing a new McLaren F1 car in any livery other than Marlboro red-and-white quite hid the detailed news that McLaren's own way of

describing its F1 cars had changed – from what might have been MP4-12 to MP4-12. Launching the new car, complete with silver West (cigarette) and Mercedes-Benz livery was a real show-business affair, that included an ear-splitting singing display from the Spice Girls, this quite obscuring the fact that the V10 engine was now much lighter and a lot more powerful than before. From Barcelona, in F-spec., it was accepted as the season's most powerful F1 engine.

Although Adrian Newey was said to be on his way from Williams to McLaren, he

McLaren MP4-12-Mercedes-Benz of 1997, Mika Hakkinen driving.

Aerodynamically the MP4-13 went its own way. All other teams had to comply with narrow-track cars and grooved tyres – but air-flow expert Adrian Newey seemed to know even more. McLaren was first to sign up with Bridgestone, and gained a winter's valuable testing time, Newey opted for a low nose/narrow tub bottom shape, which worked well. With all the power that the Mercedes-Benz (Ilmor, really) engine could offer, the advantage was built in, but more was found with a new front suspension, incorporating horizontal torsion bars, and space-saving packaging. This was a car that handled superbly, rode the bumps and the kerbs better than any other, and never looked like being beaten.

MP4-14 How to improve on a winning car? Not easy, though with MP4-14, Adrian Newey set out to do just that. The result, with ever so slightly mixed fortunes, was that Mika Hakkinen won his

power from the German-backed Ilmor V10 engine, all backed by one of the best budgets in the business, this looked crushingly advanced.

Amazingly, though, there was less reliability than in the past (critics suggested that this was because of the ultra-light construction, where carbon seemed to be everywhere one looked), though there was little criticism of the drivers. All of which made Hakkinen's spin in Italy (where he missed a gear entering the first chicane, crashed in front of TV cameras, flounced away, and hid in the bushes in distress) more difficult to understand.

If it wasn't accidents, it was brushes with Schumacher's Ferrari and, if neither, there were tyre, electrical, refuelling, and other gremlins all present. Like other teams, McLaren grappled with grooved tyre problems too, running a longer wheelbase at times to refine the handling.

stunning new MP4-15 was worth waiting for, and competitive from Day One. Visually very similar to the 1999 car, it was nevertheless full of Newey touches (this was the third McLaren he had inspired), and was bound to be as aerodynamically effective as before. Underneath the skin there was yet another new generation of Mercedes-Benz/Ilmor V10 (some people dared to suggest it was less powerful than before, but McLaren brushed that off), there were funnel-type hot-air radiator outlets in the top of the side pods, and the aerodynamics of the rear end had been tidied up. Suspension components had been reshuffled to save space, but this was not a revolutionary machine in any respect.

It was expected to be one of the two outstanding cars of 2000 (the other being Ferrari's F1-2000), and with Mika Hakkinen at the wheel it was always likely to be on pole position, and to win races. So, too, were both the drivers, David Coulthard being amazingly up-beat after

McLaren MP4-14-Mercedes-Benz of 1999, Mika Hakkinen driving.

second consecutive drivers' crown, though McLaren slipped (by their lofty standards) to a mere second in the Constructors' Championship.

Lighter and even more tightly packaged than its predecessor, this latest Newey masterpiece depressed its rivals before it even turned a wheel, for all the established virtues were there, along with innovative torsion bar rear suspension, and the ability to move the ballast around to balance the car. Along with the same driving team as before, and even more

Statistics? Hakkinen won five races, finishing second twice and third three times, while the unlucky Coulthard won only twice, and took four second places. Narrowly shaded by Ferrari in the constructors', McLaren saw their drivers take first and fourth in the drivers' series.

For team boss Ron Dennis, though, all this smelt of failure, so there would be yet more innovation for 2000.

MP4-15 As was traditional, McLaren was late in launching its latest car, but the

cheating death in an executive jet crash in which both the pilots were killed.

The fight with the Ferrari/Michael Schumacher combination went to the very end of the season, and Hakkinen would dearly have loved to win a straight hat-trick of driver's titles. But it was not to be. Battle was only resolved in the sixteenth race (Japan) when Hakkinen's close second place was just shaded by Schumacher's victory, while Ferrari finally clinched the constructors' title in the last race, in Malaysia.

McLaren

See pp.157–167.

Mercedes

Before the name Mercedes was adopted in 1901, the great German company had built a racing version of the Daimler Phoenix, and the first racing Mercedes as such made its debut in the 1901 Pau GP. Competition cars were built through the Edwardian period, most notably perhaps the 90 in its early years. A reputation for invincibility certainly does not date from the first Grand Prix seasons, for Mercedes were the last classified finishers in the two major races in 1906 and only one of three cars finished the 1907 Grand Prix, in tenth place.

A first Grand Prix victory came in 1908, when a Mercedes headed a Benz pair in France. The Grand Prix cars built that year were evolutionary machines, for Mercedes was seldom innovative; they were to be successful for several years, notably in the USA, in the Vanderbilt Cup rather than the Grand Prize, where third place in 1911 was the best showing.

The revived Grand Prix in 1912 was ignored, as was the 1913 race, although a quartet of cars was prepared for an independent entrant that year for the confusingly titled Grand Prix de France at Le Mans. Mercedes' triumph in the 1914 Grand Prix closed an era in Europe, although there were successes in America.

After the First World War there were few opportunities for German teams on the international stage, but Mercedes built new competition cars surprisingly soon. The period was notable for the introduction of the supercharger, used on some of Mercedes' 1922 Targa Florio cars. As far as Grand Prix racing was concerned, Fiat entered supercharged cars in 1923 races, and Mercedes followed with a tricky Porsche-designed car that contested only two major races.

In 1925 German teams were free to compete anywhere, but Mercedes still concentrated on home events and Italian races and its rising star, Rudolf Caracciola, scored his first Grand Prix victory, driving one of the straight eights in his home race. From 1927 the car company was to be Mercedes-Benz, following the amalgamation of the two companies. Impressions that Mercedes was a dominant force in Grand Prix racing in its first two decades are perhaps misleading,

but take nothing away from its very real achievements before the First World War.

120   The cars that ran without distinction in the first Grand Prix were actually 1905 types, that had been laid down for the Gordon Bennett races. This was a wholly orthodox design, with a pressed-steel frame, rigid suspension and artillery wheels, and a four-cylinder engine with a slightly enlarged stroke in 1906 giving a 14,432cc capacity (and 120bhp), and chain final drive.

Jenatzy and Burton shared the best-placed car in the Grand Prix, finishing tenth, more than four *hours* after the winning Renault; Mariaux was eleventh and last, and Florio retired when a wheel collapsed. Jenatzy ran with the early leaders in the Vanderbilt Cup, but fell away to be classified as the last runner, with the only surviving Mercedes.

The 1907 cars were similar, still deriving from the 1903 Rennwagen, but with new engines that had the same dimensions as the 1906 unit. They were also lower and shorter. They were never in the hunt in the Grand Prix – a technical post-mortem blamed the fuel mixture for their poor performance – and only one of the trio finished, driven into tenth place by Hémery. De Caters did win a poorly supported category in the Circuit of the Ardennes in one of these cars, with Jenatzy third in another.

135/150   A new design was called for by the 1908 Grand Prix rules, and Paul Daimler's team turned away from their traditional oversquare engines to meet the 155mm bore limit. The four-cylinder engine was built in 12,781cc and 13,533cc forms (rated at 135bhp and 150bhp in the Grand Prix cars, hence the dual designation). The larger type had a longer stroke, and was offered in 'customer' cars as an alternative to a production unit. Mercedes stuck with chain drive. The cars were more compact, although the reduced overall height gave an impression of more length. Detachable-rim wheels were fitted, and the Grand Prix team ran its tyres at very high pressures, to preserve them at a time when they were still notoriously fragile components (a ploy that contributed to Grand Prix success).

Mercedes learned lessons from the 1906 and 1907 Grands Prix and prepared thoroughly for the 1908 race, to the extent that 1907 cars with the new engine were run in training. The approach paid dividends, and Mercedes cars were first and fifth in the Grand Prix, while Otto Salzer

retired with a damaged wheel. The winning car was driven by Christian Lautenschlager, a company employee from the end of the nineteenth century who would still be racing for the company in the 1920s; Willy Poge recovered after an early off-course excursion, to finish fifth.

Three customer cars were run in the Vanderbilt Cup, but Mercedes did not really feature in that race until de Palma won it in 1912. By that time various modified cars had become prominent in the USA, one leading the opening laps of the first Indianapolis 500 while de Palma placed one third in the 1911 Grand Prize.

A modified 1908 Grand Prix car was in the quartet run by Theodore Pilette in the 1913 Grand Prix de France at Le Mans – these were not manufacturers' entries, and so were not accepted for the 'proper' Grand Prix that year. Two of the cars had 7,250cc straight-six engines designed for aircraft, a 1908-type chassis had a production-based 9,530cc four-cylinder engine, another had a 9,230cc engine developed from a 1908 Grand Prix unit. Independent team or not, Mercedes was using this race as part of a development programme. All the cars had chain drive – virtually the last in main-line racing. The best placing in the Sarthe race was Pilette's third, behind two Delages. De Palma took one of the six-cylinder cars to Indianapolis, but found shortcomings that caused it to be withdrawn before the race.

18/100   The Mercedes built for the first capacity-limit Grand Prix in 1914 have become legendary. Paul Daimler oversaw the design, and used a four-cylinder sohc 16-valve engine, with input from the company's relatively new aero engine department. It developed 105bhp, and drove through a four-speed gearbox (until a late stage the car was to have chain drive, but a more modern faction prevailed). There was a transmission brake and rear wheel drums – still no front wheel brakes. The cars presented at the Grand Prix varied in details.

The team practised assiduously for the 1914 Grand Prix at Lyons. Although Boillot led at half distance in a Peugeot he was hanging on, and the Mercedes quintet really dominated this race. Lautenschlager won his second Grand Prix, team mates Wagner and Salzer were second and third. Pilette retired his Mercedes with transmission failure (ironically, as he was a great advocate of chain drive), while Sailer fell out with engine failure. But the 1-2-3 gained Mercedes a firm place in racing history.

(Above) Mercedes Grand Prix car of 1908, Salzer driving.

Mercedes straight eight of 1926, Rudi Caracciola driving.

The cars were still raced. De Palma won several US races with one, including the 1915 Indianapolis 500. Another car was in England when the First World War started, and its engine was analysed by Rolls Royce (this car was later raced at Brooklands). Three were modified, notably with four-wheel brakes, and run in the 1922 Targa Florio. Masetti drove the car that had finished third in the 1914 Grand Prix to victory in Sicily, effectively running as a works car, and beating the actual works pair. Proved in widely varying races, the cars continued to be used in minor German events into the mid-1920s.

1924 Straight Eight Mercedes' return to Grand Prix racing came in Italy in 1924, with the company's first straight-eight cars, and its first supercharged Grand Prix cars. Daimler had used superchargers on late First World War aero engines, and Mercedes had started experiments with

automotive types in 1919, with a production engine coming for 1922. Ferdinand Porsche was in overall charge of the design of the Grand Prix car and its engine.

The M218 engine was a dohc 1,996cc unit, with a Roots-type supercharger at the back and intruding into the cockpit, as the

engine was set well back in the chassis. It compressed mixture from the carburettor. The official rating was 170bhp, and surprisingly a three-speed gearbox was felt to be adequate.

The car was low-slung and hardly handsome, especially with the bluff nose first fitted. In details of appearance there were to be several changes. In its layout, Porsche concentrated weight within the wheelbase, to the extent that there was a fuel tank under the seats. The intention was to reduce the possibility that an end would break away; in this car the result was that one end could break away so suddenly that recovery was difficult.

The cars were completed late, but the Fiat entry for the Italian GP was also in trouble, so the Monza organizers simply deferred the race, but not for long enough for Mercedes to even start to sort out the car. Alfred Neubauer – later to be Mercedes-Benz team manager – frightened himself so much in practice that he stood down in favour of Otto Merz. In the race Count Louis Zborowski was thrown from his Mercedes as it crashed, and Like his father he died racing a Mercedes. Masetti retired, Werner was flagged off as Alfa Romeos finished 1-2-3-4.

Werner was allowed to develop one car, which he did by moving the fuel to the tail and introducing a four-speed gearbox. He was successful with this car in minor German events.

Two of the cars were converted into sports cars for the first German GP, at Avus in 1926. Rosenberger crashed his into a timekeepers' box, killing its three occupants. Caracciola stalled his engine at the start (the straight eight was always prone to this), but earned his 'rain master' sobriquet with a stirring drive to victory, the only one for this Porsche-designed Mercedes in a race of any significance.

Mercedes-Benz

See pp.171–175.

Merzario

Arturo Merzario drove in fifty-seven Grands Prix, for half a dozen teams from Ferrari to Shadow, to score eleven championship points in the early 1970s. His career in sports-car racing lasted much longer, and generally he was rated more highly in that field. His attempts to establish a Merzario marque on shoestring budgets in the late 1970s were sadly misguided, and as far as Formula 1 was concerned lasted for two seasons. For his last years as a constructor (1980–83) he concentrated on Formula 2. 'Little Art' seemed perpetually cheerful, and faithful to his personal sponsor, despite the dismal record of his F1 cars: in 1978–79 these were entered in thirty World Championship races, failing to qualify to start in twenty of those and retiring from the other ten.

A1 Concept drawings by the respected Giorgio Piola in 1977 promised a sleek car, but the 1978 reality was an inelegantly bulky device that dwarfed its driver. Expediently, Merzario utilized some components from his March 751 in the first car. This was conventional, with an aluminium monocoque, double wishbone front suspension, upper and lower links at the rear, and outboard springs all round. A DFV engine drove through a Hewland FGA five-speed

gearbox. A second car had revised front suspension, and it was further modified for the last races of 1979, with smarter bodywork. This A1B was the only Merzario to qualify to start in Grands Prix in 1979, in the Argentine and US West races.

A2 Merzario and mechanic Simon Hadfield designed this ground-effects car, necessarily on economic lines and naturally with a DFV/Hewland combination. There were lower wishbones and top rocker arms front and rear, and springs were obviously inboard. However, it seemed that the monocoque was too broad to allow for adequate airflow.

Merzario tried to qualify it twice and, when he was injured, Gianfranco Brancatelli also made an unsuccessful attempt to get the A2 to a grid. A second car was never completed.

A4 Merzario acquired Kauhsen material when that hapless team collapsed early in 1979, and its WK was the basis of the ground-effects A4 (so Dallara's name was linked to Merzario). This car had a slender aluminium monocoque, with the fuel cell behind the cockpit and side pods that allowed for an adequate airflow. Suspension was on A2 lines. The DFV/Hewland combination was also similar, and probably transferred. Seven attempts to qualify this car for grids were unsuccessful.

Merzario let it be known that his M1 for 1980 was a dual-category car that could be adapted to take a DFV in place of the BMW F2 engine, but that never came to pass.

Merzario A1-Ford of 1977, Arturo Merzario driving.

Mercedes-Benz did not pick up Grand Prix themes where Mercedes and Benz had left off, but through the rest of the 1920s and into the 1930s looked to sports-car events. The company essayed a particularly hideous streamlined SSKL single-seater in 1933, following von Brauchitsch's independent one-off, and veteran driver Otto Merz was killed in it, practising for its debut race at Avus.

By then the Daimler-Benz board had looked at several Mercedes-Benz possibilities to take the place of the big sports cars, but none were followed through. The '750kg Formula' (1,654lb) promulgated late in 1932 was attractive, and early in 1933 Mercedes-Benz was committed to it. A State grant contributed towards costs, and so it is assumed did a favourable official road vehicle purchase policy (it had been suggested that the grant actually covered less than 10 per cent of team costs).

Mercedes Benz returned to top-flight racing in May 1934 with a car that may not have been avant-garde alongside its Auto Union contemporaries, but was much more advanced than the Italian types that the team under Neubauer challenged, and it was more handsome, too. It was not invariably successful in that first season, then the team was beaten only four times in 1935, before fortunes slumped in 1936 and entries for late races were withdrawn.

A new racing department under Rudolf Uhlenhaut was responsible for a new car for the last year of racing under this '750kg Formula'. These 1937 cars had power in abundance, and they put Mercedes-Benz back on top. And there the team stayed in 1938–39, with sophisticated 3litre V12 cars.

As the 1950s opened, a return to racing was mooted, and 1939 cars were run in two Argentine *formule libre* races in 1951. Time had caught up with them, and apparently they were not quite *à point*, for in both events they were beaten by an independent 2litre Ferrari.

A new Formula 1 gave Daimler-Benz the opportunity to commit Mercedes-Benz to Grand Prix racing again, in 1954. Its new car was the result of painstaking research and development, and by mid-1950s standards the programme was most generously funded – in 1954 the racing department was staffed by as many skilled personnel as most 1990s F1 teams.

The W196 was not invincible, and in its first season that team relied on the talents of Juan-Manuel Fangio for its race successes. The main driver pairing was much stronger in 1955, when sense overruled misplaced nationalism and the team took a firm grip on Grand Prix racing.

However, that was a dark season and the Daimler-Benz board decreed a withdrawal from Grand Prix racing as it ended. Its mighty investment had been rewarded with nine World Championship race victories, from the dozen entered. And hindsight suggests that however much the car impressed contemporary observers, it was not a great step forward (that was coming in simple machines built by humble British constructors).

That team was Mercedes-Benz's last in Grand Prix racing, but there was a return to Formula 1 in 1994, as engines were supplied to the Sauber team. In 1995 there was a new association, to McLaren, and that matured in 1998 when Ilmor Mercedes-badged engines powered the winning McLarens in nine Grands Prix, and a championship title. In the following year the commitment became even stronger, as Mercedes-Benz acquired a substantial holding in McLaren.

W25 Design director Hans Nibel had overall responsibility for the 1934 Grand Prix car, with Max Wagner (chassis), and Albert Heess and Otto Schilling (engines) reporting to him. Some of the elements of their 1934 single-seater had appeared in the production Typ 380 touring car, announced early in 1933 – it had a straight eight with the option of a supercharger,

Mercedes-Benz SSK of 1929, Rudi Caracciola driving.

Manfred von Brauchitsch crashed the first car at Monza in early tests and there were other incidents, and the planned first race entry was put back. As the W25s were presented for their debut, in the Eifelrennen in May 1934, they were fractionally overweight; white paint was stripped off, and the bright aluminium bodies (with just a touch of matching paint) then suggested the 'Silver Arrows' name.

Von Brauchitsch won that debut race, but the team's first race outside Germany was a disaster – the whole team retired from the French GP. It had to give best to Auto Union in three Grands Prix, but Fagioli won the Coppa Acerbo and the Spanish GP for Mercedes-Benz, and shared the drive in the winning M25 with Caracciola in Italy.

The revised car for 1935 – four new cars and four rebuilds, incidentally – was more powerful and had better brakes, and under the overall direction of Max Sailer work began on further revisions for 1936. In 1935 Fagioli won the Monaco GP, the Penya Rhin GP and the Avusrennen, but was overshadowed by Mercedes-Benz favourite Rudi Caracciola, who won the Tripoli, French, Belgian, Swiss and Spanish GPs, and the Eifelrennen.

The 1936 car was lighter, had a shorter wheelbase, transmission improvements and the M25C engine (initially 4,310cc, then 4,740cc, giving some 430bhp or 400bhp in race trim). However, there were shortcomings such as poor handling, and Caracciola won just two races, the Monaco and Tunis GPs. The team was withdrawn before the end of the season. Nevertheless, a 1935 car did appear in a secondary race in 1937.

W125 The central design department continued its role and laid down a new car for 1937, while the new racing department under Uhlenhaut developed it. This W125 had a stiffer chassis, with oval tubular main members, a de Dion rear axle, and the M125 engine. This was a 5,660cc dohc straight eight, and by the early summer it had superchargers that compressed mixture from the carburettors. The quoted power output was up to 592bhp, depending on the fuel; a bench test figure of 646bhp is often quoted, but that was approached only in late-1930s hill-climb cars and the 1937 race trim output was around 570bhp. Whatever, these were the most powerful engines used in Grand Prix racing until the turbo

Mercedes-Benz W25 of 1935, Caracciola driving in the French GP.

Mercedes-Benz W125 of 1937 in the Monaco GP.

wishbone independent front suspension and swing axle at the rear, which were to feature in the Grand Prix car (the 380, incidentally, was not a success, fewer than 100 being sold, 1933–34).

The M25 engine for the W25 was a 3,360cc dohc straight eight, with a Roots-type supercharger feeding the carburettors. In early tests this engine gave 325bhp, well above the first 280bhp target, which took account of Alfa Romeo and Maserati, but not Auto Union. To counter that car, there was a 354bhp development, then a 3,990cc engine

(M25B) with an output approaching 400bhp was rushed through.

In the chassis, the main longitudinal members were drilled to save weight, and linked by tubular cross members. There was wishbone and coil spring front suspension and a swing axle at the rear with quarter-elliptics. This was the first Mercedes-Benz competition car with hydraulic brakes. None of the components were new, but the combination of independent suspension all round, the brakes and the gearbox integral with the final drive was new.

engines of the 1980s. A W125 geared for the Avus track, and with streamlined bodywork, had a potential maximum speed of 340kmh (211mph). In the car's single racing year, Mercedes-Benz won seven races to Auto Union's five. Caracciola won the German, Swiss, Italian and Czech GPs, rising new driver (promoted from the ranks of mechanics) Hermann Lang won the Tripoli GP and the Avus-rennen (at 262kmh/162.6mph) and von Brauchitsch won the Monaco GP. As was then normal, team cars were also run in hill climbs – the W125s were run in this form of motor sport through to 1939, in some very special forms – and a W125 chassis was the basis of a record car.

W154 Once the 1938–40 Grand Prix formula was announced in autumn 1936, Daimler-Benz studied a variety of proposals, including a Porsche rear-engined design, a streamlined car, and an unsupercharged 4.5litre engine to take advantage of the formula option, despite work in hand on a supercharged V12 and a strong inclination to choose the 3litre supercharged engine option.

The car that eventually appeared had strong family resemblances, and the chassis and suspension of the W154 followed the W125 pattern. However, the V12 was angled to allow the transmission to run to the left of the cockpit, making for a noticeably lower overall height, and while the body was wider than the W125, this was reckoned to make for stability. The M154 60-degree V12 was a quad-cam 2,862cc unit, with Roots-type superchargers. It gave 425bhp early in 1938, and just over 470bhp was produced in a race car later that year. Incidentally, fuel injection was envisaged for a later development. The 1938 season belonged to Mercedes-Benz, with honours spread among the drivers; Caracciola won the Swiss GP and the Coppa Acerbo, Lang won the Coppa Ciano, von Brauchitsch the French GP and Richard Seaman won the German GP. There was an embarrassing defeat in the first race of the new formula, at Pau, and the last two races of 1938 fell to an Auto Union driven by Nuvolari. Mercedes built fourteen of these cars, and it was sensible to use them beyond 1939, especially as fewer races were run to the Grand Prix formula. However, there were sleeker bodies, and the cars were sometimes referred to as W163, as the two-stage supercharged M163K engine was used. This was rated at 483bhp (163bhp/litre), to give the W154 a maximum speed of 330kmh (205mph) – lap times achieved with these cars remained unequalled into the 1950s.

Early in 1939 the single-stage engines were still used, and the season opened with a 'revenge' 1-2 at Pau. Lang won that race, and the Eifelrennen, and the Belgian and Swiss GPs, while Caracciola scored his sixth German GP victory. He also set records in the spectacularly streamlined W154R early in 1939. Plans to send a team to Indianapolis in 1948 and 1951 came to nothing, but an independent

Mercedes-Benz 'streamliner' of 1937 at the Avus GP, Caracciola driving.

Mercedes-Benz W154 of 1938, original small-grille style, Hermann Lang driving.

Mercedes-Benz W154 of 1938, the definitive style, seen here at the French GP.

followed its late-1930s policies in having a design group and an experimental department to build and develop the cars. Hans Scherenberg had overall design control, with Ludwig Kraus responsible for chassis and Hans Gassmann for engines. Uhlenhaut was again responsible for development, and Neubauer was team manager (very much a figure from the past, but respected in spite of some of his antics). The W196 had a tubular space frame, independent front suspension by wishbones and torsion bars and a swing axle with torsion bars at the rear. Massive drum brakes were mounted inboard. The engine was a dohc 2,490cc straight eight, traditional in that it was made up of two blocks of four cylinders with integral heads and welded-up water jackets. However, it had fuel injection and desmodromic (positively operated) valve gear. Its early output was 257bhp; later 290bhp was claimed. There was a five-speed gearbox, in unit at the rear.

The car appeared with full-width bodywork, ideal for the fast open Reims circuit, where Fangio and Kling duly finished 1-2 in the French GP. Other teams' fears seemed justified, but then the bodywork proved to be a handicap at Silverstone, where Fangio could only manage fourth place. Thereafter, streamlined bodies were used only at Avus and Monza, as open-wheel bodies were quickly built. Fangio won the German, Swiss and Italian GPs to

W154 was run in the 500 in 1947–48. After the Second World War this car was found in Czechoslovakia, was taken to England and was then bought by Tommy Lee, who entered it in the 500. It retired in both races.

However, a works team did run three of the cars in Argentina in 1951, on a circuit modified to handicap them. driven by Lang, Kling and Fangio, these recorded two second places, two third places and a sixth in six starts in two races. This venture marked a step towards Mercedes's full return to top-flight racing.

W196 For its team's return to the Grands Prix in 1954, Daimler-Benz deployed unparallelled resources, and also

Mercedes-Benz W196 of 1954, the original streamline shape; Juan-Manuel Fangio is at the wheel.

Mercedes-Benz W196, Stirling Moss driving the short-wheelbase open wheel version of 1955.

follow his French victory, while Kling was allowed to win the Avus GP 'demonstration race'.

Thorough preparation showed in 1955, when chassis with three wheelbase lengths were available to the team, the short-chassis variant having outboard front brakes. Fangio won the Argentine, Belgian, Dutch and German GPs, and was a close second to Stirling Moss in Britain, where there was a Mercedes-Benz 1-2-3-4. Only six championship Grands Prix were run that year, and at the end of a sombre season Daimler-Benz retired the team.

In two years, the team had a 75 per cent success rate, with fifteen cars. That suggests an overkill approach, yet those mid-1950s Silver Arrows were not all-conquering – in 1952 Ferrari had a 100 per cent record in championship races, and an 87.5 per cent record in 1953. Nevertheless, with these superb cars, the German marque did lift the Grand Prix mechanical art to a new level.

Milano

The Ruggeri brothers were tempted by the generous starting money offer to the entrant of two new cars in the 1949 Italian GP, and modified a pair of 4CLT/48 Maseratis to the extent that they were accepted as new cars. They were named for Ruggeri's Scuderia-Milano, but were sometimes referred to as Maserati-Milano, with equal justification.

Outwardly there were few signs of change. The wheelbase was shortened and larger brakes were fitted, but the major changes were in the engine. This was developed by Mario Speluzzi, with high supercharger pressures, to give a claimed 290bhp. At Monza for the Italian GP, the cars proved faster than standard Maseratis, but failed to match the Ferrari 125s – that apparently led Farina to just give up when he was running third in one Milano! Taruffi did take third place in the other car, despite problems.

The cars were used in 1950, Felice Bonetto placing one fifth in the Buenos Aires GP, scoring a World Championship point with fifth place in the Swiss GP, finishing eighth in the Grand Prix des Nations, and showing well in lesser events. That 1949 Italian GP showing convinced the Ruggeris that a new car would be a realistic proposition, and two were laid down for 1950. Broadly, these followed Maserati lines, with oval-tube ladder frames and wishbone and torsion bar front

suspension. The only one of the pair to be completed and raced had a de Dion rear axle with a transverse leaf spring; the other was to have a refined version of the Maserati suspension. Speluzzi developed the engine, eventually with a new twin-plug head that was rated at 320bhp late in 1950.

That year Alfa Romeo 158s were again setting the yardstick in top-flight racing, with an engine that gave up to 350bhp. Driving the Milano with the twin-plug engine in the Italian GP, Comotti could not remotely match Alfa speeds (his best race lap time was 22sec off Fangio's fastest race lap in a 158).

After that, Jose Jover finished tenth in the Penya Rhin GP at Barcelona, and that first Milano was not raced again. The second was the basis of the hapless 1955 Arzani-Volpini. A chassis was built for a Milano that was to be powered by a rear-mounted air-cooled flat-eight built by Enrico Fraschini, but the two main components never came together in a complete Milano-Fraschini.

Miller

Harry Armenius Miller never built a Grand Prix car, but in the 1920s Millers were sometimes raced in Europe, among them the first private entry in the French GP.

The straight eights built to the 1922 AAA 122cu in regulations were also eligible for the 2litre Grands Prix, and three were fitted with two-seater bodies for Grand Prix racing. These cars had relatively light bodies and superb 1,983cc dohc straight eights producing some 120bhp, that more than matched European contemporaries, except the supercharged Fiat 805 in 1923, when Millers first ran in a Grand Prix.

That was the Italian (and European) GP at Monza, a European circuit best suited to these track- and board-bred cars. Count Zborowski entered and drove one, Argentinian Martin de Alzaga entered the other two, for himself and Jimmy Murphy, who finished third in the Grand Prix behind two Fiats. Later that year Zborowski drove his car to second place in the Spanish GP at Sitges. In 1924, Zborowski's Miller was admitted to the French GP, albeit the support of a letter from Miller giving it the quasi-works status was required. Disregarding that face-saving detail, this Miller was the first privately entered car to run in the once-august Grand Prix. It was quite unsuitable for the Lyons circuit of true roads, was never in the hunt, and was retired just before half distance as the front axle was about to part company with the car.

Two front-wheel-drive Cooper-Millers, modified 1926–27 cars, started in the 1928 Italian GP, Kreis retiring one on the first

Miller Grand Prix car of 1923, Count Zborowski at the wheel.

lap and later taking over Cooper's car to finish third. Leon Duray took a pair of four-wheel-drive 91cu in (1.5litre) Millers to France and Italy in 1929, breaking class records at Montlhéry. He then entered the Monza GP, retiring one from the first heat after leading and setting fastest lap, and retiring the second from the second heat! That race exhausted his budget, and he swapped the cars for three T43 Bugattis. That enabled Bugatti to build a dohc engine, at last, by copying the head of a Miller straight eight.

Minardi

See pp.177–180.

Monnier

This Formula 2 one-off was raced spasmodically from 1950 until 1954, and for its last two years would have been elegible for World Championship Grands Prix. From 1952 it was run with a Bristol engine in place of the original BMW unit, but it was entered in just a few second-line races (and

some very minor events). Builder Maurice Monnier finished ninth in the 1953 Avusrennen, and that seems to have been its only worthwhile placing in the period.

Monteverdi–Onyx

Despite many problems, the Onyx team was good enough to score six championship points in its first year, 1989, but soon after the start of the next season its major sponsor pulled out, and Peter Monteverdi took control of the team. He attempted to run it as Monteverdi–Onyx, but the financial resources proved quite inadequate. Cars designated ORE-2 were introduced at the third race but the ill-equipped team foundered in mid-season.

ORE-2 This car was a rerun of the Alan Jenkins-designed ORE-1 – a conventional machine with double wishbone pushrod suspension all round, a Cosworth DFR V8 and an Onyx six-speed transverse gearbox.

In the team's first race under its new name, at Imola, Lehto finished twelfth, but he retired from the next three Grands Prix and after his last start for it, at Hocken-

heim. He failed to qualify an ORE-2 three times. Swiss driver Gregor Foitek joined after two races and scored the team's best placing, seventh and last at Monaco after colliding with Bernard (and six laps down). That apart, he was fifteenth in the Mexican GP, retired three times and failed to qualify three times, the last when his suspension broke in practice in Hungary and he walked away from the team.

Montier

Charles Montier built Ford Spéciales from 1923, when his first types were based on Model T components. Sports cars followed, then a first single-seater in 1927. A 'Grand Prix' car came in 1930, and two of these 3.2litre cars started in the *formule libre* French GP at Pau (Charles Montier retired during the second half, his son was flagged off in the other car).

One of these cars reappeared in 1933, modified to take a straight eight made up of two Model A engines mounted end-to-end. Charles' son Guy drove this car in some minor events, and secondary Grands Prix at la Baule and Dieppe, without success.

Giancarlo Minardi built his team on the basis of its Formula 2 programmes – it built its own cars in 1980–85 – and became a Formula 1 constructor in 1985. It survived in the World Championship through to the end of the century, although its cars were seldom competitive – enthusiasm carried it, when resources were usually limited. At least it had a confidence cushion in its membership of an exclusive group, with entry costs that would have been completely beyond such a modest team in the late 1990s. And, of course, FOCA membership was a valuable asset.

Enthusiasm was a key. Giancarlo's father Giovanni Minardi had built a sports car and competed in saloons, and Giancarlo had set up Scuderia del Passatore in

But in fifteen seasons it scored only twenty-eight points, and too often its cars were to be found on the last rows of grids. Out of necessity, the team's policy had been to use young, thrusting drivers, although it has sometimes contracted experienced men.

A liaison with Scuderia Italia seemed to ease financial pressures in 1994, but it lasted for only two years (Scuderia Italia maintained a small interest in Minardi after that). In 1996 Gabriele Rumi bought into Minardi, fulfilling his ambition to return to the Grands Prix, despite his unhappy Fondmetal experiences. The whole operation was expanded, for example, with access fo the Fondmetal wind tunnel. Two years later Rumi gained a majority holding in Minardi Team SpA. The team persevered through barren late-

was selected for the first F1 Minardi. As it was not ready for the first races of 1985, the car was adapted for a Cosworth V8. When it came, the MM V6 was the least powerful turbo engine of the year.

The car was conventional, outmoded to an extent in the use of some aluminium body panels, and with double wishbone suspension. Four were built, for the inexperienced Pierluigi Martini. He failed to qualify only once, but retired from twelve races. As he was not running at the end of another, his real placings in 1985 were eighth and twelfth.

The car was revised as the M85B for 1986, with minor changes such as pushrod suspension all round. Weight was increased, and the MM V6 was no more powerful. Minardi ran a two-car

Minardi M86-turbo Moto-Moderni V6 of 1987, Adrian Campos driving.

1972. This was renamed Scuderia Everest as it moved into Formula 2 in 1975, when it was also loaned an F1 Ferrari to develop the careers of promising Italian drivers.

Minardi's base was at Faenza, where the family has car and truck businesses. Its F1 cars have tended to be well made, but development has inevitably been hamstrung by modest resources, and it has never had top-flight engines. Landmarks came when Pierluigi Martini briefly led a 1989 Grand Prix in a Cosworth-powered Minardi, and that year both of its cars finished in the points in the British GP. In 1991 Minardi was seventh in the Constructors' Championship and in 1993 achieved its highest points score, seven.

1990s seasons, when the principals often seemed happy just to be in Formula 1.

M85 Despite its designation, the first F1 Minardi was completed in July 1984, so it should have been well prepared for the 1985 season. Giacomo Caliri followed the 1983 F2 Minardi lines to a degree, and laid the car down as a dual-purpose design, intended for F3000 as well as Formula 1. However, the project was set back by the choice of engines. An Alfa Romeo V8 was envisaged, but then Carlo Chiti was dismissed by the disillusioned Milan company and set up Motori Moderni; Minardi's partner, Gianpiero Mancini, had an interest in Motori Moderni, and its turbo V6

team in 1986, when an M85B finished just one race (Nannini was fourteenth in Mexico).

M86/M87 The 1986 car did not appear until the eleventh Grand Prix of the year, and only one was run in the final races. The type was to serve in 1987. It was lighter than the M85B, and looked neater, but the MM V6 was still used.

De Cesaris finished just one race in an M86 in 1986, placing it eighth in the Mexican GP (the race where Nannini recorded Minardi's only other finish of the year!).

As the M87, the design was little revised. Three more cars were built, and the team's achievement rate was still low.

(Above) Minardi M188-Ford of 1988, Luis Perez Sala driving.

Minardi M189-Ford of 1989.

M189 The definitive 1989 Minardi by Costa and Couperthwaite was a slender car, and one of the most effective in the team's history. Few elements save the suspension were carried over, Pirelli tyres were used, side fuel tanks were abandoned in favour of a single cell, and DFRs were used again. The M189 was introduced at the Mexican GP, and at the mid-season British GP Martini and Sala were fifth and sixth; Martini scored in two other races. The retirement rate was high, but Minardi was tenth in the Constructors' Championship.

M189s were used in the first two 1990 races, when Martini placed one seventh and ninth, while Barilla retired twice.

M190 Once again the little team had the luxury of a new car, largely the work of Costa on lines generally similar to the 1989 Minardi. In common with most of the 1990 field, double wishbone pushrod suspension was used, and the Pirellis that were used by only two other minor constructors. DFRs drove through six-speed gearboxes.

No points were scored by Minardi drivers in 1990, Martini's eighth place in Japan being the best result achieved with an M190 (he did finish five races; Barilla managed four modest placings in fourteen attempts, but also failed to qualify six times; Ferrari test driver Gianni

Nannini took the flag once, but was classified eleventh in two races; team mate Campos was fourteenth in the Spanish GP.

M188 Changes in the regulations called for a new design for 1988, and this car proved to be Caliri's last Minardi. His rather quirky front suspension, with interlinked dampers, was a failure, and when Aldo Costa took on the design role he soon introduced a conventional double wishbone pushrod layout. The Cosworth DFZ 3.5litre V8 drove through a Minardi–Hewland six-speed gearbox.

Overall, the car appeared more compact than its predecessors, and it was more effective. Martini rejoined the team after four 1988 Grands Prix, finished five races, and scored Minardi's first point, in Detroit. Luis Sala drove for the whole season, and finished seven races (with a best placing eighth in Portugal), but Campos made little impression in his four drives.

A Subaru flat-twelve engine designed by Chiti was tested in an M188, with a view to its use in 1989. But for the early races that year the uprated M188s, notably with substantially revised rear suspension by Nigel Couperthwaite, were run with Cosworth DFRs.

Martini and Sala failed to finish a race in one of these M188Bs.

Morbidelli was brought in for the last two Grands Prix, and posted two retirements).

M191 Morbidelli's place in the team at the end of 1990 reflected Minardi's coup in obtaining Ferrari V12s for the new 1991 car. In many aspects of its specification there were few departures in chassis and running gear, and Costa still had to work with limited resources. Beyond that, the Ferrari engines were not front-line units, 1989 036 engines for much of the year and then 1990 037 engines, and neither type had been developed after service with the Ferrari team. The car development was hampered by lack of testing, so much of the promise was illusory.

Nevertheless, Minardi gained its highest Constructors' Championship placing – seventh, in 1991 – and its cars sometimes ran the Ferraris close. Martini scored six points with two fourth places; Morbidelli failed to score and Moreno failed to finish the last race of the year. The retirement rate was over 50 per cent.

The M191 was adapted to take the Lamborghini 3512 engine for the first four races of 1992 (funds did not allow the Ferrari arrangement to be extended). Christian Fittipaldi and Morbidelli each recorded three retirements and one finish, the Italian's seventh in Brazil being the best result.

M192 Aldo Costa's new car for the Lamborghini V12 had the virtue of a stiffer chassis, and shortcomings in areas from aerodynamics to component reliability, and another budget that did not allow sufficient testing for these to be sorted out. An unusual feature was the outboard mounting of springs/dampers in the double wishbone pushrod suspension. Lamborghini's transverse six-speed gearbox handled the power of the V12 – as much as 730bhp was claimed.

Fittipaldi scored the team's only point in Japan, but he failed to qualify the new car three times and retired once. Zanardi took his place for three races, recording two DNQs and a retirement. Morbidelli managed seven finishes, in a downbeat season.

M193 The 1993 car was ready and tested before the first Grand Prix. Designed by Costa and Gustav Brunner, it was simple, with passive suspension and no traction control, but with a large plus factor in a return to Cosworth V8 power (actually second-hand Ford HB engines) after unhappy seasons with Italian V12s.

Fittipaldi drove in fourteen races, finished ten, and scored five points (fourth in South Africa and fifth at Monaco). Barbazza was his team mate in the first eight Grands Prix, and was sixth twice. Martini drove in eight races achieving a 50 per cent finishing rate but failing to score, while Gounon had two fruitless drives. Minardi was eighth in the Constructors' Championship, with its highest-ever points score.

M194 In 1994 the team became Minardi Scuderia Italia, in an *accordo* – rather than a merger – with Beppe Lucchini's outfit that did not bring all of the anticipated benefits and in any case was to be short-lived. Costa overhauled the 1993 design, and was able to introduce a hydraulic suspension system (that was set aside) and develop a semi-automatic gearbox. Ford HB engines were retained, and the relative lack of power was a handicap on the fastest circuits.

In driving experience, Pierluigi Martini and Michele Alboreto made up an unmatched pairing, but Martini scored just four points (two fifth places) and Alboreto one, while the two recorded eighteen retirements in the sixteen race series. Minardi was tenth in the championship.

M195 This car served through a difficult year for Minardi, as ever beset by financial problems, and for half the season with legal problems. These centred on engines. The Mugen V10s that Minardi expected to have were acquired by Walkinshaw and Briatore for the Ligier team, and that led to legal claim and counter-claim. Might prevailed, and Costa had to revise the rear end of his design for the Ford ED V8 and Xtrac six-speed transverse gearbox before the first Grand Prix.

To some observers, Martini seemed to have lost his touch; he started the first nine Grands Prix in Minardis, but his best placing was seventh. Badoer drove for the whole season, and his best finish was eighth. It was left to Pedro Lamy to score the team's only point, in the last of the eight races he drove for it in 1995.

M196 Long-serving designer Aldo Costa moved on to Ferrari, and the technical director sensibly made minimal changes to the 1995 design as he looked ahead to 1997. The engine was the Cosworth ED (from ED2 at the beginning of the season to the ED4 at its end).

Four drivers, Fisichella, Lamy, Lavaggi and Marques, drove Minardis in 1996, and failed to score. Fisichella came closest, with an eighth place in Canada from his eight outings, while Lamy managed ninth at Imola. Between them the quartet managed a better-than-50 per cent finishing rate, a record marred by Lavaggi's three DNQs.

M197 In 1997 the Minardi situation improved, as Rumi and his associates brought in capital, and then it slipped back as these resources were applied to a conservative car designed by a group headed by Tredozi. The result did not sparkle, and the Hart 830 V8 was not the most powerful engine on 1997 grids (moreover, there was a surprising electronic incompatibility for half the season).

Jarno Trulli impressed in his first Grands Prix, his two ninth places being Minardi's best of the year (in mid-season he moved to Prost). Katayama's best was tenth (twice), and Marques also finished tenth in one race.

M198 Gabriel Rumi was in overall control by 1998, and he brought in Gustav Brunner, albeit when the M198 had been laid down. Other specialists joined, as the whole operation was expanded, notably on the R&D side. Giancarlo Minardi's role became team manager, incidentally, at least until Cesare Fiorio took on that role at the end of the year.

The car evolved from the M197, with some components that had served rather longer. There was a return to a Cosworth engine, in the shape of the Ford Zetec-R V10, initially in the form used by Stewart at the end of 1997, later in versions giving more power across the range.

Shinji Nakano was the lead driver, and he twice finished eighth; moreover he retired only six times. Esteban Tuero showed flashes of speed, but finished only four races, his best placing being ninth. A year when Minardi might have expected a Constructors' Championship placing turned out to be disappointing.

M199 Minardi's survival into its fifteenth Formula 1 season surprised many people, for its record of achievement was modest, and other teams had fallen by the wayside. But there it was in February

Minardi M197-Hart V8.

1999, launching a smart new car, preparing optimistically for a new season, and looking for regular points-scoring finishes. A design team under Brunner made full use of the team's increased resources, and the M199 looked the part. The Ford Zetec-R V10 engine was developed by a dedicated Cosworth team, with Minardi input.

Yet Minardi generally remained a back-of-the-grid team. There were top-ten finishes, notably by newcomer Marc Gene in his first three finishes. Gene and Luca Badoer at least achieved reliability rates bettered by few teams in 1999, and in a remarkable European GP at the Nürburgring both were in points-scoring positions in the closing phase. Badoer

retired but Gene scored his first World Championship point, and Minardi's first Constructors' point since 1995.

M02 Nothing exceptional could be expected in 2000 from this brave, but underfinanced team – and nothing was delivered. Like other 2000-generation F1 cars, this latest Minardi was an evolutionary step forward from the 1999 variety, with a similar style – but easily identifiable by its yellow (Telefonica) colour scheme, and a lower nose.

Early plans by designer Gustav Brunner to use Supertec/Renault engines had been scrapped, so for the second year in succession a 1998-specification (ex-Stewart SF-2) Ford-Cosworth V10 engine was

employed, with exhausts exiting, Ferrari-fashion, through the top of the side pods. This was mated to a new six-speed longitudinal gearbox.

As ever (unhappily, this has to be repeated) the Minardis looked good, handled well enough, but were never remotely on the pace. Gene and Mazzacane were well-liked, almost always helpful when being passed by faster cars, but no points were scored. Those who knew little blamed the use of 1998-specification engines, those who knew more were simply impressed to see Minardi plugging on.

For 2001, it was said, Minardi would use 'customer' Ferrari engines. But would they even be as successful as Sauber, who had been using this trick since 1997?

PIERRON sur voiture MOTOBLOC

L'Hirondelle - Paris

Motobloc Grand Prix car of 1908.

Mors

Mors was one of the leading marques of early racing, Emile Mors competing in one of his cars in 1897. However, the company's effort was almost spent by the time Grand Prix racing was introduced, and although it contested the Kaiserpreis equivalent in 1907 it entered the premier race only once, in 1908.

Its two cars for the Grand Prix had 12,798cc four-cylinder ohv engines, three-speed gearboxes when most entrants used four speeds, and chain drive. One was driven by the great Camille Jenatzy, the 'Red Devil', past his best in 1908 and dropped by Mercedes. He was a late entry for Mors, for his last major race, and in a car that was not competitive. At half-distance he was twentieth, and destined to finish sixteenth, almost one-and-a-half hours behind the winning Mercedes. His team mate Landon was seventeenth. Mors's factory racing efforts ended with that mediocre result.

Motobloc

This French company was sometimes tempted into racing in the Edwardian period, and it entered the Grands Prix in 1907–08 with cars that were distinguished by an appearance of long and low lines, rather than by any detail of specification.

The 1907 type had a relatively small (11,974cc) straight-four engine, and chain final drive. even its appearance was misleading, the Motobloc had the shortest wheelbase of any of the cars at Dieppe. In the race it was outclassed: Pierron was the team's leading driver at half-distance, sixteenth and more than 50 minutes down on the leader. Page had already retired one Motobloc, Pierron retired on the second day, leaving Courtade to finish, eleventh and 118min behind the winner.

The 1908 car was more sophisticated, with a hemispherical-head 12,831cc engine but still with chain drive. Pierron crashed on the fourth lap of the Grand Prix, while Courtade and Garcet ran through to finish thirteenth and fourteenth, well out of touch with the leaders. After that the cars were seen in odd local French events.

◆ N ◆

Nagant

The modest Liège company flirted with top-line racing with its licence-built Gobron-Brillié types early in the twentieth century, and ventured into the Grand Prix arena once, in 1914. Its pair of cars gave an impression of being heavyweights from an earlier era, with high bonnets and bolster tanks. In fact they weighed in at 1,055kg (2,326lb) – lighter than the outwardly sleeker Mercedes and Peugeots, and well within the 1,100kg (2,425lb) maximum – and they had twin overhead camshaft engines, 4,433cc four-cylinder-long-stroke units.

These obviously did not give competitive power, but their drivers persevered in the Grand Prix and Dragutin Esser climbed the order, from sixteenth at quarter-distance, to tenth at half distance, and was rewarded with sixth place at the end, half an hour down on the winning Mercedes. His team mate Elskamp retired with two laps to go. After the First World War, Nagant briefly turned to sports-car racing.

National

National was an Indianapolis company, and its major efforts were naturally in the local race – Joe Dawson won the 1912 '500' for National, albeit with a strong dash of good fortune, for de Palma's Mercedes failed in the closing laps when he was leading by four laps.

Nationals did face Grand Prix opposition in American road races, with orthodox stock chassis cars. A National started in the 1908 Grand Prize but failed to finish and another was third in the 1910 Vanderbilt Cup, two entries that merit the inclusion of National among Grand Prix cars. The company's best road race result was Len Zengle's victory in the 1911 Elgin Trophy, with one of the 7,325cc cars.

Nazzaro

Felice Nazzaro was one of the leading drivers in the Edwardian period, particularly with FIAT and in 1907 when he won the year's three principal races, including the Grand Prix. He established his own marque in 1912, and that year drove one of his own cars to score its first major race victory, in Sicily. Two years later Nazzaro entered a three-car team in the Grand Prix. It arrived at Lyons just in time for scrutineering, but too late for the official practice periods (familiarization, really) a fortnight before the race.

The car appeared compact and up-to-the-minute beside some of the 1914 Grand Prix entries, low and rakish, while in common with Fiats the Nazzaros carried spare wheels alongside the scuttle rather than in or on the tail. The engine was an sohc 4,441cc four-cylinder type, driving through a four-speed gearbox in unit. In other respects such as channel-section chassis, rigid front suspension and live rear axle the cars were orthodox, and in common with most entries at Lyons had transmission and rear wheel brakes. They weighed in just below the 1,100kg (2,425lb) limit.

Felice Nazzaro headed his team, and was the first to retire, after only three laps, with engine failure. De Moreas almost reached half distance before his engine failed, and after an undistinguished run Porporato's engine stopped when he was running last with two laps to go (he had two very slow mid-race laps, but otherwise was the quickest Nazzaro driver, yet seldom within five minutes of the leaders' times in one 20–21min lap).

The cars appeared in minor Italian events after the First World War, but Felice Nazzaro had left during the war and returned to Fiat in 1922 – he won the French Grand Prix for Fiat that year, and was twice second in the Italian GP before becoming the company's competitions manager.

Netuar

Rauten Hartmann reversed the spelling of his forename to label a one-off on Cooper lines that he built for South African races in the early 1960s, and was perhaps ill-advised in his choice of a Peugeot engine, which never developed competitive power. The car was entered for the Rand GPs, 1961–64, and it finished twice – last in 1963 and last in a heat in 1964 (Hartmann failed to qualify in 1962, retired in 1961 and in the second heat in 1964).

◆ O ◆

OM

This Brescia company (Officine Meccaniche) was prominent in sports-car racing in the 1920s, but its one venture into Grand Prix racing was hardly successful – second and fourth in the 1927 European GP might sound impressive, but that was a race with a thin grid.

The OMs appeared on entry lists for some time before that actual appearance, and when they did come to the line at Monza they proved to be orthodox 1.5litre Grand Prix cars in most respects. There was a channel-section chassis and non-independent suspension with semi-elliptic springs. The dohc straight eight had a Roots-type supercharger blowing air into the carburettor. A three-speed gearbox was used, when others had shown that more was needed, and the torque characteristics of the engine probably called for the car to be rowed along.

These cars were expected in 1926 (they were entered for the French GP that year), but even so were apparently little developed when they started in the Grand Prix d'Europe, and reputedly had poor handling. This shortcoming may have been alleviated by the wet conditions at Monza, and on this 'top gear' circuit the three-speed gearbox was presumably not a handicap. Giuseppe

Morandi finished second in one OM, some 22min behind the winning Delage, and Ferdinando Minoia was fourth. That was the only Grand Prix appearance for these OMs. The British concessionaire for OM, R.F. Oates, later developed one to perform respectably at Brooklands.

Onyx

Mike Earle, a widely experienced team manager, took his Onyx Race Engineering company into Formula 1 in 1989, after two years' planning and finally with backing from the Belgian, Jean-Pierre van Rossem in the name of his Moneytron finance company. Van Rossem acquired a major shareholding, and the team became Moneytron Onyx. The relationship between van Rossem and Earle and his partner Joe Chamberlain was soon strained, and the British partners left late in 1989. Van Rossem soon followed, claiming the decision was forced on him when an agreement he felt he had with Porsche fell through, that after it had been signed the German company negotiated with Arrows (an assertion denied by that team).

As Moneytron Onyx the team enjoyed mixed fortunes in its only season, with a third place to offset failures to qualify. Early in 1990 there were rumours of a merger with Brabham, but the team was sold to Peter Monteverdi, and the cars carried that name from the third race of the season. The first year had held out promise for the future, but under its new owner the team did not survive the summer of 1990.

ORE-1 Alan Jenkins designed a neat and largely conventional Cosworth DFR-powered car for 1989, around a carbon fibre and aluminium honeycomb monocoque and with double wishbone pushrod suspension all round. A new transverse six-speed Onyx-Xtrac gearbox was developed, rather than an off-the-shelf unit.

The cars seemed to need development as the season opened, and neither driver progressed beyond the pre-qualification phase of the first three races (Johansson's first race start for the new team came in Mexico, but Gachot did not reach a grid until the French GP). Johansson was fifth in the French GP and third in Portugal, giving

Onyx ORE-1-Ford of 1989, Bertrand Gachot driving.

Opel GP car of 1914.

Onyx six points for tenth place in the Constructors' Championship. Gachot started in only five races and finished in two, before losing his place to Lehto, who failed to qualify twice and retired twice. Onyx cars started in fifteen races, finished in seven. Three cars came out again as the 1990 season opened, when neither entry qualified for the first two races. They then gave way to the closely similar ORE-2, soon known as a Monteverdi.

Opel

Opel-Lutzmann cars were run in Germany's first international motoring event in 1899, and that year one of these cars won a hill climb. Modest successes with licence-built Darracqs followed, then true Opels appeared, and in the important Herkomer Trials in 1905 and 1906 Opels were placed fourth. An 8litre racing type was produced for the 1907 Kaiserpreis (taking third and fourth places behind a FIAT and a Pipe), and this design was developed for touring cars and a Grand Prix car, for 1908.

Modest results in 1908 were overshadowed by other German marques, but were the best for Opel at this level. The Opels for the 1913–14 Grands Prix were smart, but their specifications were 'ordinary' when something more was called for. Unusually among racing marques of the period, Opel

showed little interest in US competitions, although Len Ormsby qualified a 7.3litre car well at Indianapolis in 1912 (it failed to finish the 500). Opel did not return to Grand prix racing after the First World War. Its sports cars enjoyed some success in the 1920s, but the General Motors takeover late in the decade led to a concentration on production models. Five decades on, Opel became a leading rally marque.

1908 The first Grand Prix Opel was straightforward, with channel-section chassis members, beam front axle and live rear axle. It had a 12,045cc four-cylinder engine, with a four-speed gearbox and shaft drive. Crews were even more exposed than in most rival cars, but in other respects these were typical bluff-nosed Grand Prix machines.

Before the event the Opel team was not highly rated, but the experienced Carl Jörns drove a steady race to finish sixth, while Fritz Opel was twenty-first and Michel Opel retired with a broken radiator.

1913 A single car was entered for the 1913 Grand Prix, although a back-up was taken to Amiens and put through scrutineering. This was a pretty little car, its lines spoiled by the obligatory bolster tank. The chassis and suspension were conventional, and like most Grand Prix cars the Opel had wire wheels. Only one car (the

Mathis) had a smaller engine. Opel's 3,970cc inclined ohv four-cylinder unit drove through a three-speed gearbox.

The car was completed late, and preparation was hasty. Jörns's race was short. He completed the first lap in last place, and the engine problems that delayed him proved terminal during the next lap.

1914 In 1914 the Opel team was ready in good time, with cars that appeared to be more solid versions of the 1913 car. The sohc four-valve 4,441cc engine was a slow-revving unit that gave some 90bhp (100bhp was claimed at the time, but performance hardly bore that out). The 1914 car had a four-speed gearbox.

At half distance in the Grand Prix the three Opels were fourteenth, eighteenth and nineteenth, but only Jörns finished, tenth and more than 70min behind the winner. Breckheimer and Erndtmann both retired on lap 13.

Two of these cars found their way to Britain, and after the First World War Segrave won Brooklands races with one of them.

Osca

Osca built just a handful of Grand Prix cars, and the best World Championship race placing with one of these was tenth, so only nostalgia gives the marque importance. Freed of their commitment to the original Maserati company in 1947, the three surviving Maserati brothers, Ernesto, Ettore and Bindo, set up Officine Specializate Costruzione Automobili Fratelli Maserati, which was condensed to OSCA Maserati, then to Osca. It was a typical Italian performance-car boutique, concentrating on small sports cars, for competitions rather than general road use. Some single-seaters were built, ranging from a 4.5litre V12 F1 car to Formula Junior cars in 1959–60, and Osca also made efficient little engines. The brothers sold their company to Agusta in 1963.

4.5litre The first F1 Osca was an upgrade of Bira's Maserati 4CLT/48, primarily with an sohc 4,472cc V12 that had the hallowed Maserati 78 × 78mm cylinder dimensions. It had been laid down as a collaborative venture with Gordini, but the French constructor never used one in a car. The claimed output of 300bhp fell well short of Ferrari's supercharged 4.5litre V12 that gave up to 380bhp in 1951. Installation in the Maserati called for changes to the front bodywork. Bira won in the car's debut race, against a weak field in a very short Goodwood event, he was third in two other British secondary races, and fourth in the Bordeaux GP. This car was entered for one title race, the Italian GP in 1951, but failed to complete a timed practice lap

It was followed by another one-off, with an original chassis, wishbone and coil-spring front suspension and a de Dion rear axle. This was raced by Franco Rol, starting with the 1951 Italian GP when he finished ninth, but thirteen laps down. It appeared occasionally in 1952, and was then converted into a sports car (a third 4.5litre Osca was completed as a sports car).

2litre For the Formula 2 Grands Prix, Osca produced two workmanlike but uncompetitive cars that were sold to Elie Bayol and Louis Chiron. The engine was a 1,987cc dohc straight six, with a claimed output varying from 'more than 150bhp' to 170bhp. The chassis and suspension were based on the V12 car, but Bayol's car initially had inboard rear brakes.

Bayol managed minor placings in French provincial races with a stripped sports Osca before his F2 car was delivered. His best 1952 result was sixth in the Modena GP, and in 1952 he did win a race at Aix-les-Bains, beating a fairly nondescript field once Behra's Gordini ran into trouble. Chiron's

best result was second at Syracuse, but three laps down and three laps ahead of the third driver (that must have been enthralling!). He scored that tenth place in the 1953 Italian GP, when his fastest race lap was 17.5sec

slower than the best – that really sums up the potential of the F2 Osca.

Osca engines were used in 1.5litre F1 cars in 1961, ineffectively. Or perhaps the de Tomaso cars were ineffective?

Osca 4.5litre of 1949, 'B. Bira' driving.

Osca 2.0litre of 1953, Louis Chiron driving.

Osella

A minor Italian constructor, Osella had a surprisingly long career in Formula 1, sustained more by enthusiasm for simply being part of the Grand Prix circus rather than by a record of success: in eleven seasons, 1980–90, it entered cars in 132 races, and featured in the Constructors' Championship end-of-season listings just twice, in eleventh and twelfth places.

Enzo Osella ran the Abarth sports-car team in the 1960s, and this became Abarth-Osella in 1969. Under Fiat control, Abarth efforts were then diverted to rallies, leaving Osella to continue with small-category sports-racers under his own name, with some success. But however popular these cars remained in Italy, he had to look to single-seaters to maintain his operation based at Volpiano, near Turin.

Osella's first Formula 2 car came in 1974, and fortunes in that category were mixed. There were no outright race victories until 1979. Nevertheless, in the following year a one-car Grand Prix team was entered in the World Championships. That year it recorded just one finish. Osella pressed on, and points were scored in a 1983 race. The next year was its best in championship terms, as its drivers each scored points … once each.

Barren years followed, but that did not deter Gabriele Rumi, who took a major stake in the Osella F1 team in the name of Fondmetal in 1989. At the end of the next year Rumi took over completely, and the Fondmetal cars were to carry a Fomet name. The base was moved to Bergamo, and Enzo Osella left, and so did Antonio Tomaini, who had designed the first Osella Formula 2 car back in 1974 and its last Formula 1 car for 1990.

FA1 Giorgio Sirano collaborated with Osella in the design of this first F1 car, which had rather bulky lines disguised by smart livery. The monocoque comprised a tubular steel frame with a stressed aluminium skin – a simple and low-cost approach that carried a weight penalty. The suspension was by lower wishbones and upper arms. DFV engines were used, with Hewland gearboxes. The FA1 was run in eleven races, Cheever failing to qualify it four times and retiring seven times.

FA1B Giorgio Valentini collaborated in this design that followed FA1 lines in components such as the suspension, but had a conventional aluminium monocoque that was narrower, allowing for side pods that were more effective in 'wing' terms. It was a lighter car. The Cosworth-Hewland combination was still used.

The type was introduced at the 1980 Italian GP, when Cheever passed the flag in twelfth place, to record Osella's first finish in a Grand Prix (but he was also last, and lapped three times).

The car was mildly uprated for 1981, when a two-car team was run, albeit with inexperienced drivers. Beppe Gabbiani stayed for the year, DNQ appearing against his name twelve times, while he retired in the other three races. Guerra brought backing, qualified to start once in four attempts, and retired from that race. Francia tried once, then Jarier was brought in. He was eighth in his first two Grands Prix with Osella, then tenth and retired once before a new car came.

FA1C Jarier gave this Valentini-designed ground-effects car its debut in the 1981 Italian GP, when he finished in an encouraging ninth place. Overall, and in most details, it was similar to FA1B, still with lower wishbone and top rocker arm suspension. After the Italian GP, Jarier drove it in the last two races of 1981, retiring from both.

Three more cars were built to this specification for 1982, and Jarier drove one to fourth place at Imola – Osella's first scoring finish. But in the rest of the season the Frenchman retired ten times, failed to qualify twice, and did not start in the last race after a practice accident.

Riccardo Paletti was entered for eight races, started one (he retired) and then was killed in a Canadian GP start accident. For the rest of that year Osella ran one car.

FA1D Although it was given a 'D' designation, this car was an uprated FA1C, introduced at the 1982 German GP. It was further revised to meet the 1983 'flat bottom' regulations by Giuseppe Petrotta, and it was the last Osella to have a Cosworth DFV engine.

Corrado Fabi failed to qualify one of these interim cars three times, and retired five times in eight attempts. Ghinzani was entered in an FA1D three times, but failed to qualify to start a race.

FA1E The first FA1E was a D converted to take the Alfa Romeo 1260 V12; two more cars designed by Tony Southgate but carrying the same designation followed (and were the race cars by midsummer 1983). The monocoque, slender by Osella standards, had sheet aluminium sides and a carbon-fibre top. There was double wishbone pushrod front suspension, with lower wishbones and top rocker arms at the rear. The Alfa Romeo engine had a 540bhp rating (only the Cosworth units gave less power in 1983), and drove through an Alfa gearbox.

These cars were qualified to start eleven times in nineteen attempts, and finished three races, with best placing Fabi's tenth in the Austrian GP. Ghinzani's only finish was one place lower in the same race. One car was run once in 1984, until its engine gave up in the San Marino GP.

FA1F Osella's first turbo car with this designation was in fact an adapted Alfa Romeo 183T that had been destroyed in a practice accident at Kyalami. The definitive 'F' had Alfa Romeo's turbocharged V8, with a paper output of 670bhp. The monocoque was conventional, and there

Osella FA1C-Ford of 1982, Jean-Pierre Jarier driving.

Osella FA1I-Alfa Romeo of 1988, Nicola Larini driving.

was double wishbone suspension all round (pullrod at the front, pushrod at the rear). Alfa Romeo gearboxes were still used. Save for obscenely large rear wings, the lines were cleaner than previous Osellas.

By that modest yardstick, it was a successful car, in that Ghinzani finished fifth in the US GP at Dallas and Gartner was fifth in the Italian GP. Osella's four-point score in the Constructors' Championship was a high point in its history. Otherwise, Ghinzani was seventh in two Grands Prix, but Osella drivers also retired fourteen times.

The FA1F served on in 1985, in slightly modified form. Ghinzani finished two races in it (best placing ninth in Portugal), while Rothengatter drove one at Spa, ineffectually. One was brought out again in 1986, when Ghinzani failed to finish in his seven starts in it. Alan Berg managed three finishes in it, and Caffi drove to an unclassified finish at Monza.

FA1G Giuseppe Petrotta, who had developed the FA1F, was responsible for this one-off that was another evolution in the Alfa turbo-engined sequence. It was a little lighter and outwardly cleaner, and among detail changes there was pushrod suspension all round. A Hewland FGB gearbox adapted by Osella was used.

FA1G was driven by Christian Danner in five races, each time to retirement, and he failed to qualify it once. Berg drove it twice, Ghinzani seven times, to just one finish (eleventh in Austria).

It was used again in 1987, driven by Tarquini (one retirement), Caffi (one retirement) and Forini (two retirements and one DNQ).

FA1H This short-lived car by Petrotta was laid down for a Motori Moderni engine but was actually powered by the Alfa V8. Double-wishbone pullrod rear suspension on this car was an Osella departure. Danner qualified it twice in 1986, Berg once, Ghinzani twice. It did not finish a race, and was written off in a Brands Hatch crash.

FA1I Petrotta reworked the FA1H design for this car that had the Alfa Romeo 185T turbo with a claimed output of 700bhp driving through a Hewland gearbox, and improved suspension and aerodynamics. In 1987 it was driven by Alex Caffi, who was classified once, although the car had stopped running before the end of that race. Otherwise, he failed to qualify twice, retired twelve times, and did not start once. One of the 1987 cars was brought out for the first race in 1988, when Larini failed to qualify it.

FA1L Antonio Tomaini designed the team's new car for 1988, with a slender carbon-fibre monocoque, pullrod double wishbone suspension all round, Osella's version of the Alfa Romeo V8 and a longitudinal Hewland six-speed gearbox.

When it was first presented for a race, at Imola, the scrutineers regarded it as a new car rather than an evolution, and therefore

it should have had the driver's feet behind the front axle line. It was eligible for the next race, at Monaco where Larini placed it ninth. The rest of the season brought four failures to qualify, seven retirements, and two unimpressive placings.

The Osella Squadra Corse budget was a little larger in 1989 when a two-car team was run. Tomaini's car, sometimes referred to as the M89, was neater with a high engine cover and short side pods, a refined version of the pullrod front suspension, and Cosworth DFR engines.

Fortunes plummeted. Ghinzani usually failed to qualify (thirteen times), and retired from the three Grands Prix he did start. Larini was disqualified from the Brazilian GP, excluded from the Portuguese race, had DNQ against his name seven times and retired six times – really seven, as he had spun out of the race at Imola where he was classified twelfth and last. That at least gave Osella one finish in a truly dismal season.

FA1M Renamed Fondmetal Osella, the team ran a single car again in 1990. Tomaini's car was evolutionary – the same from the cockpit back – with a reversion to a normal front suspension arrangement.

Olivier Grouillard did not qualify or pre-qualify seven times, but at least he finished in four races. He was thirteenth twice, the second time in the Australian GP, which proved to be the last Grand Prix for an Osella. At the end of the season, Rumi took over and the Osella name was discarded.

Pacific

Keith Wiggins ran effective teams in secondary categories into the 1990s, and his ambition to enter Formula 1 seemed to take shape for 1993. However, he did not get a foot on the lowest rung of the Grand Prix ladder until 1994, and then the foothold was precarious.

The first car had started life three years earlier as a Reynard project, set aside during an acute financial crisis. Wiggins had won championships with Reynard cars, up to F3000 level, but the 'economical' approach – running cars that had to all intents and purposes been set aside, with obsolescent engines – proved to be a mistake. Not only did Pacific seldom qualify a car for a grid (seven times in thirty-two opportunities) and fail to get a car to the finish of a race, but the team's costs for 1995 were higher, as effectively it had to start again from scratch.

Preference had to be given to drivers who could bring finance that year, and there were five finishes, two in promising eighth places. But throughout, the team was just clinging on. Financial problems were against its survival, and towards the end of 1995 Pacific GP was put into voluntary liquidation.

PR01 This might have been the 1991 Reynard Formula 1 car and the qualification of its designer, primarily Rory Byrne, was beyond dispute. Built by Reynard then 're-assembled' by Pacific, it was wholly orthodox by mid-1990s standards, although high-nosed when that form was not fashionable. There was a carbon-fibre monocoque and pullrod double wishbone suspension. The engines were 'customer' Ilmor 72-degree V10s, and these drove through Hewland-Reynard six-speed transverse gearboxes. Adaptation to install the Ilmor engine meant that some chassis rigidity was lost, and there were aerodynamic shortcomings – and no wind-tunnel tests to investigate these. After a season like this, would 1995 be better?

All the race starts – five for Bertrand Gachot and two for Paul Belmondo – came in the first half of the 1994 season. From the French GP to the Australian GP dismal successions of DNQ appeared against both drivers' names. After a season like this, would 1995 be better?

PR02 Frank Coppuck designed a new car for 1995, again on conventional lines. Ford (Cosworth) ED engines were used. There seemed to be aerodynamic problems again, and cost considerations meant that some detail refinements were not incorporated. And costs ruled out extensive testing to sort things out.

Two of the drivers might have brought in finance, but beyond that Lavaggi and Deletraz contributed five retirements and one unclassified finish. Gachot retired nine times, but one of his two finishes, eighth in Australia, was one of Pacific's best – as well as its last. That placing was equalled by Montermini in Germany, and the young Italian finished two other races, although he usually failed to qualify or retired (ten times).

There were slight signs of progress in Pacific's second season, but the money ran out.

Panhard

The great days for Panhard et Lavassor in racing were behind the company when it entered cars for the first three Grands Prix, and those three events closed the chapter. Emile Levassor had won the first motor race as such – the distinction is needed because of reliability contests and odd non-events – when he drove one of his 1.2 litre vee-twin cars in the 1895 Paris–Bordeaux–Paris, averaging 15mph overall. In a nice conceit, the ACF was later to refer to that race as its first Grand Prix. Another Panhard in the event was the first car to race with a steering wheel, rather than tiller steering.

Panhard won the premier races in 1896, 1898 and 1899, then was runner-up to Mors in the following years. Meanwhile, Maurice Farman had driven a Panhard to win the first race to actually carry the title 'Grand Prix', a minor event in the 1901 Pau speed-week programme.

A good pioneering record did not lead to success in the age of giants, and Panhard entries did not get beyond the French trials for the French Gordon Bennett race in 1904–05, although American driver George Heath did win the Circuit des Ardennes and the first Vanderbilt Cup in 1904, driving a 15,435cc Panhard '90' that, unlike most of its rivals, had shaft drive. There was a second place in the Vanderbilt race in 1905, and that was the last top-three placing for a Panhard in a major race.

When Panhard entered the 1906–08 Grands Prix its engineers seemed to have lost their touch. Or perhaps just lost touch after the omnipotent days? in 1906 they tried very large engines, but lost to smaller cars. In 1907 the cars were just not competitive. In 1908 they were outclassed, and Panhard gave up racing for decades. There were record cars in the 1920s, and one of these was used in track races, and after the Second World War Dyna Panhards won rallies and class honours in major sports-car races. Even that passed, inevitably soon after Citroën took over in 1965.

1906 For the first Grand Prix, Panhard stuck to cars on its 1904–05 pattern, with the T-head four-cylinder engine bored out to 185mm to give a capacity of 18,279cc and an output of the order of 130bhp. Four-speed gearboxes were used, with shaft drive. Brakes followed the common pattern – a pedal-operated transmission brake and lever-operated rear wheel brakes. These big bluff-nosed cars had substantial frames and rode on wooden-spoked artillery wheels and – importantly – to get within the 1,007kg (2,220lb) weight limit, Panhard had to discard detachable-rim wheels, and thus accept the delays of many minutes when crews had to change tyres.

Heath's Panhard was seventh at half-distance, and he got through that first Grand Prix to finish sixth, five and a half *hours* behind the winning Renault. Tart and Teste both retired before half-distance.

One of these cars was entered in the 1906 Vanderbilt Cup, but Heath was out of contention when he retired on the penultimate lap.

1907 In its car for the fuel-consumption Grand Prix, Panhard reverted to an older version of the engine, in 15,435cc form, and mounted the radiator behind it, Renault-fashion. Save that it had detachable-rim wheels, the rest of the car followed the 1906 pattern.

Heath retired from the Grand Prix after one slow lap. Le Blon retired after three laps. Duray at least completed eight laps of the ten-lap race, but was last when he gave up.

1908 The limitation on cylinder bore led to the smallest Panhard racing engine for years, a 12,831cc four-cylinder T-head unit, for which 120bhp at 1,300rpm was claimed. The radiator was back in the nose after the 1907 experiment. There was a reversion to chain drive. A new chassis was reputedly lighter.

Before the Grand Prix, this car seemed more competitive, and Heath was sixth at half-distance. He was to finish ninth (only an hour after the winner!). Farman was twenty-third and last. Henri Cissac ran as high as sixth before crashing when a tyre blew on the penultimate lap. Cissac and his mechanic, Schaube, were killed, in the first fatal accident in a Grand Prix.

Parnell

Like most other Formula 1 entrants, Reg Parnell saw the introduction of the mono-coque Lotus 25 as a setback, and as the Lolas and Lotus 24 he was running obviously could not be driven to compete with the 25s, his reaction was to commission a design on 25 lines. Les Redmond, who had some respectable Formula Junior designs in his name, undertook this and a car began to take shape in the Reg Parnell (Racing) workshop. It followed Lotus lines closely, and incorporated Lotus components, but it was never completed as Colin Chapman sold Parnell a pair of 25s. Some components from the Parnell were used in a sports-racing car, and the chassis was presumably scrapped.

Parnelli

Velco Miletich, a successful entrant in US racing in the 1960s, set up an ambitious new team with his former driver and USAC champion Rufus Parnelli Jones in 1969. They had substantial Firestone backing to compete in USAC, Formula A and drag races, and success led to a venture into Formula 1 in 1974. Several former Lotus personnel were recruited, and designer Maurice Phillippe laid out a car very much on the lines of the Lotus 72, a car with which he had been deeply involved.

At the end of 1974 the Vel's Parnelli team was undermined as Firestone unexpectedly and abruptly withdrew from racing. Jones, who had never been enthusiastic about Formula 1, left that side of affairs to Miletich,

Parnelli VPJ4-Ford of 1974, Mario Andretti driving.

Parnelli VPJ4B-Ford of 1976, Mario Andretti driving.

and increasingly Mario Andretti kept the show on the road. Little development work was undertaken, although work that was done pointed in the right direction. Achievement in 1975 was modest, but should have been encouraging. Yet after two races in 1976 – and sixteen Grands Prix in its short history – the team was wound up.

VPJ4 The first three VPJ cars were for USAC racing, and this Grand Prix car came late in the 1974 season. It had overall wedge lines, hip radiators flanking the Cosworth DFV engine, Hewland FG400 gearbox, double wishbone and torsion bars front suspension with upper and lower links and torsion bars at the rear, and inboard brakes – all reminiscent of the Lotus 72.

Modifications in 1975 included the introduction of outboard front brakes, and late in the year coil springs in the rear suspension. In the single VPJ4B for 1976 there was coil spring suspension all round, and some bodywork refinement.

Andretti finished seventh in the car's debut race, the 1974 Canadian GP, and early in 1975 he was third in the Silverstone International Trophy. His best placings in championship races were fourth in Sweden and fifth in Britain. The five points scored gave Parnelli tenth place in the Constructors' Championship.

The VPJ4B was run in South Africa, where Andretti scored the team's only 1976 point, and at Long Beach, where he retired. Then the team that had shown more promise than many F1 newcomers was disbanded.

Pearce

John Pearce was a London motor trader with ambitions to enter Grand Prix racing, and to a tiny degree he achieved this with a Cooper-Ferrari put together for the first season of 3litre racing, using a 250GT V12 in a 1964 Cooper T73 chassis. Chris Lawrence drove this car in secondary British races with modest success, and he started it from the back rows of the British and German GP grids (finishing the Brands Hatch race in eleventh and last place).

Encouraged, Pearce laid down a simple space-frame car for 1967. There were to be three, one for his existing Ferrari engine and two intended for the Martin light-alloy twin-cam V8. This had been raced twice in minor events in a Lotus 35 chassis that was then written off in a test accident. At the time, the engine was felt to be 'promising', but it was never taken up by a major team before the Cosworth DFV arrived.

Three cars, the Cooper and two new cars, were entered for the 1967 Silverstone International Trophy, although it was never clear that all three were finished: together with the team's transporter, they were destroyed in a mysterious and fierce fire at the circuit two days before the meeting formally started.

Penske

Roger Penske raced in SCCA sports-car categories in the 1960s before becoming an entrant late in that decade, running sports cars, TransAm cars and USAC cars, above all for talented engineer/driver Mark

Donohue. He retired after winning the 1972 CanAm championship, but was tempted back to racing when Penske decided to enter Formula 1, as a constructor with a programme largely built around Donohue.

A European base was essential, and Penske took over the base used by Graham McRae for his F5000 team. The Penske F1 cars were designed and built at this Poole plant, which continued in use until the end of the century, for the Penske Indycars and those the team bought in and assembled to its own requirements.

Penske Cars was to enter thirty Grands Prix, 1974–76, and win one. Its first car was not a front runner and, ever pragmatic, Penske and Donohue ran a March 751 as a yardstick. Donohue crashed fatally in a 751 when a front tyre failed during the warmup for the 1975 Austrian Grand Prix.

PC1 Geoff Ferris designed a conventional and neat Cosworth-powered car for Penske's entry into the Grands Prix. It had an aluminium monocoque, double wishbone front suspension and upper and lower links with radius arms at the rear. The second PC1 had a wider track and modified front suspension, and was tried with an extended wheelbase while a narrow track was used at appropriate venues (such as Monaco). Driver-adjustable roll bars were planned, but not used in racing. The DFV drove through a Hewland FGA400 gearbox. The body followed refined wedge lines, with hip radiators.

The race debut came in Canada late in the 1974 season, when Donohue finished eleventh. He then retired for the US GP. Early 1975 results were similar, with seventh in Argentina being the best among

Pearce-Martin V8 of 1967 (right of picture).

This could have been a bodyblow to the new F1 team, but Penske persevered. A new car appeared at the end of the year, to be followed by a third type in mid-1976. This was a front-running car, and John Watson drove it to win the Austrian GP. At the end of the season, Penske was fifth in the Constructors' Championship – a noteworthy achievement for a relatively new team – but nevertheless Roger Penske withdrew from Formula 1, to concentrate on Indycar racing, which related much more directly to his major business interests.

retirements. The first points-scoring finish came in the Swedish GP, when Donohue was fifth. By that time a March had been tested and proved faster than the PC1, so Penske bought a 751 to use in the summer. A PC1 was taken to the US GP for display purposes but had to be pressed into service without running in practice. John Watson had taken Donohue's place, and he drove this car through to finish ninth.

PC3 This car should have made its debut at Watkins Glen in 1975, but refused to

Penske PC4-Ford of 1976, John Watson driving.

function in all electrical respects on race day. It largely followed March lines, with some elements carried over from the PC1, and the Cosworth and Hewland five-speed combination was retained. It was laid out by Ferris, with some input by Don Cox.

This proved to be an interim car, and was not fully competitive. It was run through the first half of the 1976 season (Hayje hired one for the Dutch GP, retiring from that race). Watson was fifth in the PC3's second race, the South African GP, after retiring in Brazil. He failed to score in his next four Grands Prix with the PC3, before turning to the PC4.

PC4 Notable for its elegant lines, the PC4 followed on from the PC3, for example using the suspension with outboard springs all round that had been inherited from the March 751.

Its first race was the French GP, when Watson started from eighth on the grid and finished third, only to be disqualified for a dimensional infringement and then reinstated. He was third in the British GP, then won in Austria; his only other scoring finish was sixth at Watkins Glen, then Penske's Formula 1 effort ended with his retirement from the Japanese GP.

PC4s were raced ten times, retiring only three times, and with only one finish outside the top ten. They were then sold to ATS. Penske's fifth place in the championship was earned with twenty points, and Formula 1 was poorer for the team's departure.

La Perle

The 1930 French GP was a *formule libre* affair which attracted a mixed field –

seventeen Bugattis and odds and ends ranging from the La Perle to a 'Blower' Bentley, but not the pace-setting new straight-eight Maseratis.

La Perle thus warrants a marginal entry in a survey of Grand Prix cars, simply because a car ran in the 1930 Grand Prix de l'Automobile Club de France. The car was a one-off, built after La Perle production had ended. It had a new chassis, functional if not handsome bodywork, and a 1,483cc sohc straight six that had its origins in 1924. A Cozette supercharger was added for this 1930 use, but even so its 85bhp output was hopelessly inadequate. De Caroli was flagged off in the Grand Prix (nevertheless, the La Perle was classified second in class to an old Delage).

Peugeot

Peugeot was involved in motor sport from its very beginning, yet had built cars under four company titles before it built a Grand Prix car. From 1906 until 1910 it had been prominent in *voiturette* racing, and it seems that when there was talk of a Grand Prix revival in 1911 thoughts turned to that category. Certainly, when the Automobile Club de France firmly decided to revive the Grand Prix in 1912 several strands came together and led to a Peugeot team entry for that race, and to the creation of epoch-making cars.

The L76 owed much to driver/engineer Paul Zuccarelli's Hispano-Suiza experience, to Peugeot drivers Georges Boillot and Jules Goux, and to Ernest Henry, a designer who had been involved with engine projects for obscure companies. It seems that Robert Peugeot gave this quartet – unfairly dubbed

les Charlatans by rivals within Peugeot – a free hand to build a Grand Prix car to carry the name of his marque, with provisos that its potential had to be demonstrated before it was raced.

In its chassis, running gear and transmission, the L76 was not startling, but it had a twin overhead camshaft, fast-revving, engine. That pointed the way ahead. The L76 was the first of a new generation, and in the 1912 Grand Prix it was pitted against one of the best of the era of 'giants'. The car was historic, and so was Boillot's victory at Dieppe. Then Goux drove one to win at Indianapolis in 1913.

Two consecutive victories in the Grand Prix – a 'first' – seemed to lead to an overconfident approach to the 1914 race, and to a defeat that was almost as famous as the 1912 victory had been. To all intents and purposes, that marked the end of Peugeot's Grand Prix involvement, but the influence of its 1912–14 cars was to linger, especially in the USA. Stripped sports cars were run independently in odd Grands Prix at the end of the 1920s, looking remarkably like replicas of the pre-First World War types.

Then, eighty years on from that crushing 1914 Grand Prix defeat, Peugeot entered Formula 1, supplying engines to leading teams. But with McLaren, Jordan and Prost, 1912's instant success was not repeated.

L76 The car for the 1912 Grand Prix was competent, with a light channel-section frame, rigid front axle and semi-elliptics, live rear axle and semi-elliptics, wire wheels, a transmission brake and large rear wheel brakes. The engine set it apart. Mounted in a subframe, it owed something to Peugeot and Hispano-Suiza *voiturette* engines, something to Zuccarelli's inspiration, and a lot to

Henry's experience and execution. It was a 7,600cc four-cylinder, long-stroke unit, with twin overhead camshafts and four inclined valves per cylinder, and hemispherical combustion chambers. The generally quoted output was 130bhp at 2,200rpm (the engine in the Fiat S74 1912 Grand Prix car was a 14.1litre unit that produced 190bhp at 1,600rpm). Henry used a remote four-speed gearbox.

In appearance, the car did not match up to its advanced engine. The valve gear led to a high bonnet line and there was a bolster tank behind the very open cockpit.

Peugeot's victory in the 1912 Grand Prix was by no means clear-cut. Zuccarelli retired early with engine failure and Goux was disqualified for taking on fuel away from the pits. Boillot ran second to Bruce-Brown's big Fiat at half-distance in the two-day event, then traded the lead with him in the second part until Bruce-Brown was disqualified. Boillot enjoyed a comfortable win, ahead of Wagner's Fiat. Incidentally, the smaller Peugeot L3 run in the concurrent *Coupe de l'Auto* also retired.

Goux drove an L76 with a 7.4litre engine to win the 1913 Indianapolis 500.

L56 The 1913 Grand Prix Peugeot was similar to L76 in most respects, with a refined version of the dohc engine. This was

Peugeot Grand Prix car of 1912, Georges Boillot driving.

a 5,654cc unit for this fuel-consumption formula race, giving some 115bhp at 2,500rpm.

During pre-race tests, Paul Zuccarelli died when he collided with a hay cart, and his replacement, Delpierre, crashed on the second lap of the race. A challenge by Guyot with a Delage faded in bizarre circumstances, leaving Boillot and Goux to finish first and second for Peugeot. Goux finished fourth at Indianapolis in one of these cars in

1914 (Arthur Duray was second in that 500, driving an L3 *Coupe de l'Auto* Peugeot).

L45 For the first Grand Prix under engine capacity regulations (4.5litres maximum), Henry refined the basic design. The 4,465cc engine was another four-cylinder long-stroke unit, producing 112bhp at the still higher speed of 2,800rpm. Transmission, chassis and suspension were similar to the 1913 cars, but this Peugeot had four-wheel brakes. The body lines were clean, with crews seated well down behind the scuttle, and there was a sleek tail, housing two spare wheels fore-and-aft. Perhaps too much has been made of the effect that this had on handling, but might road-holding deficiencies have been sorted out if Peugeot's leading drivers had not been committed to a race at Indianapolis? And the cause was not helped as Peugeot patriotically switched from Pirelli tyres late in the day.

Two of the Peugeots did finish in the Grand Prix, Goux fourth behind three Mercedes and Rigal seventh. Boillot fought hard, and led twelve of the twenty laps, and was second at the end of seven. But he was always under pressure, and drove his car into the ground, retiring with the end almost in sight (Henri Petiet once listed half a dozen failures or impending failures for me). More than one era ended on that hot summer of 1914.

174S This sports car had been raced in appropriate events – at Le Mans and Spa for example – in the mid-1920s, and later

Peugeot GP car of 1914, Georges Boillot driving.

Peugeot of 1931 at the Monaco GP.

appeared in odd *formule libre* Grands Prix. It had a 3,990cc sleeve-valve engine with a quoted output of 110bhp, and its chassis and running gear specification might also have been carried over from the 1914 Grand Prix cars. In appearance, too, there was a strong resemblance once wings and lights were stripped and bolster tanks added (required for the two Grands Prix run under fuel-consumption rules in 1929).

In the French GP that year André Boillot pressed Bugattis in this unlikely contender, and finished second. The *formule libre* French race in 1930 saw Peugeots finish eighth and ninth, while in the Spanish GP two were third and fourth. These cars should have been out of their time by 1931, yet that year Boillot took sixth place with one at Monaco while Rigal and Ferrand shared the Peugeot placed ninth in the ten-hour French GP. Then the Peugeot name really disappeared from Grand Prix racing until the 1990s.

Piccard-Pictet

This Geneva company had actually built Dufaux racing cars and SAG Pic-Pic road cars before the Piccardi-Pictet was used from 1910 (Pic-Pic remained in popular use). Its cars were usually *grandes routières*, high-class vehicles with above-average refinement and performance, built in very small numbers. Cars were run in hill climbs from 1912, notably driven by Paul Tournier.

That year a sleeve-valve engine was introduced, and this type was used in 4,441cc form in the three Grands Prix cars built for the 1914 race at Lyons. An output of 150bhp was claimed, but that would have made it far and away the most powerful in the race, in one of the lightest cars, and performance suggests that the actual power was little more than two-thirds of the claim. It drove through a four-speed gearbox. A rigid front axle and live rear axle were normal, but in common with only three other mar-

ques in the 1914 race, the Pic-Pic had four-wheel brakes (plus a transmission brake).

Thomas Clarke ran last from the second lap until he retired before half-distance. The more experienced Tournier generally ran in mid-field with the second car, and his lap times were hardly competitive (his best was 24:01, compared with a Mercedes fastest race lap in 20:06). He was in fourteenth place when he retired with two laps to go.

After that Pic-Pic never ran another works team, although these rare Swiss cars were still seen in competition, notably in Argentina during the First World War years. In the 1920s one of the 1914 Grand Prix cars was converted for road use, with a four-seat body.

Politoys

Frank Williams names his 1972 Formula 1 car for its principal sponsor, an Italian toys company, but this FX3 was the first Williams. Designed by Len Bailey, it was a no-frills Cosworth-powered car with a 'Coke bottle' aluminium monocoque and the then-inevitable double wishbone front suspension complementing upper and lower links and twin radius arms at the rear. A Hewland FG400 gearbox was used. The car's lines were fittingly modest (the FX3 was not completed as intended, for the late 1971 race). Ron Tauranac was to be involved in its modest development.

The FX3 made its debut in the British GP, when Pescarolo crashed. At the end of the year, Amon drove it in a non-title race at Brands Hatch, when it was retired less dramatically.

In 'FX3B' form, the erstwhile Politoys appeared as an Iso-Marlboro in the first 1973 races, when it was joined by a sister car, run until new deformable structure regulations made it obsolete in the spring.

Pope

This American marque rates a footnote in Grand Prix history as a Pope-Hartford appeared in two Grand Prize races. Cars built by factories in Col Albert A. Pope's combine carried names indicating location, and Pope-Toledo and Pope-Hartford (known for medium and luxury models

respectively) both appeared in racing. Pope-Toledo was first, notably when Herbert Lytle drove a 24hp car to third place in the first Vanderbilt Cup in 1904, beating several good Europeans, then in the following year the Soules brothers drove a stock model to win the first American 24-hour race, Lytle finished twelfth and last in the Gordon Bennett and Dingley won the 1905 US Vanderbilt eliminating race. Pope-Toledo faded away after Lytle led the 1906 trials in a 120hp car, described as a car with a strange frame and valve gear in its engine, finished fourth but was disqualified after a tow start.

The first Grand Prix phase was over when Louis Disbrow ran a stock-based 6,375cc Pope-Hartford in the 1910–11 Grand Prize races, retiring with engine failure in 1910 and placing the 'Hummer' fifth in 1911. He also had unsuccessful outings in events such as the 1910 Vanderbilt Cup.

Porsche

The German company never enjoyed success in single-seater racing to remotely match its sports-racing record, at times partly because of refusal to budge from its own methods and principles. Quite early in the 1950s, independent builders tried Porsche engines in one-off cars, then there

were central-seat RSKs in Formula 2, and most notably the 'Behra-Porsche', a wholly professional car using RSK components. It came as the factory was undertaking a modest Formula 2 programme with 718/2 single-seaters, and in this it was encouraged by the performance of the 'Behra-Porsche'. These first Porsche single-seaters generally matched British and Italian F2 cars, notably the car run by Rob Walker and driven by Stirling Moss. This contributed substantially to Porsche's tally of F2 championship points in 1960, when it took the title. Incidentally, Porsche success led the AvD to run the German GP for Formula 2 cars that year, thus offering spectators the possibility of a German victory.

The introduction of the 1.5litre Formula 1 for 1961 meant that these Porsches became Grand Prix cars, with minor modifications to meet the regulations. But something more was called for, especially competitive power units. That was promised for 1962, with a flat-eight engine. But outputs fell short of promise or targets. There was a rather fortunate Grand Prix victory, but before the end of the 1962 season Ferry Porsche had recognized that success in Formula 1 called for greater resources than the company could or would devote to it. There was a successful return, as an engine supplier in the 1980s, with turbocharged engines labelled 'TAG' in McLarens, in a programme closely monitored by McLaren – anathema to Porsche people, perhaps, but absolutely vital. Porsche was allowed to go it alone with an early-1990s programme for Arrows, and the engine that resulted proved heavy, unreliable and impotent. And Porsche's own Indycar device was never even raced; the company could have learned so much from the TAG programme.

718/2 This was the mildly revamped F2 car, mildly reworked for the first 1.5litre Grand Prix season, overweight and with 1,488cc air-cooled flat four giving some 155bhp. The steel space frame was retained, and outwardly the cars still appeared corpulent. While the wishbone set-up was kept at the rear, wishbones and coil springs were to take the place of the trailing arms in the front suspension. Variations were introduced through the year, in engines and most notably in the mid-season introduction of disc brakes – Porsche was the last constructor to use drums in Formula 1.

The cars were used in early-season non-championship races, when they were not

Porsche 718/2-cylinder of 1961, Jo Bonnier driving.

quite competitive, then for most of the rest of 1961 after the 787 was set aside. In championship races, the best placings were achieved by determined Dan Gurney, runner-up at Reims and Monza. Bonnier contributed three points, and Porsche's net twenty-two points gave third place in the Constructors' Championship. The cars were sold to independent entrants for 1962, when Carel Godin de Beaufort placed hs orange car sixth in his native Holland and in France. He was to score two more points in 1963, and that year Gerhard Mitter drove a de Beaufort car to take fourth place in the German GP. De Beaufort continued with his 718/2 in 1964, when he was fatally injured in a German GP practice crash.

787 This was a derivative of the 718/2, with the wishbone front suspension and an extended chassis (it was also to serve as a development car, so could accommodate the flat eight). Fuel-injection four-cylinder engines were fitted, but were still below par, and like the preceding cars the 787s had six-speed gearboxes. Handling was reported to be poor. Later the fuel injection system was changed, and with other modifications the engine was to give more than 180bhp – an output achieved only with difficulty with the 1.5litre version of the flat eight. After running in two Grands Prix, the 787 was set aside.

804 This was the purpose-designed Formula 1 Porsche, with a space frame designed by Tomola and the flat eight designed by Hans Mezger and Hans Honick. Porsche 'family' practices had to be followed, and this meant that the dohc 1,492cc flat eight was air-cooled, so Porsche drivers were handicapped with around 180bhp, less than their rivals. It drove through a six-speed gearbox. The suspension was by wishbones and torsion bars, front and rear, and disc brakes were outboard all round.

Forceful driving by Gurney sometimes put the 804 in contention and at Rouen he won a Grand Prix, albeit when Ferrari was absent and the British teams were tired as they had raced at Reims a week earlier and there were few healthy cars running at the end. Generally the Porsche Systems Engineering team struggled, and it did not enter all the championship races. Gurney was also third in Germany, and he won the non-championship Solitude GP. Bonnier scored just one point in an 804 (but two in an independent 718/2, at Monaco), and de Beaufort scored two, making Porsche's net

Porsche 804 8-cylinder of 1962, Dan Gurney driving.

total eighteen, giving fifth place in the championship.

Some development work was done for 1963, but Gurney's fifth place in the US GP was the last for a works Porsche F1 car. The team just did not travel to the last Grand Prix of 1962.

Porthos

Porthos's first car-building period was brief, 1906–09, but in 1907 this little French company entered Grand Prix racing ambitiously with straight eight. This one-off was not successful, nor were the three cars run in the 1908 Grand Prix. Then Automobiles Porthos disappeared from racing history, although it returned to manufacture with a few sporting cars just before the First World War.

1907 The first Grand Prix Porthos was conventional in all respects save its engine, with a long and apparently none-too-rigid channel-section chassis and non-independent suspension wih semi-elliptic springs. The engine was made up of four pairs of cylinders, and was a T-head unit (side valves and two side camshafts). At 9,123cc it was the smallest engine in the 1907 Grand Prix. There was a four-speed gearbox and shaft drive.

In his four Grand Prix laps in the Porthos, Emile Stricker's times were not impressive, and he was running in twentieth place when he retired with steering failure.

1908 Porthos was back in 1908 with a three-car team. The engine was a 9,121cc straight six, basically a touring car unit, and a three-speed gearbox was obviously felt to be adequate. The cars were the lightest at the weigh-in and one was right on the 1,100kg (2,425lb) minimum limit.

Gaubert in that lightest car failed to complete a single lap in the Grand Prix, and Jules Simon completed only two laps (water pump failure was blamed in both cases). Stricker fared better, surviving to the ninth of ten laps, although there were only three cars behind him when he retired from twenty-fourth place.

Prost

In 1996 the Ligier team was in turmoil, and while Flavio Briatore and Tom Walkinshaw manoeuvred, Guy Ligier kept his remaining holding to ensure that the team continued as a French team. The outcome was that the Scot departed, while Briatore sold his majority holding to four times World Championship Alain Prost. The team was soon to be overhauled and moved from its Magny-Cours base, while at the first Grand Prix of 1997 the car designed as a Ligier carried the new name of Prost.

The first season was not without teething problems, but there was promise for the future, in performance on the circuits, and in ample sponsorship, carried over and attracted by the Prost name. But there was also reorganization and necessary expansion on the technical side that seemed to lead to some confusion, and there was a change of engine from Mugen-Honda to Peugeot which might have given a patriotic fillip but did nothing to improve performance. And Gauloises Prost Peugeot was perceived as the French national team, so often a burden.

From a respectable sixth in the Constructors' Championship in 1997, Prost slumped to ninth in 1998, with just one point to its credit. At least 1999 was better in that respect.

JS45 The Ligier designation was retained for the 1997 car naturally, as it was a Ligier design. Loic Bigois, deputy technical director in the closing Ligier days, oversaw completion of the car that had been put in hand in the summer of 1996.

The JS45 was a handsome car with its dark blue colour scheme, with a nose that seemed higher than most and was aggressively pointed. Its monocoque, double wishbone suspension and body construction were conventional and its dimensions close to the JS43. Problems with that car, notably with handling, were ironed out. Mugen 72-degree V10s were used, with a lighter and more reliable 'B' version coming in mid-season. There was a six-speed semi-automatic transverse gearbox.

Olivier Panis made a good start to the season, fifth in Argentina and third in Brazil, then fourth at Monaco and second in Spain, before he was in an accident in Canada (he returned for the last three races, to score another point). Trulli stood in for seven races, and was fourth in the German GP.

Honda nominee Shinji Nakano scored two single points, and his nine retirements dented a good Prost record in this respect (the other two recorded just three retirements). The team scored twenty-one championship points, for sixth place on the table.

AP01 The 1997 season seemed to provide a good platform, but in 1998 fortunes slipped, dramatically: Trulli scored just one point, Panis none, and the Prost retirement rate reached almost 50 per cent. The car, designed under Bigois (who answered to a new technical director, Bernard Dudot), was similar to the JS45 in most respects – sensibly, as a change of engine and a new in-house gearbox brought problems in train. The engine was the Peugeot A16 72-degree V10 that originally had a reputation as a strong power unit and was to be uprated in mid-season. The longitudinal gearbox proved unreliable, and its weight upset car balance.

Through much of the season, Prost was seen as a team in disarray, and from the summer was working towards 1999, and effectively another fresh start. The single point was scored by Trulli, simply by surviving a chaotic Belgian GP, when most of the field retired.

AP02 For 1999 Dudot and Bigois looked to a more conventional car, longer and described by Bigois as 'narrower as far as aerodynamics are concerned'. Moreover, there was to be development input from John Barnard's B3 Technologies company, under an exclusive contract that

effectively added some thirty people to the 170 already committed to the project.

Obviously there was a carbon-composite monocoque, and in this car some suspension members in the same material. The Peugeot A18 engine was an evolution of the A16 used in 1998, some 5kg (11lb) lighter and with a wider useful revs band, but by no means the most powerful in Formula 1 in 1999. A new longitudinal six-speed semi-automatic gearbox was less 'radical' than the 1998 item, and more reliable.

For much of the season, the results still did not come. Panis was sixth in two Grands Prix, and until the fourteenth championship race that was also Trulli's best result. Then he was second in the European GP – Prost's best in its first three seasons. Seventh place in the championship was a welcome improvement for Prost Grand Prix.

AP03 Although Alain Prost was originally bullish about the prospects for his new Peugeot-powered car in 2000 (it had come together under the control of ex-Stewart technical chief Alan Jenkins), his smiles turned to frowns before mid-year. Simply, the AP03 was a real dog, back-of-the-grid sitter of a car – slow because of the inadequacies of its Peugeot V10 (33lb/15kg lighter than the '99 units, they claimed, but with less than 780bhp), and unreliable to boot.

Yet the shape looked right (Jenkins claimed there was much Stewart SF-3 in it), it was significantly lighter than the little-loved AP02, there was John Barnard-provided torsion bar front suspension, and every rear-suspension component was in carbon fibre. The exhaust system, too, exhausted through the top of the side pods, as on the 1999 McLarens.

Even so, there wasn't a single point to show for all the effort, where the Peugeot engines often let the side down in a cloud of blue smoke and flames, regular and annoying behaviour that was nearly enough for Alain Prost, one of F1's most successful drivers, to disappear into the sunset. After acting as McLaren's 'apprentice' for some time, this was an awful baptism for the German, Nick Heidfeld.

Yahoo, the Internet search-engine giants, must already have been regretting their £25 million three-year sponsorship deal, and Gauloise finally withdrew after many years with Ligier and its successors.

But if these engines were so awful, why did Arrows decide to use a rebadged development of them in future years?

Prost-Peugeot AP01 of 1998, Olivier Panis driving.

◆ R ◆

RAM

Raph Macdonald Racing was a successful Formula 3 entrant in the early 1970s, run by garage trade partners Mick Raph (manager) and John Macdonald (driver). They moved up to F5000 in 1975, when the team became RAM Racing and its driver was Alan Jones. Success at this level led RAM into Formula 1 with Brabham BT44s in 1976, and on to another unsuccessful venture with a March 781 in 1987. There was another return in 1980, with Williams FW07s, and this led to RAM running March cars again in 1981.

These were not March types as such, for they were built for RAM by Robin Herd's March Engines and in many respects followed the Williams FW07. The March name was retained for the 1982 car, although this time there was not even a link to March through Herd (Adrian Reynard was the chief engineer).

The record with these cars was dismal, but RAM survived to introduce a car carrying the RAM name in 1983. The team struggled on until the beginning of 1986, with cars that were always well presented to belie thin resources, until it collapsed as a hoped-for sponsorship deal failed to materialize. RAM failed to score a single championship point.

01 The March name lingered, and this Dave Kelly-designed car was known as the RAM-March 01 or March-RAM 01. It was a 'Cosworth kit car', with a Hewland gearbox. The specification was straightforward, for example with double wishbone suspension all round, and the three cars built had clean lines set off by smart livery.

In the Grands Prix they were ineffectual. Eliseo Salazar was entered six times, recording four DNQs, a retirement and a fifteenth place. Kenny Acheson failed to qualify six times, and his only start yielded twelfth place (in South Africa). Jacques Villeneuve, of all people, failed to qualify for his home Grand Prix, and Jean-Louis Schlesser failed once. But the Frenchman did finish sixth (of seven) in the Race of Champions.

One car was adapted for the Hart 415T engine and run in the first two Grands Prix of 1984, when Jonathan Palmer placed it eighth in Brazil and retired in South Africa.

02 There was no March association when RAM introduced its turbo car for 1984. This time a carbon-composite monocoque was used, and outwardly Kelly's lines were again attractive. The suspension was similar to the 01. The Hart four-cylinder engine was the least powerful turbo unit of the year, so the car's outright speed was not impressive, nor apparently was its ground-effects qualities. Hewland gearboxes were used. The RAM record was better. Palmer failed to qualify only once, retired four times and was twice ninth in his five finishes. Alliot failed to start three times, retired ten times, and the best of his three finishes was tenth. Thackwell recorded one retirement.

03 A pair of these cars was ready for the first Grand Prix of the 1985 season. Gustav Brunner was the designer, with Sergio Rinland and Tim Feast in his team, and they came up with another good-looking car. The Hart 415T gave near-competitive power in 1985, but it seems that an optimum installation eluded the RAM team.

RAM results were poor. In fourteen attempts, Alliot retired twelve times, and had a DNQ and an eighth place in the first Grand Prix against his name. Acheson twice failed to qualify, retired once. Manfred Winkelhock also failed to qualify once and retired five times, but finished twelfth and thirteenth and was an unclassified runner in the Portuguese GP in his other three races before his death in a sports car.

The team did not attend the last two races in 1985, and although a car was tested before the 1986 season opened, RAM did not enter another Grand Prix.

Realpha

In that it was built in Rhodesia this car was a rarity, but in other respects it was a southern African special for the F1 races in South Africa. In its space frame, Ray Reed followed Cooper practices – a little passé by 1964 – and like earlier one-offs in the region an Alfa Romeo Giulietta engine was used. This led to its failure in the 1964 Rand GP. As the RE, it was entered for the South African GP in 1965, but (realistically) it was withdrawn.

Rebaque

Mexican Hector Rebaque was an independent driver/entrant in Grands Prix at the end of the 1970s, one of the last of a once-important breed. He first raced in Formula 1 in 1977 (qualifying a Hesketh Racing car only once in five attempts), before turning to a Lotus 78 run under the Team Rebaque banner in 1978, when he made progress, for his nine starts yielded four finishes and a championship point. In 1979 his little team ran a Lotus 79 for most of the year (he finished three races in this car, and his best placing was seventh).

Then the Rebaque HR100 was introduced at the 1979 Italian GP. This one-off was designed under Geoff Ferris's supervision at Penske's base – that far its credentials were good. It followed the Lotus 79 in its monocoque, with side pods and ground effects, aerodynamic aids on Williams lines, suspension comprising lower wishbones and top rocker arms front and rear, a Cosworth DFV engine and Hewland FG400 five-speed gearbox.

Rebaque failed to qualify it for that 1979 Italian GP by a fairly wide margin, got his new car into the Canadian GP grid (five other drivers did not get that far), but retired before half-distance in the race, then failed to qualify it at Watkins Glen.

Rebaque talked of a new car for 1980. But Formula 1 had turned against independent ventures, and he reappeared halfway through the season in the Brabham works team, continuing with it in 1981 with commitment and some success.

Reif

This Formula 2 one-off originated in East Germany and started in the 1952 German GP, driven by Rudolf Krause. It was a BMW/EMW-engined special, and was little seen outside the DDR .

Krause qualified it twenty-third (of thirty) on the 1952 German GP grid, but he was two minutes off Ascari's lap speed in that race at the Nürburgring, and in any case completed only three laps. Krause later drove it to finish eighth in the Avusrennen, albeit three times lapped, and then he turned to another BMW/EMW special, the Eigenbau.

Renault

See pp.198–201.

Reynard

Adrian Reynard's cars for categories from Formula Ford in the early 1970s to Formula 3000 and Indycars were invariably successful, and his Formula 1 car was eagerly anticipated. But as such, it never came.

It might have come too early, as a Hake or BAF car in 1975–76. Then work on a Reynard F1 car started in 1990 with a view to entering it in 1992. But a sponsor could not be found, and Reynard could not finance the programme. So some of the

Rial

Hans Gunther Schmid turned away from racing after his 1977–84 ATS experiences, perhaps bruised but not knocked out, for he came back in 1988 with a team and cars named for his Rial wheels company. This team lasted for two years, and with one notable exception in each – both in the USA, by coincidence – its record was abysmal.

The 1988 car designed by Gustav Brunner seemed promising, but a one-driver team was run, and while Andrea de Cesaris could be quick on occasion, consistency was alien to his nature and he had a tendency to damage cars. In the second season two cars were run, and the record was worse.

ulation but was allowed to run, and next time all was in order. By that time it had an adequate fuel cell, too – it was suggested that Brunner was preoccupied with keeping weight to the formula minimum and producing a compact car, so the original cell was small.

The season can be summarized simply: eleven retirements, five finishes. De Cesaris was fourth in the US Grand Prix, and his other placings were eight, ninth, tenth and thirteenth. Three points gave Rial ninth place in the Constructors' Championship.

ARC2 Three more cars were built for 1989, in effect the ARC1 uprated by a trio including aerodynamicist Bob Bell. There were aerodynamic revisions in this notably

Rial ARC2-Ford of 1989, Volker Weidler driving.

'research in hand', which included an active ride system, was sold to Ligier, while the design became the basis of the hapless Pacific in 1994.

That year a DAMS Formula 1 car to a design by the Reynard team was put in hand. A car was built, but never raced.

Much was expected of the BAR 01 in 1999, for Adrian Reynard was technical director of this generously funded new team, and he oversaw the design by Malcolm Oastler, who had been responsible for a string of Reynard cars from 1988. In terms of continuity, this BAR was a Reynard F1 car. It was also cruelly disappointing in 1999.

In the thirty-two Grands Prix run in those two years, Rial recorded nine finishes, four in the year when two cars were entered. At the end of 1988 Schmid gave up again.

ARC1 There were similarities to Brunner's Ferrari F1/87 in major parts of this smart car, such as its monocoque. Unusually, the double wishbone pullrod front suspension had its shock absorbers positioned horizontally along the lower edge of the hull. Double wishbone were also used at the rear. A Cosworth DFV drove through a Rial-Hewland six-speed gearbox. First time out, the car infringed a reg-

sleek car. A short wheelbase version was available for tight circuits. The Cosworth DFR was used, with the Rial-Hewland gearbox.

Christian Danner drove most races for Rial in 1989, failing to qualify nine times but finishing fourth in the US Grand Prix at Phoenix that was notable for its low survival rate. None of the other drivers qualified to start a race: Weidler failed ten times, Raphanel six times, Gachot twice and Foitek once. Rial again scored three championship points, but in 1989 this was good for thirteenth place on the table. The marque's passing was not mourned.

A Renault won the first national Grand Prix, in 1906, and that alone assures the marque an honoured place in motoring history. The Renault brothers had raced their cars since 1899, usually in light car classes, although the 1903 Type O in which Marcel Renault died in the Paris–Madrid race was a 6.3litre machine. After that, the company did not stay away from racing for long, and in 1904 it built a racing type for independent drivers before its own return in 1905. The car supplied to Brokaw for the 1904 Vanderbilt Cup had the radiator-behind-engine arrangement introduced on that year's production Renaults, and used it on its racing cars through the next few years (Brokaw retired from that first Vanderbilt race). The Renault entry for the 1905 Gordon Bennett and Vanderbilt Cup was a 13litre car; François Szisz's Renault was the only car of the trio to survive the Gordon Bennett Eliminating Trials, in fifth place, and after holding second place in the opening stages of the American race he finished fifth in that, too.

That car led to the 1906 AK, which Szisz drove to that historic victory in the Grand Prix de l'ACF at Le Mans. In 1907 he was second in the Grand Prix, in a car that was virtually a replica of the 1906 AK, as Renault had sold the 1906 team cars. A modified derivative in 1908 did not feature in the Grand Prix, and this led Renault to turn away from top-flight racing after the

Grand Prize at Savannah, when one car was sixth. In any case, the French gave up the Grand Prix until 1912.

Renaults appeared in other types of racing, and later in rallies, and in the 1970s a sports-racing programme led Régie Renault back towards the Grands Prix. Its sports cars had turbocharged engines, and so did the Formula 1 RS01 for a careful entry into the Grands Prix in 1977. In 1978 a whole-hearted effort was made, and in 1979 Renault scored its first Grand Prix victory since 1906, and in France.

The programme was successful in many respects, Renaults starting in 123 Grands Prix and winning fifteen. Yet it was never better than second in the Constructors' Championship, and there was never the French-mounted French world champion that the French public wanted. Unfulfilled expectations led to tension and key personnel left, while Renault's commitment was cut back. None of these factors contributed to making the team competitive, and as it declined it was wound up at the end of 1985.

Renault turbo engines were supplied to other constructors, most notably Lotus 1983–86, while other teams were supplied with these V6 units by the Mecachrome company. Then there was an interlude until 1989, when Renault returned in a highly successful partnership with Williams – this produced sixty-

two Grand Prix victories, 1989–97. In 1995–97, these Renault engines were also used in the Benettons that won a dozen Grands Prix. But as this engine operation was passed to Mecachrome, lack of development meant that the edge was lost. Nevertheless, Renault made a great contribution to World Championship racing through most of the 1990s. They took control of Benetton in 2000, and a serious programme ensued.

AK The 1905 cars had some advanced features, such as deep tapered chassis frames and underslung rear axles, but these were abandoned in favour of convention in the 1906 Grand Prix AK. In this a channel-section chassis frame was used, with rigid front axle and live rear axle, semi-elliptics with hydraulic dampers (a racing novelty) and artillery wheels. The front wheels were normal, but at the rear the Grand Prix cars had Michelin's *jante amovible*. In this, the tyre was mounted to a detachable rim; the circuit was cruel, and tyres were flimsy, so much time was spent by car crews mounting replacement tyres on wheels. At some cost in weight, this system made for considerable gains in racing. The car had rear-wheel and transmission brakes.

The engine was a 12,970cc side-valve four-cylinder unit, with a 90CV rating and actually producing more than 90bhp. Shaft drive was used, in common with a majority of 1906 Grand Prix cars, and there was a three-speed gearbox.

Szisz led the Grand Prix from the third lap to the end, by 26min at the end of the first day and by 32min at the end of the second, completing 1,238km (769 miles). His Renault team mates fell out, Edmond after five laps with an injured eye and Richez when he crashed on the ninth of the ten long laps.

In 1907 the Renaults were painted blue rather than red, and had detachable-rim wheels all round. The Grand Prix was a fuel consumption race, each car being allowed 231litres (51gal) for the 770km (487 miles). Renault seem to have miscalculated, for Szisz was in a position to challenge Nazzaro (Fiat) for the lead in the closing phase, but eased – and he had some 30litres of fuel left as he finished second. Richez recovered from an accident to finish thirteenth, while Farman retired the third Renault.

For 1908 these Renaults had slightly smaller (12,076cc) engines, with the maximum cylinder bore (155mm) allowed by

Renault Grand Prix car of 1906, driven by François Szisz, winner of the first Grand Prix.

the regulations. Szisz completed only two laps (he was unable to replace one of the new-style detachable rims on a distorted wheel), Dimitriewich and Callois were eighth and thirteenth. Later in the year, Lewis Strang drove one of the earlier AKs in the Vanderbilt Cup, retiring, and the Grand Prize, when he was sixth. Szisz had a 1908 car for the Grand Prize, and was second before he retired. That ended Renault's first Grand Prix foray.

The Formula 1 programme in the second half of the 1970s had its origins in the Renault-Gordini CH1 V6 designed by François Castaing and used in sports and Formula 2 cars. In 1975 a turbocharged version, CHS, was introduced for sports-racing cars. In the following year, this turbo engine was used in the Alpine A500 test car, a single-seater that was a direct forerunner of the Grand Prix RS01 that was first raced at Silverstone in 1977 (the RS designation indicated Renault Sport). Eventually every constructor had to follow the Renault lead, and use turbocharged engines.

RS01 Designer André de Cortanze followed the general lines of the Alpine A500 in the first Renault Formula 1 car. It had a simple aluminium monocoque, with double wishbone front suspension and upper and lower links at the rear. Bernard Dudot undertook engine development, and in its first F1 form the 1,492cc V6 had a single Garrett turbocharger and was rated at 500bhp (it was designated EF1, incidentally, for the ELF fuel company contributed substantially to

development costs). It drove through a Hewland FGA400 six-speed gearbox. The RS01 body was workmanlike rather than handsome.

'Throttle lag' was to become a familiar refrain in the turbo era, and Renault also had to overcome heat problems. These remained when the car ran its first races. Jabouille retired it when it made its race debut in the 1977 British GP, and the car failed to finish a Grand Prix that year. Development did not get up pace until Renault won the Le Mans 24-hour Race in 1978, so perhaps that first five-race half-season in Formula 1 was premature.

At least there was only one failure to qualify in 1978, when Jabouille was again the team's only driver. He retired nine times and finished five races, scoring Renault's first points with fourth place in the US Grand Prix. That gave Renault a modest twelfth place in the Constructors' Championship.

The RS01 was used by the two-car team in the opening races of 1979. By no means had all the problems been ironed out, and the engine gave little more power than in 1977, but at least Formula 1 now had the undivided attention of Renault Sport. In eight race starts there were just two finishes (Arnoux ninth in Spain, Jabouille tenth in Brazil), before second-generation Renault turbo cars took over from the RS01s.

RS10 This was actually the first of four cars, numbers RS10–12 and RS14, that first appeared at the fifth Grand Prix meeting. Designed by Michel Tétu, this was a

ground-effects car, built around a slender aluminium monocoque, with suspension comprising lower wishbones and top rocker arms and, of course, inboard springs/dampers. With twin KKK turbochargers, the EF1 developed more than 520bhp, and throttle response was improved. The outward lines were sleeker than RS01, and the cars carried large rear wings.

These Renaults were the fastest F1 cars of the year, and front-row contenders, but reliability was still suspect: there were fifteen retirements in 1979. However, one of Jabouille's three finishes in an RS10 was a victory, *and* in the French GP. Arnoux was third in that race, second in the British and US GPs and sixth in Austria. The twenty-six points scored lifted Renault to sixth place in the championship.

RE20 The new cars for 1980 had an RE (Renault Elf) prefix, and were again numbered individually, RE20–RE25. This was a developed version of RS10, with little more outright power, but improved ground effects, aerodynamics and bodies.

Engine unreliability undermined the season, but Arnoux won the Brazilian and South African GPs, while Jabouille won in Austria. The former had three other points-scoring finishes, but Jabouille had just that victory to his name, to offset eleven retirements (Arnoux retired just twice). Their thirty-eight points brought the team fourth place in the championship.

The RE20B was developed for use in the first four Grands Prix of 1981, primarily

Renault RE20 of 1980, Jean-Pierre Jabouille driving.

Renault RE30 of 1981, driven by Alain Prost.

Renault RE40 of 1983, driven by Eddie Cheever.

with a longer wheelbase. Arnoux was fifth in Argentina and twice finished eighth; Prost was third in Argentina, and retired three times.

RE30 This was a new design by Tétu, lighter and more compact than the RE20s. The claimed output of the engine was no more than 540bhp, and it drove through a Renault Type 30 gearbox that still used Hewland internals. The RE30 was designed to run without ground-effects skirts, and had to be modified when Brabham responded to the regulations with a hydro-pneumatic suspension system, which meant effective skirts when a car was up to speed. Arnoux scored twice with these cars in 1981 (fourth in France, second in Austria) and was upstaged by Prost, winner in France, Austria and Holland, second in Britain and the season's last race at Las Vegas. With the points scored with RE20Bs, Renault's total was fifty-four, earning third place in the championship.

Modifications made through 1981 were carried through to the RE30B used in 1982, when there were further changes to the front suspension, side pods and brakes (carbon-fibre brakes were tried, but not used in races). Ballast had to be carried in early races. There was no significant increase in the output of the EF1.

Prost won the first two Grands Prix, and later in the year was second in the French and Swiss GPs. Arnoux also won twice, in France and Italy, and also had a second and third to his name. But the pair also recorded seventeen retirements. Renault was third on the table again, with sixty-two points. The 'C' version was a flat-bottom car for the first races of 1983 (Prost was seventh in the first race), while Cheever retired from the two races he started in it.

RE40 This purpose-designed flat-bottom car had a carbon-fibre monocoque, double wishbone pullrod suspension at the rear, improved aerodynamics and engines giving around 650bhp (surpassed by only the TAG V6 at the end of the year).

Prost drove RE40s to win the French, Belgian, British and Austrian GPs, and scored with a third, fourth and fifth place, yet failed to take the drivers' title by two points. Cheever gained points with second place in Canada, three third places, fourth and a sixth. But there were also eleven retirements, often with turbo overheating, and Renault was second in the Constructors' Championship, with seventy-nine points. That turned out to have been its

best chance of the title, and the team could ill-afford to lose Prost in an outburst of recriminations at the end of the year.

RE50 Tétu designed another new car for 1984, and this had to be substantially reworked at mid-season, as suspension mountings failed. An alloy-block version of the EF4 engine, with Garrett AiResearch turbochargers, gave as much as 750bhp, but that year fuel-consumption rules made for problems.

In thirty-one starts, Derek Warwick and Patrick Tambay finished only twelve times (six each), but in three cases those were paper classifications as the cars were not running as races ended. Warwick was second in Belgium and Britain, Tambay in France. Together, they scored thirty-four points, and fifth place in the Constructors' Championship pointed to a Renault decline.

RE60 Tétu completed the design for a 1985 car before he left to join Ligier, but

build and development had to go ahead without his input. The first cars were overweight, but that was corrected in the mid-season RE60B. Under Dudot – the one senior technical man to serve throughout the Renault F1 programme – the EF4 engine was uprated to give 760bhp, while the EF15 was rated at 810bhp, or as much as 1,000bhp in 'qualifying trim'. Tambay finished eight races, scoring in four with third places in Portugal and Imola his best, while Warwick's best was fifth (at Monaco and Silverstone).

In the summer, Renault announced its intention to retire from Grand Prix racing at the end of the year, so through the autumn the team was already demotivated. Perhaps seventh place in the Constructors' Championship, with just sixteen points, proved that the management decision was correct?

The way ahead for Renault was as an engine supplier, and in that role its partnership with Williams was to prove very rewarding.

Rolland-Pilain

The Tours company had an erratic racing history, and its Grand Prix machines ranged from one of the last chain-drive cars to engines in the 1920s that were original, if not highly successful. Although it was operating in 1906, Rolland-Pilain did not join the French rush into Grand Prix

racing, entering the sport with *voiturettes* in 1908. It built a Grand Prix car in 1911, and in modified form this had a less than distinguished run in the 1912 race.

The cars built for the 1922–23 Grands Prix were no more successful – a 1-2 in the poorly supported 1923 Spanish GP hardly rates. The 1923 cars re-emerged in 1924 with Schmid engines and a Schmid

badge, and there were no more Grand Prix Rolland-Pilains.

1912 Rolland-Pilain thought about a car for the aborted 1909 Grand Prix, and actually built new cars for the 1911 Grand Prix de France – not the 'real' Grand Prix, but the race often referred to as the Grand Prix de Vieux Tacots ('old crocks' race).

Rolland-Pilain, 1922.

One of these 6litre cars did lead that odd 1911 event at Le Mans, but the best final placing was Gabriel's distant third.

The 1911 design was overhauled for 1912, and the Rolland-Pilain looked up to the minute, with a low bonnet line, spare wheels alongside the scuttle allowing for a pointed tail, and a less exposed cockpit than most. But the chain drive was anachronistic. The engine was a 6,272cc four-cylinder unit.

Fauquet and Pilain shared the car that finished eighth in the Grand Prix (four of the cars ahead of it were 3litre types in the concurrent *Coupe de l'Auto*); Guyot retired the other Rolland-Pilain on the first lap, with engine failure.

1922 The 2litre Grand Prix regulations, which were to remain in force for four years, brought stability, which encouraged originality. Rolland-Pilain's 1922 cars were low-built, with left-hand drive (that has been attributed to Albert Guyot's 1921 experience with Duesenberg). Chassis and suspension were normal, but there were hydraulic front brakes (cable at the rear). Grillot designed the 1,982cc straight eight with desmodromic valves, but reliability could not be guaranteed, so the cars were raced with normal valves. The claimed output of 90bhp made these engines the second most powerful in the 1922 Grand Prix.

They let the trio of veteran drivers down very early in the race: Wagner and Guyot completed two laps of the sixty, and Hémery just got to quarter-distance. Rolland-Pilain did not enter the Italian GP that turned out to be farcical. However, two improved cars were entered for the 1923 French GP. They looked cleaner, some excess weight had been shed, and the engines were rated at 100bhp.

The race was run at Tours, and failure in front of a 'home crowd' must have been doubly disappointing. Guyot did run fourth early in the race, but fell away before retiring, while Hémery completed only five laps. Guyot finished a lacklustre seventh in the Italian GP, while Delalande was unplaced. This pair then finished 1-2 in the Spanish GP, beating negligible opposition.

A third car that had been entered for the 1923 French GP failed to appear. This comprised one of the existing chassis, with a straight six that had Ernest Schmid's cuff valves. Rolland-Pilain withdrew from Grand Prix racing, and in 1924 a pair of these cars appeared as Schmids.

Rondel

Rondel Racing is recalled as an early-1970s Formula 2 team run by Ron Dennis and Neil Trundle, who had ambitions to enter Formula 1. To this end a car designed by ex-Brabham engineer Ray Jessop was laid down. Realistic financial assessments meant that when a car was almost complete the project was passed on, and it appeared in 1974 as the Token (qv). In time, Ron Dennis, became a major player in Formula 1.

Rover Special

This homely device, familiar in British historic racing for decades, appears among Grand Prix cars because it ran in two minor Formula 1 races in 1954. That was six years after it first ran, largely built with Rover production components. Three enthusiastic Rover engineers, Spencer King, Peter Wilks and George Mackie, were responsible for it, and they had a degree of company support.

An ioe Rover 75 engine with reduced bore to give a 1,996cc capacity (for Formula 2) was used, in a simple box-section chassis and Rover production independent front suspension and a de Dion rear axle.

It was run in minor races until 1951, when it was sold to Gerry Dunham, who renamed it DHS. He used it in secondary F2 races, until 1954 when it was run in two low-level F1 races, finishing fourth in a short Goodwood race. Frank Lockhart then

acquired it, and in his hands the light green car was raced in historic events through to the 1990s.

RRA

The first of three 'Richardson Racing Automobiles' specials had its origins in the 1930s, as Geoff Richardson modified the Maclure 'IFS Riley Special' out of all recognition in the late 1940s and early 1950s, with a new single-seat body, then a new chassis, an ERA engine and an Alta engine. In that form it was run in odd British second-level F1 races in 1954, when it was hardly competitive (13sec off the fastest lap time in the Silverstone International Trophy, for example) but gave an amateur entrant pleasure. It was followed in 1957 by an RRA made up of an Aston Martin Tasman chassis with a Jaguar 2.4litre straight six. This was run in minor races, and the 1957 International Trophy, when Richardson qualified it well but retired from a heat. It was later converted into an Aston Martin DB3S, or a replica of a DB3S.

The last RRA was a Cooper T43 with a Connaught version of the 2.5litre Alta engine. This came for the last year of the 2.5litre Formula 1, when Richardson finished fourteenth in a secondary race at Brands Hatch and retired from similar events at Snetterton and Oulton Park. It was also run in two Inter-Continental races in 1961.

RRA-ERA of 1950, driven by owner Geoff Richardson.

Sacha-Gordine

This was a great 'might-have-been' of the 1950s, an advanced Formula 2 car that should have appeared when F2 was the World Championship category and Ferrari dominated it with essentially simple cars.

The programme was funded by film producer Sacha Gordine, who hyphenated his name to avoid confusion with Gordini. Designer Vigna brought his experience of the Cisitalia 360 to this French venture. The car was rear-engined, with trailing link front suspension and a de Dion arrangement at the rear, with torsion bars all round. The engine was a magnesium-block 1,970cc dohc 90-degree V8, with a 190bhp target output. A five-speed gearbox was to be used.

None of this was speculative, for two cars were almost complete when Gordine called a halt, apparently realizing that the programme would bankrupt him. The low cigar-shaped car had unproven features, and obviously much development work could have been called for, but if it had run and succeeded, racing history would have been different.

Sadler

Canadian Bill Sadler competed in North American sports-car races in his Corvette V8-powered cars in the second half of the 1950s, and aspired to enter Formula 1. To that end, he embarked on the construction of a front-engined car, with a space frame, wishbones and coil springs front suspension and a swing axle system at the rear, a Maserati 250F engine and his own gearbox/final drive.

The car took shape slowly, and by 1959 it was clear that it would be obsolete when it was completed. Sensibly, Sadler abandoned the project, and turned to a *formule libre* car for North American races.

Safir

The Token RJ02 low-budget 'Cosworth kit car' of 1974 was bought by John Thorpe, renamed for his Safir Engineering company and run in two British non-championship F1 races in 1975. Tony Trimmer drove it, to last place in the Race of Champions and last place in the International Trophy at Silverstone. Safir then concentrated on a Formula 3 car.

Sauber

See pp.204–206.

Scarab

Lance Reventlow was a competent amateur driver in the sports-car racing that flourished in America in the 1950s, and visits to European constructors convinced him that all-American cars could beat the products of Modena and the small British companies. Others had similar thoughts, but Reventlow was a Woolworth heir, and he had the means. Sports cars came first in the Reventlow Automobiles Inc. programme, then in 1958 work started on a Formula 1 car to carry the Scarab name, after a beetle.

Leo Goossen, one-time Offenhauser engineer, undertook the engine – a 2,441cc four-cylinder twin-cam unit with desmodromic valve gear and fuel injection. Its development threatened to spin out through the last year of the 2.5litre Formula, so the project had to be forced along.

Renowned fabricators Troutman and Barnes built the space frame. The engine was steeply canted ahead of the cockpit, with the drive carried to the left, to a five-speed gearbox. Suspension was independent by wishbones and coil springs all round. Aircraft-style drum brakes plus a disc brake on the final drive could not be developed in time, so Girling discs were adopted, undermining Reventlow's 'all-American' approach.

The smart car finally appeared for the 1960 Monaco GP, when Reventlow and Daigh could not remotely approach a qualifying time (a 1min 39sec lap got the slowest car onto the grid, neither American could break 1min 50sec). Both qualified for the Dutch GP, but the team withdrew in a starting-money dispute, and both started in the Belgian GP, when the two cars retired with engine failure. The French GP entry was scratched, and the team returned to the USA, presumably wiser.

Daigh drove one car to a finish in 1961, in an Inter-Continental race in Britain. RAI then developed a rear-engined car for the predecessor of Formula 5000, but it was raced only once. Reventlow turned his back on motor racing.

Scarab of 1960, Lance Reventlow driving.

Peter Sauber entered racing as a driver, with a VW Beetle in very minor events, and the first racing car in his C-designated series was a sports car built around Brabham components ('C', incidentally, for his wife Christiane, in the series followed through to C18 at the end of the century). He moved on to BMW M1s, and in 1982 introduced the Ford-powered Sauber C6 Group C car. That also brought the first contacts with Mercedes-Benz engineers, and he was to abandon the BMW engine of his C7 in favour of a Mercedes turbo V8 in the C8 in 1984. Sauber-Mercedes won the sports car championship in 1989–90, and the Le Mans 24-hour Race.

As sports-car racing went into decline, Sauber looked to Formula 1 to keep his team in being, and early in 1992 he confirmed his intention to enter the premier category in 1993. The record in international sports-car racing meant that the Hilwil-based team was not received as a raw newcomer, and the point was made when one of its C12s was driven to a points-scoring finish in its maiden Grand Prix. The black cars proclaimed a Mercedes association – 'Concept by Mercedes-Benz' – and the Ilmor engines were soon to be labelled Mercedes-Benz. Then there were Ford V8s in 1995–96, followed by Ferrari V10s which Sauber developed and renamed for a major partner, Petronas.

During these years, Sauber was a solid middle-order team, never attracting top drivers and never quite threatening the established pattern – its 1993–98 Constructors' Championship positions were sixth, seventh or eighth, with points scores ranging from ten to eighteen, so the 1999 total of five points marked a downturn.

Throughout, Peter Sauber kept firm control while his partner Fritz Kaiser played a quieter role (principal sponsor Dietrich Masteshtiz has been the other major shareholder, in the name of Red Bull). Sauber Petronas Engineering is responsible for design and development. Success as a Swiss Formula 1 team is a major objective, and a challenge that has proved greater than any that Sauber faced in sports-car racing.

C12 Although Sauber personnel had no experience of Formula 1, the entry into Grand Prix racing in 1993 was convincing. Sensibly, there was an adequate acclimatization period, with a car running months before its race debut. Harvey Postlethwaite and Steve Nichols contributed some initial design work, but the C12 was essentially Leo Ress's car.

It conformed to the early 1990s pattern, with a narrow monocoque and double wishbone pushrod suspension. The engine was an Ilmor 72-degree V10 that was to carry a Sauber badge in its 'B' form later in the year, in a move that was a prelude to Mercedes-Benz badging in 1994. Sauber's own longitudinal six-speed gearbox was original, and one component that was to prove troublesome. The team took time in coming to terms with aerodynamics and suspension tuning as it visited circuits strange to it.

J.J. Lehto scored its first points in its debut race, with fifth place in the South African GP, was classified fifth in the San Marino GP and finished five other races. Karl Wendlinger's best placing was fourth in the Italian GP, and with three other placings he contributed seven points to a Constructors' Championship total of twelve, for an encouraging sixth place in Sauber's first season.

C13 Ress developed his 1993 design for a new season, and for Mercedes-badged engines. This Ilmor unit was a shortstroke version of the V10, and development during the year included pneumatic valves. However, this was to be Sauber's only season with 'Mercedes' power units. The car's body was refined in details, and there were mid-season suspension changes.

Heinz-Harald Frentzen drove a full race programme (the team missed the Monaco GP following Wendlinger's practice accident). He scored in four races, fourth in France, fifth in the Pacific GP and twice sixth. Wendlinger started well, sixth and fourth coming from his three race starts. De Cesaris took his place, contributing a sixth-place finish and eight retirements before Lehto returned for the last two races without scoring. Sauber's 1993 championship score was equalled, but in 1994 the twelve points were good for only eighth place.

C14 Mercedes's partner from 1995 was McLaren, and so that year Sauber became Ford's favoured team. Because this arrangement was concluded when Ress's design had been completed, the C14 had to be adapted for the heavier Ford-Zetec-R 75-degree V8. Balance was upset, and this was only partly countered by aerodynamic work. In other respects, the specification of the cars was similar, while outwardly there was a high nose end and, of course, there was a radical change of colours.

Frentzen was again the key driver: he scored in eight races and retired only five times. His best placing was third in Italy, there was a fourth, two fifths and four sixth places. Wendlinger was entered for the first four races, and finished just once

Sauber C13-Mercedes-Benz of 1994, Heinz-Harald Frentzen driving.

Sauber C15-V10 Ford of 1996, Heinz-Harald Frentzen driving.

before Jean-Christophe Bouillon took his place. His best placing was fifth, in Germany, and he scored one other point in his eleven Grands Prix (Wendlinger returned for the last two races). Sauber's eighteen points, its highest score, placed it seventh on the championship table.

C15 Sauber came to terms with the new Ford-Zetec-R 72-degree V10 engine in 1996 – although it was described as 'gutless' early in the season – only to have to face losing it to Stewart at the end of the year. There were handling problems with the C15, too. The make-up was largely familiar, but there was a new longitudinal semi-automatic six-speed gearbox.

Frentzen scored in three races (fourth in the Monaco and Spanish GPs), while his new team mate Johnny Herbert found his place in the team once he had taken third place at Monaco. The pair failed to finish sixteen times – a 50 per cent record. Their eleven points meant that Sauber was seventh in the championship.

C16 Ress produced a competent car for Sauber's first season with another new engine, but there was to be little development progress with the C16 in 1997. After

an off-season furore, there was agreement that the Ferrari 046 V10 was to be developed by ex-Honda, ex-Ferrari man Osamu Goto, as a Petronas engine. This was more powerful than the Ford V10 but, except in straight-line speed, this was not translated into better performance. There seemed to be aerodynamic shortcomings that were never fully ironed out, and once again Ress produced an understeering car.

Herbert was the number one driver, and responded by scoring six times, notably third in Hungary and fourth in Argentina and Belgium. Nicola Larini contributed a point in the first Grand Prix, but left after four more Grands Prix. Morbidelli crashed heavily in his second race for Sauber, came back for the last six Grands Prix but failed to score. Norbert Fontana stood in for him, but failed to score in his four races. Once again Sauber was seventh in the Constructors' Championship, this time with sixteen points.

C17 While it had to have a new monocoque to meet new regulations, this was another evolutionary car, but this time a development agenda was followed through the season, with considerable effort put into aerodynamic work. Sauber

took time to come to terms with the grooved tyres called for in 1998. Perhaps later than desirable, a revised V10 was introduced in the autumn, and then it still needed development time – Sauber habitually did not respond rapidly to change in most departments.

Before the season opened, team manager Max Welti left, Peter Sauber effectively took his place, and Ress became technical director with an enlarged staff. Herbert scored a point in the first Grand Prix, but after that his best finish was seventh and he was outshone by Jean Alesi. He was third in Belgium, twice fifth and once sixth. Sauber was sixth in the championship, but with just ten points, when progress might have been expected as the team matured.

C18 The 1999 chassis was developed from the C17, although few parts were carried over, and Sauber claimed that twenty weeks of wind-tunnel work had been completed before the season. Like the C17, it had torsion bar springing, mounted horizontally, with double wishbone suspension. The 80-degree Ferrari V10 designated Sauber Petronas SPE 03A came into full service. It was lighter and

Sauber C18-V10 Ferrari of 1999, Jean Alesi driving.

had a lower installed height, and drove through a new and more compact seven-speed semi-automatic gearbox.

The season was disappointing. Alesi scored single points in two Grands Prix, Pedro Diniz single points in three. Although Sauber was eighth in the Constructors' Championship, its five-point score was its lowest since it entered Grand Prix racing.

C19 Although merely a logical evolution on the C18 layout of 1999, Sauber's 2000 F1 car was considerably lighter, aerodynamically neater, and better packaged under its skin.

Powered by a late-1999 version of Ferrari's V10 engine (the 80-degree version, therefore, not the 90-degree version used in the official Ferrari F1 cars of 2000), the C19 also used a brand-new, slimline, longitudinal seven-speed transmission.

Visually, this was a rather square-rig car (on McLaren/Stewart lines), though aerodynamicist Seamus Mullarky had been able to do a good deal more wind-tunnel development than on previous models.

In 2000 Sauber performed much as they had done in 1999, and 1998 ... competent mid-field runners early in the sea-

son, a clear lack of ongoing development by mid-year, and a gradual slippage towards the back of grids in the autumn.

No podium positions, just a handful of points (all of them to new recruit Mika Salo's credit), and few smiling faces from within. All this presumably meant that, if

these were late-1999 'works' engines from Ferrari, then the rest of the car was not up to scratch.

Salo obviously thought the same, jumping ship at the end of only one season, to join the nascent Toyota operation for 2001 and beyond.

Schmid

Dr Ernest Schmid acquired two of the 1923 Rolland-Pilain Grand Prix cars, to demonstrate his 'valveless' engine in racing. This was a cuff-valve type, with moving segments to open and close inlet and exhaust ports; the type had first been exhibited by Peugeot in 1919, and it led to the Grand Prix Schmid sometimes being listed as the 'SS' (*sans soupapes*). The Grand Prix version was a 1,978cc straight six, and its 1924 output was stated to be 100bhp, hardly competitive power, especially as the Schmid car was overweight. The cars were rebuilt at Annecy, in most respects retaining the Rolland-Pilain chassis and running gear, with bulkier bodies.

Only one started in the 1924 French GP, as Foresti crashed in practice, leaving Goux to take the start. He made an early pit stop to look at the engine and then ran at the tail

of the field until he retired on the twentieth of the thirty-five laps. The pair also retired from the Spanish GP, then the Grand Prix career of Dr Schmid's cars ended when Goux and Foresti were fifth and sixth in the Italian GP, well behind four Alfa Romeos.

Th. Schneider

Théophile Schneider entered racing with a pair of cars run in the *Coupe de l'Auto* section of the 1912 Grand Prix. These were little more than tuned versions of the company's touring models, but then the objective of the three Schneider Grand Prix efforts was sometimes felt to be to demonstrate reliability rather than aim or hope for victories. The 1912 cars had 2,993cc T-head engines and a combination of short wheelbase, small bonnet and large scuttle radiator making for a curious appearance.

Croquet placed one fourth in the *Coupe*, behind three Sunbeams, and seventh overall in the Grand Prix. Champoiseau retired the other car early in the race.

Th. Schneider was encouraged to enter the 1913 Grand Prix with purpose-built cars. These had 5,501cc side-valve engines, conventional chassis and suspension, wire wheels that looked very spindly, and better overall lines than the 1912 cars, largely as the radiators were less prominent.

These cars were not notably fast, but they were reliable and finished seventh (Champoiseau, after an off-course excursion and almost an hour behind the winning Peugeot), ninth (Thomas) and tenth (Croquet). Gabriel retired on the fourth lap. Remarkably, the three classified Schneiders ran through without changing tyres, which seems to have been a Grand Prix 'first'.

In 1914 Schneider tried again, running a trio of cars with 4,441cc sohc four-cylinder engines and orthodox chassis, transmission and rear-wheel and transmission brakes. Champoiseau was again the best driver, lapping two or three minutes off the leader's times (in a 20-minute lap), and fifteenth of the twenty-three cars that reached half-distance. He finished ninth, while Gabriel and Juvanon retired just before half-distance, both with engine failure.

Th. Schneider then disappeared from the Grand Prix world; before the company disappeared altogether in 1931 a few of its sporting cars were raced.

Scirocco

American Hugh Powell, young and rich, took over Emeryson in 1962, at the behest of his guardian Tony Settember, who had racing ambitions. For 1963 an 'improved' version of the 1962 F1 Emeryson was devised by Hugh Aiden-Jones, with some chassis strengthening, more attractive bodywork and, above all, a BRM V8.

Two cars were completed, but normally the Scirocco-Powell team ran one. Settember crashed out of an unimpressive debut race in the Belgian GP (on paper he was classified eighth). He retired early in the French GP; both cars (Ian Burgess in the second) also retired in the British GP and Settember failed to qualify for the Italian GP.

There were finishes in non-championship races. Settember's second place in the Austrian GP was not, in fact, impressive, for winner Brabham lapped him five times and there was only one other finisher. Burgess was a modest eighth in the Oulton Park Gold Cup, while Settember retired. Hugh Powell called a halt, and the cars were sold.

André Pilette acquired one for the Ecurie Scirocco Belge, and installed a Coventry Climax FWMV engine. He was the slowest qualifier for the 1964 Belgian GP and completed eleven laps in the race, and failed to qualify for the German GP. Pilette also entered non-championship F1 races, finishing in three.

SEFAC

From a French point of view, prospects for the 750kg (1,654lb) Formula that came into force in 1934 were not encouraging. There was Bugatti, and the T59 was a pretty car, but there was a realization that

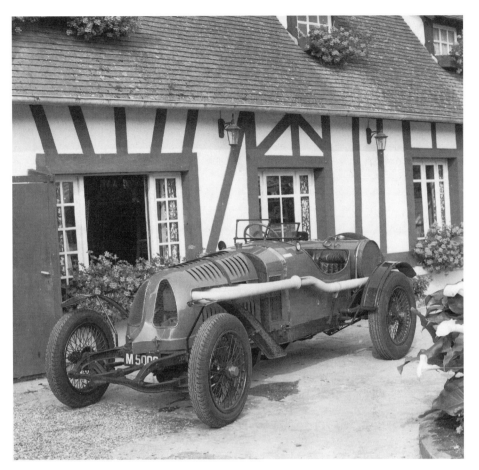

Th. Schneider of 1913.

something more would be needed to uphold national prestige. This led a group of patriotic enthusiasts to form the 'Société d'Etude et de Fabrication d'Automobiles de Course', SEFAC, to build a Grand Prix car. This was to be designed by Emile Petit (engine) and Edmond Vareille (chassis), both former Salmson designers. The first car was promised for the 1934 French GP, when it was anticipated that another member of the group, Raymond Sommer, would drive it.

The SEFAC did appear for the 1935 French GP, when Marcel Lehoux completed a few practice laps before it was withdrawn, for the most ardent officials could hardly hide the fact that it did not meet the maximum weight regulation, by a wide margin.

The car had an orthodox chassis of main channel-section members, with an odd independent front suspension by forward-facing radius arms and coil springs, and a live rear axle. Petit's engine was a 2,771cc parallel eight, comprising two blocks of four

cylinders side by side, with camshafts rotating in opposite directions and linked by gears. There were twin overhead camshafts, and another approach to desmodromic valves, which were positively closed. A large supercharger was mounted behind the engine. The claimed output was 250bhp. An offset Cotal electro-magnetic clutch was used. The body was plain.

After the 1935 fiasco the car was put away, only to be brought out again in 1938, as it conformed to a new formula. Save for a semi-streamlined nose it was little changed, and the power/weight ratio – 250bhp/931kg (2,053lb) – meant that it could hardly be competitive.

Early in the year it was run in the Pau GP, and retired. In practice for the French GP at Reims Eugène Chabaud was not given a time, and started from the back of the grid. For two laps the SEFAC lost ground to the Talbots running at the tail, then its engine gave out. It was entered for the 1939 French GP, with little expectation that it would actually appear.

Ten years later it reappeared as the Dommartin, with an attractive new body and the engine in unsupercharged form, bored out to 3,619cc. It was entered for the French GP, but true to form it did not turn up. Almost fifty years on, and without its engine, it posed problems for a British restorer.

Serenissima

Scuderia Serenissima was twice connected with Formula 1 projects in the 1960s, and the first materialized as the hapless 1963 ATS, given that name rather than Serenissima as Giorgio Volpi withdrew his financial support before it was completed.

In 1966 Bruce McLaren briefly used a 2,996cc Serenissima V8 in an M2B, and despite its output being well below the publicized 300bhp, he scored his marque's first championship point with this car, in the British GP. Three years later, a Serenissima F1 car was reported to be well advanced, and described (a car with conventional monocoque and suspension, and a 380bhp V8). It was even expected at the 1969 Italian GP, but it did not appear there, or anywhere else, and in 1970 Serenissima faded away.

Shadow

See pp.209–210.

Shannon

This one-off almost completed one lap in a Grand Prix. It was created by Aiden Jones and Paul Emery for the first year of the 3litre Formula, 1966, around an aluminium monocoque chassis and a Coventry Climax FPE 'Godiva' V8. This had been laid down as a 2.5litre unit for 1954, when it was abandoned. Emery dusted it down, enlarged it, and modified it to run on the obligatory pump fuel. The car somehow looked tired before its debut, in practice for the 1966 British GP.

Trevor Taylor must have found the effort amateurish after his seasons with Lotus and BRP, but there were two slower cars on the Grand Prix grid. He retired the Shannon on lap 1, with engine failure or a split fuel tank. It later turned up in Formula 3 guise!

Sima-Violet

Marcel Violet built and raced small cars in the 1920s, and produced a novel Grand Prix car in 1926. He pursued his lightweight approach tenaciously, but pointlessly, for the car was reported to weigh just over 500kg (1,102lb) for a season when the Grand Prix minimum weight limit was 700kg (1,543lb). There was a tubular backbone chassis and transverse leaf front suspension, both a little reminiscent of the first Tatra three years earlier. The driver was seated low to the right. The engine was a 1,484cc flat-four two stroke, said to produce 100bhp, but perhaps delivered two-thirds of that. A four-speed gearbox was in unit with the back axle, and there was no differential. Nor were there adequate resources in the SIMA bank. The entry for the French GP was withdrawn – perhaps unfortunately, for that was the farcical race with a grid comprising just three Bugattis, and as one of those retired M. Violet's creation would have been at least third if it had lasted beyond half-distance.

SEFAC of 1938.

Don Nichols's Advanced Vehicles Systems first racing car appeared in the 1970 CanAm sports-car series, named UOP Shadow for its sponsor, Universal Oil Products. Two years later an AVS base was set up in Britain, to build Formula 1 cars and race them. Initially the UOP title was used, but this was soon discarded and the cars were run as Shadows. Nichols's principal associates were Jackie Oliver (who had raced the CanAm car), Alan Rees and designer Tony Southgate.

With one exception, the cars were straightforward Cosworth-engined types, and the team learned lessons from the first and produced competitive follow-up cars. There were enormous setbacks in fatal accidents to drivers Peter Revson and Tom Pryce, while finance was marginal, especially as UOP support was withdrawn at the end of 1975.

A moment of real success came when Alan Jones won the 1977 Austrian GP in a Shadow. But then Nichols's lieutenants defected to form the Arrows team. There was little consolation for Nichols in a High Court judgement in his favour, finding that the first F1 Arrows was too similar to Southgate's last Shadow design and ordering its withdrawal.

Nichols struggled on, and the team survived into 1980. It had contested 104 Grands Prix when it was sold to Teddy Yip. In the Constructors' Championship it had generally achieved lowly placings, seventh in 1977 being its best, and its total points score in seven seasons was 67.5. It was a brave try.

DN1 The first black car looked the part, with a fine nose running back to 'Coke bottle' lines. Double wishbone front suspension followed the early-1970s norm, while at the rear there were lower wishbones, top links and radius arms. So far, so good, but the monocoque was not stiff enough, and Southgate had no previous experience with the DFV engine, so did not take its notorious vibrations into account. Stiffening had to be added, notably in the car Graham Hill bought for his fledgling team.

George Follmer scored points in the team's first two races, finishing sixth in the South African GP and third in Spain, but failed to score again that year (in thirteen starts, he retired seven times). Jackie Oliver finished four Grands Prix, finishing third in Canada towards the end of the season. Graham Hill entered his white

Embassy DN1 for a dozen Grands Prix, failed to qualify once and finished six races, with his best placing ninth in Belgium. Shadow was eighth in the Constructors' Championship, with nine points – a reasonable start for a new outfit.

In 1974 Jean-Pierre Jarier started two races in DN1s, and failed to finish in either.

DN3 Southgate modified his first Shadow design for the 1974 car that had a stiffer monocoque, longer wheelbase and wider track, and outwardly an even longer slim nose and more prominent engine airbox (on which the stars and stripes was displayed). The Cosworth-Hewland combination was retained.

Peter Revson retired from the first two Grands Prix in 1974, then was fatally injured in practice for the South African GP. Brian Redman took his place for three races (his only finish was seventh in the Spanish GP), and Bertil Roos retired in his native Sweden. Then Tom Pryce joined Shadow, to finish three times in eight attempts, and score a point. Meanwhile, Jarier led the team after Revson's accident. He finished seven times, was third at Monaco and fifth in Sweden. The season brought seven points for Shadow, and eighth place in the championship again.

A DN3B that incorporated some DN5 parts was run in Argentina and Brazil in 1975. Pryce failed to finish either race.

DN5 The design was further refined for the 1975 car – the specification was almost identical – with changes in areas such as aerodynamics and weight distribution. This was the first wholly competi-

tive Shadow, but the team did not gain full rewards with it.

Jarier and Pryce both qualified among the top cars at some events, both led a Grand Prix, and the Welsh driver won the non-championship Race of Champions. In the Grands Prix, however, Jarier scored only once, finishing fourth in the 'half-points' Spanish GP, and retired eleven times. On the other hand Pryce retired only seven times, was third in the Austrian GP, fourth in Germany, and sixth three times. Shadow was sixth in the championship, with 9.5 points.

DN5Bs had to be run for most of 1976, when Jarier finished twelve of the sixteen Grands Prix but failed to score a point (his best placing was seventh at Long Beach). He was fifth behind Pryce in the International Trophy at Silverstone. Pryce scored well – third in Brazil and fourth in Britain in DN5Bs – and he retired only twice before the DN8 came in. So DN5Bs contributed seven points to Shadow's total in 1976, when there was another eighth place on the final table.

One of these cars was driven by Renzo Zorzi in Argentina and Brazil in 1977, and he scored his only World Championship point at Interlagos.

DN7 This one-off was built in 1975 for the Matra MS73 V12 that rated at 500bhp compared with the 470bhp credited to the DFV, and was felt to be an ideal power unit for fast circuits. In other respects the car followed DN5 lines, even to the Hewland TL200 gearbox. Fuel tank capacity was increased by 130litre – not enough for the thirsty V12, it was suggested.

Shadow DN5-Ford of 1977, Renzo Zorzi driving.

The car was never developed, or proved; Jarier retired it from two races, and after the second of those, at Monza, French self-interest dictated that a Matra engine should henceforth be supplied exclusively to Ligier.

DN8 This was intended to be the 1976 car, but a tight financial situation meant that the first was not ready until the summer of that year, and a second car did not appear on a circuit until 1977. The basic design was by Southgate, and was in line with his earlier Shadows, but the work was completed by Dave Wass. It was a little lighter and narrower, but the specification could almost have applied to the earlier cars. Outwardly there was a humped bonnet cover, but that went when Southgate returned to oversee development in 1977, and contributed neater oil and water cooling arrangements.

Tom Pryce's fatal accident overshadowed the early part of the season, Alan Jones's victory in Austria lifted spirits. The Australian was also third in Italy and sixth at Monaco. Other drivers were Oliver (fifth in the Race of Champions, ninth in the Spanish GP), Patrese (sixth in Japan, four other finishes, four retirements), Merzario (retired in Holland) and Jarier (ninth in Canada). Shadow scored its highest points total, twenty-three, but was still only seventh on the championship.

Clay Regazzoni started three early 1978 races in a DN8, placing fifth in Brazil, while Hans Stuck started in two (neither driver qualified in South Africa).

DN9 For the second time Southgate laid down a car, and left it for another to complete, this time John Baldwin. The DN9 was necessarily a ground-effects car, and the outward continuity of the Shadow lines was sacrificed to a more angular shape. There were now lower wishbones and top rocker arms at the front, with upper and lower links and radius arms at the rear. In this car the DFV drove through a Hewland FGA400 five-speed gearbox.

Neither driver finished in the DN9's debut race, the Silverstone International Trophy. The Grand Prix debut should have come at Long Beach, but Stuck failed to qualify, while at Monaco Regazzoni failed to qualify. After that, Regazzoni scored just once in eleven races, with fifth place in Sweden. Stuck also finished fifth in one race, in Britain, and had a run of retirements in the last six Grands Prix. Shadow's eleventh place in the championship, with just six points, accurately suggested a team in decline. Incidentally, Danny Ongais twice failed to qualify a DN9 entered by Interscope.

Richard Owen and John Gentry were responsible for the 'B' modification for 1979. Revised suspension and side pods were the main changes, and efforts to create more downforce with further side pod revisions came quite late in the year.

The season brought little joy to the team. Elio de Angelis did finish sixth in the Race of Champions (he retired from the other non-championship race, at Imola), and he did score Shadow's only points, three at Watkins Glen that gave the mar-

que tenth place in the championship. He had two other top-ten finishes, but also a DNQ and seven retirements. Jan Lammers's best finish was ninth, he failed to qualify three times and retired five times.

DN11 There was a pair of new cars for the opening race of 1980, to a design started by John Gentry and completed by Vic Morris. This DN11 had bottom wishbone and top rocker arm suspension all round, the rear being carried over from the DN9B, and there was a needle nose.

The car was not competitive. Geoff Lees qualified once in five attempts, and went on to finish thirteenth in South Africa. David Kennedy did not qualify once in seven attempts, Stefan Johansson failed twice. There was no effort to improve the cars after Yip took over, and in any case the team did not complete a full season.

DN12 This car was put in hand hastily, as shortcomings in the DN11 became apparent. Vic Morris and Chuck Graeminger designed this not unattractive short-wheelbase car, but it was rushed into service with no development. A DN12 first appeared at the 1980 Belgian and Monaco GPs, when Lees did not qualify. There were two at the Spanish GP, entered by Theodore Shadow, and neither finished. When Lees and Kennedy both failed to reach the grid for the French GP Teddy Yip withdrew the team for the rest of the year.

A DN12 was to run as a Theodore in the 1981 South African GP, in a footnote to the story of Don Nichols's Shadow team.

Shadow DN8-Ford of 1976, Tom Pryce driving.

Simplex

The famous American marque's cars were sometimes seen in the Vanderbilt Cup races, and once in the Grand Prize. The first was Fred Croker's 14.7litre '75' in the 1904 Vanderbilt race, when the chassis that had been excessively lightened for hill climbs failed on the Long Island road circuit. There were retirements for 10litre '50hp' cars in the 1908 and 1910 Vanderbilt races. Louis Disbrow ran an updated 1910 '90' in the 1914 Vanderbilt Cup, finishing eighth, and in the 1915 Grand Prize, when he was sixth.

Simtek

Nick Wirth's Simtek Research company brought design and engineering expertise, as well as experience in research work for the FIA, to its first car. This direct entry into Formula 1 was an enormous challenge, but that seemed to have been met as it moved into a second season, with a tragedy behind it and the odd top-ten finish as some encouragement. In its second season, with a car drawing benefits from the 1994 experience, Simtek seemed poised to make real progress. But a major sponsorship deal was not finalized, and Simtek struggled on with mounting losses until it was put into voluntary receivership in the early summer of 1995.

S941 The design of this conventional 1994 car with distinctive lines was attributed to Nick Wirth. The team had to accept second-best in its engines, outmoded Ford HB 75-degree V8s. Xtrac six-speed

Shannon-V8 Climax of 1966.

transverse gearboxes were used. Double wishbone pushrod suspension was fitted all round, high-mounted at the front with the aim of providing a clean airflow.

Drivers who brought finance were welcome. David Brabham served through the whole 1994 season, qualifying for every race, but retiring from ten; his best final placing was tenth, in Spain. Roland Ratzenberger started only once in three attempts (placing eleventh in Japan) before he was fatally injured in an Imola qualifying session accident. Andrea Montermini tried once, and wrote off a car in practice in Spain. Jean-Marc Gounon showed

promise, finished four times in seven races and gained Simtek's highest placing, ninth in the French GP. Schiattarella had two pointless outings, Inoue one.

S951 The 1995 car looked similar and was equally straightforward, as the design was based on the first Simtek by Paul Crooks. This time Cosworth ED engines drove though Benetton six-speed gearboxes, and an arrangement resulted from a deal to run Benetton's test driver, Jos Verstappen. Although he retired from the first three Grands Prix, Verstappen showed the

Simtek S941-Ford of 1994, Jean-Marc Gounon driving.

potential of the car in qualifying sessions, after the first outing, when the car was very new. His only race placing was twelfth in Spain. Domenico Schiattarella was back, and he finished ninth in the Argentine GP. Neither driver could take the restart at Monaco, and the team did not appear at the next Grand Prix. Simtek had entered twenty-one Grands Prix, and shown promise – but that was not enough with a thin budget.

Singer

Five British companies entered teams for the *Coupe de l'Auto* race within the 1912 Grand Prix, among them Singer, which had five years of racing behind it. The car had no really outstanding features, and behind its large pointed radiator it was not the most elegant in the race. It was also substantially overweight, at more than 1,100kg (2,425lb) when the minimum weight for these 3litre cars was 800kg (1,764lb). The T-head four-cylinder 2,986cc engine drove through a four-speed gearbox.

At quarter-distance in the race, Frank Rollason was sixteenth of forty-seven starters, and ahead of some full Grand Prix cars. But his race ended after another lap when a con rod broke. Bramwell Haywood was starting to climb the order, and was twenty-third on lap 5 when his race ended against a tree that broke the external gear and brake levers.

Sizaire-Naudin

Another marque that briefly appears in Grand Prix history because it ran a team in that 1912 *Coupe de l'Auto*, Sizaire-Naudin had been enormously successful in Edwardian *voiturette* racing. The 1912 *Coupe* entry was designed by Georges Sizaire, one of the brothers whose name was coupled with Louis Naudin in the company title, with Causan responsible for the engine. The car had odd lines, with the radiator apart from the separately enclosed engine, and a long, tapered tail. There was sliding pillar and transverse leaf spring front suspension and a combined gearbox/rear axle, and like most *Coupe* entries it had wire wheels. The engine was a 2,982cc four-cylinder 16-valve unit, driving through a four-speed gearbox. This was another overweight car.

There were also suggestions that it was underpowered, but Georges Sizaire was seventh overall on lap sixteen (of twenty). He

lost one place on the next lap, then retired when his car shed a wheel. The other two cars were not prominent, Naudin's engine failing on lap 7 and Schweitzer's on lap10.

Spirit

John Wickham and one-time McLaren and March designer Gordon Coppuck formed Spirit Racing in 1981, with encouragement and assistance from Honda and Bridgestone, to contest the Formula 2 championship. They moved up to Formula 1 in 1983, bringing Honda back to the Grand Prix scene, in a move that proved to be a prelude to a significant and successful period for the Japanese company, albeit not with Spirit after that first exploratory season. Spirit failed to score points in its 1983 F1 half-season, but the engine was proved, and Honda established its association with Williams.

At least Honda helped financially Spirit to continue in Formula 1, as the 1984 car had to be reworked to accept an alternative engine at short notice, when the 101 had been designed. Inadequate funds meant that Spirit struggled through the 1984 season, but lasted only to the spring of 1985. Spirit Motorsport later ran a Formula 3000 team.

201 Two of Spirit's F2 cars were converted for the Honda RA163-E turbocharged V6, the first as a test and development car, the second to be raced in six Grands Prix in the second half of 1983. In F2 form the 201

was neat and attractive; for Formula 1, wide side pods and extravagant three-tier staggered rear aerofoils mounted on large end plates made it look outlandish. There was lower wishbone and top rocker arm suspension all round. Some 600bhp was claimed for the KKK-turbocharged engine (it was by no means the most powerful turbo engine in 1983), and a Hewland gearbox was used.

First race for the car was the Race of Champions, when Stefan Johansson retired it early. A lighter 201C was built for Spirit's first Grand Prix, the British race, when it was qualified in mid-grid, briefly ran tenth, then retired with turbo failure. In his other five Grands Prix, Johansson retired twice and his best finish was seventh, in Holland.

101 This was purpose-designed for the Honda V6 for a full 1984 season, but it then had to be revised to take the Hart 415T, rated at 600bhp that year (a Cosworth DFV had to be used for one meeting, when a Hart engine was not available). The rest of the specification followed 1983 lines, but with angled radiators in place of the large side pods it was a better looking car.

Mauro Baldi was entered in the first six and last two Grands Prix, and he finished in three of them; he had one other finish, one DNQ, and three retirements. Huub Rothengatter failed to qualify the car when it was run with a DFV, and then had two classified finishes in seven starts, the best being eighth at Monza.

The car was revised to 'D' specification for 1985, primarily with changes to the

Spirit 101-Honda of 1983, driven by Mauro Baldi.

front suspension and radiators. Baldi started in three Grands Prix, but failed to finish any of them. The entry for the Monaco GP was withdrawn, marking the end of another Formula 1 effort that deserved to succeed.

Stanley-BRM

The last of the BRM Formula 1 line, the ineffectual P207 was the only new car to be introduced after the original company was put into liquidation when Rubery Owen support was withdrawn in 1974. A P201 was also run spasmodically, as Louis Stanley made grand statements and the team slipped towards sad but predictable oblivion. These cars are described with the other BRMs.

Stebro

The possibility of adapting Formula Junior designs for Grand Prix cars was obviously tempting in the early 1960s, for construction was similar and could be modified for an appropriate engine and transmission, larger tanks and so on – after all, there was the Lotus 18 example. Those tempted ranged from André Pilette, who looked to the possibility of an F1 version of the Merlyn Mk 3, to Ausper which envisaged changes to its FJ car to take the Clisby dohc 1,476cc 120-degree V6 (it seems a pity that a basic flaw in the engine ruled that out). Canadian Peter Broeker took his FJ Mk IV Stebro as the basis for a Formula 1 car that was raced in one Grand Prix – and finished one place away from scoring a point.

This Stebro Motors entry in the 1963 US GP was a low space-frame car, with a Martin-prepared Ford 105E engine. The promise of a performance that it held out was confirmed in practice: Graham Hill took pole in 1min 13.4sec, Broeker's back-of-the-grid time was 1min 28.6sec. For most of the race he ran last, but survived while others retired, to be classified seventh, completing 88 of the 110 laps. The F1 Stebro was not seen again.

Stewart

Stewart Grand Prix entered the Formula 1 arena in 1997, when it became established as a serious contender. It did not win races, but if not reliable, its car was competitive. For a team started from scratch, that was

Stanley-BRM Type 207 of 1975, Teddy Pilette driving.

perhaps achievement enough. The Stewarts – Jackie and Paul – had decided against buying their way into Formula 1 by taking over an existing team.

Maturity came in the third season, when there was a Grand Prix victory and Stewart Grand Prix was a solid fourth in the Constructors' Championship. Only one other team launched in the 1990s won a Grand Prix in that decade, and it took Jordan eight seasons. But Stewart's third Formula 1 season was also its last, for at the behest of Ford, which had taken control, it was to be transformed as Jaguar Racing for 2000.

Jackie Stewart had been ever-present in the background while Paul Stewart Racing was successful in minor single-seater categories in Formula 3, and as the Grand Prix team was announced late in 1996, he became Executive Chairman while son Paul took the Managing Director title (for the third year he became Deputy Chairman while David Ring briefly became Managing Director). Paul largely created the team's structure. The blue ovals on the cars made the point that this was also Ford's favoured team, and in 1999 Ford's team. There must have been times in the first season when the Cosworth commitment that came with Ford was an embarrassment.

Jackie Stewart always maintained that the second season would be difficult, and

it was. Stewart Grand Prix and Cosworth learned, and worked closely. There was a personnel shake-out.

In 1999 Stewart drivers scored points ten times (in eight races), and Johnny Herbert won the European GP. There was Stewart family delight that the team had won while it still carried its name, for Ford was in control and weeks earlier the rumours that SGP would become a Jaguar team had been confirmed at the Frankfurt Motor Show.

SF1 The white cars with carefully integrated sponsor colours that stood out on 1997 grids were designed by Alan Jenkins. The SF1 broke no new ground in its make-up, with a carbon-fibre monocoque that had an important aerodynamic role (and was manufactured by SGP personnel) and double wishbone pushrod suspension all round. The Ford Zetec-R 2,998cc 72-degree V10 was not the most potent F1 power plant, and constant attempts to update it meant that some development work was carried out in the field. It drove through a Stewart/Xtrac longitudinal semi-automatic six-speed gearbox.

The 1997 season was notable for one race result, and for twenty-five retirements (twenty-six if a restart DNS is added). Many were due to engine failures. Rubens Barrichello scored the teams six points when he

Stewart SF1-Ford of 1997, Rubens Barrichello driving.

SGP was to run a separate test team from its new base in 1998.

This team with high aspirations saw its cars finish just twelve times in 1998. Barrichello finished six races, and was twice fifth. Magnussen started seven races, finished three, and scored a point in the last one before he was replaced. Verstappen started nine races, and finished three (best placing twelfth). Stewart was eighth in the championship, with five points.

SF3 Alan Jenkins and aerodynamicist Eghbal Hamidy left just before the 1999 car was announced, when Gary Anderson (ex-Jordan) took over as Technical Director and Darren Davis became responsible for aerodynamics. The awkward timing of the changes could have made new car development difficult, but things 'came good'. The SF3 was run before the end of 1998, and much was new, although the shape was only subtly different, for example at the nose. The monocoque was stiffer and stronger. The engine was Cosworth's all-new Ford CR-1, a 2,998cc 72-degree V10 that was lighter than the Zetec-R – weighing less than 100kg (220lb) – and smaller in every dimension, length, height and cross-section. There was a pressurized cooling system, making for smaller radiators. The gearbox had a magnesium casing.

In only its third season, the team lived up to Jackie Stewart's hopes, and Ford's expectations. In 1999 its drivers scored ten times, in eight races, and its scores were spread through the season. Barrichello was third in the San Marino, French and European GPs, fourth once and fifth three times. Johnny Herbert seemed to settle in slowly, first scored with fifth place in the Canadian GP and was third in the first Malaysian GP late

finished second at Monaco, in that most important showcase race for teams and sponsors. Beyond that he was classified just twice. In that respect, Jan Magnussen did better, finishing five times (his best was seventh at Monaco). In its maiden season, Stewart Grand Prix was ninth in the Constructors' Championship.

SF2 Jenkins's second F1 Stewart was similar to his first in many respects, and visually there are details to distinguish it, in the nose, the side pods and so on. The new and lighter Zetec-R V10 for this car did not run until the end of 1997, and it still needed development time as the 1998 season opened. Stewart's six-speed gearbox needed even more time. This slender longitudinal 'box had a carbon-fibre casing that served to reduce the weight bias to the rear, but in return for this small advantage it gave disproportionate trouble (ten retirements were attributed to the transmission in 1998). There were also software problems. Ancillaries were repositioned, to the benefit of weight distribution and allowing the rear bodywork to be narrower between the rear wheels. Incidentally,

Stewart SF3-Ford of 1999.

Stewart SF3-Ford of 1999, Rubens Barrichello driving.

for the 1912 race. These had neat slim bodies, with the riding mechanic's seat staggered partly beside the driver's seat to cut down frontal area, a tapered tail, and steel wheels that resembled the old 'artillery' type and detracted from the car's appearance. The engine was a 2,986cc four-cylinder side-valve unit, and a four-speed gearbox was used.

Four cars were run in the Grand Prix, and one retired before half-distance with engine failure. But at that stage, the others were fourth, fifth and sixth overall, with only three full Grand Prix cars ahead of them. They were, of course, 1-2-3 in the Coupe class, and that position was held to the end. Overall, Rigal, Resta and Médinger finished 3-4-5, and Victor Rigal was only 40 minutes down on the 7.6litre Peugeot in 14 hours' racing.

in the season. Before that he had won the European GP at the Nürburgring, giving Stewart Grand Prix its first victory. The team was fourth in the Constructors' Championship, with thirty-six points.

Earlier in September, and SF3 had appeared at the Frankfurt Motor Show in a tentative green Jaguar colour scheme, with no Stewart or Ford badges.

Sunbeam

Sunbeam cars were not seen in racing before 1910, but significantly that year Louis Coatalen's overhead-valve engine was tested in a Sunbeam Brooklands car. There was a hesitant first move into International racing in 1911, then in the following year a resounding triumph in the *Coupe de l'Auto*, which was coupled with third, fourth and fifth places overall in the Grand Prix.

Full Grand Prix cars came in 1913, when a third place in the French race seemed less impressive, and there was another good finish in the 1914 Grand Prix, in some ways the greatest of all pre-First World War races. That year the first Sunbeam appeared in top-flight American races, too.

There was a return to Grand Prix racing in 1922, a year later than intended, in the confused Sunbeam Talbot Darracq situation. The 1922 car was designed by Ernest Henry, who seemed to have lost his touch. But the famous 'Fiat in green paint' model came in time for 1923 – one of the Type 804 designers, Vincent Bertarione, had been induced to collaborate in the design of the

Sunbeam – and Segrave drove one to score the first British victory in a Grand Prix.

It was not repeated in the French race with the sophisticated 1924 car, but Divo did drive one to win the San Sebastian GP, effectively the Spanish GP, and there was a third place in the French GP in 1925. That year, Sunbeam's approach to the Grand Prix was half-hearted, and it was the last year that it contested the premier category; it had briefly entered sports-car racing, but tended to concentrate on record cars for a while, then turned away from motor sport until it re-entered mainline competition in rallies in the 1950s.

1912 Sunbeam entered a single ugly 2,412cc car in the 1911 *Coupe de l'Auto*. it failed to finish, but led Coatalen towards a serious effort, and lay down a team of cars

1913 Coatalen's car for the 1913 Grand Prix was similar to the 1912 Coupe type, obviously with a larger engine, a 4,479cc side-valve straight six (100bhp was the claimed output). The fuel consumption regulations called for a bolster tank, otherwise the Sunbeam was a slender and neat car. There was a four-speed gearbox, and no differential. Chassis and suspension were as conventional as in 1912, and there were brakes to the rear wheels only.

Two of the four cars finished the Grand Prix, third (Chassagne) and sixth (Resta); Guinness crashed, and Caillois's fuel tank was ruptured. Marquis ran one of these cars in the USA in 1914, retiring from the Vanderbilt Cup with rear axle failure and crashing out of the Grand Prize when he was leading. Two also ran in the Indianapolis 500 that year, with modified

The Sunbeam Grand Prix team of 1912.

engines: one retired when a wheel collapsed, Harry Grant was seventh in the other.

1914 The engine of the 1914 Grand Prix car closely resembled the 1913 Peugeot unit, in elements from its gear-driven twin overhead camshafts to its dry-sump lubrication. It was a 4,441cc long-stroke four-cylinder unit, driving through a four-speed gearbox. In its lines, the car resembled the 1913 type, even to the bolster fuel tank. However, wire wheels were used. Coatalen stuck with the trusted rear-wheel and transmission brakes arrangement.

Only one Sunbeam finished, driven into fifth place, 20min behind the winning Mercedes by Dario Resta. The engines failed on the other team cars (driven by Guinness and Chassagne).

Two of the 1914 Grand Prix cars were fitted with 4.9litre dohc straight-six engines for racing in the USA, where one was fourth in the 1916 Indianapolis 500.

1921 In 1920 the STD combine – Sunbeam, Talbot, Darracq – was created, and it entered two Sunbeams, two Talbots and three Talbot-Darracqs for the 1921 French GP. These were all identical, with 2,973cc 108bhp straight eights, and the cars that started in the race looked old-fashioned alongside the Duesenbergs and Ballots. Those starters were the Talbots and Talbot-Darracqs, for the Sunbeams did not appear 'owing to the coal strike'.

1922 Ernest Henry was retained to design the first Sunbeam for the 2litre Grand Prix formula. His car had a dropped chassis, normal semi-elliptic suspension all round and unusual servo-assisted four-wheel brakes. The engine was a dohc 1,975cc long-stroke four-cylinder unit, for which 84bhp was claimed, substantially less than the Fiat 804 that was to set the standard in 1922. Two of the cars retired early in the French GP, and Segrave's just before half-distance, all when inlet valves failed.

1923 Fiat's success in the French and Italian GPs in 1922 led Coatalen to invite Bertarione to design the 1923 Sunbeam. Naturally, this echoed Fiat practices in its 1,988cc straight six, that gave 102bhp for the French GP. It was installed in a chassis on 1922 lines.

Once again the cars were outpaced by new Fiats, but these were destined to retire. At quarter-distance Guinness led in

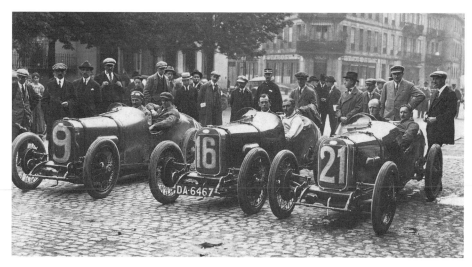

The Sunbeam Grand Prix team of 1922.

Sunbeam of 1923, Henry Segrave winning the French GP.

a Sunbeam, at half-distance Sunbeams were 2-3-5, and at the end Segrave won for Sunbeam, from team mate Divo with Guinness fourth. Divo then drove one of these cars to win the first Spanish GP to be run as a formula race.

1924 Once again a Fiat lead had to be followed, and Sunbeam adopted the supercharger. This was a Roots-type instrument, and it set a trend as it compressed the mixture. It increased the output of the straight six to 138bhp. There was a four-speed gearbox, the chassis and running gear were revised in detail, and the cars were thoroughly tested before the French GP.

Segrave led the opening laps of that race for Sunbeam, then made the first of a series

of pit stops. Practice seemed to have shown a weakness, and this led to a change of magneto type for the race, when wiring proved fragile. Segrave finished fifth, and must have been frustrated as his lap record proved that the car had real potential. Guinness, second at half-distance, retired with engine failure; Resta was running at the end, but was flagged off. Segrave later won the San Sebastian GP with one of these cars.

The 1925 Sunbeams showed little change, and were outclassed. Only one of the trio reached half-distance in the French GP, and Count Masetti drove it on to finish the race in third place. Sunbeam entries for the European and Italian GPs were withdrawn, and a single car was sent to Spain for Masetti, who retired. Sunbeam's Grand

Sunbeam of 1924, Henry Segrave driving.

Prix history ended on that low note, with little consolation to be found as the cars won minor events.

Surtees

See pp.217–219.

SVA

Information on this obscure one-off car is elusive, but at least Mike Lawrence has established that it had a supercharged Fiat engine. It started in one Formula 1 race, the 1950 San Remo GP, when Rudolf Fischer retired it on the first lap.

SURTEES

The Surtees Racing Organisation built its first single-seater, the TS5 Formula 5000 car, in 1969 and the first Formula 1 car came in the following year, to be run by Team Surtees and driven by John Surtees. He won the Oulton Park Gold Cup with it, and scored his team's first Constructors' Championship points. Surtees soon gave up driving, to concentrate on his team and its engineering and his businesses – 1971 was his last full season as a driver, and his last Grand Prix was the 1972 Italian race.

Generally, in those years, Surtees's cars were successful in F5000 and F2. In the Grands Prix his team's best seasons were 1971–72, and in both years Mike Hailwood came close to making the final breakthrough, close to a victory in a World Championship race. The cars were neat – John Surtees played a substantial design role – but the team sometimes did not have the best of DFV engines, nor later the best tyres, and seldom had adequate sponsorship in a period when Formula 1 was increasingly costly if it was undertaken with whole-hearted professionalism, and John Surtees could never take a dilettante approach. Beyond that there were accidents, two of them tragic.

A decline started in 1973, and signs of a recovery in 1976 proved illusory. Beyond

that, John Surtees was unwell in 1978, and at odds with FOCA colleagues over financial aspects of Formula 1. That year his team scored only one championship point, bringing the tally with Surtees cars from 118 Grands Prix in nine seasons to fifty-three, and Surtees decided to call it a day. Fortunately, he remained involved with the sport, notably as a most welcome figure at historic events, where his forceful driving at the end of the twentieth century belied his years.

TS7 John Surtees was largely responsible for his first F1 car, with detail draughting by Peter Connew and Shahab Ahmed. It had distinctive lines, appearing low-built around its angular aluminium monocoque, with a near-flat radiator in the nose. Orthodox double wishbone suspension was used all round. The Cosworth DFV drove through a Hewland DG300 gearbox.

John Surtees drove the car in its first races, qualifying well back on the 1970 British GP grid first time out but climbing to seventh place before the engine failed. In the German GP Surtees was third when he retired, and in the second and lighter TS7 was sixth when he retired from the Austrian GP, while he completed only one lap at Monza. Then in the Canadian GP

he finished fifth, and while he retired from the US Grand Prix, Derek Bell scored a point for Team Surtees. Thus it claimed eighth place in the championship, with three points. The late summer also saw John Surtees score a convincing victory in the Oulton Park Gold Cup.

A TS7 was run in the first Grand Prix of 1971, when Rolf Stommelen finished twelfth (he had earlier won a heat of the non-title Argentine GP). Van Lennep placed one eighth in the Dutch GP.

TS9 This was a straightforward evolutionary car, with a new rear suspension (upper and lower links and radius arms) and a Hewland FG400 gearbox. Late in the summer of 1971 one car appeared in side-radiator form. It overheated in practice at Monza, where it was raced with a nose radiator, but side radiators were used for the last two Grands Prix in 1971, and in 1972.

The TS9 was first seen in the first race of 1971, and normally a two-car team was run. Surtees's car was entered by Rob Walker, while Stommelen's was an Eifelland entry, and confusingly there was a third Team Surtees car later, for Derek Bell in the British GP and Hailwood later. John Love raced a Team Gunston TS9 in South Africa.

(Above) Surtees TS9-Ford of 1971, John Surtees driving.

Surtees TS9B-Ford of 1973, James Hunt driving.

In his last full season as a driver, Surtees was fifth in the Dutch GP and sixth in Britain, and he was seventh in two other Grands Prix. In non-championship races, he won at Oulton Park again and was third in the Race of Champions.

Stommelen also recorded a fifth (in Britain) and a sixth (at Monaco). When he was injured in a Monza practice accident, Sam Posey took his place, only to retire from the US Grand Prix. Bell also retired in his one Grand Prix, then Mike Hailwood was given a drive in the Italian GP, and was fourth, just 0.18sec behind the winner. He was also classified fifteenth in the USA.

The TS9B was the normal car in 1972, in side-radiator form. Hailwood's first full season with the team was a good one, with second place in Italy, two fourth places and a sixth in Grands Prix, and second in the

Race of Champions. Tim Schenken was fifth in the first Grand Prix and finished five other Grands Prix; Andrea de Adamich was fourth in Spain and finished four other Grands Prix. Posey and Love failed to finish in their single races. In championship races, the TS9s had a 50 per cent retirement rate. In 1971 they earned Surtees eighth place in the championship (eight points) and in 1972 the team's best placing was fifth with eighteen points.

TS14 This car for 1973 was ready well in advance, too far in fact, as the regulations were relaxed before the start of the season and Team Surtees found itself running an overweight car. The first TS14 actually started in two late-1972 races, Surtees (in his last Grand Prix) retiring it at Monza, while Schenken failed to finish with it in the USA.

The TS14 was a deformable-structure car, with a sandwich construction monocoque, a broad nose and side radiators, like its contemporaries with an inelegantly exposed engine topped with one of the less pretty engine airboxes. Suspension was outboard all round, and inevitably a Cosworth–Hewland combination was used. During 1973 the team suffered a lot of accident damage, and had tyre problems. Hailwood was involved in two early accidents, when he was leading the Race of Champions and in a collision in South Africa. He was placed in only five Grands Prix (best placing seventh in Italy). Carlos Pace scored all of Surtees's seven points (for ninth place in the championship, incidentally) in two races, third in the Austrian GP and fourth in the German GP. Jochen Mass drove once, to seventh place in Germany, while de Adamich was eighth in South Africa before he turned to Brabham.

TS16 In a line of succession from the TS14, the TS16 was to serve Team Surtees for two seasons, and reduced circumstances in 1975 meant that a single car was run. The TS16 appeared with nose radiators, but in 1975 the water radiators flanked the DFV. Save in details of geometry, the suspension followed the TS14. Once again Hewland FG400 gearboxes were used.

The 1974 driver pairing was strong, but the results were poor. Jochen Mass did finish second in the Silverstone International Trophy, but that result was not repeated in championship races. In those, Mass finished twice (fourteenth and seventeenth) and retired nine times, then took to a McLaren. Pace again scored the team's points, with fourth in Brazil; after two more finishes and four retirements, he left for Brabham. Bell failed to qualify four times and was eleventh in the race he started; Kinnunen failed to qualify a Surtees three times and retired after his only start; Quester was ninth in his home Grand Prix; Koinigg's record was a tenth place and a retirement, Dolheim's a DNQ and a retirement. At Watkins Glen, Helmuth Koinigg was killed as his TS16 crashed.

John Watson drove in eleven of the 1975 races, finishing seven with a best placing eighth in Spain (he was second in the Race of Champions, fourth in the International Trophy and fifth in the non-championship Swiss GP). Dave Morgan was entered in the British GP, and finished eighteenth. Team Surtees did not score in the Constructors' Championship, where the TS16 had brought it eleventh place in 1974.

TS19   This was a different Surtees, outwardly reminiscent of the 'pyramid cross section' Brabham BT42, and with a broad nose and high cockpit surround. John Surtees and Ken Sears laid it out, using a Cosworth–Hewland combination, of course.

Alan Jones's first Grand Prix with Team Surtees was the third in the 1976 series, but before that he had finished second in the Race of Champions. His Grand Prix record included three scoring finishes (fourth in Japan, twice fifth), and he retired from only three Grands Prix. Brett Lunger started ten times, but had two DNQs against his name; he finished seven races, with tenth in Austria his highest classified position. Pescarolo drove a Norev-entered TS19 nine times, twice failing to qualify and twice to retirement, with his best finish ninth. Conny Anderson started one race, and retired. Divina Galica failed to qualify for the British GP. Jones's seven points brought Surtees back onto the Constructors' Championship list in 1976, tenth.

The cars served again through 1977, with detail changes to the nose, the cooling arrangements and the brakes. Vittorio Brambilla drove a full season, qualifying every time, retiring only five times, and scoring three times (fourth in Belgium was his best result). Hans Binder started nine races and finished four. Larry Perkins did not qualify twice and was twelfth once. Vern Schuppan had a DNQ against his name, three finishes, with seventh place in Germany. Leoni failed to qualify once, as did Tambay and Trimmer. Oh, and Divina Galica was twelfth in the Race of Champi-

ons. Brambilla's efforts brought eleventh place in the championship, with six points.

Until the T20s were ready, the TS19s were used in 1978. Brambilla and Keegan each suffered a DNQ, between them accounting for five retirements, leaving the Italian to finish two races, outside the points.

TS20   A development of the TS19, this car came late – appearing first at Monaco – and it was not a ground-effects car. Moreover, the team was not favoured with the best tyres. John Surtees's health could have been better, and so could his relations with other FOCA people.

Brambilla finished seven races, and scored Team Surtees's last point, in the Austrian GP. Keegan finished just one race, and his failures to qualify marked his decline, as well as the team's. Gabbiani stood in after Brambilla was injured at Monza, and did not qualify to start a race. René Arnoux finished ninth in Italy, showing that the car could be quick, and retired in Canada. 'Gimax' failed to get a car to the Italian GP grid. That single point gave Surtees thirteenth place in the Constructors' Championship.

A TS20 was adapted for ground effects following design work on a TS21, and wind-tunnel tests with a model. The TS21 was abandoned, but the 'TS20+' was run in a British national series, in a downbeat end to the Surtees Formula 1 story.

Surtees TS19-Ford of 1976, Alan Jones driving.

Talbot

See pp.221–223.

Tec-Mec

When the Maserati Formula 1 effort ended, its chassis engineer Valerio Colotti set up Studio Tecnica Meccanica, and one of his first projects was an extension of the Maserati 250F theme in a lightweight car, that might have been Maserati's own next F1 type. It was commissioned by driver Giorgio Scarlatti, and built by ex-Maserati personnel.

In effect, it was a space-frame Maserati special, with wishbone and coil-spring front suspension and wishbone and transverse leaf spring rear suspension. A Maserati 250F engine was mounted ahead of the cockpit – a distinctly passé layout by 1959, when the car was completed. It was compact, but its lines were hardly attractive.

Scarlatti backed away, and Colotti left to concentrate on his gearbox work. George Pennington took over Studio Tecnica Meccanica, and was to rename it Tec-Mec Automobili, and the car was completed slowly. Seemingly the testing was less than thorough, but even so a reputa-

tion for tricky handling circulated. It was not ready when it was first entered for a race, the 1959 Italian GP. However, it did appear at the first US GP to be a World Championship race, at Sebring late in 1959. Brazilian Fritz d'Orey was 33sec off the 3min pole time in practice (two other cars were slower), and he retired from the race with an oil leak after seven laps. Pennington lost interest. Much later the car became a museum exhibit.

Tecno

The Pederzani brothers' pugnacious cars were effective in Formula 3 and then Formula 2 in the late 1960s and into the 1970s and this tempted Tecno – founded by Lucciano and Gianfranco Pederzani as Tecnokart in Bologna in 1962 – into Formula 1. That swallowed all their resources, to no useful end.

Various chassis were numbered in a PA123 sequence (001–006) and in the second (last) year there was E731. Common to all was a 2,967cc flat twelve, on the lines of the contemporary Ferrari boxer unit. In 1972 its claimed output was 460bhp, while the supposed 1973 maximum power was 475bhp. But it was always

a weak link in the Tecno chain. Its cooling demands led to the use of a large nose radiator, rather than the hip radiators proposed, and this contributed to the PA123's unattractive lines. Hewland FG400 gearboxes were used through the programme.

The engine was a stressed member, mounted to a tubular frame with welded bottom and sides, making up a hybrid monocoque. There was double wishbone front suspension, and lower wishbones with upper links and radius arms at the rear (Ron Tauranac was to redesign the rear suspension during 1972). The first body looked bulky, and as it exceeded the maximum permitted width, it had to be revised.

Tecno's F1 debut came in the 1972 Belgian GP, when Nanni Galli retired. His only Grand Prix finish that year was in Austria, where his Tecno was running at the end but, nine laps down, was not classified. He did finish third in the minor 'Grand Prix of the Republic of Italy'. Derek Bell was entered in a second car five times, and actually started twice, retiring from both races. So the 1972 record was ten entries, and one real finish, in a nontitle race.

Alan McCall designed a proper monocoque chassis for 1973, but driver Chris Amon persuaded Tecno to put a second chassis in hand. The 'McCall car' had a similar suspension to the 1972 cars, the engine was more powerful (on paper) and had a better torque range. The car was said to have been extensively tested before its first race, in Belgium. There Amon persisted despite considerable discomfort, and scored Tecno's only Constructors' Championship point. By that time McCall had left.

The 'Goral' Tecno, the E731, was designed by Gordon Fowell, and looked better than the 'McCall car'. But it was never actually raced. Amon drove it in practice for two Grands Prix, but his race starts were in the last PA123. Apart from that Belgian GP sixth place, he retired three times (the team did not appear at every meeting).

The inevitable end came at the Austrian GP meeting, where Amon managed a back-of-the-grid qualifying time in the PA123, but was 5sec slower in the E731. When the PA123 was withdrawn, with engine problems, Amon walked away from the team, and then the team was wound up.

Tecno PA123 flat-12 of 1971.

TALBOT

Talbot-Darracq came into existence in 1920, as Sunbeam, Talbot and Darracq merged in the STD group, and the first major racing venture was a trio of cars for Indianapolis (two Sunbeams and a Talbot-Darracq), closely followed by a Grand Prix car in 1921. This was a shared design, with little more than a pointed tail to distinguish the French Talbot-Darracq from its British sisters (though the British tended to regard Talbot as French). There was a fifth place in the French GP, but really this effort was a failure, and there was a pause until 1926, when a straight-eight 1.5 litre Grand Prix Talbot was designed and built in France. This was campaigned half-heartedly for less than two years – Talbot gave up after one car finished fourth and last in the 1927 French GP, and sold the cars to an Italian team.

The STD combine withered in the late 1920s, and collapsed in 1935, but Talbot returned to formula racing in 1938. Antonio 'Tony' Lago rescued the company and ventured into the Grand Prix field that was dominated by two German teams. Limited resources meant that despite a grant from the French racing fund a 'pure' Grand Prix Talbot was not built, and the marque relied on sports-related cars.

As the production cars became known as Talbot-Lagos (later Lago-Talbots), big cars on pre-Second World War lines contested the Grands Prix again – some late 1930s cars were still run, Talbot-Lago built some new ones and there were independent conversions of sports cars. Outclassed in terms of sheer speed, but tough, reliable and above all frugal compared to supercharged cars, these Talbots were successful in secondary races and sometimes in major Grands Prix, notably the French GP in 1947 and the Grand Prix de France in 1949 (when it was not the ACF race).

They were raced until the first Formula 1 lost its World Championship status, and well beyond in lesser events. By the early 1950s they were hardly competitive – single-seater development had never been more than modest, and ended before Lago announced that support for the Grand Prix cars would not continue into 1951. There were overbearing company reasons, and there was also a recognition that the old cars – splendid representatives of a past era though they might have been – could never be made competitive. And there was no chance that a successor would appear.

1921 The first Grand Prix Talbot/ Talbot-Darracq was of an unadventurous design, with a channel-section chassis and non-independent suspension. The dohc straight eight closely resembled the contemporary Ballot engine in many respects, even to its 65 × 112mm (2,973cc) dimensions. However, it was sturdier and had better lubrication arrangements, which meant higher revs and a little more power – offset by the substantially greater weight of the STD cars, as much as 190kg (419lb) above the minimum in the case of the two Talbots.

The STD team was simply not prepared for the French GP, and Coatalen withdrew its entries. However, four were reinstated, at the drivers' insistence, and two Talbots and two Talbot-Darracqs started. André Boillot finished fifth in a Talbot-Darracq; Guinness and Segrave were eighth and ninth in Talbots, around an hour behind the winner.

1926 The 1.5litre Grand Prix Talbot was indisputably French, although designed by Bertarione and Becchia, and it was built at Suresnes. It was a notably low car with a stiff chassis comprising parallel longitudinal members linked by vertical members (in a single pressing per side), not unlike a Lancia Lambda, and generously cross-braced. The axles passed through the side members, and the front axle was split at the centre. The engine was a 1,488cc supercharged dohc straight

Talbots of 1921: Rene Thomas (left) in a Talbot-Darracq and K.L. Guinness (right) in a Talbot.

eight that was second only to the similar Delage unit in terms of power output in 1926. The radiator was steeply raked, the driver sat very low, and there was a nicely shaped tail.

Completion was delayed, in part as finance was a problem for STD by this time, and the intended French GP debut was abandoned. The first race for these cars was the first British GP, when they were obviously underdeveloped, and in particular had serious braking problems. Moriceau retired after one lap, with front axle failure, Divo fell out eighty-eight laps later, and then Segrave, both with supercharger failure. At least Segrave set the fastest race lap. A month later he won a secondary race at Brooklands, while Divo headed a 1-2-3 in the Grand Prix du Salon at Montlhéry.

Little development work was done for 1927. Moriceau won a heat of a minor race at Miramas, and Divo won a minor Montlhéry event. Then STD ran the cars for the last time, in the French GP. Two of the Talbots retired with engine failure, while the third car, shared by Williams and Moriceau, was fourth and last.

STD sold the cars to Scuderia Materassi, and in Italy they were developed to become effective racing cars in 1928–29. Count Brilli-Peri won the 1929 Tripoli GP in one, but died in it during practice for the 1930 North African race. Emilio Materassi was successful in secondary races, but was killed in one of his Talbots in the 1928 Italian and European GP at Monza.

Arcangeli had some success, and Nuvolari raced a Talbot twice, finishing second in the 1929 Monza GP 1,500cc heat and second in the final. Later, Enrico Platé, usually associated with Maseratis, substantially modified one of these cars, and raced it successfully as a Talbot-Platé.

Monoplace Sports-car successes in 1937 led to a grant from the ACF Racing Fund Committee, which was a contribution towards the development of a French Grand Prix car (the major prize was to go to Delahaye), and Lago put in hand work on two projects. Walter Becchia, responsible for the 1926 Grand Prix straight eight, laid down a 4.5litre unsupercharged straight six and a supercharged V16, while work started on a chassis. Meanwhile, a pair of stripped sports cars was entered in the 1938 French GP, a race with only nine starters. The Mercedes team finished 1-2-3, and the only other finisher was Carrière's Talbot, ten laps in arrears in a 64-lap race.

Two of the three 1939 chassis were to have the cross-over pushrod ohv 4,483cc six-cylinder engine. The third was intended for the V16, and was eventually completed with a 4.5litre unit. These three had channel-section chassis frames, with wishbone and transverse leaf front suspension and live rear axle with semi-elliptics. The first two were offset single-seaters, with the transmission running along beside the driver's seat, and pre-selector gearbox. The third had its cockpit on the centre line.

The offset cars were first raced in the 1939 Pau GP, one finishing third, and then they were third and fourth in the Coupe de Paris. The real baptism of fire came in the French GP, where the third car also appeared, and all qualified well off the German team's pace. A Mercedes-Benz collapse let Auto Unions finish 1-2, with le Begue and Etancelin third and fourth in Talbots. May retired the centre-cockpit car with a split tank.

The first two cars were sent to Indianapolis, where they failed to qualify for the 1941 500 (just think about that date!). When they returned to France, one was run by Ecurie France 1947–51, the other less frequently from 1949. They were to be joined by open-wheel conversions of Talbot T150C sports cars.

The third 1939 car was driven to finish second in a race at the first post-Second-World-War meeting, in the Bois de Boulogne in 1945. Louis Chiron had some success with it in 1946, and even more in 1947 when he won the French GP and a secondary race, while Chabaud drove it to win two regional Grands Prix. Incidentally, five Talbots ran in that French GP, and finished third, fourth and sixth. In 1948 Chiron was second at Monaco in the Ecurie France car, and he won the French GP again. The old warhorse was sold, gained a T26C chassis and was later rebuilt as a sports car.

T26C Tony Lago and Carlo Marchetti laid this car out on classic – less politely, near-archaic – lines, broadly following the 1939 single-seaters in chassis, suspension and transmission, while the 4,483cc engine had high-mounted camshafts (reports suggested that Lago could not finance a dohc engine). The claimed power output was 240bhp, to propel a car weighing more than 900kg (1,984lb); an uprating in 1949 gained perhaps 20bhp.

In view of the cars available from Italian constructors, Lago's production seemed ambitious, but these were sound and reliable cars for independent entrants, and they served well. The T26C was first raced at Monaco in 1948 (Louis Rosier retired it). Within weeks T26Cs were fourth, fifth and sixth in the French GP, and those placings almost set a pattern. The only victory that year came in the minor Coupe de Salon.

Alfa Romeo's withdrawal in 1949 generally opened the door for Ferrari, but Rosier won the Belgian GP in a Talbot with a

Talbot of 1927, René Wagner driving.

steady and economic run (and it was apparently decisive in persuading Enzo Ferrari to turn away from supercharged engines). Beyond that, Chiron won the 'Grand Prix de France', and there were good placings in other major races – Sommer's third in the Swiss GP, and Etancelin's runner-up finishes in the European GP at Monza and the Czech GP.

In the first Drivers' Championship season the cars were not old, but the concept was ancient, and unlike the equally old Alfa Romeo 158 original design, little development work had been put into the Talbot. Among the Talbot drivers, Rosier scored best, with third places in Switzerland and Belgium, fourth in Italy and fifth in Britain. Grignard and Cabantous each scored three points. Sommer had a heat win at Albi, Rosier was second at Pescara and third at Pau, 'Levegh' was fourth at Bari, Cabantous fourth in the Grand Prix des Nations.

There were crumbs in 1951, a fourth and fifth (Rosier and Cabantous) in the Belgian GP being the only scoring finishes for Talbot drivers. Rosier did win the

Talbot T26C of 1949, Raymond Sommer driving.

non-championship Dutch GP, and at Albi and Bordeaux, and was second at Pau. Hamilton was second and Rosier fifth in the curtailed International Trophy at Silverstone, and Talbots headed by Gonzalez were 2-3-4-5-6 in the very minor Paris GP.

Although Whiteford won the 1952–53 Australian GPs in a T26C, and some Talbots were still run in the few Formula 1 races in 1952–53 as well as in *formule libre* events, the only real successes for these cars came as they were run in sports-car form.

Theodore

Far East entrepreneur Theodore 'Teddy' Yip raced at a modest local level and backed a Formula 5000 team before he became involved with Formula 1, with the second car of the Ensign team in 1977. That led to the first Theodore car, which was designed by Ron Tauranac. It made no impression in championship races early in 1978, although there was a victory in a non-championship race, and in the second half of the year Theodore Racing ran Wolf cars.

Yip next took over the Shadow team, and ran DN12s until a new Theodore appeared, and made little impact in 1981. An amalgamation with Ensign for 1983 also brought few rewards, and as this Yip and Mo Nunn team could not obtain turbo engines for 1984 the pair turned to CART racing, and – perhaps at the margins – Formula 1 was the poorer for the loss of an enthusiastic sponsor and constructor.

TR1 This Tauranac design was a typically solid-looking car, and entirely conventional in its make-up, with a Cosworth DFV engine and Hewland FGA400 six-speed gearbox.

The little team gave Keke Rosberg his first experience of Formula 1, but the

Theodore N183-Ford of 1983, Brian Henton driving.

combination usually seemed out of its depth. Rosberg qualified the car for the penultimate row of the grid at its South African GP debut in 1978, but retired from the race with assorted mechanical

ailments. He got over the pre-qualification hurdle once more, but then did not reach the grid. His victory in the Silverstone International Trophy owed everything to his skill in heavy rain.

After six attempts, the team gave up the TR1 and later in the year Rosberg drove Wolf WR3 and WR4 for Yip, finishing just one Grand Prix (in Germany) in six attempts. Early in 1980 Geoff Lees was entered in a DN12 by Theodore Shadow, but failed to qualify for a championship Grand Prix. He did start in the non-title South African GP, in a DN12 redesignated TR2, but failed to finish.

TY01 Yip tried again in 1981, with a ground-effects car designed by Tony Southgate. At first this stood out with a pylon-mounted aerofoil above its short nose, but that soon gave way to a more normal nose. The car had generous side pods, and the suspension followed common ground-effects cars lines, with lower wishbones and top rocker arms all round. The Cosworth DFV drove through a Hewland FGB gearbox.

The first car was completed only just in time for the first Grand Prix of the season, at Long Beach. Patrick Tambay qualified it well, and finished sixth in a promising debut race (that point was to give Theodore twelfth place in the championship). Tambay finished four more races of the seven he drove for Theodore. Marc Surer took his place, had a DNQ against his name but was classified in five Grands Prix (best placing eighth in Holland) and retired only twice.

Derek Daly drove a TY01 early in 1982, when his only finish was fourteenth in South Africa.

TY02 This Southgate design was similar, save for its aluminium honeycomb monocoque and generally more attractive lines. However, there were handling shortcomings, and the 1982 record was dismal.

Daly retired a TY02 twice, then joined Williams. Lammers failed to qualify five times and retired from his only race. Lees retired once. Byrne had three DNQs to his name, and two retirements.

N183 The Ensign designation was used in 1983, for uprated versions of Nigel Bennett's N181/N182 design. The two new cars built had reinforced tubs, but other changes were in details. This was a Cosworth-powered car in the turbo age, so the team faced a battle against heavy odds.

Robert Guerrero finished eight races (best placing twelfth), albeit he was not classified twice; he failed to qualify twice, and retired seven times. Johnny Cecotto scored a point at Long Beach, to give Theodore another foot-of-the-table placing; that was the best of his six finishes, he failed to get to a grid four times, and retired from three Grands Prix. Quite incidentally, Brian Henton was fourth in a one-off drive in the Race of Champions.

Sensibly, Teddy Yip turned away from Formula 1 at the end of 1983.

Thin Wall

The four Thin Wall Specials were really Ferraris, but earned an individual place in history.

Before G.A. 'Tony' Vandervell broke with BRM he had acquired a 1949 Ferrari 125 to give that beleagured team some experience – it was run in the British GP as the Thin Wall Special Ferrari. The second was another supercharged Ferrari that was rebuilt as a 4.5litre unsupercharged car. Another followed, and this unsupercharged Thin Wall Special was to be extensively modified, for example with disc brakes long before Ferrari would countenance them, as the team worked towards Vanwall. The fourth Thin Wall was one of the long-wheelbase Ferrari 375s, run from 1952.

Reg Parnell was fourth in the 1951 French GP in Vandervell's third Ferrari, and Peter Whitehead qualified it well for the British GP, although brake problems dropped him to ninth at the end of the race.

Thin Wall Specials became familiar in British secondary races particularly when the Grands Prix were run to Formula 2 regulations, battling with BRMs. These green Ferraris played a useful role in honing the team that was to build and run Vanwalls in the coming years.

Thomas (GB)

J.G. Parry Thomas is usually recalled for his untimely death in a record attempt, but this talented engineer also built a Grand Prix car. It promised much, but its development was cut short when he died on Pendine Sands in 'Babs'. The Thomas Special was low-built – its bonnet was below the tops on the front tyres – with an underslung chassis and transmission run to the left of the driver. It was nicknamed

Thin Wall Special of 1953, Mike Hawthorn driving.

Thomas (GB) Special of 1927.

'flat iron'. Suspension was non-independent, with semi-elliptic springs at the front and quarter-elliptics at the rear. The engine was a 1,494cc straight eight, with two Roots-type superchargers ahead of the crankcase. It was an sohc type, with Thomas's leaf-type valve springs. There was a four-speed gearbox.

Thomas's entry for the 1926 British GP was withdrawn, because of gearbox problems. Parry Thomas raced 'flat iron' for the first time in the Brooklands 200-mile race a few weeks later, finishing a rather troubled eighth. He then had a car running properly for a later, and insignificant, Brooklands handicap race that he won.

Two cars for the 1927 British GP, which was run after Thomas's death. They obviously needed the development they never received. Driven by Scott and Purdy, they both retired before half-distance, with transmission failures (although some reports suggest that Scott just gave up because his car was slow or because he found driving it difficult, as he was a big man in a small cockpit). The cars were raced at Brooklands on into the 1930s.

Thomas (USA)

The first Thomas entered for a major race appeared in the 1905 Vanderbilt Cup eliminating trials, and was remarkably unorthodox – there was a straight six under an immensely long and slender bonnet and the crew sat behind the rear axle, in a layout that was to be tried by Alfa Romeo four decades later. Montague Roberts finished fifth in the trial, and was eliminated only because the organizers decided that a car which had retired should be allowed to run in the main race.

The 1906 Vanderbilt cars were conventional, but they were modified touring cars to be pitted against some of the best from Europe. Le Blon led the eliminating race, dropping to second on the last lap (Caillois lasted to half-distance in the other Thomas). European drivers and cars dominated the final, and Le Blon's Thomas in eighth place was the first American car to finish.

A single car was entered for the 1908 Grand Prix, for Lewis Strang. This low-built car had an 11,176cc four-cylinder engine rated at 115bhp – no improvement on the 1906 Vanderbilt car there – with chain drive. It was running thirty-second – next to last – when the clutch failed on the fifth lap. There was little European interest in the 1908 Vanderbilt Cup, when Salzmann was fourth in one Thomas of the trio that started. Thomas did not enter the Grand Prize, but then it hardly needed publicity, for three months earlier one of its touring cars had won the New York–Paris 'race'.

Token

Ron Dennis and Neil Trundle initiated the design of this car in 1974, for their Rondel team, intending to move it up from Formula 2 to the Grands Prix. However, as adequate sponsorship could not be found (there was an energy/oil crisis), they sensibly backed away. The project was handed on to Tony Vlassopoulo and Ken Grob, and a car was completed in 1974, with a name combining elements of theirs.

This RJ02 was designed by Ray Jessop, and was an attractive Cosworth-powered car that perhaps, because it was so neat, looked smaller than it actually was. It had a slender monocoque, double wishbone front suspension, with upper and lower links and radius arms at the rear.

Tom Pryce drove it in its first race, starting from the back of the Silverstone International Trophy grid and retiring before half-distance. David Purley narrowly failed to qualify it for the British GP – he equalled the time of the slowest car on the grid, and eight cars were slower. Ian Ashley did start in the German and Austrian GPs and finished in both races, fourteenth and thirteenth respectively.

The car was taken over by John Thorpe, and when it appeared in 1975 it was renamed for his Safir company.

Toleman

Ted Toleman first backed a single-seater team in 1977, and in the following year Toleman Group support was moved up to Formula 2, sponsoring a March, while designer Rory Byrne was taken on, with a view to building Toleman cars. Meanwhile, quasi-works F2 Ralts were run, successfully, in 1979 as the first Toleman F2 cars were built. These TG280s were the dominant Formula 2 cars of 1980, and that year Toleman was preparing for its entry into Formula 1, which came in 1981.

Grand Prix racing proved to be a much greater challenge – as it should be. Toleman's budget was not generous, and there were to be problems in areas from engine reliability to tyres, where broadly Toleman had to live with 'the wrong ones'. Its first ugly cars seldom qualified in its first season, and its second was a struggle. Eventually there was progress, and the team's last cars looked much better.

Ayrton Senna came close to wining a Grand Prix (Monaco) for Toleman in

1984, but as the next year opened Toleman found itself without a tyre supplier. That major problem was improved as Toleman bought the expiring Spirit team's tyre contract. But the team missed races, and through the rest of the series a Toleman finished in just two Grands Prix. The 1985 cars were run in Benetton colours, foreshadowing the team's future as Benetton.

TG181 The F2 TG280 had been a good-looking car, but this first F1 Toleman was extraordinarily ugly. Rory Byrne and John Gentry laid it out around a straightforward aluminium monocoque, with lower wishbones and top rocker arms suspension front and rear. Brian Hart was commissioned to design and build a turbocharged engine, and used his successful F2 four-cylinder unit as a basis. The 415T was the first purpose-designed British turbo engine, and it suffered teething problems from its first tests in an unadapted TG280 on through the 1981 season.

In racing, Toleman's F1 baptism was hardly encouraging. Brian Henton qualified to start in one Grand Prix (he finished tenth in that Italian GP). Derek Warwick qualified to start once, at Las Vegas, where he retired.

One of these cars, revised to 'B' specification, was run in the first race of 1982, when Teo Fabi failed to qualify it. That year the T181C had more powerful engines, but qualifying was still a struggle for Fabi (he failed seven times), and so was finishing a race – he did not see the chequered flag all year. Derek Warwick, on the other hand, qualified for all save two races, and before he turned to the TG183 for the last two Grands Prix he finished twice (fifteenth and tenth). In mid-season the team was withdrawn from the US and Canadian GPs.

TG183 Byrne and Gentry laid out a stronger car for 1983, notably with a carbon-fibre composites monocoque and double wishbone pullrod suspension all round. The first car was running in the summer of 1982 and late that year the 'flat bottom' regulations were adopted for 1983, so that the car had to be modified, and T183Bs were run. Hart 415Ts were still used, but with Holset turbochargers in place of Garrett units. The power output – 580bhp was quoted – was still not competitive, and ungainly rear wings had to be dragged around.

Warwick retired in his two 1982 races with the first car, but 1983 was a much better season. He started all the races, retired from nine, then at the end of the year put together a string of four scoring finishes, fourth at Zandvoort and Kyalami, fifth in the European GP at Brands Hatch and sixth at Monza. Bruno Giacomelli failed to qualify only once and finished six races (best placing sixth in the European GP). Toleman's ten points gained ninth place in the Constructors' Championship.

With just a little more power, TG183Bs were used for the first four Grands Prix in 1984. Ayrton Senna scored two sixth places with them, Johnny Cecotto retired four times.

Toleman TG181-BMW of 1981.

Toleman TG184-Hart of 1984.

TG184 The 1984 car appeared late, but soon proved to be competitive. Its monocoque followed TG183 lines, but the suspension was modified and there were pullrods at the front, while the radiators were in side pods. Double rear wings were still used. The race-trim output of the Hart engine was some 600bhp.

Ayrton Senna came within a lap of victory in the truncated Monaco GP with a TG184. He was second there, and third in the British and Portuguese GPs; he retired seven times. Cecotto started four times, finished once, and crashed heavily in practice for the British GP, ending his Formula 1 career. Martini stepped in, failed to qualify in his one attempt, and Stefan Johansson drove in the last three Grands Prix, finishing fourth at Monza. Toleman was seventh in the championship, with sixteen points.

TG185 This car was described as a refined derivative of the TG184, and it was the most handsome Toleman by a wide margin. The aerodynamic appendages were much neater, and this was the first of Byrne's F1 Tolemans to have a full engine cover. The Hart 415T was substantially more powerful, and there was a Toleman five-/six-speed gearbox in place of the Toleman-Hewland five-speed 'boxes used previously. The downside was the life-threatening tyre problems; this meant that the team did not race until the fourth Grand Prix of 1985 and that instead of the strong two-car effort that had been planned, there was just a single car for much of the year.

Teo Fabi started thirteen races, but finished only two, and his best placing was twelfth in the Italian GP. Ghinzani started six races, and retired every time. In its last, sad, season Toleman failed to score in the Constructors' Championship.

Toyota

During the 1990s rumours about Toyota's impending entry into Formula 1 occasionally circulated, then the subject was dropped. There was a short-lived TOMs Formula 3 programme that could have provided a basis – certainly the British factory and plant would have been adequate. But clarification of the company's intentions did not come until 1999, and late that year the decks were cleared of impediments such as the rally programme, for an entry into Formula 1 early in the twenty-first century, to be based at the Toyota Motorsport GmbH subsidiary in Germany.

Trebron

The history of Formula 1 is littered with aborted projects, such as that of the early-1990s Trebron. This was to be a Judd-powered car, and it was backed by Canadian Norbert Hamy and there was to be Japanese input, as well as sponsorship. Published impressions show a cockpit surround on Kojima lines, and aerodynamic treatment in other areas that promised to be highly original. The origin of Trebron? Norbert in reverse.

Trojan

When McLaren abandoned its sports-racing cars and concentrated on Formula 1, Trojan's customer car build programme ended. Peter Agg looked to extend it, and Trojan adapted the McLaren M21 F2 car as its T101 Formula 5000 car, and then commissioned Ron Tauranac to design the T102 for the same category. That design was seen as the basis for a car giving a very low-key entry into Formula 1. Agg always made it clear that this programme would run to the extent of a modest budget, and no further. And so it proved, with the car run through the European season, sometimes by no means disgraced.

T103 The T102 monocoque served for this F1 car that was very straightforward in components, such as the suspension. A Cosworth DFV and Hewland DG300 gearbox were used. The body was essentially simple, with twin radiators in the broad nose.

The Trojan was entered for eleven Grands Prix in 1974, to be driven by Tim Schenken; the entry for the Swedish GP was not accepted, and Schenken twice failed to qualify. He finished fourteenth in the Trojan's debut race, the Spanish GP, was twice tenth, and retired three times. The car was last seen as it retired from the Italian GP.

Trossi Monaco

This startlingly original device was completed early in 1935, but never raced. It was designed by Augusto Monaco and built at Count Carlo Felice Trossi's castle near Biella in northern Italy (the Count was wealthy, a very capable driver and an engineer, sometime President of Scuderia Ferrari, and he backed this project when other support was withdrawn).

The car had a Zoller-supercharged air-cooled 3,982cc engine – a double piston two-stroke, no less. It was mounted at the nose and drove the front wheels. Two-stroke engines have never been recipes for Grand Prix success, nor has front-wheel drive.

The car had a low and compact body built around the tubular chassis (in effect a space frame) and independent suspension all round. The engine was reported to develop 250bhp, at a time when the dominant German cars had engines giving more than 300bhp; moreover, consistent outputs with racing split-single two-strokes were achieved only in motorcycles in the 1930s. The Trossi-Monaco was tested and set aside, but it survived as a fascinating museum exhibit.

Turner

John Webb (not of Brands Hatch) commissioned special builder Jack Turner, who had converted his MK K3 Magnette into a single-seater, to build him an F2 car for the 1953 season. Like Turner's sports specials, it had a lozenge-shaped ladder frame and transverse leaf springing, and was fitted with an aluminium block 1,750cc Lea Francis engine enlarged to 1,960cc with a twin-plug aluminium head by Turner himself.

It also had SU fuel injection adapted from the SU aircraft system and supervised by the works. In this form the engine gave a claimed 145bhp at 6,500rpm, and drove via a Wilson/Armstrong Siddeley preselector gearbox to an ENV differential mounted on the chassis.

Webb drove it in some minor British F2 events in 1953 where it was always at the back of the field. The following year he tried a 2.5litre Alta engine, but the story was the same and his best performance in this 'F1' car was in the 1954 International Trophy when Jack Fairman drove it, and came thirteenth from fifteen finishers in the final. At least on that occasion it finished – most of its other races ended in retirement.

Tyrrell

See pp.228–234.

Throughout his long career in motor racing, Ken Tyrrell was an enthusiast and a fighter, and as far as his Grand Prix team and its survival was concerned, the two always went hand in hand. Too often, particularly in the 1980s and 1990s, the team was grievously under-financed, and there were also times when it was at the receiving end of some questionable rough justice.

In many seasons its equipment was not of the best, and although there was a point at which stagnation seemed to have set in, that impression was misleading. This was always one of the friendliest teams, perhaps because commercialization and profit was not its only motivation.

Tyrrell turned his back on driving racing cars – he had been good but not outstanding in 500cc F3 cars – to build up a sound reputation as an entrant/team manager in the 1960s, running Formula Junior, F3 and F2 Coopers, and then F2 Matras, for drivers of the calibre of John Surtees, Jacky Ickx and – above all – Jackie Stewart. He was ambitious to take the Tyrrell Racing Organization into F1, and his opportunity came with the availability of the Ford-Cosworth DFV – ordered in 1968, before Tyrrell had a car for it, or the finance to run a car. The car came in the form of a Matra, and the chassis cost him nothing.

Jackie Stewart drove the blue Matras to nine F1 Grands Prix victories in 1968 and 1969, but for 1970 the French team was not prepared to build a new car to be powered by Ford-labelled engines – nor was Tyrrell prepared to abandon the proven engine, and his relationship with the Ford company. For 1970, therefore, he turned to using March 701s, but these were never more than stop-gaps, for late in the summer of 1970 the very first Tyrrell – 001 – appeared.

The 001 was the first of a long line, the early chassis being individually numbered. Type numbers arrived, almost incidentally, with 006 of 1973, and then more deliberately (and consistently) with 007. These early cars were designed for Elf-Team Tyrrell by Derek Gardner, who stayed long enough to see them succeed, then to see his six-wheeler racing car theories put into practice, succeed to some degree, and then become a dead end as tiny-tyre technology lagged.

Maurice Phillippe (ex-Lotus) then took his place, and remained with Tyrrell through a long period that saw more disappointments than triumphs. One of the lowest points came in 1984, when the team's Championship race placings were retrospectively disallowed as an alleged 'illegal' additive was found in the water-injection system of one of its cars.

Throughout, Tyrrell persevered, sometimes with front-line drivers, sometimes with understanding, adequate sponsors, but often struggling to stay in business. In 1988, too, he became the elder statesman among F1 constructors as Enzo Ferrari died, and in that year changes were made. Harvey Postlethwaite joined him as chief designer, while Phillippe and his designer colleague Brian Lisles soon left.

Then came the transformation of the base at Ockham, which had always looked temporary since Jackie Stewart was the leading driver. By 1989 the premises were once again appropriate headquarters for a modern F1 constructor; there was a new management structure, with Ken becoming the Chairman, his son Bob becoming the Managing Director, Postlethwaite, Engineering Director and aerodynamicist Jean-Claude Migeot in charge of research and development. Former Ferrari chief mechanic Joan Villadelprat soon joined as team manager.

Early in 1990 came news of an association with McLaren, in a marketing department linked with TAG/McLaren Marketing Services, though this advance was illusory, achieved nothing, and was shortly abandoned.

Throughout the 1990s, Tyrrell clung on to its place in F1 racing, the sport that Ken Tyrrell loved so much, yet it became increasingly marginalized and, somehow, pitied, by younger, less experienced, but much more brash rivals. The miracle was that the team stayed afloat, seemed to be able to pay its bills from year to year, and seemed to enjoy itself so much.

At no time did the team get its hands on front-line 'works' engines (though it achieved value-for-money deals from second-line machinery), which meant that it could no longer attract top drivers, or generous sponsorship. This early-1990s situation initiated a spiral decline from which there was no recovery. The 1990s was a period in which Tyrrell used six different engines – Ford DFR V8, Mugen-Honda V10, Ilmor V10, Yama/Judd V10, Ford ED V8 and Ford JD V10 – which was very unsettling and, ultimately, unsuccessful.

Certain engine supplies implied the use of drivers who were, shall we say, less than competitive – Satoru Nakajima (who came up with the rations when Tyrrell had Mugen-Honda engines) and

Ukyo Katayama (Yamaha) being two such. Not even the welcome return of Harvey Postlethwaite (from Ferrari) to design the 022 of 1994, and its successors, could balance that.

During the 1990s, Tyrrell's best drivers were Jean Alesi (1990, moved to Ferrari), Mark Blundell (1994, moved to McLaren) and Mika Salo (1995–97, moved to Arrows), but Ken could not afford to keep any of them.

The last podium position came in Spain in 1994, the last year of independence was 1997. By this time the team's future seemed to be in doubt, and Ken Tyrrell must have been tempted to close down, but before the end of the year he sold control to British American Tobacco (which was avid to get into F1 grids). Predictably, Ken could not live with the brashness of the new, and walked out early in 1998, leaving technical chief Harvey Postlethwaite to hold the reins for the last year. By the end of the year many of the team personnel had already defected to other teams, so a complete close down in November was swift, and complete.

It was a sad ending for the company which had provided Jackie Stewart with each of his three World Championships.

001 The original Tyrrell was designed in great secrecy, for Gardner worked entirely from home, where the first wooden mock-up was constructed in his domestic garage. In some general respects, he followed the lines of Tyrrell's erstwhile Matra MS80, for 001 had a similar 'coke-bottle' platform, while another distinctive feature was the broad-nose aerofoil above the radiator intake.

Construction was conventional, around an alloy monocoque, with a double wishbone front suspension, along with single top links, twin lower links and radius arms at the rear. The car was first run in the (non-Championship) Oulton Park Gold Cup, then in three late-1970-season Grands Prix, where it showed potential, but failed to finish a race.

002–004 These cars were, in effect, refined versions of 001, longer (002 was built specifically for Cevert, who was taller than Stewart), and with numerous detail improvements. Black engine airboxes were used from the 1971 Dutch GP onwards, and full-width noses in racing from the French GP, while components such as double-disc brakes appeared, and novelties such as a rear wing incorporating radiators were also tried.

The first GP victory for a Tyrrell fell to Stewart, driving 003 in Spain: in short order he also won Championship races in Monaco, France, Britain, Germany and Canada, to secure the Drivers' title, while Cevert won the US GP in an 002. Tyrrell won the Constructors' Championship, scoring more than twice as many points as the runner up.

These cars came out again in the first half of 1972, when Stewart brought his tally of Championship race victories with 003 to eight, as he won the Argentine and French GPs. 004, originally built as a spare, raced three times for the team before it was sold off to South Africa.

005–006 These new cars, much more angular, shorter and lower than the previous types, came in mid-1972. In detail they retained nose water radiators but had oil radiators alongside the rear of the cockpit, clean lines around the engine bay, large engine airboxes by 1973 and, save for a brief period, brakes were outboard all round, as was the suspension itself.

Two duplicates of 006 were built for 1973, when the team won in South Africa, Belgium, Monaco, Holland and Germany, yet the team was only second in the Championship. Cevert crashed fatally in 006/3 at Watkins Glen, Jackie Stewart retired from driving, and Tyrrell had to face a complete rebuild of the team around two new drivers, though the 006 types were used for the opening races of 1974.

007 This was the first Tyrrell type number intended to cover all the cars in one batch – four being laid down and raced from the start of the 1974 European season. That year they had torsion bar suspension and inboard front brakes, replaced in 1975 by coil spring/shock absorber suspension and outboard brakes.

In 1975 two more 007s were built, to serve through the year and into 1976. Two were entered independently in Grands Prix when sold out of Tyrrell 'works' service. Scheckter won three Grands Prix in 007s, in Sweden and Britain in 1974, and in South Africa in 1975, but in Constructors' Championship terms the team slipped, to third in 1974 and fifth in 1975.

P34 This boldly engineered car was the F1 sensation of 1976, probably earning a worthwhile return for its sponsors

Tyrrell 006/2-Ford of 1973, driven by Jackie Stewart.

through photographic exposure even before it raced. From the cockpit backwards it was conventional, but behind its broad nose Derek Gardner used four small front wheels, to improve aerodynamic penetration and, through increased tyre contact, to improve cornering and braking. Suspension was by double wishbones and coil spring/damper units.

Scheckter and Depailler placed P34s first and second in the Swedish GP, and through the rest of the year the cars were placed second in six further races. Development lagged in 1977, especially with the small tyres, while the cars (in new sponsorship colours) grew bulkier and heavier, in part as the front tracks were increased in efforts to get the tiny tyres to work better. This was the first season when a Tyrrell car failed to win a race.

008 Phillippe's first design for Tyrrell was compact but quite conventional, and was never a real Championship contender in 1978. It had a shallow monocoque, double wishbone front suspension with inboard springs/dampers, and upper and lower links, radius arms and outboard springs at the rear.

Depailler drove 008/3 to his first GP victory at Monaco, but overall this was the year in which Lotus's ground effects advance arrived, and this Tyrrell was outmoded. Five cars were built, and a succes-

sion of scoring finishes earned Tyrrell a respectable fourth place in the Constructors' Championship – but the team was not to equal that in the next decade.

009 Introduced for 1979, this was an early ground-effects design inspired by the Lotus 79, and followed its lines, with rocker-arm front suspension, and double wishbone rear suspension. It seemed competitive as the year opened up, but after that it never looked like being a winner.

The four third placings gained were just about what this design merited, and other points-scoring finishes saw Tyrrell fifth in the Constructors' Championship again.

010 Another clone, this time clearly inspired by the Williams FW07, and first used in 1980. It appeared to be as well built as all Tyrrells, but was uncharacteristically involved in two heavy accidents attributed to structural failures. The 010 also had to serve on into 1981 because financial resources were very limited, and the team was battling to survive.

One of the bright spots was that Tyrrell attracted Michele Alboreto into its driver line-up, but this immediately underlined the need for a better car. In 1980–81 Tyrrell was sixth and eighth in the Constructors' Championship. All but two of the 1981 points, in fact, were scored in old-type 010s.

(Above) Tyrrell P34-Ford six-wheeler of 1976, Patrick Depailler driving.

Tyrrell 009-Ford, 1979.

011 The '1981 Tyrrell' was late, and did not appear until halfway through that season. Compared with 010, it was a stiffer car, complying with drive safety cell regulations due to come into force in 1982, and its efficacy in that respect was proved very early in a testing accident. It had a narrower track, pullrod suspension,

and fixed skirts. An 011 was placed in the points just once during 1981.

The car was then substantially modified for 1982, when Alboreto scored in the last seven races of the year, and won the final Grand Prix, at Las Vegas, USA. The 011 was then further modified, into 'flat-bottom' form for 1983. That was the year in

which a Tyrrell was the last Ford-Cosworth DFV/DFY-powered car to win a Grand Prix, when Alboreto won in Detroit, USA.

012 Shorter, slimmer, with a carbon-fibre/aluminium honeycomb monocoque, and still relying on non-turbo Ford-Cosworth power, 012 appeared for the last four races of 1983, and than ran throughout 1984, which was a year of strife as Tyrrell was made to forfeit points scored (notably, this included a fine second place in Detroit, USA) after a so-called 'hydrocarbon content' was found in the engine's water injection system.

These cars were powered by the ultimate Cosworth DFY, and for a time were the only normally-aspirated entries running in Grands Prix (hence Tyrrell's reluctance to agree to a reduced fuel-capacity limit, which possibly cost him the support of the turbo teams in his battle with FISA). The cars continued in 1985, until 014 was ready, and two were used in the first season of F3000.

014 Tyrrell arranged to use Renault turbo engines in 1985, albeit not as a favoured customer for the most modern units (those engines went to Lotus), but supplied through Mecachrome. In most respects, 014 followed established Tyrrell lines in chassis and running gear, with wider tracks and a longer wheelbase.

The first 014s raced in mid-season, and ran on into 1986, when the team once again had a major sponsor in Data General. At least Tyrrell returned to the top ten in the Championship, ninth in 1985 when Bellof scored all the points in Cosworth-engined cars.

015 This can really be seen as a modernized 014, with pushrod suspension all round, rear brakes moved outboard, softer body lines with the Renault V6 turbo completely enclosed, and with radiator air exhausted through the top of the side pods. It was run in Data General colours, with some success – Tyrrell was seventh in the 1986 Constructors' Championship table, Brundle's fourth in Australia being the best individual race placing.

016 Tyrrell turned away from turbocharged engines with apparent relief, to contest the new non-turbo division of F1 in

(Above) Tyrrell 009-Ford, 1979.

Tyrrell 012-Ford, 1983.

1987. The new car was designed by Brian Lisles and Maurice Phillippe, and powered by a Cosworth 3.5-litre DFZ V8. Construction was conventional, and while the cars looked bulky they were reliable and effective, the team clearly winning the Colin Chapman Cup (for entrants). Jonathan Palmer equally clearly took the Jim Clark Cup (for drivers), while Tyrrell was equal sixth in the overall Constructors' Championship.

017 The 1987 season had been encouraging for Tyrrell, but it was followed by a slump in 1988, with the new 017. This car appeared less convincing, despite its sleeker lines that did not in fact give any aerodynamic advantages, and it seemed not to benefit from clever detail work (including lowering the engine in the chassis). Palmer did score some points, but his team mate often even failed to qualify, so although the team retained its top-ten place in the Constructors' Championship, it was beating only the no-hopers on Grand Prix grids.

From the summer, Harvey Postlethwaite was already hard at work on a successor, but until that was ready, three 017s had to be used in early 1989 races. The principal modification in '017B' was the introduction of a Tyrrell-designed six-speed gearbox mounted longitudinally (this was an advance development for the next car, 018). The only race for these cars was the Brazilian GP, when Palmer finished seventh.

018 The Tyrrell Racing Organization's team was fifth in the 1989 Constructors' Championship, their highest place since 1979, yet the outcome of the season was still something of a disappointment. Harvey Postlethwaite laid out a state-of-the-art car, with the slimmest nose among grids of cars all noted for this characteristic, on a carbon-composite monocoque, powered by a Cosworth DFR engine, and the Tyrrell-developed gearbox first seen in 017B.

A front suspension novelty accounted for the fine front-end lines – it was a double-wishbone layout, but there was only a single damper, mounted just ahead of the instrument panel and operated by a transverse rocker and pushrods. There was a more normal double wishbone pushrod arrangement at the rear. In 1990 Pirelli tyres were used.

The team was not generously financed in 1989, indeed to all outward appearances hardly financed at all until mid-season, when sponsors were proclaimed, and Camel (cigarette) yellow was spliced to Tyrrell blue.

A driver change after six races turned out not to be a great setback, for new boy Jean Alesi finished fourth in his very first Grand Prix (in France), after running as high as second. The best final placing of

Tyrrell 018-Ford, 1989.

the year was achieved by Alboreto, third in Mexico, and in 1990 the team had its best result for years when in the first race Alesi led to half-distance, and finished second, the other team car finishing sixth.

019 It might not have looked much, but Tyrrell 019 ushered in a new fashion for F1 – the high nose/dropped front wing layout that proved to have several aerodynamic advantages.

Making its debut at Interlagos (Brazil), the new Postlethwaite-designed machine caused a real stir. It was small, neatly-detailed, handled well and was very nimble.

Although Brian Hart's massaging had worked wonders, its engine – Ford's ageing DFR, which Benetton had first used in 1988 – was nothing special, but its fiery young Corsican driver, Jean Alesi, truly was. Unhappily for Tyrrell, Alesi soon decided to seek his (larger) fortune elsewhere, and would defect to Williams for 1991.

Tyrrell, as often at this stage, had very little obvious financial support on his cars. This, coupled to the use of an engine lacking at least 70/80bhp compared with Honda and Ferrari units, meant that results were always going to be a struggle. Yet Alesi managed a miraculous second place at Monaco, and Nakajima scrab-

bled a couple of sixth places at the end of the season.

020 Although it wasn't quite all change for the Ockham-based team, there was no air of calm and permanency about the 1991 effort. Compared with the remarkably effective 019, the 020 was awful. Modena achieved second in Canada, and fourth in Phoenix and that was really all.

The reason for the Japanese driver, Nakajima, being hired finally became crystal-clear, when Tyrrell adopted Mugen-Honda V10 engines (heavy, but powerful) to use instead of their previously reliable Ford DFRs. Not that one could blame Ken, for considerable money changed hands, to keep him afloat – and if Honda technology had worked such miracles with McLaren, why should they not do so with him?

Modena and Mugen-Honda, frankly, were disappointing substitutes for Alesi and Ford DFR, and there was only a 50 per cent finishing record, so it was really a miracle that the team scored twelve points in the Constructors' series – half of them coming from one result (in Canada).

020 itself was a simple update of the innovative 019, though this could not make up for the sheer lack of engine grunt, and lack of driving talent. Nakajima, by the way, retired at the end of the season,

so had the deal with Honda been worthwhile, after all?

020B and 020C Not an all-new car, for sure, but because it used a totally different engine (and the drivers were all-change too), it deserves separate study.

Ever-low in the pecking order, little-sponsored, and short of funds as usual (though rent-a-driver Andrea de Cesaris helped considerably), Tyrrell had to rework the season-old design for 1992. Mugen-Honda having taken their engines away (Footwork/Arrows would use them instead), Tyrrell signed a deal to lease Ilmor V10s instead. In later years, of course, Ilmor would transmute into 'Mercedes-Benz' and produce peerless power units, but that position was still years into the future.

Tyrrell might have been sold up in 1991/1992, so precious little new engineering was done, and Mike Coughlan had to scheme up the cheap-and-cheerful 020B in double-quick time.

Tyrrell's gentle downward slide continued, for the cars only reached the finish half the time, there were no podium positions, and De Cesaris scored all of the team's eight points. Grouillard was described by one close observer as a 'liability', and no-one else argued with that – four accidents and eight engine/transmission failures summing up his dismal short stay.

Re-engined with the Yamahas intended for the 021, and renamed as 020C, the old designs soldiered on for the first nine races of 1993 – more than half the season – and even though these V10s improved significantly as the summer progressed, they still delivered no points. The 021 that followed was really no better.

021 Once again, the need for cash caused another cataclysmic change at Tyrrell. Here was yet another new engine – the fourth in four years, this time from Yamaha/Judd – and yet another pay-for-drives pilot, Katayama from Japan. Though he was not a beggar, Ken could not afford to choose – the engines came free, and Cabin (cigarette) money followed Katayama.

Even this, though, could not deliver new cars before mid-season, for the Japanese-engined 021s did not race until Germany in July. Strangely, in view of Tyrrell's early successes, they were not high-nose machines.

But, the fact that no points at all were gained tells its own story: we knew that De Cesaris was at least competent, and the chassis was tolerable if not technically up-to-the-minute, but with the cars 3.5sec off the pace in Germany, one had to blame the engines.

Tyrrell 021-Yamaha of 1993, Andrea de Cesaris driving.

Tyrrell 022-Yamaha, 1994.

022 Altogether neater and more effective than the short-lived 021, the 022 was a good Grand Prix car, the result of a happy liaison between Harvey Postlethwaite (now happily free of Ferrari, and a major shareholder in the Tyrrell team) and Jean-Claude Migeot.

Yamaha power, still carefully nurtured and developed by Judd in Rugby, was better and more reliably present even than in the latter part of 1993, which almost helped to make the 022 into a mid-field runner. The arrival of Mark Blundell instead of the erratic De Cesaris, too, was a real bonus. Money, and a lack of major sponsorship, though, was still a problem.

All in all, a better year than in 1993 when, with the same basic engine, there had been no scores at all. This time, at least, there were thirteen Manufacturers' points, shared between Mark Blundell (eight) and Katayama. With a third, for

Tyrrell 026-Ford of 1998, Ricardo Rosset driving. This was the final Tyrrell model.

Blundell, in Spain, that was quite an improvement that pleased everyone.

023 An ordinary car, this, with few redeeming features, and Tyrrell was now on the slide towards 1998 oblivion. Tyrrell had hoped for much under the new 3-litre formula, but the latest Yamaha was much less competitive than its 3.5-litre ancestor. The aerodynamic performance, in particular, let the side down.

A new 'Hydrolink' suspension system, by Harvey Postlethwaite and Mike Gascoyne, that used high-pressure fluid instead of steel springs, was never properly explained (though it was claimed to have 'active' benefits without being active, which was banned!), and the transverse six-speed gearbox of previous years was retained. Hydrolink was abandoned halfway through the season, for it had shown no advantages.

A new driver (Mika Salo in his first full season) could not match the Yamaha's unreliability. Mika scored all the points – two fifths and sixth, at the end of the season: Katayama, who came in with the Yamaha package, failed miserably. Certainly no advance on 1994.

024 No improvement really – five points, undistinguished race performances, and the usual adjectives of 'brave', 'friendly' and 'honest' all being applied – really sum up Tyrrell's 1996 season. Harvey Postlethwaite's high-nose 024 was described as a 'low-risk' project, was as neat as expected, and great things were forecast of the latest high-revving OX11A Yamaha engine during the season, especially as it was now linked to a longitudinal six-speed transmission – yet virtually nothing was delivered.

Tyrrell had lost their Nokia sponsorship, which didn't help when funds were really needed to go testing, but it was the Yamaha engine's lamentable reliability (and lack of competitive power) that really proved to be the killer.

As in four previous years, driver Katayama was a grave disappointment, and when Tyrrell decided that he had to leave, Yamaha engines left with him.

On the showings of 1996, neither was a great loss, especially as there had been fifty engine failures during the season.

025 Still going down, but clinging on to the sport that they loved, Tyrrell produced a 1997 F1 car that was adequate but no more. Reverting to a Ford-Cosworth 'customer' V8 – the ED4 (the ED5 would follow later in the year), which was itself a final evolution of the early-1990s HB –

and running with the usual lack of sponsorship, they notched up only two Championship points – a fifth place for Mika Salo at Monaco when (in a wet race) he ran through non-stop.

Postlethwaite's 025 was announced early, with a near-white livery in which Ford was barely mentioned, and where PIAA was the main supporter. It looked neat, partly because of the compact 75-degree V8, it was small and compact, but it never looked as if it was about to win anything. The engine was described as 60–100bhp down on the best V10s – and it showed.

025 was no more than a development of 024, though choosing Cosworth's V8 engine meant that almost every item, and its packaging, had been changed. Here was a mediocre, safety-first car, and it showed in its performance.

There had been no scope (or money) to be adventurous (though infamous 'X'-wings were tried, briefly, in mid-season), and there would be even less in 1998, as Ken Tyrrell sold out to British American Tobacco, so that 1998 would be the last year for a Tyrrell-badged car.

026 So this was to be the long goodbye, a complete 1998 season controlled by British American Tobacco, and without Ken Tyrrell himself, who walked away from the company which he had founded, in February.

Tyrrell himself regretted that his favoured driver, Jos Verstappen, could not be retained for 1998, and there was no doubt that this was justified by the performance of the chosen duo. Takagi, like all Japanese drivers who have tackled F1, had an unimpressive driving record. Rosset, well, he did not even qualify for five of the races – though he was impressively financed!

Like its immediate predecessors, 026 was a typically conventional car, not special in any way, and obliged to rely on 720bhp 'customer' Ford V10 power, the type that Stewart (and Ford) had already cast aside in favour of lighter, higher-revving, machinery.

At the end of the season Tyrrell had scored no Championship points at all, so disappeared with a whimper. The writing, in any case, had been on the wall for months, as a modified 026 had been seen testing, with Renault V10 power, as a lash-up for the first of the BARs that would replace the Tyrrells on the grids of 1999.

Vanwall

Guy Anthony Vandervell was a hard-nosed industrialist who originally supported the BRM project until he could no longer stomach the committee-minded bureaucracy mixed with an element of gentlemanly amateurism. He then set out to build up his own team to beat the Italians – who were the target that he thought mattered in the 1950s.

His very first Grand Prix car had been a Ferrari, that he called the 'Thin Wall Special' (q.v.), a name inspired by the shell bearings his company manufactured, and that he had purchased to give the BRM team some experience of actually running a modern Grand Prix car. Other Ferraris (also nicknamed 'Thin Wall') followed, and were raced, mainly in the UK.

Vandervell then set up his own design team to manufacture the Vanwall cars, first in F2 and ultimately in F1 guise. The original car took ages to be completed, and the original 2.0litre type was not ready until the 2.5litre F1 came in. Progress thereafter was rapid, this car being raced in 2.0, 2.3 and 2.5litre form – all these being versions of the same four-cylinder engine, that had Rolls-Royce (crankcase) and Norton motorcycle (cylinder head) influences, and had been designed by Leo Kuzmicki.

From 1956 four new cars were built, with chassis and suspension designed by Colin Chapman of Lotus, the tall sleek bodies being shaped by aerodynamicist Frank Costin (who had already worked wonders on a series of Lotus racing sports cars).

These were the basis of the improved cars constructed in 1957 and 1958, that went on to win nine World Championship races, and the very first Constructors' Cup of 1958.

After spending a great deal of money, Tony Vandervell's prime racing ambition was finally satisfied, but since his health was precarious he then ran down the team's efforts, the cars only ever appearing sporadically from 1959, and the last of all being built in 1961.

The original Vanwalls never carried year-on-year type and chassis numbers, though the ever-expanding fleet of Chapman/Costin machines eventually took on a series of VW numbers that were often repeated and swapped around from season to season. Each year's cars tended to be used as mobile parts bins for the following season's machinery.

1954–55 The first Vanwall of all ran as the 'Vanwall Special', had a chassis built up by Cooper on Ferrari lines of the day, and in its first 2litre form was distinguished by an ugly surface cooling radiator for the engine. This was used throughout 1954, then written off in a Spanish GP practice accident.

Four more closely related cars were built for 1955, all of them with conventional radiators, and 2.5litre engines, but at the end of the season all were broken up to provide parts for the next-generation machinery.

Although powerful and fast, they had handling and reliability deficiencies, which explains why their only successes came in small British events, first in a heat at the Crystal Palace International Trophy meeting of July 1955, and later at Castle Combe, Harry Schell being the driver in each case.

1956–58 The four original Chapman/Costin cars, which still used developed versions of the original engines and transmissions, were much more serious propositions than the original, for they were no longer copies of any other make of racing car.

Stirling Moss drove one to Vanwall's first significant victory, in the 1956 International Trophy (at Silverstone); Harry Schell battled for the lead with the Lancia-Ferraris in the French GP, Schell also being ultra-fast in the Italian GP. Although the cars were very fast in a straight line, and their standard of workmanship was high,

Vanwall of 1956, Stirling Moss driving.

they were let down, far too often, by niggling faults and breakages.

The same cars were refurbished, redesigned and further improved for 1957, with new examples also being built. Coil spring rear suspension was added, Stirling Moss and Tony Brooks joined the team, and for the very first time this was an organization that could match anything put up by the Italians. One car was tried at Rheims with a streamlined body, while another was built with a lightweight chassis.

Stirling Moss took over the unwell Tony Brooks's car in the British GP, to record a famous and historic victory, adding to that success with further victories at Pescara (Italy) and Monza later in the summer.

For 1958 the team was even more formidable than before, there now being the makings of eight cars, whose engines and details were shuffled, not only from 1957 but from race to race in 1958 too. Even though the rules had changed, the engines being obliged to run on AvGas instead of a methanol mix, with peak power down from about 285bhp (methanol) to 260bhp (AvGas), the latest cars were no lighter but somehow faster than before.

It was a season of triumph, for Vanwall dominated F1. Moss and Brooks shared the victories, but there was tragedy at the end of the year when Stuart Lewis-Evans was fatally injured in an accident in the Moroccan GP. During the next winter Tony Vandervell formally announced the end of a full team effort.

1959–60 One car was rebuilt in a more compact and lighter form, and driven by Tony Brooks in the 1959 British GP and secondary British events in 1960. It was also used to test and prove a new independent rear suspension designed by Valerio Colotti.

Together with a new gearbox, mounted behind the final drive, this was used on 'VW11', the 'low-line' car that was the last Vanwall actually to start in a Grand Prix, the 1960 French race. This was its only race.

1961 Vanwall experimented with a rear-Vanwall-engined Lotus 18 in 1960, then for 1961 came up with a new rear-engined car of their own (VW14), that had a 2.6litre engine intended for the abortive Intercontinental Formula. It raced once only, finishing fifth in the International Trophy at Silverstone.

Vauxhall

How times change. At the end of the twentieth century Vauxhall was only one part, and a minor part at that, of the colossal General Motors multinational corporation. Yet in 1914 the same company built a Grand Prix car, and would have developed it further if the First World War had not intervened.

There were, in fact, two separate Vauxhall entries in Grand Prix racing – one by courtesy of French regulations, the other as a dedicated effort.

In 1912 the ACF found themselves short of entries for the French GP at the Dieppe circuit, so decided to run the *Coupe de l'Auto* alongside the main event, and make all such cars eligible for the big race. Vauxhall, therefore, who prepared three 3litre cars, took advantage of this.

The *Coupe de l'Auto* Vauxhalls had 90 × 118mm (2,991cc) four-cylinder engines with side valves, driving through four-speed gearboxes, and although 80bhp was talked of, there was little evidence of this on the track. Visually these two-seaters had the famous Vauxhall flutes on their radiators, the drivers being the much-respected Percy Lambert, A.J. Hancock and W. Watson.

Hindsight tells us that these cars were ill-prepared. Although Hancock's car was well-placed after five laps, fourth overall and actually leading every other 3litre engined car, Watson's car retired with engine trouble, and Lambert's car was near the tail.

Hancock's car was sixth overall after the first day, but was eliminated on Day Two with a broken piston. Three Vauxhalls had started, but not one finished.

In the meantime, chief designer Laurence H. Pomeroy had designed a new overhead-camshaft Vauxhall engine as early as 1910, but this performed poorly, and it was not until 1913/14 that his plans to use it were revived. In the meantime the Prince Henry sports car had been launched, and prospects looked good.

For 1914 Vauxhall proposed to build a team of cars to compete in two races – the RAC Tourist Trophy in the Isle of Man (for 3.3litre cars) and the French GP at Lyons (for 4.5litre machines). By current standards the chassis were conventional enough, though made to be as light as possible, with narrow two-seater bodywork, half-elliptic leaf springs all round, and without front brakes of any sort.

By converting the engines between races – different blocks, pistons and crankshafts – the same basic engines could be used for both events. It was planned, and it was achieved, that conversion would take place in a matter of days after the TT, and before trials for the French GP began.

Twin overhead camshafts and four-valves per cylinder made these engines as up-to-the-minute as possible. In 3.3litre form they

Vanwall 'lowline' of 1960, Tony Brooks driving.

Vauxhall, as raced in the 1912 GP.

gave 90bhp at 3,600rpm, while in 4.5litre Grand Prix form they produced 130bhp at 3,300rpm, which was fully competitive for the period. The four-speed gearboxes were separated from the clutch by a short shaft, and there was torque tube drive to the rear axle.

Three cars, none of them (as it transpired) well-prepared, started the TT race in June 1914, two retiring with engine problems almost at once, the third car rolling into retirement on the second day. For the French GP, there were only three weeks to convert the engines and find some reliability, but all was in vain, as two stuttered appallingly slowly around the first long lap in Lyons, the third car also expiring during the event. Later it was discovered that a simple carburettor problem, that should have been discovered if enough testing had ever taken place, was the culprit. Perhaps it was a mercy that the First World War intervened, as the press was extremely critical, and although the cars performed better post-war, no more was heard of Vauxhall's Grand Prix ambitions. Perhaps it was as well, for the British firm was neither worldly nor technically capable at this time.

Veritas

In 1948 two former BMW engineers, Ernst Loof and Lorenz Dietrich, built a number of sports cars, using the pre-war-type BMW 328 engine in a tubular chassis,

based on the design that had won the 1940 Gran Premio de Brescia (that has sometimes been called the '1940 Mille Miglia').

These were highly successful in Germany, in both sports car and F2 races. Despite a ban on their export, some were nonetheless dismantled and exported as 'spares', to appear in France under other names.

Loof developed the BMW engine and then designed his own unit, that was built for him by Heinkel. This followed broadly the same lines as the BMW engine, but was cast in alloy, and had 'square' dimensions of 75 × 75mm, giving it a capacity of 1,988cc. In competition trim, and when using three Solex carburettors and running on methanol it gave a useful 140bhp.

This was fitted into a new single-seater that had a ladder-style chassis and independent suspension all round, by double wishbones and longitudinal torsion bars. Some BMW components were used, but Loof also designed his own five-speed gearbox.

As Germany was still banned from international competition until 1950, Veritas had to be content with success at home, and as a competent limited-production car it helped to develop a number of leading German race drivers.

However, Veritas became too ambitious for its own small facilities to cope (it was also making a 750cc-engined sports car using French Panhard parts), and it folded in 1950.

Dietrich left the wrecked concern, but Loof revived it in a small workshop at the

Nürburgring. Later in 1950 he unveiled a single-seater, with an all-enveloping body style and de Dion rear suspension, that became known as the Veritas-Meteor to distinguish it from the RS open-wheelers. The apex of Veritas achievement came when Paul Pietsch won the 1951 Eifelrennen in a Meteor.

By the time F2 was elevated to World Championship status, however, the drive had gone out of the Veritas marque, and it was struggling to survive. International events rarely saw a Veritas, though the Belgian amateur, Arthur Legat, entered his home Grand Prix with one in 1952 (he was extremely slow). Five Veritas cars started the German GP, but only one finished, Fritz Reiss being seventh and two laps down.

Legat entered his car in the Belgian GP of 1953, but was again very slow and retired after only one lap. Six of the cars started the German GP and three finished – in ninth, twelfth and sixteenth places.

During 1953 Loof realized that he could not keep pace with new developments, so he closed his works, and returned to work for BMW. He died only three years later, and nothing more was ever heard of Veritas.

Vinot-Deguingand

Like Vauxhall, this bustling little French concern took advantage of the ACF's decision to run 3litre *Coupe de l'Auto* machines in with other French GP contenders in 1912, and entered a team of three cars.

To meet *Coupe de l'Auto* regulations, the Vinots had four-cylinder, 89 × 120mm (2,996cc) engines with overhead valves, and three-speed transmissions. These cars had somewhat curious styling, with a humpback shape behind the cockpit, which served to cover the twin spare wheels.

Naturally they could not hope to keep up with the vast-engined Grand Prix cars of that year, but on the Dieppe circuit they hoped that reliability would be in their favour. Unhappily, only one of the three cars reached the finish – way down in twelfth place, more than five hours behind the winning Peugeot.

By the middle of Day One (of a two-day event) only two of the cars were still running, well down the field, and only Vonlatum's car survived the first day on the rough, stony circuit. Struggling on to the finish, it achieved some honour for the company, but no glory. Vinot-Deguingand never came back to repeat this fruitless exercise.

Voisin

Gabriel Voisin was already famous as a French pioneer in aviation circles before he turned to building and selling cars. Starting in 1918 by acquiring the rights to the still-born Citroën model that used a sleeve-valve power unit, he soon made his reputation, especially with sporting derivatives that followed.

Launching into Grand Prix racing early in the 2litre era, in 1923 he entered no fewer than four cars for the French GP at Tours. These were astonishing-looking machines, to which *The Autocar* devoted four entire pages of technical analysis, for they hid a sleeve-valve straight-six-cylinder engine under body shells having a carefully calculated aerodynamic form (quite befitting an aeroplane specialist) in that the rear wheels were almost totally enclosed, and the front end was both low and brutally angular. The front track was a conventional 4ft 9in (145cm) the rear track was a mere 2ft 6in (76cm)!

The structure was an early-type monocoque, there being no separate frame, but a complex amalgam of wood, pressed-steel members, steel tubes and aluminium panelling. The sleeve-valve engine itself (62 × 110mm, 1,993cc) was claimed to use many parts from Voisin road cars of that period, had a compression ratio of 7.0:1, and used twin Zenith carburettors.

The French GP itself, remembered mainly for the quite unexpected victory of Segrave's Sunbeam (and the failure of the supercharged Fiats), was a disappointment for Voisin, as only one car (that driven by G. Lefebvre – who had also designed the race car for his *patron*) finished, in fifth and last place, at an average of 63.2mph (102kmh).

Even after five laps, all the Voisins were a long way behind the leaders (for many laps they rather depressingly held all the last three places), and in the end more than two hours separated winner from last.

Humiliated, and unable to finance the development of supercharged engines that would surely be required in future years, Voisin never again tackled full-blooded Grand Prix racing.

Vulpes

This small, but ambitious, French concern was so inspired by the decision to organize *the* first-ever Grand Prix on French soil, that it set out to prepare a car to compete on the special, long circuit close to Le Mans.

Faced with team competition from experienced marques such as Renault, Fiat and Mercedes, this was a brave move. Even so, there was an almost complete lack of thought about detail behind this entry, for at pre-event scrutiny it was turned away for weighing more than the maximum of 1,000kg/2,205lb stated in the regulations.

If it could not even meet the one regulation that mattered (for there were no limitations on engine size), it could not have been a serious contender – and nothing more was ever heard from Vulpes, that itself went out of business in 1910.

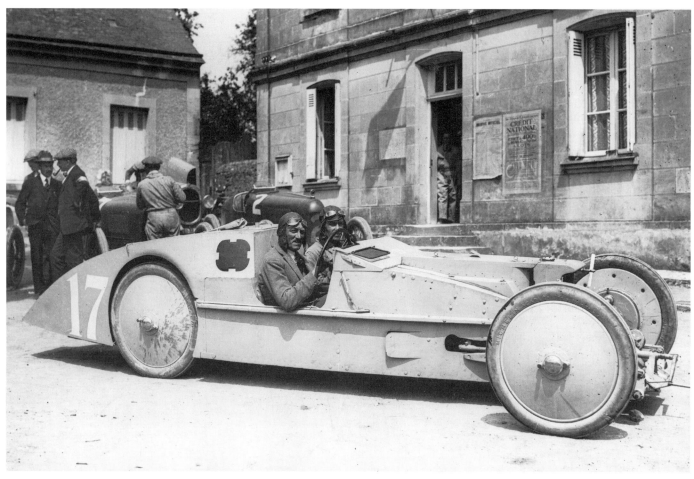

Voisin of 1923.

Wolf WR1-Ford of 1977.

Walker-Climax

In 1959 Rob Walker, the most successful of all post-war private entrants, ran F1 and F2 Coopers for Stirling Moss and Maurice Trintignant to drive. They rewarded him, and enjoyed themselves, by winning regularly, but the behaviour of the cars was not up to his expectations, so Alf Francis (his chief mechanic) and ex-Maserati designer Valerio Colotti designed a replacement.

The resulting 'Walker-Climax' looked somewhat like the Cooper of the period, but it had a more scientifically designed space-frame chassis, all-independent suspension by coil springs and double wishbones, and used Borrani wire wheels. The 2.5litre Coventry-Climax engine sat upright in the frame, thus ensuring a high-engine cover, while the bulbous pannier fuel tanks were held in place by rubber bands. As with the existing Walker Coopers, a Colotti five-speed gearbox was used.

Work on the car – only one of them was completed – was slow, partly because the arrival of the Lotus 18 made it virtually redundant before it could be completed. When tested in 1961, the new 1.5litre F1 formula was already in force, and the

Walker became too bulky and heavy to be competitive.

The original car therefore did not race, though it was preserved, while a second, lighter, example was never completed because Stirling Moss was happy with the Lotus that the team had purchased.

Weigel

Although Weigel was a British-based company, its founder, D.M. Weigel, was the first managing director of Clement-Talbot Ltd, which had strong French connections.

The first two Weigel Grand Prix cars (driven by Laxen and Pryce-Harrison, neither of them 'racing aces') were long and low, with straight-eight engines of 14.9litres, allied to two-speed transmissions, and had their designs rooted in Itala principles. These were entered for the 1907 French GP, on the Dieppe circuit, where the only regulations were concerned with fuel consumption (cars had to achieve better than 30litres/100km or 9.4mpg).

At half-distance, only Harrison's car was still running, in twenty-fourth place out of twenty-seven survivors, and even

that machine disappeared, *en panne*, minutes later.

Weigel tried again for the 1908 race that was once again held at Dieppe, in a race that limited maximum piston area to 117sq in, and minimum weight to 1,150kg/2,534lb. Although the cars were new, their basic layout was not changed. The 12,781cc engines were now four-cylinder units with single overhead camshaft valve gear (a real advance) and three-speed transmissions. This time three cars started the race, driven by the 1907 duo, Laxen and Pryce-Harrison, along with Shannon. The latter's car soon retired with a deranged steering system, while Laxen's car retired on the fourth long lap after an accident due to brake failure; the third car also retired, on lap six, when it rolled, tossing out driver and passenger. Humiliated by all this, and with its company finances in trouble, Weigel never again tried to break into front-line motorsport.

Williams

See pp.240–247.

Wolf

Austrian-born Walter Wolf came into Grand Prix racing when he backed the struggling Williams team from late in 1975. He acquired the equipment of the dissolved Hesketh team for use in 1976, when the cars carried Williams designations, and were sometimes referred to as 'Wolf-Williams'.

Wolf took over 60 per cent of the Williams company, and within a year Frank Williams found himself in an impossible position, and quit to regain his much-cherished independence.

For 1977 Wolf set up a powerful new team, with Harvey Postlethwaite to design a new car, Peter Warr tempted from Lotus so that he could manage affairs, and just one driver – Jody Scheckter – hired. The team won three Grands Prix. That, however, was their only good season, for Wolf had no immediate response to the 'ground effect' revolution ushered in by Lotus in 1978.

The F1 team failed to score a single point in 1979, and during the winter that followed it was merged with Fittipaldi, as Walter Wolf turned his back on motor racing.

continued on p.247

Frank Williams started out as a racing driver, fast but not outstanding, soon realized that he was not World Championship material, and turned to become an entrant, an entrepreneur and, later, a constructor.

First of all he ran a Brabham F2 car for Piers Courage, following it with an ex-works Brabham BT26 F1 car. This enterprise worked well, for Courage placed the immaculate car second in two World Championship races in 1969.

Tragedy then followed. Williams's ambition to become a fully-fledged team owner saw him run the 'works' de Tomaso cars in 1970, but Piers Courage was killed in an accident in the Dutch GP. For 1971 Williams reverted to his role as a customer-car entrant, with a March.

Then came his own 'Politoys' project in 1972, followed by the awkwardly named Iso-Marlboros. These were later redesignated Williams FW01–FW03 (the first cars to carry what became a famous series of type numbers), and in 1975 they were joined by the first 'new' Williams, the FW04.

Because of Williams's own precarious finances (he once admitted that his 'office' was a kerbside telephone box …), the team was run on the tightest possible budget, so the opportunity offered by joining forces with multimillionaire Walter Wolf for 1976 seemed miraculous (the erstwhile Wolf-Hesketh 308Cs were run as FW05s), although this was not a partnership that would last for long.

In 1977 Williams was again on his own, and ran a March. Though his season was totally without success, he somehow founded an association with Saudi Arabian businessmen, who provided financial stability for the next five years, and allowed the team to lay down their first in-house F1 cars, that were designed by Patrick Head.

This new car, the FW06, was promising, but the FW07 that followed was outstanding. The team's first-ever Grand Prix victory was scored by Regazzoni at Silverstone in 1979, and in 1980 and 1981 Williams won their first Constructors' Championships. A period of relative disappointment then followed, and ironically it was the TAG company, that Williams had brought into Grand Prix racing, who caused much of it by backing a turbocharged Porsche engine – that was used by McLaren. Rather than become a second (customer) user for these German engines, Williams chose to develop a new

relationship with Honda, and in time that was to be very rewarding, for Williams-Honda cars won the 1986 and 1987 Constructors' series.

By then the company was operating from a sophisticated base at Didcot in Oxfordshire, where fortunately they had the managerial strength in depth to ride the terrible blow of Frank Williams's crippling road accident in 1986.

After Honda moved its F1 association to McLaren in 1988, Williams suffered a lean year, for its FW12s had to be powered by normally aspirated Judd engines in what was the final 'turbo year' in F1. Frank Williams then developed a new relationship with his one-time arch-opponent Renault for 1989, when they developed a new normally aspirated V10.

This liaison proved fruitful in the very first year, for Williams-Renault victories followed suit almost at once, which fittingly rounded off a decade in which the Williams team was usually at the forefront of all major F1 successes and developments.

In the next few years, Williams surged on to establish complete F1 dominance. With technical wizard Adrian Newey joining Patrick Head from 1990/1991, and with ever-improving Renault V10s behind their shoulders, a series of superstar drivers won race after race, and championship after championship, for the team. Not that most of them reaped much praise for this, as Frank Williams showed a rare genius for sacking, falling out with, or simply losing drivers after they had proved to be the best in the world.

Nigel Mansell returned to the fold for 1991 and 1992 (when he became World Champion), but then stormed out in a dispute over money (Frank Williams called him, 'a genius in the car, a pain in the arse out of it'). Alain Prost joined the team for a single year in 1993 (becoming World Champion, and then retiring), then the great Ayrton Senna arrived for 1994, only to be tragically killed at Imola in his third race.

Damon Hill, the much underestimated 'apprentice' (he had been the team's test driver) then shouldered the burden, nearly won the Driver's Championship in the next two years, and finally delivered in 1996 – whereupon Frank Williams sacked him because of his salary demands. No matter, thought Williams, for they had already hired Jacques Villeneuve, who then won the Drivers' crown for them in 1997. This, though, had to be balanced

against the loss of Adrian Newey, who moved to McLaren in 1997, once again following a salary dispute.

For two years thereafter, the team went into decline, for Renault withdrew their 'works' support, Hill's replacement Heinz-Harald Frentzen did not get on with the team, Villeneuve left voluntarily to help start up the BAR team, and another much-hyped Williams 'miracle' signing, Alex Zanardi, proved to be a grave disappointment.

The real miracle was that, in 1997, Williams had announced that they were forging a strategic alliance with BMW for 2000 and beyond – and that against all the odds it was a success. 2000 was the year in which the FW22s were better than any Williams since 1997, and when the team's coherence seemed to return. In the early 2000s, perhaps, this famous pedigree would once again be recording victories.

FW01–FW03 There were the erstwhile Iso-Marlboro cars, redesignated after Iso abruptly stopped paying contributions in the spring of 1974, and uprated for use by the team in 1975, when the regular drivers were Arturo Merzario and Jacques Laffite, though with eight (sometimes paying) stand-ins.

The team was trying to run on a budget that would have been inadequate for a single top-line F3 season in the 1980s – and Williams was even forced into buying scrubbed, sometimes old, tyres from other teams. Late in 1977 FW03 reappeared as the Apollon-Williams, entered for the Italian GP for Loris Kessel, who did not remotely approach a qualifying pace before crashing his car.

FW04 A one-off development of the existing FW cars, carried out by Ray Stokoe, whose main contribution was with a lighter, slimmer and more angular monocoque. Just once, in the 1975 German GP, other teams suffered enough problems for Jacques Laffite to drive FW04 through into a well-merited second place.

This car was later acquired by Brian McGuire, who attempted to uprate it for Grands Prix as a McGuire in 1977, but died in it in a Brands Hatch accident.

FW05 This designation was applied to the Hesketh 308Cs when they were taken over by the Wolf team (q.v.), and when Frank Williams joined in that project.

Williams FW03-Ford (also Iso-Marlboro) of 1974.

GP), his driving coupling with the car to serve notice that the revived and now well-backed Williams was henceforth to be taken seriously.

The cars were later sold on, and had useful second lives in the British national series.

FW07 Williams's – and Head's – first ground-effects car was exemplary, and to a greater extent than the earlier FW06 it marked the team's transition from being a mere 'British kit car' builder to a fully-fledged constructor, with the resources to dedicate time and effort to research and evaluate test programmes.

The FW07 had an aluminium monocoque, with conventional suspension (upper rocking arm/lower wishbone/inboard coil spring-damper) that was necessarily very stiff so as to remain consistent with the very heavy aerodynamic downloads that were developed.

The side pods were broad, yet the overall lines were still elegant. A large radiator was positioned at the front of each pod, for oil on the left, and for water on the right. The cars were revealed as the 1979 European season opened – a little late as there followed minor failures and incidents that meant that despite their obvious speed, results did not come until high summer.

Before that, this had become the first Williams F1 car to lead races, then Regazzoni won the British GP, and in the

FW06 During 1977 Patrick Head designed his first Williams, and the first Williams to have any real impact on F1 racing – the neat, straightforward, light and above all reliable FW06. It had a conventional monocoque and suspension, the engine, inevitably, being a Cosworth DFV.

Three cars were built and driven by Alan Jones through 1978, and they served on until the next Williams, the FW07, was ready in the spring of 1979. By that time the FW06 was outclassed by the ground-effects cars, but Jones had already scored points (notably a second place, in the US

Williams FW07C-Ford of 1981, Carlos Reutemann driving.

second half of the year Jones won the German, Austrian, Dutch and Canadian GPs. Because of this, the team were runners-up in the Constructors' Championship.

Williams went one better in 1980, when the Constructors' title fell to them by a wide margin, while drivers Jones and Regazzoni were first and third respectively in the Drivers' Championship. Between them, they won Grands Prix in Argentina, Monaco, France, Britain, Canada and USA (East). The car used was designated FW07B, due to its stiffer monocoque, and extended under-car aerodynamics. It was not, however, perfect, for it suffered from 'porpoising', but shorter underwings seemed to cure this trait.

Reutemann drove an FW07B to win the 1981 South African race, before the FW07C appeared to comply with the newly imposed ban on skirts. In that form, Jones and Reutemann drove FW07Cs to win in Long Beach (USA) and Brazil, after that the team was caught up in the scramble to develop a suspension-lowering system, to emulate the Brabhams that had pioneered this installation.

In aerodynamic respects, therefore, the cars were not properly effective again until the end of the summer. Reutemann won the team's fourth Grand Prix of the year in Belgium (that brought his personal run to fifteen consecutive points-scoring finishes) – but the next victory did not come until the very last race of the season, when Alan Jones won in Las Vegas; this was also Jones's last race for Williams. For the second year in succession, Williams Grand Prix Engineering became Champion Constructors.

The ageing FW07Cs were run for the first three Grands Prix of 1982, when Reutemann and Rosberg each finished second in a race. At this point (pre-Falklands war, or was this a coincidence?) the Argentine driver abruptly retired, and Mario Andretti stood in for a single race.

FW08 Once again Williams waited for the European season to start before launching a new car, the short-wheelbase, short-chassis FW08. In most design respects it followed FW07, but apart from being more compact than before, it was also a stiffer car, and eventually proved to have better aerodynamic qualities. It was right down to the minimum weight, so could also carry the 'water ballast' that DFV users employed for a brief and technically dubious period.

Keke Rosberg was the principal driver in 1982, and consistently successful, so that although he only won one race (the 'Swiss GP', at Dijon, actually in France), he amassed enough points to win the Drivers' Championship, though Williams slipped to fourth place in the Constructors' table.

FW08 had always been designed with a possible six-wheeler (four rear wheels) configuration for later development, and FW08/1 was actually converted to run in that guise, in a test programme in the autumn of 1982.

As well as the lower drag and higher tyre contact patch advantages that such a layout gave, from using four small (front-size) wheels at the rear, there was also the possibility of gaining increased downforce from a larger shaped underside. All this was nullified, in fact, when six-wheeler cars were immediately barred from F1 in 1983.

For 1983, therefore, an FW08 was modified to comply with new 'flat bottom' regulations, and a series of new FW08Cs were then built. Outwardly these cars looked markedly different from before, with very short side pods containing radiators, beside the engine.

The engine, still the DFV, was now coming to the end of a distinguished career, and in power terms was outclassed by the latest turbo units. The only Grand Prix that Williams won in 1983 was the Monaco race, with Rosberg. Otherwise he and Laffite struggled to gain enough points to secure fourth place for Williams in the Constructors' table.

FW09 Williams's first turbo car was ready for tests in the autumn of 1983, and actually competed in a 'race test' in the

South African GP that wound up the Championship season: Rosberg drove it to an encouraging fifth place.

The power unit was the Honda RSA163-E 80-degree V6 with IHI turbochargers – an improved version of that earlier used in the Spirit 201 of 1983. It was undoubtedly very powerful, but had a very abrupt power delivery.

For the chassis, Patrick Head still employed an aluminium honeycomb monocoque (but this was not stiff enough), and there was a new pullrod rear suspension. This was superseded by the FW09B in 1984, and also had Williams's own six-speed gearbox.

From late 1983 the team was based at its new Didcot factory. In 1984, the racing season was not rewarding, partly because the team had to learn how to use the new power unit. Understeer was a particular problem. Rosberg won one Grand Prix – at Dallas (USA) – but Williams was only sixth in the Constructors' Championship.

FW10 Head finally turned to using a carbon-composite monocoque for the 1985 car, and the nine chassis were all made in-house, for the new Williams factory now included an autoclave. Pushrod suspension, naturally with inboard spring/damper units, was used at the front, while at the rear top rockers operated the inboard spring/damper units until mid-season, when pullrod rear suspension was introduced on the FW10B. The gearbox was revised, and carbon brakes were usually used.

Early in 1985 the cars did not seem to be wholly competitive, then Rosberg won

Williams FW10-Honda, 1985.

Williams FW11-Honda of 1986, Nigel Mansell driving.

in Detroit, and the team then came on very strongly later in the year, when Nigel Mansell won the European and South African GPs, and Rosberg won the Australian GP. The team was equal third in the Constructors' Championship.

FW11 In a year, 1986, when Frank Williams was largely absent, recovering from his road-car accident during the winter, his team pulled together strongly, and dominated the Constructors' Championship.

The FW11 evolved from the FW10, was even more neatly packaged, albeit slightly longer and wider in track and wheelbase dimensions, and had 'F'-spec Honda engines that were powerful even in race-boost trim (this was the year in which fuel allowances fell to 195 litres per race). Most problems resulted from minor failures, but it was not until the Austrian GP that both cars failed to finish.

Nelson Piquet (new to the team) won in Brazil, Germany, Hungary and Italy, Nigel Mansell won in Belgium, Canada, France, Britain and Portugal. Mansell's championship hopes were shattered, spectacularly, when a rear tyre exploded in the last race, in Adelaide.

For 1987 the design was improved in details such as cooling arrangements, and seven of the new monocoques built were for the FW11B, while the revised Honda V6 was more powerful *and* more fuel-efficient. The new factor was in the use of hydraulic computer-controlled active (or 'reactive', as the team responded to complaints from Lotus) suspension system, which was intended to provide a constant chassis-to-road ride height throughout a race, and was extensively tested before it was raced, at Monza, where Piquet used it on his race-winning FW11B.

By that time it was known that Honda would break its contract with Williams (even though the contract was not at its end), despite the success of the partnership. In 1987 Williams was once again Championship constructor, and Piquet was World Champion driver (with victories in Germany, Hungary and Italy), while Mansell was runner-up, with victories in Imola, Paul Ricard (France), Silverstone, Austria, Spain and Mexico City.

FW12 The team was perhaps misled by the performance of the 'reactive' suspension in the 1987 cars, so for the next season (and having lost their supply of turbo-

Hondas), when they were obliged to use an interim normally aspirated engine, they concentrated on reducing weight.

The engine was the Judd KV8 3.5litre V8, that drove through a Williams transversely positioned gearbox (that incorporated Hewland gears).

From the very first race, the electronic controls of the gas/hydraulic suspension installation behaved unpredictably, and half the season passed before an instant decision was taken at the British GP – and the cars were converted to conventional suspension, literally overnight.

This worked, in that Mansell was second in the British GP, but there were no victories for Williams that year – seventh overall in the Constructors' Championship was another trough – but this was only a temporary blip, as 1989 would see an upsurge.

FW12C During 1988 Williams Grand Prix Engineering and Renault signed an agreement covering collaboration, development, and the supply of F1 engines for three seasons, starting in 1989. Williams once again had an exclusive, and it was soon shown, competitive engine; Renault had found themselves a front-line team, which was vital if their programme was to succeed.

The normally aspirated 3.5litre Renault RS1 was a 67-degree V10, that first ran on a testbed dynamometer in January 1988 and began circuit testing in a modified FW12 in the autumn of 1988.

The FW12 was modified, for example with a wheelbase extended by some 5.9in/15cm to accommodate the new French V10, and a new designation might really have been expected – but Head's new FW13 was programmed to follow later in the 1989 season.

Meanwhile, the so-called FW12C was competitive. Early in 1989 Patrese finished second in three consecutive Grands

season's use. There was a new front suspension, but the FW12C's rear suspension was used for the first few races.

The settling-in period was not too happy as there were handling problems to be resolved, and both cars were put out of their debut race (in Portugal) with clogged cooling radiators. Nevertheless, the FW13s were second and third in their third race (Japan), while Boutsen won in Australia. With the FW12C and FW13 types, Williams finished second in the 1989 Constructors' Championship.

Still with the same well-respected drivers, the cars appeared in FW13B form in 1990, with modified bodywork, and aerodynamic appendages, enjoyed more power

between them, though Frank Williams was disappointed with fourth in the Constructors' tables.

FW14 The big surge back to Williams's late-1980s dominance began with FW14, an efficient and attractively detailed car that Nigel Mansell (and to a lesser extent) Riccardo Patrese used to the utmost. All the elements were favourable – ample funding, a still improving Renault V10 engine (now it was the RS3 type, with a lot more top-end power), an efficient change-by-wire gearchange – and the first aerodynamic input from new recruit Adrian Newey, who had arrived from the Leyton House F1 team.

Williams FW12-Judd of 1988, Nigel Mansell driving.

Prix, while Thierry Boutsen scored his maiden Grand Prix victory in Canada. However, throughout the summer the car was already at the limit of its capability. Because of 'new car' problems with the FW13, the FW12C was used as late in the year as the Spanish GP, when Patrese placed it fifth.

FW13 and FW13B Although purpose-designed around the Renault V10 RS1 engine, this was nevertheless an evolutionary car. Its chassis was slimmer than that of the FW12, and intended for a full

from their ever-improving Renault V10s, and once again notched up two outright victories. We did not know, at that point, how much more there was to come from Renault, and how much Patrick Head's design team still had in mind for this generation of single-seaters.

Perhaps there wasn't quite the buzz (aggravation?) of having a Mansell in the team, though he would be back, but there was plenty of driver consistency. Sixth and seventh in the Drivers' series meant that Boutsen and Patrese amassed fifty-seven points (which included the two wins)

Maybe the new car's carbon chassis wasn't rigid enough, and there were often worries about the gear change, but it all came right in the end.

Meanwhile, Mansell the wanderer returned, won five times and Patrese twice, the result being that they finished second and third behind Ayrton Senna's McLaren in the Drivers' series, while the team also trailed behind McLaren-Honda in the Constructors' series.

If Mansell hadn't lost a victory through waving prematurely to the crowd in Canada (and stalling the car), and the gearbox had been more reliable (four failures), it might have been a different story. There was also the occasion when Mansell changed wheels at an Estoril pitstop, then lost one of the new ones as he accelerated away.

FW14B More dominant than any previous F1 car had been since the Lotus 79 changed the technical face of Grand Prix racing in 1978, the FW14B made mincemeat of the 1992 Constructors' Championship, and (in spite of what he would say) provided Nigel Mansell with comfortable transport towards his Drivers' Crown.

Tested exhaustively before the season started, technically superior to every rival, and backed by the huge backlog of experience from Didcot, the FW14B was, in every way, 'The Best'.

The figures tell their own story. Mansell secured the Drivers' crown with five (of the sixteen) races to spare. Along the way he won nine races – including *all* the first five – and three second places. Patrese, elegantly playing second fiddle, had only one victory (Japan) but six other second places and two thirds. This, by any standards, was complete success.

Why? First of all there were Patrick Head and Adrian Newey to refine the car that was a logical, far-reaching, evolution over the 1991 machine. Renault's latest V10, the RS3B, was the most powerful on the grids, the semi-automatic gearbox was now bombproof, there was traction control – and there was active, self-levelling suspension.

Yet, through all this, Mansell and his complaints were insufferable. The press reviled him, and Frank Williams was glad to see him go, so he went off to CART racing in the USA, where it took Newman-Haas less than two years to learn why they should not have hired him.

FW15C An interesting model number this, noting not only a new design, but that this was effectively the third derivation of FW14 as well. The title, though, doesn't matter for it was results that counted.

One really doesn't have to detail them but – victory in the Constructors' Championship, with more points than the next two rivals put together (McLaren-Ford and Benetton-Ford, respectively), victory in the Drivers' series, where Alain Prost won seven races, and the arrival of Damon Hill (ex-test driver) with three victories and third in the standings.

In later life, people who suggested that Damon Hill only won because of the seat he was in might have had a point, for all but one of his career victories came in these wonderful Renault V10-engined machines. Between them, the two drivers led races for more than 64 per cent of the total laps involved!

For ambitious drivers, there was nowhere else to be in the early/mid-1990s – that explains why Alain Prost came rushing in as Mansell left, and why Ayrton Senna would make haste to move to Didcot as soon as Prost then retired.

The car was, as expected, formidably fast, complicated – and effective, though an early FISA announcement of rule changes for 1994 meant that several developments were never made (not needed, anyway!). It was a pretty car, too – but that didn't matter, and in any case Frank Williams never cared for such things. All he wanted was results, and the FW15C delivered – almost all the time.

FW16 It is impossible to discuss this car on its own, for it was in an FW16 that Ayrton Senna was killed at Imola, in only his third race for Williams. To this day no-one is sure why the car sheared off the road and hit the wall: what is for sure is that a suspension member pierced his helmet, injuring him fatally.

The original team line-up – FW16 + Senna + Damon Hill + huge exclusive new sponsorship from Rothmans (cigarettes) – looked ideal, especially as the cars were still class-of-the-field, but the death crash changed everything. Hill became de facto team leader, David Coulthard was promoted from test driving – and towards the end of the season even Nigel Mansell (who had fallen out of love with American CART racing) started four races.

As ever, the Renault was the most powerful F1 engine of the year and (also as ever, it seems) the Williams chassis was not the best. As ever, too, Head, Newey and their team grappled with its shortcomings throughout the year, turning it into a very effective race car.

The long-running battle of this 1994 season, therefore, was between Damon Hill's Williams-Renault, and Michael Schumacher's Benetton-Ford, the issue only being resolved in Australia when the two collided and both cars were eliminated. Along the way, Hill won six races and took five second places.

Apart from Hill's fine showing, Coulthard felt his way competently into contention until displaced by Nigel Mansell, while Mansell managed a victory and a fourth place in his last two starts. All four team drivers led races at one time or another. No wonder, then, that Williams-Renault once again lifted the Constructors' Championship with this car, their third in succession.

FW17 and FW17B Frank Williams and Patrick Head might have been disappointed by 1995, as they were 'only' second in the Constructors' series – but they were beaten by a car using similar Renault engines.

Benetton (or should we say Michael Schumacher?) may have shaded the FW17, though with its latest Renault V10 (the RS7 3litre), it was still considered a very fine machine, though season-long unreliability was a problem. Its British drivers delivered five victories and twelve other podium finishes, the FW17 starting from pole position twelve out of seventeen times during the year. Later in the season, with mechanical updates including a new gearbox, and with a revised aerodynamic package, it progressed to FW17B status.

This was Adrian Newey's first high-nose Williams and, with its smaller fuel tank, it was smaller than other recent Williams-Renaults. Perhaps its abilities flattered Damon Hill's true standing as an F1 driver, and it was certainly a car other teams would have loved to run.

FW18 A perfect season really, with the FW18 winning the Constructors' Championship by a distance (175 points to Ferrari's 70 and Benetton's 68), and with Damon Hill winning the Drivers' Championship, clocking up eight outright victories and two second places. Fresh from CART/Indycar racing in the USA, Jacques Villeneuve also won four times.

Headlined 'Simply the Best' in so many post-season reviews, Williams's 1996 performance was as dominant as any in the previous decade, proving that their engineering (led by Adrian Newey) and their engines (Renault's latest 67-degree V10 was reputed to develop 750bhp, and to spin up to 17,000rpm) was of the very highest standard. Depressed rivals who trailed, all confirmed that the FW18 handled better, was faster, and was altogether better-balanced than their own: simple,

Williams FW18-Renault of 1996, Jacques Villeneuve at the wheel. Williams won the Constructors' Championship with this car, Damon Hill becoming Drivers' Champion.

really, if only they had known how to match it.

During the year individual cars differed in detail, for Hill preferred a foot clutch, while Villeneuve preferred two-pedal control with a paddle (behind the steering wheel) change. Villeneuve looked scruffy, and was flamboyant behind the wheel, Hill militarily smart and similarly inclined on the race track.

Amazingly – and this was so typical of Frank Williams – the team did not appreciate Hill enough to want to keep him for 1997, even though he had won the World Championships for them. It was a great loss for both – for Hill never got on well with his next employers, while his replacement at Williams failed the tests too.

FW19 Any new car faced with the problem of beating the record of Williams's 1996 F1 car, FW18, was in big trouble. Amazingly, with the FW19, Williams achieved the double. As in 1996, the cars and drivers lifted the Constructors' and the Drivers' titles yet again.

Jacques Villeneuve fulfilled all the promise he had shown in 1996, by winning the Drivers' Championship, even though Michael Schumacher blatantly tried to push him off the road in the season's last event. Totally unfazed by this – as, indeed, he seemed to be about everything – Villeneuve not only defeated the German, but won seven races. His new team mate, Heinz-Harald Frentzen, who soon

discovered that the Williams team was not prepared to love and nurture him, began to wilt, and won only one race and six other podium places with near-identical cars.

Like many other F1 cars of this period, FW19 evolved directly from the team's previous F1 machine. It was the last Williams to have been influenced by designer (and aerodynamic genius) Adrian Newey, who had left Williams before it was unveiled. Power-assisted steering was new, with almost every other aspect of the car an improvement on the old.

There was, however, a downside, for even before the start of the year Renault announced that the new RS9 V10 was their last effort, and that they would withdraw from the highly charged F1 scene at the end of 1997, though they also guaranteed to support efforts to provide 'customer' V10 engines in the future.

And, if they meant it, the FW19 proved to be the perfect car with which to bow out.

FW20 Oh dear! By Williams's own exalted standards, the FW20, and the 1998 season, would become unmitigated disasters, for this was the first time since 1988 – ten years, in fact – that there was not even one race victory to celebrate.

It was not that the FW20 was a bad car, but that its engine – a Mecachrome 'customer' V10 instead of a 'works' Renault equivalent – lagged behind the opposition. There was also the fact (something

that the team did not like to acknowledge) that their design genius Adrian Newey had been attracted to McLaren, where his knowledge was already beginning to show through.

FW20 was not only new, but looked new, as the livery had changed from Rothmans (1997 and FW19) to another related cigarette brand Winfield (1998 and FW20). It was, in fact, the first product of the 'post-Newey' design team, where Patrick Head's principal associates were Gavin Fisher and Geoff Willis, who surprised everyone by retaining a transverse gearbox, instead of the new fashion of a slimline longitudinal box that many teams were choosing for aerodynamic reasons.

Throughout the year the drivers complained steadily about oversteer (there seemed to be an insoluble lack of rear-end grip), and there is no doubt that this car did not balance as well as its predecessors.

In spite of the formidable driving team – Jacques Villeneuve and Heinz-Harald Frentzen – the season was a great disappointment, for 'Winfield-Williams' dropped to third in the Constructors' Championship – scoring 38 points to McLaren's dominant 156. Villeneuve (already tipped to go off to the new BAR team – which he duly did in 1999) never scored higher than third (twice), while Frentzen, who had fallen out of love with the team, had only a single third place.

Neither Frank Williams nor Patrick Head seemed to cosset their drivers – and it showed – for there were usually more frowns than smiles in the Williams camp in 1998. At the end of the season Villeneuve jumped ship, and Frentzen was eased out – both of them moving happily to new employers, BAR and Jordan respectively.

FW21 For the second of its 'interim' years, 1999 (Williams's long-term future deal with BMW had been announced in mid-1997, to take effect in 2000), the FW21 was effectively a backward step, for in a year when some teams (notably Ferrari, McLaren and Stewart) could use at least 60bhp more power, the same Mecachrome 'customer' V10 (of Renault parentage) had to be used.

By the end of the year, the FW21 was seen as a disappointment, not fast enough in a straight line. Although lighter, and lower, than before, it was not a stable car, particularly under heavy braking – this being a function of having to work with Bridgestone tyres for the very first time.

Compared with the glorious mid-1990s Williams cars, FW21 was simply not competitive, and it showed. In a full season, new-signing Ralf Schumacher (Michael's younger brother) took only one second place, and two thirds. The team slipped to fifth place in the Constructors' series, and didn't enjoy that at all.

The biggest disappointment of all was that the other signed-up driver – Alex Zanardi, fresh from success in the American CART series – did not gain a single point. He finished seventh once, and eighth twice and he rapidly slumped from being a newcomer from whom much was to be expected to a man who was virtually ignored by his team. As with Michael Andretti's terrible year in the 1993 McLaren, CART fame simply had not translated to the F1 circus, and the marriage was swiftly dissolved during the next close season.

Could it get better for 2000? With BMW not only due to supply engines, but to become title sponsors, it surely *had* to be.

FW22 Almost submerged under the pre-season hype of a new commercial partner/engine supplier (BMW), and a new young driver signing (Jenson Button), the FW22 car itself was almost ignored at first.

As expected, FW22 was a progressive update from FW21, with a 2.75in/7cm longer wheelbase, though the BMW V10 engine (itself a complete update from that originally designed in Munich) was all new, and there was a longitudinally positioned seven-speed gearbox to match. Like all currently fashionable F1 cars, there was torsion bar suspension all round, with horizontal inboard dampers.

In what had always been seen as another Williams transitional year, the FW22 BMW combination amazed everyone (even, if they had admitted it, top team personnel). Before it was even installed in a race car, the BMW engine was rumoured to be too heavy, and not reliable enough, but from the very start it proved to be powerful and (increasingly, throughout the year) durable too. The chassis, without doubt, was already competitive, and it was clear that Williams (more properly known as BMW–Williams, by the way) was on its way back towards race victories.

Although there were none in 2000, Williams at least finished third in the Constructors' series (though, let us be honest about this, well over 100 points behind McLaren and Ferrari, who dominated), Jenson Button's pace and maturity was a revelation, and there were regular finishes in the top six to back this up.

Ralf Schumacher, seemingly with more reliable cars, finished fifth in the Drivers' series. Button deserved a second chance but (as so often with drivers at Williams) he was dumped at the end of the season in favour of the much-hyped Juan Montoya, who had been starring in USA CART racing.

Williams FW21-Renault of 1999, driven by Alex Zanardi.

continued from p.239

FW05 Carrying the (later) famous Williams type numbers, two of the three cars had originally been built as Hesketh 308Cs, and modifications made for 1976 only seemed to make them heavy and less competitive. This was a poor programme – five drivers achieving ten finishes, but there were eight retirements and no fewer than five DNQs.

WR1–4 This was a distinctive and workmanlike new design from Harvey Postlethwaite, with a 'wedge' theme to its outward lines, in plan as well as in profile, though it hid a conventional Cosworth DFV/Hewland FGA400 engine/transmission package.

Jody Scheckter drove WR1/1 to a sensational debut victory in Argentina in 1977, and used the same car to win in Monaco (that was the DFV's 100th F1 Championship success) and Canada. Beyond that, he scored two second places and four thirds in a remarkable display of mechanical and team reliability.

The cars served on for the first races of 1978, but by that time they were outmoded by the Lotus ground-effect cars. However, Bobby Rahal was given a run in one at the end of the year, while Teddy Yip (of Theodore fame) entered Keke Rosberg in one of the two Theodore team cars in midsummer races, but achieved nothing.

WR4 was run by Theodore during the first half of the 1980 British National F1 series, unremarkably except that Desiré Wilson won the Easter race at Brands

Wolf WR7-Ford of 1979.

Hatch in it, this being the first and only race won by a woman driver, in F1, in the twentieth century.

WR5–6 The opening race of 1978 showed that there was no development potential left over in the original Wolf/Postlethwaite design. Postlethwaite then quickly designed his first ground-effects car, and WR5 was equally rapidly built. It was an ugly machine, largely because the oil cooler was mounted ahead of the cockpit on a flat, plain, surface.

WR5's circuit behaviour was so tricky that WR6 was hastily completed with wider tracks (there were two cars that carried this number, incidentally – the first car being written off in a warm-up accident at Monza). Scheckter was second in the German and the Canadian GPs, which were the team's best results of the 1978 season.

In mid-1979, David Kennedy drove WR6/2 in British national races, and he too found that its ground effects were not consistently effective.

WR8–9 These three cars were at least much better looking machines than their predecessors, though much less effective on the track. In 1979 the team's record comprised twelve retirements (and one DNQ) to set against only two finishes.

There seemed to be persistent aerodynamic balance and suspension problems – while the cars were not even competitive in straight-line speed terms.

Postlethwaite introduced his folded honeycomb aluminium monocoque construction with this design, although other aspects, including the DFV engine, transmission and suspension layouts, were conventional.

Its debut in Argentina was accompanied by a furore over the use of clutch-driven impeller blades that were used to draw air through the oil cooler, this speedily being ruled out as a 'moveable aerodynamic device'.

That apart, the last Wolf F1 car was only newsworthy when ex-World Champion James Hunt suddenly gave up driving in mid-season, disillusioned both with the Wolf team, and with F1 in general. Like Hunt, his successor, Keke Rosberg, was classified only once in the second part of the season.

Through that period, Wolf team morale was always in sharp decline, as a disappointing end was in sight. WR8 and WR9 became the first two Fittipaldi F7s.

◆ Z ◆

Zakspeed

Erich Zakowski's German-based team built up a solid reputation in saloon car racing in the 1970s, first with Ford Escort RS1600s and later with space-frame Capris. Having become more and more closely involved with Ford, it developed Group 5 Escorts and turbocharged Capris, before trying to make sense of Ford's hopeless C100 Group C racing sports car of 1982–84.

By 1983 Zakspeed was already looking towards F1, and the compact Zakspeed Formula Racing Division was set up. Its own-brand turbocharged four-cylinder F1 engine (90.4 × 58.25mm, 1,495cc) ran for the first time in September 1984, and a new F1 car – the 841 – was announced later in that month.

Despite considerable experience with Ford turbo engines, Zakspeed's commitment to its own in-house power was always a risky manoeuvre, and the company was poorly served in the four seasons in which it was raced. The power output of early units may have been up to the claimed 700bhp, and in 1986 800–1,100bhp (race or qualifying tune) may well have been achieved, but in competitive terms output was never quite sufficient. The cars always looked neat, but were not very effective, despite the best and bravest effort of their drivers, and through three full seasons Zakspeed F1 cars finished in the points only once.

For 1989 Zakspeed was again innovative – this time by choosing Japanese Yamaha V8 engines – but its drivers were inexperienced. The combination of tyro driving and new machinery meant that this Zakspeed featured regularly in the list of cars that failed even to progress beyond the pre-qualifying stage (these being the days of the 'Wide Awake' club).

At the end of the season, that car/engine combination was withdrawn, and though a return, after intensive development, was promised, the Zakspeed name never again appeared on a single-seater.

841 Although it was announced in September 1984, the original Zakspeed F1 car was not raced until the following, 1985, season, and then only in the European races in the F1 Championship calendar. It was a state-of-the-art design by Paul Brown (ex-Chevron, March and Maurer), built around a carbon-fibre/Kevlar monocoque, that had double wishbone front suspension, and a pullrod rear layout. The race debut was in the Portuguese GP, but the only finish in nine Grands Prix entered came at Monaco, where Jonathan Palmer was eleventh.

861 The 841 design was further refined for the team's second season, in particular weight being shed, aerodynamics improved, and a new engine management system introduced. In detail, during the season, carbon-fibre brakes were introduced, there were new fuel injection arrangements, Garrett turbos were preferred to KKK units, and detail aerodynamic work was also carried out.

Performances did not improve proportionately to all this effort, in part because Zakspeed's resources were stretched when a second car was being run later in the season. Thirty entries resulted in only ten finishes – a one-in-three result, Palmer's eighth place at Detroit being the best. The cars were also to be used early in 1987.

871 Attributed to the 'Zakspeed Design Group', this was a further development of the existing design, though continuity paid very few dividends. The frontal area was reduced, the aerodynamic performance was improved (this was not always obvious in practice), there was revised wishbone/pullrod suspension that was to be revised yet more as the 1987 season progressed – and there was a new gearbox.

The first car was ready for the second Grand Prix of the 1987 season, when Martin Brundle drove it to secure Zakspeed's very first F1 World Championship points. Thereafter, development lagged, and although some wind-tunnel work was completed, finding adequate downforce was always a problem.

881 In its final season with the in-house turbocharged engine Zakspeed's fortunes slipped back even further – the turbocharged engines were supposed to hold a residual advantage over 'atmo' engines, but the 2.5-bar boost pressure regulations seemed to reduce the power of the Zakspeed engine to a par with the best normally aspirated units, and it was still unreliable.

The 1987 chassis had been uprated, and the bodywork refined, but the cars were never competitive. Team leader Ghinzani was classified only three times (best placing fourteenth), Schneider once (twelfth), though their respective DNQ annotations were eighth and tenth.

891 The car marked a new beginning, Zakspeed hoped, though this was in fact illusory. This was a car designed under the direction of Gustav Brunner, by Nino Frisson, who had joined the team from Ferrari in mid-1988. Outwardly this seemed a small car, less neat than its predecessors; it still used pullrod suspension, and carried the same West sponsorship colour scheme.

But the engine was the 40-valve Yamaha OX88 V8 (Cosworth had already tried this head layout, and rejected it), and it drove through Zakspeed's new transverse gearbox.

That amount of novelty called for experienced development drivers – but neither Schneider nor Yamaha-imposed Suzuki were experienced. With almost inevitable regularity, the 1989 Zakspeeds failed to get past the pre-qualifying hurdle, although Schneider actually got one car onto the grids for the last two races of 1989.

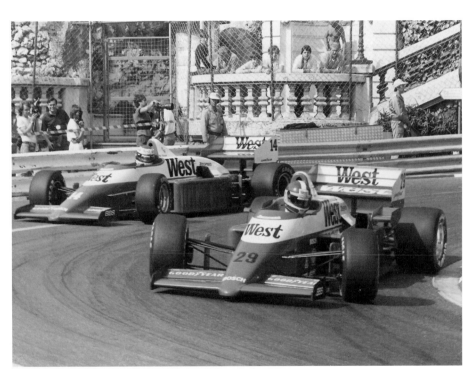

Zakspeed 861 of 1986, Jonathan Palmer and Hube Rothengatter driving.

Zakspeed 891-Yamaha of 1989, driven by Bernd Schneider.

Grand Prix Racing – Regulation Changes from 1906

The Regulations, or Formulae, governing Grand Prix racing, changed many times during the twentieth century. Looking back, limits placed from time to time seem to show little logic – though they were usually set according to the standards, and trends, of the day.

Without going into the tiny details, here are the basic GP Formulae that have applied, from 1906 to 2000:

1906	Maximum vehicle weight 2,220lb/1,007kg No limit on engine size
1907	Fuel consumption limited to 9.4mpg (Imperial) 30litre/100km
1908	Minimum vehicle weight 2,535lb/1,150kg Maximum engine piston area 117sq in/7,548sq cm
1912	Maximum width of car 68.9in/175cm No limits on engine size or vehicle weights
1913	Minimum vehicle weight 1,764lb/800kg Maximum vehicle weight 2,425lb/1,100kg Fuel consumption limited to 4.2mpg/20litre/100km
1914	Minimum vehicle weight 1,764lb/800kg Maximum vehicle weight 2,425lb/1,100kg Maximum engine capacity 4,500cc Superchargers and special fuels banned

First World War intervened

1921	Minimum vehicle weight (dry) 1,764lb/800kg Maximum engine capacity 3,000cc
1922–24	Minimum vehicle weight 1,433lb/650kg

In all the foregoing years, it was compulsory to carry two occupants (driver and 'driving mechanic'), with a minimum aggregate weight of at least 265lb/120kg. Ballast had to be carried to make up weight shortfalls. From 1925 onwards, 'driving mechanics' were banned.

1925	Minimum weight 1,433lb/650kg Minimum body width 31.5in/80cm, and two seats to be fitted Maximum engine capacity 2,000cc
1926	Minimum weight 1,323lb/600kg Minimum body width 31.5in/80cm, and two seats to be fitted Maximum engine capacity 1,500cc

1927	Minimum weight 1,543lb/700kg Minimum body width 33.5in/85cm Single-seater types now permitted Maximum engine capacity 1,500cc
1928	Minimum weight 1,213lb/550kg Maximum weight 1,654lb/750kg Minimum race distance 373miles/600km (Only used in Italian GP)
1929	Minimum weight 1,984lb/900kg Minimum body width 39.4in/100cm Maximum fuel (petrol + oil) consumption 30.9lb/14kg/100km race distance (approx equal to 14.5mpg). Pump fuel compulsory (Only used in French and Spanish GPs)
1930	Regulations as for 1929, but with 30 per cent added Benzol fuel mixture authorized (Only used in French and Belgian GPs)
1931	Minimum race duration 10 hours. No car technical restrictions
1932	As for 1931, except for race duration of 5 to 10 hours
1933	As for 1931 and 1932, but race duration to be 311miles/500km
1934–37	Maximum weight 1,654lb/750kg. Minimum body width 33.5in/85cm
1938–39	Sliding scale relationship between weight and engine capacity, but maxima were: Engines 3,000cc with superchargers, or 4,500cc without superchargers. Minimum weight for cars with such engines was 1,874lb/850kg

[*Note:* From 1934–39 minimum weights were measured without engine oil, or wheels/tyres fitted]

Second World War intervened

1947–53   Maximum engine size 1,500cc (with forced induction), or 4,500cc normally aspirated.
No weight or dimensional limits

This formula was discredited in 1952 and 1953 by a lack of competing cars, and was displaced by the existing Formula 2 that was:

1952–53   Maximum engine size 500cc (with forced induction), or 2,000cc normally aspirated.
No weight or dimensional limits

1954–60   A new Formula 1. Maximum engine size 750cc (with forced induction), or 2,500cc normally aspirated.
No weight or dimensional limits
Aviation spirit fuel became compulsory from 1958

1961–65   Minimum engine size 1,300cc normally aspirated
Maximum engine size 1,500cc normally aspirated
No provision for forced induction engines
Minimum weight (incl. oil and water) 992lb/450kg

1966–88   Initially :

Maximum engine size 1,500cc (with forced induction), or 3,000cc (normally aspirated)
Rotary and gas turbine engines also authorized
'Commercially available' fuel was compulsory
Minimum weight (incl. oil and water) 1,102lb/500kg

This formula was subject to many detail changes, refinements, and weight increases over the years. A few highlights were:

- By 1970 the minimum weight was up to 1,168lb/530kg

- From 1973, no more than 12-cylinder engines were authorized. Minimum weight was up to 1,268lb/575kg

- Sliding aerodynamic skirts were banned from 1 January 1981
Minimum weight limit was 1,290lb/585kg
All but four-stroke reciprocating engines were banned

- 'Flat-bottom' aerodynamic rules were imposed
Minimum weight (normally aspirated cars) was reduced to 1,190lb/540kg

- Maximum boost on turbocharged engines was reduced to 4.0 Bar in 1987, and again to 2.5 bar in 1988

1987   For a separate one-off 'Jim Clark' award, there was a separate category within Formula One:
Maximum engine capacity 3,500cc, normally aspirated

From this point, not only were there further Formula changes, but the regular imposition of detail rules covering everything from weights to dimensions, tyre usage, safety test requirements, and much more. The basics, therefore, of what followed from 1989 were:

1989–94   Maximum engine capacity 3,500cc, normally aspirated
No provision for forced induction cars
Engines could use no more than 12 cylinders

1995–2000 Maximum engine size 3,000cc

A compulsory V10 engine layout regulation was imposed in 1999 (all cars were already using such engines).

Formula 1 – World Champions

CONSTUCTORS' CHAMPIONSHIP This series was only set up in 1958.

YEAR	CONSTRUCTOR	YEAR	CONSTRUCTOR	YEAR	CONSTRUCTOR
1958	Vanwall	1973	Lotus-Ford	1987	Williams-Honda
1959	Cooper-Climax	1974	McLaren-Ford	1988	McLaren-Honda
1960	Cooper-Climax	1975	Ferrari	1989	McLaren-Honda
1961	Ferrari	1976	Ferrari	1990	McLaren-Honda
1962	BRM	1977	Ferrari	1991	McLaren-Honda
1963	Lotus-Climax	1978	Lotus-Ford	1992	Williams-Renault
1964	Ferrari	1979	Ferrari	1993	Williams-Renault
1965	Lotus-Climax	1980	Williams-Ford	1994	Williams-Renault
1966	Brabham-Repco	1981	Williams-Ford	1995	Benetton-Renault
1967	Brabham-Repco	1982	Ferrari	1996	Williams-Renault
1968	Lotus-Ford	1983	Ferrari	1997	Williams-Renault
1969	Matra-Ford	1984	McLaren-TAG Porsche	1998	McLaren-Mercedes-Benz
1970	Lotus-Ford	1985	McLaren-TAG Porsche	1999	Ferrari
1971	Tyrrell-Ford	1986	Williams-Honda	2000	Ferrari
1972	Lotus-Ford				

DRIVERS' CHAMPIONSHIP This Championship was set up in 1950, after the post-war Formula 1 had already been running for three years. No 'World Champion' was ever declared in years earlier than this.

YEAR	WINNING DRIVER	CAR (CARS) USED	YEAR	WINNING DRIVER	CAR (CARS) USED
1950	Dr Guiseppe Farina	(Alfa Romeo 158 and 159)	1975	Niki Lauda	(Ferrari 312B and 312T)
1951	Juan Manuel Fangio	(Alfa Romeo 159)	1976	James Hunt	(McLaren M23)
1952	Alberto Ascari	(Ferrari 500)	1977	Niki Lauda	(Ferrari 312T2)
1953	Alberto Ascari	(Ferrari 500)	1978	Mario Andretti	(Lotus-Ford 78 and 79)
1954	Juan Manuel Fangio	(Maserati 250F/Mercedes-Benz W196)	1979	Jody Scheckter	(Ferrari 312T3 and T4)
1955	Juan Manuel Fangio	(Mercedes-Benz W196)	1980	Alan Jones	(Williams-Ford FW07B)
1956	Juan Manuel Fangio	(Lancia-Ferrari D50/Ferrari 801)	1981	Nelson Piquet	(Brabham-Ford BT49C)
1957	Juan Manuel Fangio	(Maserati 250F)	1982	Keke Rosberg	(Williams-Ford FW07C and 08)
1958	Mike Hawthorn	(Ferrari Dino 246 and 256)	1983	Nelson Piquet	(Brabham-BMW BT52 and BT52B)
1959	Jack Brabham	(Cooper Climax T51)	1984	Niki Lauda	(McLaren-TAG Porsche MP4/2)
1960	Jack Brabham	(Cooper Climax T53)	1985	Alain Prost	(McLaren-TAG Porsche MP4/2B)
1961	Phil Hill	(Ferrari 156)	1986	Alain Prost	(McLaren-TAG Porsche MP4/2C)
1962	Graham Hill	(BRM P57)	1987	Nelson Piquet	(Williams-Honda FW11B)
1963	Jim Clark	(Lotus-Climax 25)	1988	Ayrton Senna	(McLaren-Honda MP4/4)
1964	John Surtees	(Ferrari 158)	1989	Alain Prost	(McLaren-Honda MP4/5)
1965	Jim Clark	(Lotus-Climax 25 and 33)	1990	Ayrton Senna	(McLaren-Honda MP4/5B)
1966	Jack Brabham	(Brabham-Repco BT19 and BT20)	1991	Ayrton Senna	(McLaren-Honda MP4/6)
1967	Denny Hulme	(Brabham-Repco BT20 and BT24)	1992	Nigel Mansell	(Williams-Renault FW14B)
1968	Graham Hill	(Lotus-Ford 49 and 49B)	1993	Alain Prost	(Williams-Renault FW15C)
1969	Jackie Stewart	(Matra-Ford MS10 and MS80)	1994	Michael Schumacher	(Benetton-Ford)
1970	Jochen Rindt	(Lotus-Ford 49C and 72)	1995	Michael Schumacher	(Benetton-Renault)
1971	Jackie Stewart	(Tyrrell-Ford 001 and 003)	1996	Damon Hill	(Williams-Renault)
1972	Emerson Fittipaldi	(Lotus-Ford 72)	1997	Jacques Villeneuve	(Williams-Renault)
1973	Jackie Stewart	(Tyrrell-Ford 005 and 006)	1998	Mika Hakkinen	(McLaren-Mercedes-Benz)
1974	Emerson Fittipaldi	(McLaren-Ford M23)	1999	Mika Hakkinen	(McLaren-Mercedes-Benz)
			2000	Michael Schumacher	(Ferrari F1-2000)

Index